The routes to exile

MANCHESTER
1824

Manchester University Press

Studies in
Modern French History

Edited by
Mark Greengrass and Pamela Pilbeam

This series is published in collaboration with the UK Society for the Study of French History. It aims to showcase innovative short monographs relating to the history of the French, in France and in the world since c.1750. Each volume speaks to a theme in the history of France with broader resonances to other discourses about the past. Authors demonstrate how the sources and interpretations of modern French history are being opened to historical investigation in new and interesting ways, and how unfamiliar subjects have the capacity to tell us more about the role of France within the European continent. The series is particularly open to interdisciplinary studies that break down the traditional boundaries and conventional disciplinary divisions.

Titles already published in this series

Catholicism and children's literature in France: The comtesse de Ségur
(1799–1874)   Sophie Heywood

The Society for the
Study of French History

The routes to exile

France and the Spanish Civil War refugees, 1939–2009

SCOTT SOO

Manchester University Press

Published by Manchester University Press
Altrincham Street, Manchester M1 7JA, UK
www.manchesteruniversitypress.co.uk

British Library Cataloguing-in-Publication Data is available

Library of Congress Cataloging-in-Publication Data is available

ISBN 978 1 5261 0684 1 *paperback*

First published by Manchester University Press 2013

This edition first published 2017

Printed by Lightning Source

Contents

Preface

On a hot day in June 2000, it took me some time to locate the monument to the refugees who were interned on the beach of Argelès-sur-Mer in 1939, and the stele marking the place where some of those refugees were buried. It would not be so difficult to find these today partly because the history of these camps and the internees has become much more widely known. In 2009, the seventieth anniversary of the Spanish republicans' arrival in France was recalled with an impressive array of commemorations across the country. The various events signalled that the Spanish republican exile in France was fast becoming an integral part of French, but also Spanish and European history.

Much of our knowledge about the history of the Spanish republican exile has come from the refugees' memoirs and the work of French and Spanish historians. While there has also been pioneering work in the English language, there are few books and only one general overview by Louis Stein published in 1979 when access to the relevant state archives in France was limited. My aim is to provide an updated account in the English language and to advance knowledge of the subject through a consideration of exile in relation to the refugees' lived experiences and memory activities. Given the contemporary trend of nation-states in neglecting refugees' rights, understanding the personal and long-term impact of the French reception of the Spanish republicans is as important now as it has ever been.

I am grateful to a number of institutions and individuals for supporting this project. The Economic and Social Research Council and the Arts and Humanities Research Council financed the postgraduate research from which this book emerged. I would also like to thank the staff at the French, Spanish and British National Archives, as well as those at the numerous *Archives Départementales*. There are three friends in particular who I would like to mention. Jean-Jacques Réal, Hélène Tallet and Francisco Perez of the former CIRAS archive guided me through the documents of the Spanish Libertarian Movement in exile under very difficult circumstances. Jean-Jacques was steadfastly enthusiastic about this project even though he was enduring the final stages of terminal cancer. Both Jean-Jacques and Hélène ('Léna') insisted that I continue working with the archives, even though these were based within their own home, and Francisco was always on hand for any questions. I very much regret that neither Jean-Jacques nor Francisco lived to see the publication of the book.

In addition to the archival work, I was very fortunate to listen to so many people about their experiences and memories. I would like to express my deep gratitude to everyone for generously giving up their time and hope they will forgive me for not being able to incorporate all of their stories here. The names of those whose oral histories feature in this book can be found in the bibliography. These oral-history interviews have provided an essential insight into exile as well as inspiring successive cohorts of students to learn more about the subject. In the process, these students have both challenged and advanced my understanding of the Spanish republican exile and I would therefore like to thank the students who have studied FREN 3025 'An ambivalent asylum: the history and memories of refugees in early twentieth-century France', and TRANS 6002 'Problematizing the national'.

I have benefited from the interdisciplinary context of the University of Southampton and the collegiate ethos of Modern Languages, and very much hope this will be able to survive the incessant market-inspired challenges to British academia. I owe thanks to virtually all of my colleagues in Modern Languages as well as others in History, Sociology and Geography. But a special mention must go to Jackie Clarke, who kindly took time from her own monograph to provide feedback on various chapters. The same applies to another good friend and historian, Evgenios Mikhail.

For his infectious enthusiasm, inspiration, invaluable advice and generous hospitality, my deep gratitude goes to Rod Kedward. Sharif Gemie also deserves a special mention for his encouragement and critical feedback during the genesis of this book. I am also grateful to all the staff at Manchester University Press and the Series Editors, Mark Greengrass and Pam Pilbeam, for their advice.

Portions of Chapter 5 appeared in my article 'Ambiguities at Work: Spanish Republican Exiles and the Organisation Todt in Occupied Bordeaux', *Modern and Contemporary France*, 15:4 (2007) (http://www.tandfonline.com/toc/cmcf20/current) and in my chapter 'Returning to the Land: Vichy's Groupement de Travailleurs Étrangers and Spanish Civil War Refugees', in S. Ott (ed.), *War, Exile, Justice, and Everyday Life, 1936–1946* (Reno, NV: Center for Basque Studies, 2010). The extracts are reprinted with the kind permission of Taylor & Francis, and the Center for Basque Studies, University of Nevada. I am also grateful to University of Wales Press for their permission to reproduce some of the text from 'Between Borders: The Remembrance Practices of Spanish Exiles in the Southwest of France', in S. Gemie and H. Altink (eds), *At the Border: Margins and Peripheries in Modern France* (Cardiff: University of Wales Press, 2008) in Chapter 7.

Friends as well as family have been incredibly supportive. *Je remercie les copains de Saint Michel* in Bordeaux and especially Fred Labes, who has followed this project from the start. Thanks also to Jean-Bernard and Marylène for allowing me to hijack their *salon* for some of the writing of this book. I can never thank enough my parents Dave and Charlotte, whose own stories and backgrounds have motivated my interest in social and cultural history. Nobody has followed the evolution of this book as closely as Flora. Flora has been tremendously patient and understanding as well as gracious in allowing her holidays to be (re)routed to places of Spanish republican interest in France: I owe her my heartfelt gratitude. Finally, no acknowledgement would be complete without mentioning Molly and Joe: I apologise for the absences and thank you both for being everything to me.

List of abbreviations

ADE	Alianza Democrática Española
AGA	Archivo General de la Administración
AGE	Agrupación de Guerrilleros Españoles
AVER	Amicale des Volontaires de l'Espagne Républicaine Orphelins, Veuves et Ascendants
CDL	Comité Départemental de Libération
CGT	Confédération Générale de Travail
CLC	Commissariat à la Lutte contre le Chômage
CNT	Confederación Nacional del Trabajo
CTE	Compagnies de Travailleurs Étrangers/Espagnols
FAI	Federación Anarquista Ibérica
FETE	Federación Española de Trabajadores de la Enseñanza
FETT	Federación Española de Trabajadores de la Tierra
FFI	Forces Françaises de l'Intérieur
FFREEE	Fils et Filles de Républicains Espagnols et Enfants de l'Exode
FIJL	Federación Ibérica de Juventudes Libertarias
FSC	Friends Service Council
FTPF	Francs-Tireurs et Partisans Français
FUE	Federación Universitaria Escolar
GTE	Groupements de Travailleurs Étrangers/Espagnols
IRO	International Refugee Organisation
JARE	Junta de Auxilio a los Republicanos Españoles
JEL	Junta Española de Liberación
JSU	Juventudes Socialistas Unificadas
MLE	Movimiento Libertario Español
MOI	Main d'Œuvre Immigrée
OT	Organisation Todt

PCE	Partido Comunista de España
PCF	Parti Communiste Français
POT	Partido Obrero del Trabajo
POUM	Partido Obrero de Unificación Marxista
PSOE	Partido Socialista Obrero Español
PSOP	Parti Socialiste Ouvrier et Paysan
PSUC	Partido Socialista Unificado de Cataluña
RMVE	Régiments de Marche de Volontaires Étrangers
SERE	Servicio de Evacuación de Refugiados/Republicanos Españoles
SFIO	Section Française de l'Internationale Ouvrière
SIA	Solidarité Internationale Antifasciste
SNCF	Société Nationale des Chemins de Fer
SOE	Special Operations Executive
SSE	Service Social des Étrangers
STO	Service du Travail Obligatoire
TE	Travailleurs Étrangers
UGT	Unión General de Trabajadores
UNE	Unión Nacional Española

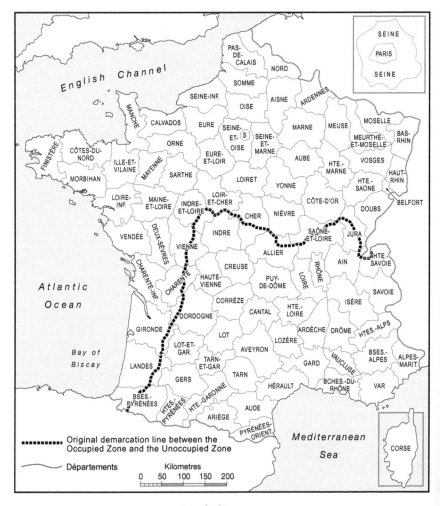

1 French *départements*

2 South-west France

Introduction

Coming to terms with the Spanish republican exile in France

Miguel Oviedo could not have anticipated the extent of exclusion and uncertainty awaiting him as he trudged over the border into France at 11.30 a.m. on Monday 6 February 1939. According to the French government everything was in place for the arrival of the Spanish republican refugees. But in the small village of Argelès-sur-Mer the local authorities had barely any time to react to events, managing to do little more than erect a barbed-wire enclosure on the nearby beach to keep the refugees apart from the local population. Photographs taken at the time show an enormous expanse of windswept beach with refugees attempting to gain some protection from the elements under makeshift bivouacs and in holes dug from the sand. Miguel set foot in the camp on Tuesday evening. Food was out of the question; the queues were enormous. Fortunately some war-wounded refugees offered him space in one of the rare barracks. Even so, Miguel's diary entry for that day presents a sense of foreboding as it closes with the words: 'under these conditions we won't last for long'.[1]

The French state was already well versed in providing refuge for persecuted peoples from across the European continent, and therefore could have received the Spanish republicans more humanely. But refugees' rights had substantially deteriorated towards the end of the 1930s as successive governments battled against a gloomy economic outlook, deepening divisions in French society, a crisis of national identity and an increasing prospect of war with Germany. More specifically, Édouard Daladier's Radical-led government set out to limit any further refugees from settling in the country by transforming France from a refuge to a place of transit: a temporary rather than a permanent place of asylum. The start of 1939 was clearly not an auspicious time for the reception of close to half a million refugees from the Spanish Civil War.

The very particular circumstances surrounding the French government's reception policy – involving the forced separation of families and friends and the ensuing internment of hundreds of thousands of people – represents a unique episode in French refugee history: never before had the country experienced a rapid influx of refugees of this magnitude; and never before had the French state responded to the call for asylum with mass internment. Admittedly, one can cite other occasions in the twentieth century when the French state placed refugees in camps during peacetime: the Armenians in the 1920s and the Harkis in the 1960s. But even so, in both cases the camps were conceived more as accommodation centres as opposed to places of internment. Neither before nor after have the French authorities and public – especially in the south-west of the country – reacted with such intensity to the reception of a group of refugees.

The staggering mass of French official documents produced in response to the Spanish refugees' arrival is a further and telling indicator of the exceptional circumstances marking the onset of the Spanish exile. The mountainous paperwork was not simply generated because of the scale of the refugee phenomenon. It reflected a level of administrative preoccupation and discrimination which bordered on the obsessive. Even after the repatriation of around two-thirds of the refugees during 1939–40, local French authorities persistently focused on the remaining Spanish republicans. This continued throughout the trails of war with Germany and the subsequent occupation of the country. Although the Liberation involved a readjustment in French perceptions of the Spanish republican exile, the onset of the Cold War was accompanied by a partial return to a vocabulary of discrimination in local authority correspondence.

However, the impact of the Spanish republicans in France cannot be gauged through the optic of French administrative correspondence alone. The modest stele on a tucked-away parcel of land outside Argelès-sur-Mer, which marks the graves of refugees who died whilst interned by the French authorities, contrasts markedly with the striking statue of the Spanish guerrilla-resistance fighter at Prayols in the Ariège. Similarly, the annual commemorations organised by local associations with the participation of local French representatives offer a different, albeit overlapping, perspective from the rituals and objects found in the homes of former refugees in France. Memorials, as well as annual and everyday forms of remembrance, are equally valid traces of a rich and varied history.

This book is about the conditions, and more specifically about the events and processes, which gave shape to the history and memory of one of the most significant exiles in French asylum history. I examine the origins and development of the Spanish republican exile as lived experience and as a subject of remembrance from 1939 to the 70th anniversary in 2009. Given that experience and patterns of remembrance are socially and culturally mediated, I attend to how the processes of mediation unfolded. I therefore privilege an interpretation of exile as a social construction grounded in the actions of both the Spanish refugees, and the institutions and people with whom they interacted in France. This focus furthers historical understanding of refugee history in France more generally and the Spanish republican exile more specifically.

In relation to the wider history of refugees in France, this study makes several contributions. First, I engage with historians' debates over refugees' rights under the Third Republic by rejecting a view of the decade as involving a linear narrative of steadily decreasing rights. While there can be no doubting the brutal consequences of the Daladier government's legislation on the arriving Spanish republicans or the coercion on them to return to Spain, I also explore the opportunities generated by the French war economy of 1939–40. Secondly, while I point towards some aspects of continuity between the Third Republic and Vichy labour strategies for refugees, there is no intent to read the last years of the Third Republic through the prism of Vichy France. On the contrary, the presence of the German authorities in France created an entirely new dynamic which produced a range of unexpected possibilities for those Spanish refugees prepared to negotiate the contradictions in French and German labour policy. Thirdly, I present a more complex and yet telling reading of Resistance narratives in post-Liberation France. The presence of Spanish republicans in local commemorations of the Liberation challenges the view of France being dominated by the Gaullist and Communist national visions of the Resistance heritage, while also revealing the origins of the current commemorative culture of the Spanish republican exile.

The analysis of Spanish republicans' life histories and remembrance practices adds another dimension to studies of refugees in France. We discover how the painful experience of forced relocation was immensely aggravated through the French government's reception strategy, which in turn created a long-standing lens through which Spanish republicans interpreted and subsequently recalled their lives in France. Because history and memory have often been conceived of as separate phenomena, historians have yet to explore fully the Spanish republicans' commemorative practices. This book redresses this neglect by recognising the symbiotic relationship between memories of the past and experiences of the present which characterised the long and uneven development of a commemorative culture of exile in France. Attention to both the public and private spaces of remembrance produces evidence which suggests the need for an alternative reading of Pierre Nora's concept of realms of memory. Nora's contention that 'there are realms of memory because there are no longer memory environments' carries little weight for refugees deprived of the institutions and cultural apparatus needed for the production of realms of memory and who arrived in France with little more than, and in some cases not even, a suitcase.[2] In a context when daily rituals and everyday objects became important vectors for remembering, is it not more appropriate to reverse Nora's maxim: 'were there memory environments because there were no longer any realms of memory'?

The discussion of remembrance does not imply that Spanish republicans were entrenched in the past. On the contrary, this book eschews any view of exile as engendering nostalgia and paralysis through an obsession with the past and returning to Spain. Instead, I adopt an interpretation which accounts for the role of historical contingency and the enabling properties of remembrance. In respect of this latter point, Spanish republicans' recollections were more frequently mobilised as a strategy for responding to contemporary and future concerns. Whether it is in relation to the paths trodden over the Pyrenees and across the south-west of France or to the array of restraints, opportunities, choices and motivations that characterised refugees' lives as they interacted with the institutions and citizens of France, the notion of trajectory is important. The temporal, spatial and social-interaction emphasis of this study is reflected in its title *The routes to exile* which adopts Paul Gilroy's use of 'routes' as a homonym of 'roots'.[3]

Searching for the Spanish republican exile in France

If we were to speak of a centre of the Spanish republican exile we could take heed of an anecdote that still circulates among surviving Spanish republicans in France: 'Where is the capital in France? Why, Toulouse of course!' Even if their representatives congregated in Paris during the first year and a half of exile, the French capital was rarely a focal point for most refugees. The French government had declared Paris as out of bounds to all but a tiny minority of Spanish republican representatives in 1939. Furthermore, the majority of refugees, together with the central offices of their political parties and trade unions, soon gathered closer to the French–Spanish border. Toulouse, a city famous for its rose-brick architecture, together with the surrounding *département* of the Haute-Garonne, thus became an important centre of exilic activity.

Unsurprisingly, much of the historical work has focused on the Toulouse region. While I will be making forays into the Haute-Garonne, as well as other *départements* of the south-west, I also trace the refugees' paths across the Aquitaine region. The rationale relates partly to the presence of a sizeable number of refugees – who were notably gathered in the region's administrative centre, Bordeaux – and partly to the lacunae in existing publications.[4] Some excellent work exists on the Spanish republicans in the *département* of the Basses-Pyrénées.[5] However, historians have largely overlooked the remainder of the region as a subject for detailed study.[6] Much of the information uncovered for this book thus constitutes fresh empirical data and is drawn from state-produced archives as well as from the refugees' memoirs, autobiographies and oral-history interviews.

Wherever possible, this book relays a sense of the terminology used by the French administration and the Spanish republicans. Most commonly, French administrators used the terms *réfugiés espagnols* (Spanish refugees) and *étrangers* (foreigners). At various junctures, other modes of categorisation were prevalent. When the French government began considering the economic potential of the refugees during the spring of 1939 officials began to refer to *travailleurs étrangers/espagnols* (foreign/Spanish workers), thereby resorting to a well-established tendency to consider asylum within the paradigm of economic migration. References to '*rouges espagnols*' (Spanish reds) can be found during the first year of exile, but became especially widespread with the Occupation and Vichy era when officials also referred to '*terroristes*'. I have also been mindful of how refugees referred to themselves. In the main, when speaking of themselves as a group, they employed the terms *refugiados españoles* (Spanish refugees) and *republicanos españoles* (Spanish republicans).

Taking the 'Spanish Republic' as an umbrella term is not without its problems. Throughout the nineteenth and twentieth centuries the development of a Spanish republican national identity consistently foundered on the divisions that ran along and across regional, social and ideological-political formations. Paradoxically, the conflict in Spain suggested a pressing need for the production of a coherent discourse of belonging while simultaneously laying bare all of the long-standing fault lines.[7] Existing divisions were accentuated by the phenomenal pressure generated by the demands of the Civil War and the *de facto* international isolation of the Spanish Republic. The victory of Franco's 'nationalist' forces, together with the onset of exile, further compromised the development of a discourse of national identity amongst the Spanish republicans. Bitter recriminations about the management of the conflict and the defeat of the republican forces stymied any significant long-lasting gesture of unity amongst the various groups in exile. Furthermore, the refugees' conflation of nationalism with the dictatorship in Spain compromised the notion of an all-encompassing identity in exile.

A form of commonality nevertheless existed and found expression at certain junctures. Refugees commonly referred to themselves as Spanish republicans as it was a term that was palatable and intelligible to their French hosts. There was also a nebulous though tangible sense of common belonging evident in the evocation of certain iconic figures. Traces can still be found in the homes of former refugees through the display of representations of Cervantes's Don Quixote.[8] The resilient idealism evoked by this archetype was also embodied in cultural icons such as Antonio Machado and Federico García Lorca, both of whom died as a result of the conflict. Sharif Gemie refers to this 'common sense of idealism' with the apt expression 'Republic of the Mind'.[9] The notion of a republican identity was certainly ambiguous and there was no consensual discourse of the Spanish Republic throughout the entire period of exile, but the Spanish Republic was nevertheless evoked and remembered within specific contexts.

A caveat is also needed when referring to the internment of the Spanish refugees in France. According to state archives, contemporaries of the Third Republic referred to the camps using a variety of different terms, of which the most common were 'concentration', 'internment', 'reception' and 'accommodation'. It is important to underline that the notion of concentration camp in France at the end of the 1930s conveyed a very different sense to the term as it is understood today. The well-known quote by Albert Sarraut, the French Minister of the Interior who dealt with the refugees' arrival, is revealing in this respect:

It will never be a question of interning prisoners. The Spanish will never be submitted to any harmful regime or to forced labour. Let us repeat that: the camp of Argelès-sur-Mer will not be a penitentiary centre but a concentration camp. It is not the same thing.[10]

The meaning of the term evidently changed in a radical sense during the post-war period as news of the Holocaust spread throughout Europe. As a consequence the general understanding of 'concentration' camp is more often than not linked to Nazi extermination policy. In order to avoid this conflation, some scholars avoid reference to concentration camps in the context of French history.[11] To be sure, more comparative research is needed on the phenomenon of the concentration camps from the late nineteenth century onwards. However, in reflection of the terminology used by administrators under the Third Republic and Vichy regime, I will use the terms 'concentration camp' and 'internment camp'.

As this study concentrates on the localities where Spanish refugees could be found, the bulk of archival material stems from the local *archives départementales* in France. Attention to local detail should not be equated with a parochial vision of refugee history. Correspondence received or generated by local officials was exchanged with government ministers and thereby reflects how national policies and strategies were implemented or sometimes challenged at the local level. Some caution is nonetheless required, and especially with documents outlining French public opinions of the Spanish refugees, as it is often unclear on what evidence the reports were based. While I have accepted the validity of direct references to specific members of the local populations, I believe the reports shed more light on the assumptions of the persons who wrote them than on public attitudes. I have therefore used statements by French officials (prefects, sub-prefects and the police) and representatives (mayors, and *députés* – the French equivalent of members of parliament) to gain an insight into how cultural boundaries were constructed and segregation justified by local authority figures. Although I make no claims to generalisation, I argue there was a general will to believe in such representations where similar and mostly pejorative comments were repeated by officials, representatives and their superiors within a given locality or across a number of *départements*.

In their memoirs, autobiographies and oral-history interviews, henceforth referred to collectively as life histories or life-history narratives, Spanish republicans often recount with bitterness stories of reification and discrimination. These narratives also contrast an undignified response of the French state with instances of solidarity by local populations in France. While the French archives lend substance to these claims, they also reveal that some French representatives and officials sought to secure the most favourable conditions for the refugees. The different ways in which Spanish republicans have recalled exile does not invalidate life-history methodology.[12] On the contrary, it points unerringly to the necessity of using oral and written narratives. The proviso about approaching sources with some distance applies to this material as it does to archival evidence. With this caveat in mind, refugees' recollections are illuminating in different ways: first, they provide an additional insight into how the Spanish republicans' experiences in France were dependent on local factors; furthermore, they show that the experience and interpretation of events could be influenced by the baggage of memories collated during the arrival and reception in France. This latter point adds a further dimension to historical studies of exile which recognise a dialectical relationship between memories of pre-exile and post-displacement identities.[13] A singular characteristic of the history of Spanish republicans is that the memories of their pre-exilic lives, and especially those of their first months in exile, exerted a potent force on how they internalised reality and created a sense of self in France.

Reflections on exile

The first academic histories of the Spanish republicans were written in Spanish and emerged as the dictatorship's stranglehold upon historical research relaxed with the demise of Franco in the late 1970s.[14] Shortly afterwards Louis Stein tackled the major episodes of the Spanish republicans in France, but with very restricted access to French archives.[15] Since Stein's work, there have been very few academic histories in the English language. David Pike's work of the early 1990s has a narrower focus on the Spanish Communists between 1939 and 1945 and is not always clearly evidenced.[16] More recently, our knowledge of French, North American and British foreign policy towards the Spanish republicans in the post-war period has been greatly enhanced by David Messenger's study.[17] The bulk of work, though, is the result of French and Spanish scholars.

The most comprehensive overview of the social and political history of the Spanish exiles in France is Geneviève Dreyfus-Armand's impressive *L'Exil des Républicains Espagnols en France*, which includes an in-depth historiography of the topic.[18] On the Spanish diaspora more widely, Alicia Alted has also made a significant contribution to this history, often drawing extensively, though by no means exclusively, on oral histories.[19] While many publications have titles referring to exile, the term is used with the traditional meaning of a person/people or place. Pierre Laborie and Jean-Pierre Amalric stand apart with the evocatively entitled 'Mémoires en devenir. La construction des sens de l'exil'. But while their chapter offers an insightful discussion of the problems in referring to a single collective memory of the Spanish republican exile, it leaves us wondering about the construction of 'senses' or 'meanings' of exile in a wider sense.[20] *The routes to exile* picks up this thread in order to understand how exile was formed, what it meant and how it has been remembered.

My purpose in privileging lived experience as opposed to a textual reading of exile in no way implies a rejection of other disciplinary approaches. Rather, I seek to reconsider how exile can be conceived from a historical perspective given that reflection on this concept has mainly come from literature and cultural studies specialists. Michael Ugarte's analysis of Spanish republican intellectuals' autobiographies, novels and poetry points to two dominant and interrelated features of the Spanish republicans' exilic literature: a close relationship to the concepts of life and death, together with the presence and self-exploration of nostalgia.[21] Shirley Mangini adopts a similar approach in a study of Spanish republican women's texts where she states that exile is a 'dialectical process: though it may represent a new life, exile also embodies the death of a former life'.[22] Both scholars identify the presence of nostalgia in the Spanish republicans' lives together with the propensity to view departure from Spain in terms of rupture.

Francisco Caudet also picks up the theme of nostalgia through attention to obsessive and stagnant representations of Spain in the literary works of Spanish republican intellectuals who were based mostly in Mexico.[23] The chapter 'The Condition of Being an Exiled Republican' is notably interesting, with Caudet's observation that refugees often espoused 'a certain moral superiority ... which was often the consequence of an incapacity'.[24] To illustrate the consequences of forced displacement, Caudet draws evidence from both Spanish republican intellectuals' texts and studies containing discussions of the socio-psychological effects of exile such as Jacques Vernant's *The Refugee in the Post-War World*.[25]

Vernant's 1953 study explored the difficulties faced by refugees across a range of different host countries and referred to a 'refugee complex': 'Neurosis is a common condition among refugees and, quite apart from

symptoms of a definitely pathological character, there is every justification for speaking of a "refugee complex".[26] The emotions underlying this
'complex' range from instability and isolation to rejection. Vernant
further suggested that the difficulties associated with acceptance and
'assimilation' into the host country emanated from the refugees' desires,
and accompanying frustration resulting from the lack of freedom to
maintain links with their countries of origin.

There is no doubt that exile influences human behaviour. A problem
with using terminology such as a 'condition' or 'complex', however, is that
it sits uncomfortably close to the framework within which the French
category of the 'undesirable' foreigner was formulated during the 1930s.
Neurosis has connotations of mental disorder and obsessive behaviour,
while pathology refers to a source of illness or disease. By referring to
complexes or conditions, a focus on abnormality is directed to the refugees' behaviour as opposed to the circumstances and surrounding environment which influenced behaviour, and in this case the conditions in
which the French government and local officials received the Spanish
republicans. These studies certainly contain compelling arguments and
informative details about the challenges of exile. What remains to be
addressed more fully, though, is the relationship between the socio-psychological effects of forced displacement on the refugees, the reactions
of the institutions and nationals of the host country, and finally, the ways
in which grass-roots refugees responded to these challenges.

Exile remains an amorphous notion, but one which may be clarified
through recourse to border theory. Shirley Mangini has suggested that
Hamid Naficy's model of exile may be useful for exploring the lives of
Spanish republicans.[27] Naficy conceives of exile as a process of perpetual
becoming involving several overlapping phases: 'separation from home,
a period of liminality and in-betweeness that can be temporary or permanent and finally incorporation into the dominant host country'.[28]
Naficy's development of Victor Turner's work on the space and time of
liminality is particularly interesting. Turner regards liminality as a
moment when people are freed from normative demands, a space betwixt
and between ordered worlds where anything can happen. He further
suggests that such moments contain the potential to produce 'commu-
nitas', a social anti-structure or bond that unites people over and above
their normal everyday relations.[29] Naficy employs this conception of
liminality to advance a more positive aspect of exile. Liminality, he states,
is 'a creative and subversive space where values of both the former and
host society may be challenged, and subverted. It creates impulses to

doubt, analyse, and transcend one's own culture and society.' Liminality thus engenders what Naficy believes to be a 'privilege of exile'.[30]

The idea of exile conferring any form of privilege seems at odds with the everyday hardships confronted by the majority of Spanish republicans in France. Caudet's caveat about the temptations of reducing the complexity of the Spanish republican exile to the realm of mythology is certainly apposite.[31] If liminality and in-betweeness could lead to a state of enlightened detachment, it more frequently engendered considerable instability. The hardships and effects of forced displacement were clearly identifiable to people working with refugees in France and elsewhere during the first half of the twentieth century.[32] It was not uncommon for refugees to experience a sense of rupture and loss during and after forced displacement from one country to another. Moreover, reconstruction was a necessary, if not inevitable, consequence as refugees responded to the loss of country, property, possessions, interpersonal networks, status, and even a sense of self. In addition, disorientation and isolation emanated from the liminal and marginal position that refugees often found themselves in as they confronted, engaged with and adapted to the new cultural environment of the host countries.[33]

The refugees' journey towards the French–Spanish border had been bad enough. Many people had no option but to travel on foot across mountainous terrain, in poor weather, without adequate provisions, and with the danger of the terrifying strafing and bombing attacks from nationalist planes which homed in on civilians and troops alike. Many of the protagonists' life histories describe the physical and psychological demands of the border crossing as a painful experience which, far from dissipating, actually intensified as the refugees stepped onto French territory. The refugees confronted and negotiated a nexus of boundaries, less visible than the geopolitical border, but nonetheless tangible, and which frequently served to differentiate, if not exclude, them from French society.

The reception and first year in France represented a formative phase in the creation of the Spanish republican exile. More specifically, I argue that the 'habitual effects' of forced displacement, that is to say, the processes of loss, marginality and liminality, were immensely aggravated through the government's reception and repatriation strategy, and then compounded through subsequent events in France. The Spanish refugees endured not one but rather a series of painful episodes. These reached as far back as the start of the Spanish Civil War, if not further, and continued into exile with the overly inhospitable and often barbaric reception in France; hardships, refusal and revolt during the Occupation and Vichy era; the refusal of the western democracies to help overthrow Franco's dictatorship in the post-war years; and finally, a form of silence (and further exclusion) as the refugees disappeared from French narratives of the Second World War.

How refugees responded to these challenges constitutes a second theme in this book. I hope to demonstrate how the shock and disappointment of the first weeks in France created a long-standing lens through which Spanish republicans interpreted and subsequently remembered events. The disappointment and mistrust generated at the border was further compounded, if not confirmed, through the Vichy period and into the post-war years. Initially, this reaction manifested itself through refugees' misunderstandings about cultural practices in France. More recently, a sense of long-term discrimination has produced highly ambivalent feelings among some Spanish republicans about acculturation in France. This legacy has been reflected in the dynamics of remembrance practices in both the public and private spaces in France since the 1970s.

An interpretative approach of this kind inevitably incorporates the interlinking processes of identity and memory. There is a certain overlap in that both exile and identity can be conceived as an ongoing process of social construction. Stuart Hall's well-known formulation is helpful here. According to Hall, identity is a matter of becoming rather than being 'never complete, always in process, and always constituted within, not outside representation'.[34] Furthermore, identity is a form of positioning constructed through as opposed to outside difference.[35] The stress on difference should not be taken to imply that identity can only exist through differentiation. Identity is Janus-faced, pulling in two opposing directions and evoking both similarity and difference.

Fredrik Barth's classic exploration of ethnic groups is also helpful.[36] According to Barth, the organisation and maintenance of ethnic groups occurs through the ascription and self-ascription of individuals to their respective groups through the process of daily interaction with others. Groups distinguish themselves from one another through processes of difference and similarity. This can take two forms. Overt signals or signs may be exhibited in representation of a collective identity. Diacritical features may include flags, dress, language, etc. Identification can also be expressed in relation to basic value-orientations that include standards of morality through which behaviour is judged.[37]

Although Barth was referring to ethnic groups, his propositions are equally relevant to the Spanish political parties and trade-union organisations in exile. When the French authorities granted permission for the Spanish republican organisations to stage meetings in French public spaces, notably after the Liberation, refugees invested considerable effort in performing identities that expressed difference but also significant similarity to the French Republic. At a more individual level, though still within the group context, refugees started creating a sense of commonality through the retelling of past experiences soon after their arrival in France. Like other minority groups, the Spanish refugees drew on memories and myths to create and reinforce a sense of self that could, at times, also be translated into strategies for survival.[38] The fact that stories and anecdotes were representational practices does not imply the absence of material implication. Memory not only served as a buffer to the blows that exile wrought on refugees' sense of individual and collective self-esteem, it provided inspiration for projects and strategies aimed at facilitating both life in France and the return to Spain.

Some scholars have, not without reason, questioned the validity of Halbwach's notion of collective memory.[39] And yet, if we substitute 'collective memory' with 'collective narratives of the past', Halbwachs's thoughts retain their salience in exploring both the actions and themes involved in group remembrance activities. Particularly pertinent to this study are his thoughts on the socially constructed emphasis on remembering, the accompanying role of memory (or narratives of the past) in cementing group identities, and lastly, the relationship between the past and the present.[40]

Halbwachs's work carries implications for exploring the Spanish republicans' remembrance patterns in France. The first relates to the proposition that there can be as many collective memories as there are groups within society. Given the relationship between identity and memory, groups tend to select and reappropriate aspects of the past in relation to their contemporary concerns and future aspirations. In the case of the fragmented composition of the Spanish republican exile, this potentially calls into question the existence of an overarching memory of exile. Refugees from various organisations, whether political, syndical or cultural, interpreted the past in accordance with the interests of their specific group. Despite the acute differences that sometimes reigned between the memories of different organisations, however, refugees created a metanarrative of exile based on a series of perceived shared experiences which served to legitimate the concerns of all Spanish republicans at various junctures.

The second implication concerns the relationship between individual and collective memory. According to Halbwachs, it is misleading to delineate any hard and distinct difference between individual and group memory due to the influence exerted by the latter on the individual. Individual thought and memory is inextricably tied to that of the corresponding group; indeed, it is projected onto the social framework or collective memory of the group in question.[41] The assumption, therefore, is that individual memory may only be formulated within the context of the collective. The oral histories collected for this study reveal that the relationship is more complex. Although the individual may recount episodes of his/her life which reflect the overarching metanarrative of exile, other and more explicitly personal memories can also be expressed. This suggests that the relationship between the social and the personal should not be viewed too deterministically.

It is a truism that memories espoused by an organisation or individuals are influenced by the context in which they occur: they are dependent on questions of time, space and social milieu. A commemoration of exile celebrated in 1945 may have constructed memory in a different way to a memorial occasion in 2005. The point to be made here is that while these different factors exercise an influence on individual and group memory, it should not be assumed that they radically change the content of the memory in question. This may partly relate to the question of duration; the longer the period in question, the more likely it is that the central themes of a memory narrative will undergo transformation. The contemporary concerns of different Spanish republican groups have influenced their representations of the past and, as will see in the last part of this book, the processes of selection and appropriation have clearly been evident. At times the Spanish republicans have emphasised certain aspects of the past to the neglect of others, and new themes have recently begun to emerge. But at the same time a kernel of themes have provided a semblance of continuity. In this study, it is therefore appropriate to regard the content of the Spanish republican exilic memory-narrative in terms of changing emphasis.

The Spanish republicans' remembrance practices clearly represent a performative phenomenon, constructed at given moments through specific kinds of memorial activities. Nevertheless, the idea of performativity, together with Halbwachs's point about the influence of the present on memory, should not be taken too far. Remembrance also serves to construct a sense of self, which in turn relies on creating a sense of continuity. In the context of rupture and exile this is particularly important.

On the other hand, focus on temporal continuity should not blur the changes that have occurred in the Spanish republicans' remembrance practices over the long duration.

In the approach that I have set out, exile becomes more than simply a referent to a place or person. The Spanish republican exile in France was much more than the product of Franco's victory in Spain, or of the refugees' preoccupations and meditations about returning. It was a socially constructed phenomenon grounded in historical contingency and dependent on the actions of the refugees, the French and Spanish authorities, and the people with whom they interacted in France. While it is necessary and unavoidable to underline the scale of exclusion confronted by the Spanish refugees, the solidarity and support shown by French representatives, associations and members of the population should also be recognised: exile involved exclusion, but also acceptance. Hence this book's concerns with the ever-changing framework of exile constructed by – and through the interactions between – the Spanish republicans and their hosts in France.

On the 'routes' to an exile

This book is organised both chronologically and thematically. Chronologically, it charts events from the last year of the French Third Republic, passing through the Occupation and post-war periods, to the development of a commemorative culture of exile and the celebration of the seventieth anniversary of the *Retirada* in 2009.[42] Thematically, it discusses the development of three different aspects of exile. Part I, 'The onset of exile,' sets out how the structural aspects of exile were established through a focus on group boundaries during the first year and a half in France. Chapter 1, 'Unravelling rights and identities: the exodus of 1939', discusses the context of early twentieth-century immigration history in France in order to understand the French government's ambivalent and improvised reception of the Spanish republicans. It then turns to the events surrounding the largest refugee influx hitherto in French history, the 1939 exodus. The last part of the chapter resonates with the refugees' voices and identifies some of their strategies for coping with the harrowing journey across the Pyrenees. I argue that this border crossing represented the culminating point in a process that involved the unravelling of both the Spanish republicans' identities and the French Republic's commitment to asylum.

The next chapter, 'Reception, internment and repatriation, 1939–40', outlines the reactions of the French authorities, press and public. Although some French nationals reacted with gestures of solidarity, the refugees faced a considerable level of discrimination and pressure to return to Spain. The most visible sign of exclusion existed on the beaches of the French Mediterranean where close to two hundred thousand refugees were penned into sprawling concentration camps. Although most women, children and the elderly were housed in reception centres elsewhere in France, conditions were often very basic. Comparisons are drawn between the reductive and scaremongering reporting of the Spanish refugees in much of the French press, and French officials' descriptions of refugees arriving in their localities. The argument here is that French officials mobilised cultural difference in order to secure the exclusion of the refugees from the French population and their return to Spain. In Chapter 3, 'Organisations, networks and identities, 1939–40', the emphasis switches to how the Spanish republicans responded with a focus on the reconstruction of their organisations, networks and collective identities. The chapter presents an overview of the Spanish republican government and the main organisations in exile before looking at the reconstruction of interpersonal networks in the camps. It shows the various ways in which refugees recreated group identities, from the telling of stories to the commemoration of dates from the Spanish and French republican calendars.

Part II, 'Working in from the margins', looks at the development of the Spanish republican exile in conjunction with wider changes in France, from the mobilisation of war against Germany through to the Liberation and post-war period. The overall premise of the two chapters is that the introduction of refugees into French workplaces opened up possibilities which facilitated adaptation to daily life in France. Chapters 4 and 5 demonstrate how governments of the Third Republic and Vichy years initially endeavoured, but ultimately failed to maintain Spanish republicans as marginal subjects whilst introducing them into the labour economy through paramilitary labour formations. While acknowledging the very different contexts of the Third Republic and Vichy, these chapters identify points of similarity surrounding the implementation of, and reactions to, the foreign labour formations.

Chapter 4, 'Ambiguities at work: refugees and the French war economy, 1939–40', questions the view that all refugees endured an increasingly repressive context at the end of the Third Republic by showing how the war economy created certain, though limited, opportunities for the

Spanish republicans. The introduction of the refugees into workplaces through the Foreign Labour Companies and other work schemes secured an end to mass internment and was followed by improved working conditions. Nonetheless, the French authorities had to contend with problems of surveillance and issues of legitimacy as some Spanish republicans protested or escaped from the Labour Companies in order to retain some agency over their lives in France.

Chapter 5, 'Work, surveillance, refusal and revolt in Vichy and German-occupied France, 1940–44', explores the refugees' experiences of working for Vichy's Foreign Labour Groups and the German Organisation Todt. An initial reluctance to employ the Spanish workers by both Vichy and German officials was rapidly replaced by a realisation of their labour potential and a corresponding amelioration of their working conditions. As under the Third Republic, the French authorities were preoccupied with surveillance and escaping refugee workers. Moreover, the motivations driving a high number of Spanish republicans to escape from their workplaces continued to stem from the need to improve material conditions or to retain an element of choice over their location of work. However, the presence of the German occupying forces and the collaborationist Vichy regime created an entirely new dynamic to organised refugee labour. A competing demand for labour combined with the development of rival refugee labour strategies essentially opened up new possibilities for those Spanish republicans needing to change their place of work. Another and fundamental point of rupture was the stridently subversive transformation of workplaces into spaces of contestation along with the decisively dangerous consequences if arrested for resistance activities. As French and German authorities became increasingly reliant on Spanish republican labour, a pronounced pattern of refugee refusal and revolt unfolded, with workplaces becoming key sites for nurturing Spanish republican resistance.

Work and resistance could be an enabling factor in forging new relations between the Spanish republicans and French nationals. An emphasis on common adversity and/or ideological beliefs combined with ostensible displays of Spanish–French republican friendship thus became a central feature of Spanish republican commemorative events during the Liberation and post-war years. The dynamics surrounding this commemorative drive, along with the ensuing development of Spanish republican remembrance activities over the long duration, are analysed in Part III, 'Aspirations of return, commemoration and home'.

Chapter 6, 'Mobilisation, commemoration and return, 1944–55', explains the different ways in which the refugees responded to the possibility of returning to Spain. The refugees' aim of returning was not accompanied by a nostalgic discourse about an idyllic homeland, but rather justified by references to atrocious conditions in Spain, and the Spanish republicans' participation in the Liberation of France and Europe. A tangible sense of an imminent return resulted in a mass incursion of Spanish republican guerrilla fighters into Spain, the reappropriation of Spanish consulates and embassies in southwest France, and a prolific round of public meetings and commemorative activity designed to call attention to the Spanish republican cause. For the first time since their arrival, the refugees began mobilising a collective memory of their exile in France as part of their strategy for returning to Spain. But as it became clear there would be no intervention by France and its allies or even any support for overthrowing General Franco, the socio-political framework of exilic memory diminished. During this short but intense bout of remembrance Spanish republicans established some of the central themes of the commemorative culture of exile that gradually emerged from the 1970s.

The title of the final chapter, 'Moving memories, 1970–2009', is a reference to the affective, changing and spatially mobile characteristics of Spanish republicans' memory activities. The chapter reflects on the place of refugees' memories within and beyond the memory framework of the French nation state. In the first place, it demonstrates both the potential and limits of Nora's work for understanding refugees' memories through a discussion of the relationship between *lieux* and *milieux de mémoire*. The emphasis then turns to Spanish republican remembrance practices in both public and private spaces in France. The chapter explains how and why a commemorative culture of the Spanish republican exile gradually began to emerge during the 1970s before observing the development of memory associations in France from the 1980s to the seventieth anniversary of the *Retirada* in 2009. The last section of the chapter reveals how Spanish republicans have constructed a sense of home through material culture and everyday rituals. Their narratives evoke the long-lasting effects of exile, but also underline how any understanding of exile necessarily involves a consideration of the attitudes and reactions of the host country.

The format of this book is not meant to articulate a teleological approach to history. There was no predetermined outcome to exile. Neither the duration nor the future events of exile could have been foreseen as refugees like Miguel Oviedo crossed the Pyrenees in search of refuge. The future was an unknown quantity, but one which refugees began to measure against the conditions of their arrival and reception in France.

Notes

1 Unpublished diary of Miguel Oviedo.

2 All translations are my own unless otherwise stated. P. Nora (ed.), *Les Lieux de Mémoire*, Vol. 1 (Paris, 1997), p. 23.

3 Paul Gilroy's use of 'routes' emphasises the processual and constantly changing nature of identity. P. Gilroy, *The Black Atlantic: Modernity and Double Consciousness* (London, 1993), p. 3.

4 In 1952, there were 13,905 statutory Spanish refugees registered in the Aquitaine, 6,145 of whom were in the *département* of the Gironde. AD Gironde, Versement 1239/42. Report from the Ministère de l'Intérieur, 17 October 1952.

5 In contemporary France the Basses-Pyrénées is known as the Pyrénées-Atlantiques.

6 For studies on the Basses-Pyrénées see: C. Laharie, *Le Camp de Gurs, 1939–45: Un aspect méconnu de l'histoire du Béarn* (Biarritz, 1993); C. Arnould, 'L'Accueil des réfugiés espagnols en Béarn et en Soule de 1936–1940', in M. Papy (ed.), *Les Espagnols et la Guerre Civile* (Biarritz, 1999); J. Ortiz 'La résistance espagnole en Béarn', in *Ibid.*; J. Ortiz, *Guerrilleros en Béarn. Guerrilleros, étranges terroristes étrangers* (Biarritz, 2007). There exists one publication dealing with a general history of Spanish migration to the Aquitaine which contains a broad, general overview of the Spanish republicans in Bordeaux: M. Santos-Sainz and F. Guillemeteaud, *Les Espagnols à Bordeaux et en Aquitaine* (Bordeaux, 2006). Otherwise some references to the Spanish republicans can be found in: R. Terrisse, *Bordeaux, 1940–1944* (Paris, 1993). D. Lormier, *La Base Sous-Marine de Bordeaux, 1940–1944* (Montreuil-Bellay, 1999) contains fleeting references to the Spanish refugees, which is surprising given that they were heavily implicated in the construction of the submarine base. C. Courau, *Les Poudriers dans la Résistance: St Médard-en-Jalles (1940–1944)* (Pau, 2001) contains some brief but interesting information on Spanish workers of the Labour Companies during the battle of France. B. Reviriego, *Les Juifs en Dordogne 1939–1944* (Périgueux, 2003) provides useful details of Spanish participation in Vichy's Foreign Labour Groups.

7 The tensions leading up to the conflict are discussed in P. Preston, *The Coming of the Spanish Civil War. Reform, Reaction and Revolution in the Second Republic* (London, 2nd edn, 1994). An authoritative account of the Second Republic during the Civil War is provided by H. Graham, *The Spanish Republic at War 1936–1939* (Cambridge, 2002).

8 See the discussion on material culture and the home in Chapter 7.

9 S. Gemie, 'The Ballad of Bourg-Madame: Spanish Refugee Writing and the Pyrenean Border, 1939', *International Review of Social History*, 51 (2006), p. 10.

10 *La Dépêche*, 2 February 1939 reproduced in M-C. Rafaneau-Boj, *Odyssée pour la liberté. Les camps de prisonniers espagnols (1939–1945)* (Paris, 1993), p. 117.

11 D. Peschanski, *La France des camps. L'internement 1938–1946* (Paris, 2002), p. 17. See Introduction to J.-C. Villegas (ed.) *Plages d'exil. Les camps de réfugiés espagnols en France – 1939* (Nanterre-Dijon, 1989). J. Rubio, *La emigración de la guerra civil de 1936–1939*, Vol. 1 (Madrid, 1977), p. 289.

12 Debates concerning the extent to which oral histories are representative, reliable and valid have been well rehearsed and therefore need not be repeated here. See for instance: R. J. Grele, *Envelopes of Sound: The Art of Oral History* (Chicago, 1985), pp. 127–54; R. Samuel and P. Thompson (eds), *The Myths We Live By* (London, 1990); A. Thomson, M. Frisch, and P. Hamilton, 'The Memory and History Debates: Some International Perspectives', *Oral History*, 22:2 (1994); P. Thompson, *The Voice of the Past: Oral History* (Oxford, 3rd edn, 2000), pp. 156–69; and K. Plummer, *Documents of Life 2: An Invitation to a Critical Humanism* (London, 2001), pp. 232–53.

13 A. Thomson, 'Moving Stories: Oral History and Migration Studies', *Oral History*, 35 (1999).

14 A. Artís-Gener, *La diáspora republicana* (Barcelona, 1975); J. L. Abellan, (ed.) *El Exilio español de 1939*, 6 vols. (Madrid, 1976–78); J. Rubio, *La emigración de la guerra civil de 1936–1939*, Vols. 1–3 (Madrid, 1977).

15 L. Stein, *Beyond Death and Exile: The Spanish Republicans in France, 1939–1955* (Cambridge, Massachusetts, 1979).

16 D. W. Pike, *In the Service of Stalin: The Spanish Communists in Exile, 1939–1945* (Oxford, 1993).

17 D. A. Messenger *L'Espagne Républicaine: French Policy and Spanish Republicanism in Liberated France* (Eastbourne, 2008).

18 G. Dreyfus-Armand, *L'Exil des Républicains Espagnols en France: De la Guerre Civile à la Mort de Franco* (Paris, 1999).

19 In particular see A. Alted Vigil, *La voz de los vencidos: El exilio republicano de 1939* (Madrid, 2005).

20 P. Laborie and J.-P. Amalric, 'Mémoires en devenir. La construction des sens de l'exil', in L. Domergue (ed.), *L'exil Républicain espagnol à Toulouse 1939–1999* (Toulouse, 1999).

21 M. Ugarte, *Shifting Ground: Spanish Civil War Exile Literature* (Durham/London, 1989). See in particular Chapter 6 'Exilic Autobiographies', pp. 82–96.

22 S. Mangini, *Memories of Resistance: Women's Voices from the Spanish Civil War* (New Haven/London, 1995), p. 155.

23 F. Caudet, *Hipótesis sobre el exilio republicano de 1939* (Madrid, 1997).

24 *Ibid.*, p. 336.

25 J. Vernant, *The Refugee in the Post-War World* (London, 1953).

26 *Ibid.*, p. 17.

27 S. Mangini, 'El exilio de Federica Montseny en Francia', in A. Alted Vigil and M. Aznar Soler (eds), *Literatura y Cultura del Exilio Español de 1939 en Francia* (Salamanca, 1998), p. 503.

28 H. Naficy, *The Making of Exile Cultures: Iranian Television in Los Angeles* (Minneapolis, 1993), pp. xv–xvi.

29 V. Turner, *Dramas, Fields and Metaphors: Symbolic Action in Human Society* (Ithaca/London, 1974), pp. 231–70.

30 Naficy, *The Making of Exile Cultures*, p. 10.

31 Caudet, *Hipótesis sobre el exilio republicano de 1939*.

32 Vernant, *The Refugee in the Post-War World*.

33 Anthropologists suggest that the phenomena of loss, reconstruction, marginality and liminality tend to be experienced by refugees generally. L. A. Camino and R. N. Krulfeld (eds), *Reconstructing Lives, Recapturing Meaning: Refugee Identity, Gender, and Cultural Change* (Basel, 1994), pp. ix–xviii.

34 S. Hall, 'Cultural Identity & Diaspora,' in J. Rutherford (ed.), *Identity: Community, Culture, Difference* (London, 1990), p. 222.

35 S. Hall, 'Introduction: Who Needs "Identity"?' in S. Hall and P. du Gay (eds), *Questions of Cultural Identity* (London, 1996), p. 2.

36 F. Barth (ed.), *Ethnic Groups and Boundaries: The Social Organisation of Culture Difference* (London, 1969).

37 See the 'Introduction' in *Ibid.*

38 Samuel and Thompson (eds), *The Myths We Live By*, p. 19.

39 N. Gedi and Y. Elam, 'Collective Memory – What is it?' *History & Memory* 8:1 (1996), pp. 30–50.

40 M. Halbwachs, *La mémoire collective* (Paris, 1950), p. 48, cited in A. L. Coser (ed.), *Maurice Halbwachs on Collective Memory* (Chicago, 1992), p. 22.

41 M. Halbwachs, 'The Reconstruction of the Past', in *Ibid.*, p. 53.

42 Spanish republicans initially referred to the 1939 exodus as the '*retirada*'. The spelling of '*Retirada*' has emerged in conjunction with the commemoration of the Spanish Republican exile over the last couple of decades.

PART I

The onset of exile

1

Unravelling rights and identities:
the exodus of 1939

Antonia Illazque's recollection of the exodus as a 14-year-old contains themes common to other Spanish refugees' narratives. She left home in Tarrasa with her family early one morning to undertake a hazardous journey on foot to the Franco-Spanish border. They endured the well-founded fear of aerial attacks, fatigue and the lack of food. Somewhere along the way, her brother asked to go back home: he was hungry. His mother tried to encourage him with positive words about France: it was a country with a rich culture, and it was a Republic, just like Spain.[1] Antonia's description of her mother's dialogue ends ominously with the words 'but then we crossed the border'. This reference to the border crossing alerts us to a profound and lasting sense of shock and disappointment. The French authorities separated the family, sending her cousin and grandmother to Grenoble, while interning Antonia, her mother and brother in the concentration camp on the beach of Argelès-sur-Mer. Her father was interned in another camp at Vernet, in the Ariège. 'Why was the family separated?' asked Antonia, 'we felt like criminals, labelled "reds" . . . No. We were republicans!'

The labelling, insults and alienation experienced by Spanish republicans was a brutal blow and an indication that crossing the Franco-Spanish national border engendered a profound change. The array of personal, domestic and military objects scattered along the pathways and roads into France – left by refugees too weary to carry them or confiscated by the French border authorities – represented perhaps the first visible sign that becoming a refugee entailed leaving something behind. Loss contained multiple layers. Along with the absence of possessions came the realisation that their rights, along with their identities, the very sense of who they were, could no longer be taken for granted.

There was nothing inevitable about the French treatment of the refugees. On the contrary, Spanish republicans had several reasons to think they would be warmly or at the very least adequately received. Throughout Europe, the politically persecuted viewed France as *the* country of asylum. More particularly, the 1789 French Revolution and ensuing Republic had long been a source of inspiration in Spain, even giving rise to the republican allegory of a Spanish Marianne on propaganda posters during the Spanish Civil War. Furthermore, the French and Spanish Republics ostensibly shared common interests. The fear of extreme right-wing authoritarianism, from both within and beyond the borders of these two nation-states, together with the accompanying desire for social justice, had been influential factors behind the election of Popular Front governments in both countries.[2] Why, therefore, was the French government extremely reticent about welcoming refugees from a neighbouring republic? Why and how did the refugees evoke so much ambivalence amongst French nationals? What circumstances led the French government to deprive refugees of a fundamental right through mass internment, thereby compromising the universal values of the Republic? After examining these issues, this chapter will return to the voices of refugees like Antonia to gain an insight into how they experienced the largest border crossing in French history, and will finish with the an assessment of the appalling conditions of the camps.

Refugee legislation and the Third Republic

In 1793 the Montagnard Constitution proclaimed that France would 'give asylum to foreigners banished from their homelands for the cause of freedom'.[3] Politicians and pro-refugee groups of the Third Republic frequently associated the Republic with refuge for the persecuted. It did not matter that the practice of providing asylum actually pre-dated the French Republic, or that the right to asylum often depended on the economic, social and political context of France as opposed to universal values, or that national identification hinged on categorising who belonged, and consequently, who did not belong to the nation.[4] Tradition operates by smoothing out contradictions and easily incorporates inconsistencies into the composite of national narrative. Asylum was an ideal rather than a given, and as such, open to interpretation and uneven in implementation. To the population in France and beyond, however, this ideal was strongly associated and perhaps synonymous with the French Republic: France was the home of universal rights and *the* refuge for the persecuted in Europe.

The country's central geographical location, its shared borders and international transport links also explain why France became the prime destination for refugees from across the continent during the first half of the twentieth century. During the decades of the 1920s and 1930s refugees became a truly mass phenomenon as the development and consolidation of nation-states across the continent led to exclusion on a previously unimaginable scale. Nation-states developed a new vocabulary, new procedures and new responses with the invention of the stateless person. In 1921, the Bolsheviks stripped Russian 'whites' of their nationality and citizenship rights resulting in the exile of more than 120,000 émigrés in France. Mussolini's regime was quick to adopt this new procedure and anti-fascist refugees increased the Italian migrant population in France to 800,000.[5] In the same decade around 65,000 Armenians sought refuge in France.[6] During the 1930s, the rise of fascism in Germany led to the displacement of German Jews and anti-fascists as well as refugees from other Central and Eastern European countries. By the time the Spanish republicans arrived en masse in 1939, governments of the French Third Republic had therefore already dealt with large numbers of refugees. France was at the forefront of refugee reception, and yet the country lacked an overall refugee statute or comprehensive policy on asylum.

At the international level, there had been some developments towards a pan-national response to refugees. In 1921 the League of Nations appointed Fridtjof Nansen, a Norwegian diplomat with a background in Arctic exploration and science, as High Commissioner to deal with the Russian issue. Nansen's response was the creation of special identity papers, the 'Nansen passport', which allowed Russian and refugee groups from the former Ottoman Empire, such as Armenians and Kurds, to travel between countries in lieu of a national passport. During the following decade, the 1933 Geneva Convention marked an attempt to define a wider refugee statute by recognising a refugee as someone 'who does not or who no longer enjoys the protection of his country'.[7] It also established social rights for the Nansen refugees and forbade governments of refuge countries from expelling them. This had little immediate impact in France, however, for the Convention was not ratified until the autumn of 1936 by the Popular Front government.

As the issue of Jewish refugees became ever more pressing, additional moves were made to extend the international refugee remit with President Franklin D. Roosevelt's impetus for an international conference. Representatives of nation-states and charity organisations met at Évian-les-Bains from 6 to 15 July 1938 to hammer out an international plan of co-operation for refugee relief and settlement.[8] The creation of an Intergovernmental Committee to look into all victims of fascism was one of the few outcomes of the conference. Even this was ambitious. The Committee achieved very little before the outbreak of the Second World War due to a lack of time and will of national governments.

The developing framework of refugee rights at the international level had limited impact on overall refugee issues in France. It may even have reduced French commitments to developing a consistent refugee policy by creating the impression that a pan-national approach removed the need for solutions at the national level.[9] At any rate, in the absence of any overall refugee statute, governments of the Third Republic consistently balanced asylum with the sovereign interests of the nation-state. French officials treated refugees from different countries on a case-by-case basis, granting juridical refugee status to the Nansen refugees, Saarlanders and refugees from Germany who had arrived in France between the start of 1933 and the summer of 1936.[10] Refugee status was denied to Italian anti-fascists for fear of upsetting Mussolini, and for similar reasons, the Spanish republicans had to wait until the end of the Second World War.

With or without legal refugee status, life in France had never been especially easy for any group of refugees. In the absence of any overall refugee statute, French officials tended to conceive of migrant workers and refugees within an overall paradigm of economic migration. During the 1920s, the favourable economic outlook undoubtedly facilitated the reception and incorporation of refugees into local employment networks. But even then the different experiences of the Russian and Armenian refugees, both of whom came under the Nansen remit, illustrates that conditions varied considerably between different refugee groups and localities.[11] The major problem with treating refugees as any other migrant worker, however, is that the refugees' official status was dependent on the possession of a work permit. In other words, the French state often provided asylum in accordance with a refugee's work situation rather than in relation to universal rights. Unemployment could thus make refugees vulnerable to repressive measures including expulsion.

Matters deteriorated in the following decade. By the start of the 1930s France had one of the highest immigration rates in the world. At the same time, the Depression had begun to bite provoking debates in France about the reception and even presence of refugees. This resulted in the law of August 1932 that limited immigrant numbers in French workplaces. The context of a declining economy and rise in xenophobic and anti-Semitic sentiment was hardly conducive to the arrival of refugees, often Jews, from Nazi Germany and Eastern Europe. Even so, the government, anxious to secure a diplomatic victory over the Nazi regime, initially posed fewer restrictions on the reception of German refugees from the spring of 1933. But this was short-lived, with the government reversing its initial stance on relaxed entry restrictions during the summer. Although the League of Nation's creation of a High Commissioner for refugees from Germany in October showed growing international commitment to the issue, it provided the opportunity for successive French governments to call on other nations to share the responsibility of refugee reception by pushing forward the view of France as a place of temporary rather than permanent asylum.[12]

The return of conservative rule in November 1934 did not bode well for refugees or immigrants more widely. The governments of Pierre-Étienne Flandin and Pierre Laval sought the reduction of foreigners as one solution to the country's economic difficulties and introduced a series of laws aimed clearly at excluding German and Eastern European refugees from the labour market. Worse still, refugees unable to renew their work permits, including refugees from Germany, were expelled. Pro-refugee voices could still be heard, though room for manoeuvre was limited. Marius Moutet, a Socialist deputy and leading member of the League for the Rights of Man, proposed a draft immigration statute that included improved rights for refugees, but it never passed the discussion stage in parliament.[13] As Vicki Caron has noted, the Flandin and Laval administrations implemented the first anti-refugee crackdown of the 1930s.[14]

The Popular Front

From the mid-1930s, France became an increasingly fractured and politically polarised country. A financial scandal surrounding establishment figures and Alexandre Stavisky, a French national of Russian-Jewish origins, stoked up xenophobic and anti-Semitic sentiment, together with hostility towards the Republican regime. 'France for the French' was one slogan chanted by militants of the anti-parliamentary far right-wing league, the Croix de Feu, as they demonstrated in front of the National

Assembly on 6 February 1934. A violent confrontation with the police ensued, resulting in 17 deaths and well over 1,000 injured.[15] As well as provoking the resignation of the newly designated premier, Édouard Daladier, the riot sparked immediate debate about whether the Republic was under threat of a fascist coup. Contemporaries on the left were convinced the Republic was in imminent danger. The PCF consequently organised a counter-demonstration on 9 February that also turned nasty, leaving six demonstrators dead, and a general strike in support of democracy followed on 12 February.[16] The month of February 1934 had involved a level of political violence hitherto unparalleled in the Third Republic, and laid bare cavernous divisions in French society, producing something akin to a civil-war mentality.

The anti-fascist reflex of 1934 led to the election of the Popular Front coalition government in May 1936 under the premiership of the Socialist theoretician Léon Blum. The working class greeted electoral success with an unprecedented wave of strikes which seemed to turn the world upside down by challenging power relations and entrenched forms of hierarchy. It was a reminder that the remit of the Popular Front stretched beyond anti-fascism to include long-awaited and necessary social and work-related reforms. The widespread optimism of this moment also spread to refugees and supporters of a more humane approach to asylum-related matters with one commentator, Ernesto Caporali, exclaiming in the General Confederation of Labour (CGT) newspaper *le Peuple*: 'A Popular Front government must give the right to asylum a real sense, fitting for a Republic which seeks to continue the great traditions of 1789.'[17]

On asylum-related issues there was good cause to be optimistic. In opposition, the Socialist Party had provided vociferous support for refugees while contesting the anti-Semitism of the right-wing press. Leading Socialists such as Blum and Moutet had repeatedly called for disentangling the right of asylum from the ability to find work. In May 1936, another Socialist, Marcel Livian, set out an immigration code that proposed a legal status for refugees, and two months later, the Communist deputy, Georges Lévy, proposed an immigration statute which included asylum guarantees. In the same year, the Popular Front government signed up to the League of Nations' provisional arrangements for refugees from Germany, and, as we have already seen, the government finally ratified the 1933 Geneva Convention for Russian and Armenian refugees on 28 October 1936. But there was also reason for disappointment. Anti-Semites continued to peddle their illusory view of a government dominated by Jews, seemingly confirmed by Blum's Jewish background.[18] The Socialists' and Communists' proposals were never implemented, and while the League of Nations agreements were undoubtedly a step forward, the pan-national response to refugee issues may have resulted in lethargy at the national level. The most contentious of the Popular Front's actions, though, was the hard-line approach towards newcomers from Germany and the decision to deny asylum to refugees arriving from the start of 1937.[19]

The historical record of the Popular Front on refugee issues has consequently been the subject of some debate. Some of the first historians to discuss this issue stress the absence of any significant reform or improvement to refugees' conditions.[20] More recent studies, however, have contained more nuanced views. Gérard Noiriel points towards the absence of any major legislative reform, but believes that more generally migrant workers' rights improved in line with French workers.[21] On the question of refugees from Germany, Vicki Caron and Mary Lewis argue that a revised and substantially more positive picture of the Popular Front emerges if a distinction is made between the intention to close the eastern border to newly arriving refugees, and the positive steps taken for refugees already in France.[22]

Echoes of the conflict in Spain

Given the reticence about accepting further refugees from Germany, how did the Popular Front government react to the prospect of refugees from the conflict in Spain? The fracturing of the political arena in France and the responses to the Spanish Civil War are cardinal to understanding this question. Even though the strikes of the summer of 1936 expressed optimism and a call for the Popular Front to introduce much-needed reforms, they were perceived by the right and extreme right wing as evidence that the country was on the verge of revolution. The cumulative tensions produced by 6 February 1934 and the carnivalesque summer of 1936 began to take on the appearance of a dress rehearsal for a wider, more extraordinary phenomenon. Within this context, the outbreak of conflict in Spain reverberated loudly in France, providing an uncanny echo of tensions at home.

An increasingly divided French society viewed the theatre of conflict in Spain through the lens of its own anxieties and aspirations.[23] As in France, the political system in Spain was based on the Republic and governed by a Popular Front government. The difference was that in

Spain an attempted coup against the Popular Front occurred. On 17 and 18 July 1936 a group of renegade generals tried to overthrow the government and the Second Spanish Republic, but failed in the face of popular opposition and support from those members of the armed forces and police who remained loyal to the Republic.

There had been a tradition of military intervention in Spanish politics, but none had developed into open warfare on this scale. The July coup occurred in the context of a society where a coalition of elite interests had consistently tried to block moves towards mass democracy and desperately needed social reforms. This was unlike previous military coups. First, myriad conflicts were unleashed: urban culture versus rural tradition; secularism against religion; liberal democracy versus authoritarianism, autonomists against centralists; revolutionaries against reactionaries; and anti-fascists against fascists. As the failed coup d'état evolved into a longer conflict these various interests coalesced into two rival sides: the republicans and the nationalists led by the rebel generals. Secondly, rapid external intervention transformed Spain into an international theatre of war which became a focus for the hopes and fears of populations across the world.[24]

Anti-fascists in France and elsewhere received news of the rapid military intervention of Nazi Germany and fascist Italy on the nationalist side as evidence that democracy throughout Europe was at stake. Accordingly, many believed Spain constituted perhaps the last opportunity to make a stand against the spread of fascism and reaction. Some anti-fascists and particularly anarchists took heart that a more progressive, egalitarian society would emerge from the social revolutions which had accompanied the outbreak of war. Among conservative and religious circles in France, however, the reports of social revolution and church desecrations further fuelled apprehensions about the fate of Christianity in Europe, thereby strengthening anti-communist and anti-anarchist resolve. In Pierre Laborie's words, Spain literally made France 'sick with fright'.[25]

Blum's first reaction was to provide war material to the Spanish Republic. But he was forced to back down because of British disapproval, a hysterical response from the right-wing press and the Radicals' reticence about intervention. The ensuing French proposal of 'non-intervention' aimed to keep weapons out of Spain, thereby exhausting the conflict and enabling the survival of the Republic. In practice, the international 'Non-Intervention' treaty produced the opposite effect, essentially preventing the Spanish Republic from purchasing weapons as the western democracies turned a blind eye to German Nazi and Italian fascist support for the nationalist camp. Russian supplies to the Spanish Republic did little more than prolong defeat, but provided ammunition to conservatives in France who believed that Stalin was seeking to establish communist power throughout Western Europe.

Defeat came in stages, as did the number of people seeking refuge in France. The rebels' gradual occupation of republican Spain pushed several waves of refugees towards France before the great exodus of 1939: 15,000 in September 1936 as the Basque country was occupied; another 120,000 as the nationalists completed their northern campaign during the summer and autumn of 1937; and a further 25,000 in the spring of the following year with the nationalist victory in Aragón. At the end of 1938, the Spanish refugee population numbered just over 40,000.[26] This final figure indicates that a high number of refugees had crossed back over the border after a relatively short period of time in France.

Offering a temporary refuge was highly consistent with the Popular Front's stance on Spanish refugees. The strategy aimed to offer a humanitarian response while at the same time limiting the cost of aid and the accompanying criticism from right-wing circles about sheltering Spanish republican or 'red' refugees. According to Geneviève Dreyfus-Armand, while ministerial guidelines were initially inspired by humanitarian concerns, it was not long before they were tainted with preoccupations about finance. The government had never envisaged the permanent settlement of the refugees and became ever keener to repatriate refugees as soon as possible to the zone (republican or national) of their choice. Where this was not possible officials transferred the refugees from the border into reception centres located between the Garonne and Loire rivers. In the spring of 1937, the government adopted a harsher position, restricting entry through reinforced border controls and stricter bureaucratic requirements for people wishing to leave Spain. By the end of the year, the Socialist Minister of the Interior, Marx Dormoy, wished to create an 'impassable barrier' along the border and to repatriate all refugees reliant on public funds, save children, the sick and the injured.[27]

There were some similarities with the earlier German refugee crisis. The government's initial liberal response soon gave way to entry restrictions, amidst criticism about the economic and political considerations of receiving anti-fascist refugees. The Spanish refugee issue also reinforced views which had been floating around the administration since 1933 that France should no longer serve as a permanent place of asylum but rather as place of transit, a stepping stone towards permanent asylum in other countries. Views of the refugees continued to be divided along ideological lines, with the left generally articulating a pro-refugee position and the right pressing for entrance restrictions ostensibly because of the economic costs involved and the fear of bringing conflict to France.[28] However, anti-refugee sentiment in France at the end of the 1930s was considerably worse than during the first years of the decade. The malign notion of the 'undesirable refugee' now featured in policy making while also permeating moderate public opinion. Claims that France should no longer offer permanent asylum gathered pace, feeding a mounting logic of exclusion which reached its apogee with the mass refugee internments of 1939. The legislative framework for these internments was put in place by Daladier's Radical-led government.

Legislating for control, surveillance and exclusion

Shortly after Daladier's administration entered office on 10 April 1938, the premier and his Minister of the Interior, Albert Sarraut, indicated they would take a strong line on immigration. In particular they argued the need to distinguish between 'good' and 'bad' foreigners. They wasted no time. Four days into office, Sarraut called for a 'methodical, energetic and prompt action with a view to ridding our country of the presence of an excessive number of undesirable elements'.[29] Several weeks later, Sarraut explained that the decree of 2 May differentiated 'the foreigner[s] of good faith, who maintained an absolutely correct attitude vis-à-vis the Republic and its institutions' from the 'clandestine foreigners, irregular guests ... unworthy of living on our soil'.[30] The new measures essentially increased police powers and strengthened procedures for dealing with so-called 'clandestine' immigration, while also containing two articles which improved refugees' rights in relation to the application for refugee status and immigrant expulsion orders.[31] Less than a fortnight later, the decree of 14 May outlined further improved conditions for immigrants through an extension of the validity of identity cards and increased rights for foreigners able to demonstrate commitment to France through length of stay and family ties.

The concessions contained in the two decrees suggest the government had not entirely evacuated the principle of asylum from policy making. In practice, however, local officials largely ignored the improved rights of immigrants while consistently applying the restrictive measures of the May decrees, thereby creating what Mary Lewis refers to as an unprecedented repression of migrants' civil liberties in France.[32] Over the following six months the logic of exclusion became more extreme as officials entertained and then implemented legislation which set the basis for mass internment. On 3 May, the Ministry of War and National Defence had already instructed generals in the southwest of France to find suitable areas for the installation of internment camps for an esti-mated population of 15,000 Spanish refugees from 'certain categories', a euphemism for those considered as a threat to national security.[33] Six months later the decree law of 12 November 1938 then established the legal framework for the internment of 'undesirable' foreigners into 'special camps'.[34] Henceforth, the French government could intern for-eigners on the basis of a suspicion rather than through a crime commit-ted: any foreigner suspected of compromising public order or considered to be a threat to national security could be locked up without trial.

What were the reasons behind this extreme measure and deepening public anti-refugee sentiment? Daladier's administration was confronted by a challenging context and concerned about the stability of the Third Republic. At the domestic level, the country's economic problems, with a declining franc and deepening public debt, continued to feed into the xenophobia of the late 1930s. However, what distinguished this bout of anti-refugee sentiment from the first half of the decade is the politicisa-tion of debates on refugees. The political landscape itself had changed since the Popular Front, with the radicalisation of the right and growing similarities in the agendas of the parliamentary right and extreme right. But perhaps more worrying for progressive refugee policy was the shift-ing constellation of the left as many Radicals, along with some Socialists and trade unionists, developed outright hostility for the French Com-munist Party (PCF).[35] The gathering wind of anti-communism sweeping through France affected not only French Communists, but also refugees identified with anti-fascism more generally, in other words, nearly all refugees seeking asylum in France at this juncture. Even though a series of political attacks involving foreigners in 1937 were not entirely the work of anti-fascists, the incidents and accompanying press reports stoked up fears of refugees importing the ideological clashes afflicting Germany, Italy and Spain into France, potentially leading the country to war and social revolution.[36] It is significant that, by 1938, right-wing and some moderate circles were more fearful of conflict from the left inside France than from a neighbouring fascist regime, powerfully illustrated by the refrain 'Rather Hitler than Blum'. Storm clouds were gathering apace, but from different directions. Daladier's preoccupations thus oscillated between preparing the country for a potential war with Germany whilst enforcing domestic stability. This latter point involved minimising the presence of refugees in French society, just at the very moment when the nationalist occupation of Catalonia pushed hundreds of thousands of refugees towards the French border.

The exodus in context

BORDER POLITICS

On Monday 16 January *The Times* referred to exhausted refugees pouring into Barcelona from the war zone. The city itself, though, was not completely separated from the front: five planes had bombed the port the previous Saturday morning, and gunfire from the war zone was clearly audible.[37] By 25 January damage to railway tracks prevented any more trains from leaving and the following day enemy troops, including Italian units, began entering the Catalan capital. Existing refugees were once again forced on the move and joined by new refugees. Hundreds of thousands headed towards the border following in the steps of government officials of the Second Spanish Republic, whose own relocation from Barcelona to Gerona and then from Gerona to Figueres had hardly inspired public confidence about the Republic's ability to stop or even delay the rebel advance.

The last session of the Spanish Cortes took place in an old fort in the frontier town of Figueres between 10.30 p.m. and 2.45 a.m. on 1 February. The premier, Dr Juan Negrín, made a speech to the members of parliament in which he outlined three conditions for a negotiated end to the conflict in Spain involving a guarantee of national sovereignty, a plebiscite for the country's political future and finally an end to persecution in order to facilitate reconciliation. He additionally vowed: 'we will fight for Cataluña, and will retain what's left of Cataluña under our control, and if we lose Cataluña, then we still have the centre-south zone where we have hundreds of thousands of fighters determined to fight on'.[38] Despite the difficulties, he assured his audience that government authority remained steadfast. It was a characteristically Quixotic speech, and perhaps necessarily so. The chief of staff, General Vicente Rojo, had already advised Negrín and the President of Spain, Manuel Azaña, that the best they could hope for was to delay defeat through buttressing short-term defences. Given Franco's ruthless campaign against a Republic he was bent on annihilating, Negrín believed that their only chance of obtaining any guarantee against reprisals rested on the Republic bargaining from a position of opposition as opposed to defeat.[39] This was not so much a strategy of resistance to the end, but rather resistance for survival. Unfortunately, the strategy also rested on republican authority, which as the presence of only 62 parliamentary deputies indicates, was in the midst of unravelling.

Two days before Barcelona fell, the Foreign Minister of the Spanish Republic, Julio Álvarez del Vayo, had asked his counterpart, Georges Bonnet, if France would accept 150,000 women, children and the elderly. This was not the first indication of an imminent crisis. The French embassy in Madrid, together with French military observers in the frontier region, had warned the French government on several occasions about the possibility of a mass exodus to France.[40] However, French ministers continued to be wilfully oblivious of the need to react. Bonnet responded negatively and offered instead a plan to create a neutral zone just inside the Catalan border. There was nothing new about the idea, though it had been largely ignored by the French government since republican Spain's consul in Perpignan, Joaquín Camps Arboix, had proposed it nine months earlier.[41] By this stage, however, Spanish republican ministers no longer favoured the idea and it was also rejected by Franco. The French government continued to hope that they could avoid receiving refugees en masse. Would the Spanish republican army stem the nationalist advance and create another front inside Catalonia, or even surrender? In short, the French government desired any possibility save that of granting refuge to Spanish republicans in France. Sarraut closed the border on 26–27 January. Given the sheer weight of people who would be caught between French border guards and the nationalist forces with little prospect of food or shelter, the closure was as inhumane as it was impractical. The anarchist Federica Montseny later tried to capture the collective atmosphere around Le Perthus with the following words: 'the terror, the desperation of the fugitives upon seeing they couldn't pass and the Francoist planes flying overhead is something indescribable'.[42] On 28 January, the French government issued orders to reopen the border for women, children and the elderly but barred the way for *hommes valides*, meaning combatants and men of arms-bearing age.[43]

Evidence from the French border town of Prats-de-Mollo illustrates that government orders could not always be implemented on the ground. While the border was officially closed, at 4 a.m. on 27 January, two French officials received three Spanish republican troops suffering from the cold after crossing the snow-capped mountains.[44] The following day, men were crossing unchecked at various points up in the mountains but were arrested once inside France.[45] According to the local newspaper, *L'Indépendant*, by 29 January combatants as well as civilians had begun arriving via the main points of passage along the Pyrenean border: Cerbère, Le Perthus, Saint-Laurent-de-Cerdans, Prats-de-Mollo and Bourg-Madame.[46]

The government stubbornly stuck to the principle of allowing only women, children, the aged and the wounded to cross the border. When Sarraut visited Prats-de-Mollo on 31 January he reminded officials of the government line. Elsewhere along the border, French guards sent several thousand refugees back into Spanish territory, including 1,800 people who had set up camp in the international rail tunnel between Cerbère and Portbou.[47] When French border guards were able to implement Sarraut's instructions it led to the painful separation of families and friends, leaving refugees to wonder when or even if they would ever meet up again. Less than a week later Sarraut relented under the pressure of unfolding events. On Saturday 4 February, nationalists occupied Gerona and Palamos, removing any hope of the Spanish Republic retaining Catalonia. The following day, the French authorities finally opened the border to combatants and men of arms-bearing age.

It was also on Sunday, at 4 a.m., when the President of the Republic, Manuel Azaña, the leader of the Cortes, Martínez Barrio, together with the Presidents of the Catalan and Basque governments, Lluís Companys and José Antonio de Aguirre, unceremoniously crossed the border on foot near the tiny village of Las Illas. On 9 February, nationalist troops reached the frontier town of Le Perthus, and by 15 February the exodus was over.[48] In the space of two weeks around 465,000 people had sought refuge in metropolitan France and a further 15,000 in French-controlled North Africa.[49] They included soldiers from the republican army, members of the International Brigades and around 170,000 civilians, of whom around 70,000 were children.[50]

It was not just the scale and speed of this exodus that was unique. The social composition of the Spanish republican exile was also different from both previous migrations from Spain, and other refugee groups in France. The refugees represented a cross-section of professions from Spanish society, ranging from agricultural labourers and industrial workers to civil servants, military career officers and the liberal professions.[51] More specifically, the presence of a high number of skilled industrial workers and a variety of middle-class workers was unusual.

Even more remarkable was the ideological and political composition of the Spanish republican exile, and notably the presence of tens of thousands of libertarians. The world has only ever seen one example of a mass libertarian movement, and that occurred in Spain during the end of the nineteenth and start of the twentieth centuries. In 1919 there were around 800,000 members of the anarcho-syndical labour union (CNT) with an even higher number of workers influenced by anarchist ideals.[52] To be sure, libertarians represented one ideological current amongst many in the various groups which fought against the nationalist forces under the umbrella of the Second Spanish Republic. There are no accurate figures of the exact political and trade-union composition of the Spanish republicans in France during 1939, but we do know about the relative size of each organisation. In descending order, the most numerically significant organisations were the Spanish Libertarian Movement (MLE) – including anarcho-syndicalists of the CNT, anarchists of the Iberian Anarchist Federation (FAI)[53] and the anarchist youth movement (FIJL)[54] – the Spanish Socialist Party (PSOE), the Socialist-linked General Workers' Union (UGT) and finally the Communists of the Spanish Communist Party (PCE) and its Catalan equivalent, the United Socialist Party of Catalonia (PSUC).[55] In addition, there were various, but numerically small, republican parties, and also the Workers' Party of Marxist Unity (POUM), an anti-Stalinist communist party with which George Orwell had fought in the Civil War. The presence of all the parties and trade organisations which had fought in the Spanish republican camp was significant enough, but even more interesting is that from 1939 France became the refuge for the world's largest mass libertarian movement in exile.

IMAGES OF THE REFUGEES IN THE FRENCH PRESS

A heady mixture of ideological hatred, xenophobia and fear of conflict being exported into France goes a long way to explaining why much of the French press reified the Spanish republicans in the most virulent terms. The qualification of republican forces as 'terrorist hordes' during the exodus was not an isolated case of reporting.[56] Neither was this form of vitriol an especially new phenomenon. Back in December 1937, Joseph Delest's article in the far-right newspaper *L'Action Française* likened republican combatants to 'deserters, assassins and burglars'.[57] The difference, however, is that the depiction of 'terrorist hordes' came not from a far right-wing newspaper but from the politically moderate *La Dépêche de Toulouse*, one of the most widely-read dailies in the south-west. In fact, the semantic framework of *La Dépêche*'s reporting of the refugees' arrival contained subtle rather than fundamental differences compared with its right-wing counterpart *L'Express du Midi*.[58]

The ambivalence towards the refugees is not solely explained by the newspaper's editor being the brother of Sarraut, the French Minister of the Interior. It represented a wider, significant shift in mainstream coverage and reflected the fact that the idea of 'undesirable' refugees had become commonplace. The pejorative reporting became notably acute when the border was opened to all refugees on 5 February. Before this, much of the press, save that of the far right, had tended to emphasise human suffering. Papers remaining steadfastly supportive of the Spanish republicans continued to focus on the human and tragic consequences of forced displacement. In contrast, the press that was opposed to the Spanish republicans or wary about offering refuge placed repeated emphasis on fear-provoking images.[59]

On the day when French officials authorised combatants and men of arms-bearing age to enter France, *La Dépêche* carried photographs of French troops digging trenches near the border in Cerdagne. The aim of this defensive manoeuvre was not as a precaution against the rebel forces which, after all, sought to destroy the Republic in Spain, but rather to prevent, in the words of the newspaper, 'a potential invasion of Spanish [republican] militia'.[60] The more conservative press also reproduced pernicious images. Wladimir d'Ormesson in *Le Figaro* called on the public to help the refugees but warned about the variety of germs being potentially carried into the country.[61] Any initial empathy for the refugees' plight amongst the far-right press, and some of the conservative press, was replaced with vitriolic hostility. 'The scum of world anarchy is in France thanks to M. Albert Sarraut', read one article from *Candide* on 8 February. Two days later, *L'Émancipation Nationale*, which was the organ of Jacques Doriot's extreme right-wing party, the Parti populaire français, carried a plea from Yves Dautun: 'France has watched by as it is invaded by the Marxist army in retreat . . . protect us from the plague!'[62]

Left-wing papers, parties, unions and other organisations tried to counteract the negative images of the refugees. In the last week of January, *Le Midi socialiste* had called on the government to open the border and help the refugees but also to tackle the crisis in its wider context.[63] At the same time, *Le Populaire* argued that whatever dignity remained in France would be lost unless the government offered refuge.[64] During the exodus, *Le Midi socialiste* asked whether *La Dépêche* had become a Francoist mouthpiece following its call for the repatriation of refugees.[65] On 5 February, the day the government opened the border to men of

arms-bearing age, *L'Humanité* printed a call by various well-known personalities calling on France to ease the 'the appalling misery' of the
Spanish republicans. The list included prominent Catholics and was also
published by the Catholic newspaper *L'Aube*. The following day, P. L.
Darnar, writing for the Communist newspaper *L'Humanité*, presented a
harrowing picture of arriving refugees.[66] It is difficult to ascertain how
much these actions countered the negative representations. Almost from
the very start of the conflict, the conservative and extreme right-wing
press had consistently circulated anti-Spanish republican reports and
photographs. This was compounded by some of the mainstream press,
which labelled the refugees as threat and a problem to France during the
exodus.

PRIORITIES: WELFARE OR SECURITY?

How effective were the French welfare measures in place? In November
1938, the Bray–Webster report to the League of Nations had identified
acute food shortages throughout republican Spain.[67] The deprivations
stemming from a war economy and a series of forced displacements
within Spain meant that refugees arriving in France would need adequate
provisions. Just before opening the border officials in Paris and the Pyrénées-Orientales expressed confidence in their contingency plans. On
paper, the plans for the Pyrénées-Orientales seemed appropriate enough,
envisaging the transfer of refugees from the border to evacuation centres
where they would receive either a cold meal or at the very least a hot
drink, along with a smallpox vaccination.[68] Officials, however, had hope-
lessly, perhaps even recklessly underestimated the scale of the event.
Predicated on a rate of 2,000 refugees arriving daily, the measures in place
could never have dealt with the 140,000 people who arrived in the first
four days alone.[69]

The French authorities were helped by a number of aid associations.
An especially active association, and one which Spanish republicans have
fondly remembered for its work in France, was the Friends Service
Council (FSC). Despite their best efforts, the FSC faced an overwhelming
task, an idea of which can be gained from the number of rations distributed on both sides of the border. While the border remained closed the
FSC managed to issue 100,000 drink and food rations to the gathering
refugees in Catalonia using canteens on lorries, and a further 96,000
rations of hot drinks, bread and in some cases cheese and chocolate to
people arriving in France once the border was opened.[70] At Prats-de-
Mollo French officials were able to provide the first arrivals, on 27 and

28 January, with hot drinks, milk, chocolate and bread, but soon ran into problems as the rate of arrivals increased.[71] An idea of the intensity of arrivals at the height of the exodus, between 6 and 9 February, is indicated by one aid worker who noted 'the streams of refugees were fifty kilometres long'.[72] Conditions varied considerably according to the specific locality and time of the crossing, but were on the whole very insufficient given the numbers and physical state of the refugees.

Preparations for the sick and wounded were equally inadequate. Refugees arrived from hospitals in Catalonia and were joined by people who fell ill or were injured en route as a result of the conditions and nationalist attacks, numbering at least 12,000 between 30 January and 6 February.[73] At the start of the exodus, the number of beds available in the hospital in Perpignan, the administrative centre of the Pyrénées-Orientales *département*, was 80. Officials organised an extra 500 places at Saint-Louis and 800 at a former military hospital in Perpignan. In addition, hospital ships at nearby Port-Vendres received 1,716 wounded on 11 February, and two other ships in Marseilles took aboard 1,212 people. Other wounded refugees were sent to hospitals further inland. The Prefect in Perpignan, possibly to deflect any criticism, optimistically reported that 'there is good reason to say that, despite the massive number of wounded, and the often lamentable psychological state and accompanying misery in which they arrived, immediate care was administered as soon as they entered France'.[74] Observations by relief workers and refugees' recollections provide a more harrowing picture.

Dr Audrey Russell's report for the International Commission for the Assistance of Child Refugees in Spain noted that medical resources were very basic and in some cases nonexistent. Blankets and bedding were needed at all of the principal refugee reception centres along the border. More specifically, at Amélie-les-Bains, 'the sick and wounded (some children with air-raid injuries) were lying in the open on the grass for two days. There is still not enough accommodation for all in the tent. They urgently need blankets.' At another border post, Le Boulou, local officials transformed the village school into a hospital, but the only supplies to hand were a few dressings brought by a Spanish field hospital. Russell wrote: 'women, children and the wounded were lying in the utmost filth in straw'.[75] Conditions in the vicinity of Latour-de-Carol have remained etched into the memories of refugees. Antonio Miró described how men sucked on snow to relieve their thirst amid the stench of gangrenous wounds during his first night in France in a snowy field devoid of shelter, while Mariano Constante remembered the substantial number of wounded men left for several days at the local station without any medical attention.[76] During these early days, the disused military hospital in the main urban centre of Perpignan was only marginally better. According to another aid worker, there were 'no sheets, no night clothes, no pillowcases, no towels, nothing in the way of linen or equipment. While we were there an ambulance arrived and some of the men they took out were already dead. Put in a little room with the five who had died the night before.'[77]

The magnitude and rapidity of events certainly posed an immensely challenging task for the officials and aid agencies working along the border. But this alone cannot explain the appalling lack of facilities and provisions. As already noted, the government had received forewarning of an exodus earlier in 1938 but had decided not to take any action. Once the exodus was under way, the local and national authorities did begin to react to events, but even then, a series of decisions by the government helped aggravate an already desperate situation.[78] The government could have used military bases and field equipment to house the refugees, but refused because of concerns for national defence. Similarly, although some military hospitals were used, the government generally sent the sick and wounded to civilian hospitals, which as we have seen, were completely under-resourced.[79] The appalling conditions underlying the refugees' reception were thus partly an outcome of the government's erroneous construction of the issue as a choice between welfare and security. And by privileging the latter, the government proved itself utterly unequal to the task of receiving the Spanish republicans humanely.

Some of the government's security objectives were left to the improvisation of local officials. Although the Ministry of Defence had been considering the question of internment since at least as far back as May 1938, ministers had refused to take heed of warnings about the likelihood of an exodus. The result was a great deal of frenzied activity to create the first internment camp. Pierre Izard, the Deputy Mayor of Argelès-sur-Mer, believes the military officer charged with constructing a camp on the nearby beach at the end of January had not received adequate directives. The officer initially ordered Izard to build barracks with a detachment of Spanish refugees who seemed to have never handled so much as a hammer before. These initial barracks were designated for wounded refugees. Despite the obvious need for more buildings, the officer re-ordered everyone to work on fencing off the camp with barbed wire in time for Sarraut's visit at the start of February.[80] Even so, in the first weeks of the camp the enclosure was largely ineffective given the ease with which internees could come and go.

Barbed wire was not, however, the only measure used for maintaining control and surveillance over the Spanish republicans. Both local and national authorities rapidly implemented procedures aimed at restricting contact between refugees and the surrounding populations, French or otherwise. The Prefect of the Pyrénées-Orientales banned any form of gathering on public highways on 28 January, and on 5 February went further by prohibiting public meetings and demonstrations.[81] Further away from the border in Bordeaux, the Prefecture produced posters and adverts in the local press warning foreigners in the city (probably a reference to the sizeable pre-existing Spanish immigrant colony)[82] to abstain from any propaganda or demonstrations.[83] Then, just before the end of the exodus, the Minister of the Interior provided all prefects with more precise instructions about issues of containment and security.[84] Officials were to ensure the vaccination of all refugees to avoid any risk of contagion to the local population, and ensure that everyone, including women and children, were searched for weapons. Refugees were to be restricted to the *département*, arrondissement or canton to which they had been assigned and issued with a provisional pass that was renewable every month. Any male refugees entering a *département* without permission would be interned. Prefects were reminded of their authority to expel from the country any refugee considered to be troublesome,[85] though in practice this meant internment. In exceptional cases, prefects could allow people with an 'impeccable' background to choose where they lived and issue an identity card.[86] But the Minister reminded prefects that refugees did not have the right to work in any job whatsoever. In addition, the Minister ordered prefects to establish a list of people who had held positions of authority in Spain: government officials, army officers, civil servants and heads of regional organisations, political parties and trade unions. Moreover, he wanted details about their activities in Spain, along with any information on their contacts with French or foreign political and trade-union organisations, and also on the refugees' attitudes towards France and their relations with French nationals, committees and associations. Sarraut's explanation for this request lay in reports that the refugees included people who had left Spain in order to escape punishment for violent crimes. This circular, which was marked confidential, emphasises where Sarraut's priorities lay. In the midst of the crisis, he publicly announced his desire to reconcile the maintenance of public order, the safety of public health and the humanitarian needs of the refugees. Two months later he stated: 'my obsession was national security'.[87]

Refugees' accounts and responses

How did refugees respond to the challenges of the exodus? A comment by Nancy Cunard appearing in the *Manchester Guardian* on 2 February is telling: 'This migration is not an hysterical stampede, but the result of knowing that they stand the very great danger, when not certainty, of being shot. These people in their vast majority have seen too much of Fascism.'[88] Whether people had become refugees out of fear of reprisals or to escape the conflict more generally, they all made a conscious decision to depart.[89] Furthermore, the mechanics of departure and travelling involved a degree of organisation, which for non-military personnel, and the first refugees arriving in France, often fell to the responsibility of women, and notably mothers. They were frequently responsible for ensuring the safe passage of their families into France. Federica Montseny, a prominent figure in the CNT and former Minister of Health, is one of the most well-known examples. She undertook the exodus with her two children, her terminally ill mother, father and other family members.[90] Many other mothers shared similar experiences. Señora Diaz, for example, was responsible for getting her 4-year-old son, sister and mother over the border.[91] Rose Duroux's mother recalled the precarious task of negotiating treacherous, snowy mountain paths with her daughter in her arms. She lost sight of the other refugees and fell several times, on one occasion hitting her head on a rock. The bleeding wound was less serious than it appeared, but worrying nonetheless.[92] Antonio Arias, aged 13, followed his mother's orders by packing photographs and other small items before leaving and then, during the exodus, attempted to find food for the family whilst his mother looked after his two younger siblings.[93]

Not all children were accompanied by relatives. The separation of mother and child figures prominently in Consuelo Granda's recollection. She was 16 and with her mother when she lost sight of her sister in the Catalan town of Molló. Consuelo simply states: 'my mother never saw her daughter again' before describing how she was then separated from her mother at the border.[94] Other children, some orphans, who had been evacuated from the war zones in Spain travelled with their respective colonies. After his mother was killed during a bombing raid in Barcelona, the 9-year-old Ángel Fernández, along with his younger sister and brother, were sent to a children's colony close to Gerona. Staff evacuated the colony at the start of the exodus, but Angel and his siblings became separated from the rest of the colony during a bombardment when the chapel in which they were sheltering collapsed, killing some of the other children.[95]

The fear of being separated from relatives was prevalent among adults and children alike. Specific to childhood accounts, however, is the presence of terror and famine as key narrative structures.[96] In this sense, the exodus constituted a continuation of the horrors of the war in Spain. Even so, no amount of previous exposure to air attacks could dampen the terror. As people pushed towards the border, nationalist planes targeted military and civilian targets alike. A French lorry driver even suspected he and his child passengers had been targeted deliberately: 'My lorry was crowded with children. The plane swooped so low that they must have seen it. But that did not stop them. Seventeen of the children were killed.'[97] One child, Marie Lafforgue, aged 12, was so affected when Figueres was bombed that she lost all recollection of the following days.[98] Some people had little recollection of crossing the border save that of feeling a sense of relief on arriving in France.[99] Eduardo Bernad experienced the French side of the border at Cerbère as a haven from the aeroplanes.[100] The lack of provisions was another common problem, pushing some children to lick oil from empty sardine tins, and explains why scenes of food in France marked their memories of arriving in reception centres. Raquel Thiercelin recalled the animated scene of a large hall decorated with different-coloured flags as if for a party in which hundreds of people were sitting eating. Although grateful for the first hot meal in days, she could not understand the meaning of the 'celebration'.[101] On the other hand, Eduardo Bernad evoked his arrival at a centre in the *département* of Yonne in relation to the sight of plates laden with food; it was a 'mundo irreal' (surreal world).[102]

The exodus was an immensely harrowing and destabilising experience. It threw into question all aspects of peoples' lives as homes, possessions, customs, and interpersonal networks were left behind. For many people, their personal and collective identities felt as though they were unravelling, being stripped away and discarded at the side of roads and paths along with the objects that had become too burdensome or were confiscated by French customs. For others, notably militants, their sense of collective identity appeared to be sustained or even strengthened by the objects they carried into exile and their experiences of solidarity en route. In a context of rupture, as refugees left their familiar surroundings, objects and interpersonal relations provided a sense, albeit tenuous, of continuity. Possessions could be a means of identification, most obviously in the case of passports or family photographs, but also a reminder of a more stable past and a source of comfort against the uncertainty of the future. The choice of object to take offers an insight into how future

lives were envisaged, but also sheds light on the process of identity reconstruction during what was an extremely challenging period.[103]

Not everyone was as fortunate as the Socialist theorist, Luis Araquistáin, who managed to transport his personal library into France.[104] More
often than not, possessions were limited to what could be physically
carried, and anything compromising was simply destroyed. Abel Paz, alias
Diego Camacho, remembered libertarians burning documents, archives
and other important papers, describing it as the 'destruction of a time
gone by'.[105] Just before leaving, Sara Berenguer, another libertarian and
member of the Mujeres Libres (Free Women), left instructions for her
mother to burn several books which might compromise her parents who
stayed behind. Among the items Sara chose to take with her was a pair
of overalls her mother had made for her during the first months of the
revolution.[106] If the decision was partly practical, it also signalled the
continuation of her libertarian identity.[107] To a certain extent, gender
influenced the type of possession, and in particular domestic objects
featured among items carried by women. María-Pilar Lang's mother used
the family's silver cutlery to pay for something to eat and a place to sleep
en route to the border.[108] The sight of women burdened with household
items stuck in the mind of Teresa García. Her mother, on the other hand,
never ceased to bemoan the sheets she had lost during the crossing for
the next 20 years.[109] Perhaps the most evident of transitional objects, and
frequently seen in photographs of the exodus, are blankets. Even if Rose
Duroux's mother jettisoned the family's suitcase and bag containing their
spare underwear, she insisted on keeping the blanket.[110] The extraordinary value of this object stemmed from its versatility – it provided
bedding, doubled up as a shawl/coat and could also be used to make a
bivouac.

Images of abandoned possessions punctuate photographs, newspaper
reports and also refugees' narratives of the exodus. Nancy Cunard's
report of 3 February from the frontier area referred to a 'litter of rags and
filth'. The side of the road was strewn with a dead ass, an abandoned van
and discarded mattresses, blankets, a typewriter and an armchair.[111] Consuelo's account of the border area moves between the collective and the
personal. She recalled sleeping out in the open on a pile of paper which
at daybreak turned out to be a pile of republican banknotes. The material
loss of the state is then juxtaposed to the loss of her suitcase containing
virtually all of her remaining possessions.[112] Abandoning objects could
be a question of survival. Ramon Moral i Querol, a non-commissioned
officer in the Republican army, was forced to abandon his belongings

following an order to discard all unessential items. The soldiers discarded
or destroyed documents, weapons, ammunition and vehicles, followed
by rucksacks containing personal effects:

> in respect of my papers, my notebook, my memoirs, the notes taken about
> the journey and events which I was carefully recording for the future, all
> that which in itself constituted an important bundle, along with clothes,
> family photos, spare tobacco and most of my money, everything, absolutely
> everything was burnt.[113]

The arrival at French border posts can be seen as the climax to this
unravelling of personal and collective identity as the actions of French
guards crushed refugees' hopes of a warm reception. At one border crossing Gustave Regler recalls how French officials emptied cases, bags and
bundles containing personal possessions into a ditch filled with chloride
and lime. He observed: 'I have never seen such eyes of such anger and
helplessness as those of the Spaniards.'[114] Similarly, French officials
ordered María Biencito's family to throw all but what was strictly necessary into a ditch.[115] The French armed forces showed particular eagerness
in seizing some of the Spanish republicans more advanced military
equipment and anti-aircraft guns,[116] but generally ensured the refugees
surrendered all arms at the border. The commander of the 18th Corps,
José del Barrio, found the confiscation of arms along with the regimental
archives particularly painful.[117] It was as if the army had been stripped
of everything that symbolised the defence of the Republic, in short, its
very identity.

The bitterness with which Spanish republicans recall the border crossing is not simply related to the separation of families and confiscation of
possessions. It also addresses the French use of colonial troops. Federica
Montseny described a group of colonial troops beating a group of
wounded soldiers back from the border, while Eulalio Ferrer recalled
seeing a refugee stabbed with a bayonet because he resisted attempts by
the Senegalese guard to take his watch.[118] The refugees' memoirs convey
a sense of surprise and anger, but also humiliation. The reasons are
complex. Historians have alluded to the possibility of racist reactions by
the refugees or to a sense that colonial relations had been inverted.[119] The
government's employment of Senegalese and Spahi troops at the border
and to guard the camps undoubtedly lacked sensitivity, given Franco's
controversial use of Moroccan soldiers to repress the Asturian revolution
of October 1934 and as shock troops during the civil war. The repeated
references to Senegalese and Spahi brutality are not confined to refugees'

memoirs. Miss Pye of the Friends Service Council reported that Dr Audrey Russell had been struck on the chest by one guard while passing the border, and also referred to several cases of colonial troops robbing refugee internees at the point of a sword.[120]

Despite the perils of the exodus, morale could be sustained through solidarity between family and friends, or between people from the same ideological or institutional network. Despite being separated from his mother and brothers during the exodus, Abel Paz's recollection avoids the emotional intensity often present in refugees' narratives. Instead he describes how his group of libertarians managed to avoid the French border authorities and remain at large with the help of sympathisers in France.[121] It is not inconceivable that his lifelong commitment to libertarian ideals has influenced his depiction, obscuring feelings of personal loss in favour of a narrative which stresses the resilience and ingenuity of libertarians. But there is little doubt that militants such as Paz met the challenges of the journey into exile through implementing values central to their ideological world-view: mutual support reinforced a sense of ideological continuity and vice versa.

A similar observation can be made about depictions of well-organised, disciplined and spirited Spanish republican troops marching across the border. The reality was certainly complex, as illustrated by Sharif Gemie's comparison of two accounts. José del Barrio, an officer in the (Spanish) Republican army, described troops marching impeccably into France, while Daniel Guérin referred to 'men who must have been soldiers: bandaged, dragging their feet, crushed, dazed'.[122] Admittedly some refugees may have reconstructed the event as a more positive experience to offset the painful experience of defeat. But on the other hand, one can find examples of both Guérin's and de Barrio's images when examining the exodus in all its spatial and temporal diversity. The municipal authorities in just one village, Prats-de-Mollo, contrasted the first contingent of arriving troops in terms reminiscent of Guérin, with the last to arrive in a strikingly similar way to that of de Barrio.[123] The exodus involved loss and despair, but also the strengthening of group identities.

In the same year when refugees such as Antonia Illazque responded to their loss of rights and status by stressing their republican credentials, the French population, notably on the left of the political spectrum, lacked enthusiasm about the state of the Republic in France.[124] Daladier's government had not simply compromised the Popular Front coalition and isolated the working class through the repression of the November 1938 strikes, but had additionally bypassed the democratic process through the widespread use of decree laws. National security was the premise on which Sarraut's response to the Spanish exodus was based. When finally driven to react, the Minister of the Interior thus made a deliberate choice to press the issue of security rather than the refugees' welfare.

The internment camps were an obvious indicator of waning refugees' rights in the late 1930s. They could also be interpreted as the apogee of a process of boundary construction under the Third Republic which distinguished immigrants from French nationals through the elaboration of a national community based on social rights. Gérard Noriel's view of immigrant legislation under the Third Republic is certainly apposite in this respect.[125] We do, however, need to be cautious about interpreting the camps, and by implication the Daladier government's stance towards refugees, as an inevitable outcome of a linear process of steadily declining refugee rights throughout the 1930s. A theme running throughout this chapter, and one which will be repeated in the focus on employment in Chapters 4 and 5, is that of historical contingency. There was nothing inevitable or natural about the fate of Spanish republican refugees in 1939. It was the result of a particular set of circumstances. These included the refusal of those in authority within France to respond to an emerging reality, with the consequent resort to makeshift solutions as the dimensions of the refugee issue forced them to act.

Circumstance is a contingent phenomenon and subject to differing interpretations. To many contemporaries the government's strategy was legitimated by the exceptional pressures exerted on the Third Republic. But to others, perhaps a minority but nonetheless a significant and very vocal minority, the undignified reception of the refugees amounted to a betrayal of the principle of asylum. As the exodus petered out, Jean Bénazet, a French Communist, reacted to the appalling way French officials treated refugees in the area around the Pyrenean town of Amélie-les-Bains by noting: 'this lack of solidarity with the Spanish Republic signals the dying toll of the French Republic'.[126] Had the seam binding the universal values of the Republic to the identity of the French nation-state started to unravel beyond repair?

Notes

1 Interview with Antonia Illazque, Bordeaux, 5 July 2002.
2 See M. S. Alexander and H. Graham (eds), *The French and Spanish Popular Fronts: Comparative Perspectives* (Cambridge, 2002).

3 G. Noiriel, *Réfugiés et sans-papiers: La République face au droit d'asile XIX–XX siècle* (Paris, 1999).

4 The practice of asylum dated back to the *ancien régime. Ibid.*

5 Noiriel, *Réfugiés et sans-papiers*, p. 101.

6 M. Mandel, *In the Aftermath of Genocide* (Durham, NC and London, 2003).

7 Noiriel, *Réfugiés et sans-papiers*, p. 105.

8 T. P. Maga, 'Closing the Door: The French Government and Refugee Policy, 1933–1939', *French Historical Studies*, 12:3 (1982), pp. 424–42.

9 G. Burgess, *Refuge in the Land of Liberty: France and its Refugees, from the Revolution to the End of Asylum* (Basingstoke and New York, 2008), pp. 170–1.

10 For details on the ratification of a League of Nations agreement on German refugees see V. Caron, *Uneasy Asylum: France and the Jewish Refugee Crisis, 1933–1942* (Stanford, CA, 1999), pp. 120–4.

11 M. D. Lewis, *The Boundaries of the Republic: Migrant Rights and the Limits of Universalism in France, 1918–1940* (Stanford, CA, 2007).

12 Burgess, *Refuge in the Land of Liberty*, p. 195.

13 *Ibid.*, pp. 186–8.

14 Caron, *Uneasy Asylum*, p. 3.

15 R. Kedward, *La Vie en bleu: France and the French since 1900* (London, 2005), p. 166.

16 J. Jackson, *France: The Dark Years 1940–1944* (Oxford, 2001), pp. 65, 72–4.

17 E. Caporali, *le Peuple* (21 May 1936), cited in R. Schor, *L'Opinion française et les étrangers, 1919–1939* (Paris, 1985), p. 640.

18 In reality there was nothing unusual in the number of Jews holding high-ranking posts under the Popular Front. See Caron, *Uneasy Asylum*, pp. 270–1.

19 *Ibid.*, p. 196.

20 J.-C. Bonnet, *Les pouvoirs publics français et l'immigration dans l'entre-deux-guerres* (Lyon, 1976), pp. 30–1. Schor, *L'Opinion française et les étrangers*, p. 633. Rita Thalmann goes as far as outlining continuities of refugee policy between the Popular Front and former administrations. R. Thalmann, 'L'immigration allemande et l'opinion publique en France de 1933 à 1936', in *La France et l'Allemagne, 1932–1936* (Paris, 1980), p. 171. R. Thalmann, 'L'Émigration du III Reich dans la France de 1933 à 1939', *Le Monde Juif*, 35:96 (1979), p. 136.

21 G. Noiriel, *Immigration, antisémitisme et racisme en France (XIX–XX siècle): Discours publics, humiliations privées* (Paris, 2007), p. 424.

22 Caron, *Uneasy Asylum*, pp. 117–70; Lewis, *The Boundaries of the Republic*, pp. 180–4.

23 For an innovative analysis of French public opinion and the war in Spain see P. Laborie, *L'Opinion française sous Vichy: Les Français et la crise d'identité nationale 1936–1944* (Paris, 2nd edn, 2001), pp. 200–4.

24 For two excellent introductions to the war in Spain see: H. Graham, *The Spanish Civil War: A Very Short Introduction* (Oxford, 2005); P. Preston, *A Concise History of the Spanish Civil War* (London, 1996).

25 Laborie, *L'Opinion française sous Vichy*, p. 204.

26 G. Dreyfus-Armand, *L'Exil des Républicains Espagnols en France: De la Guerre Civile à la Mort de Franco* (Paris, 1999), pp. 34–5.

27 *Ibid.*, pp. 33–41.

28 The government's allocated budget for sheltering the Spanish refugees increased from 13 million francs when Blum was premier to 55 million during the second semester of 1937. *Ibid.*, p. 39.

29 *Ibid.*, p. 58.

30 Caron, *Uneasy Asylum*, p. 174.

31 *Ibid.*

32 See Lewis, *The Boundaries of the Republic*, pp. 222–9.

33 AD Pyrénées-Orientales, 1287W 1. Letter from the Ministry of War and National Defence stamped 'SECRET VERY URGENT' to Generals of the 16th and 17th Military Regions of the Southwest, 3 May 1938.

34 Dreyfus-Armand, *L'Exil des Républicains Espagnols en France*, p. 59.

35 Jackson, *France*, pp. 79–80.

36 Schor, *L'Opinion française et les étrangers*, pp. 653–8.

37 *The Times* (16 January 1939).

38 J. María del Valle, *Las Instituciones de la República española en exilio* (Paris, 1976), p. 13.

39 H. Graham, *The Spanish Republic at War 1936–1939* (Cambridge, 2002), pp. 397–9.

40 J. Rubio, *La emigración de la guerra civil de 1936–1939. Historia del éxodo que se produce con el fin de la II República española*. Vols 1–3 (Madrid, 1977).

41 L. Stein, *Beyond Death and Exile: The Spanish Republicans in France, 1939–1955* (Cambridge, MA, 1979), pp.15–6.

42 F. Montseny, *El Éxodo: Pasión y muerte de españoles en el exilio* (Barcelona, 1977), p. 18.

43 All combatants and men of arms-bearing age, thereby including civilian men, were refused entry into France.

44 J.-C. Pruja, *Premiers camps de l'exil espagnol: Prats-de-Mollo, 1939* (Saint-Cyr-sur-Loire, 2003), pp. 35–6.

45 AD Pyrénées-Orientales, 31W 274. Details from the report entitled 'Exode Espagnol' from Préfet to Ministère de l'Intérieur, 6 March 1939.

46 'Des milliers de soldats et de réfugiés espagnols entrent en France par Cerbère, Le Perthus, St.-Laurent-de-Cerdans, Prats-de-Mollo et Bourg-Madame', *l'Indépendant* (29 January 1939). Reproduced in Pruja, *Premiers camps de l'exil espagnol*, p. 42.

47 *The Times* (1 February 1939).

48 AD Pyrénées-Orientales, 31W 274. Report, 'Exode Espagnol', 6 March 1939.

49 J. Rubio, 'La population espagnole en France: Flux et permanences', in P. Milza and D. Peschanski (eds), *Exils et Migration: Italiens et Espagnols en France 1938–1946* (Paris, 1994), pp. 39–40.

50 A French report of 9 March 1939 refers to a total of 68,035 children. The actual figure is likely to have been higher since some refugees had already returned to Spain by this date. Rubio, *La emigración de la guerra civil de 1936–1939*, Vol. 1, p. 70.

51 See Appendix for a breakdown of the socio-professional composition of the refugees.

52 H. Thomas, *The Spanish Civil War* (London, 3rd edn, 1986), p. 56.

53 The Federación Anarquista Ibérica was created in 1927 to defend anarchist principles in the CNT in Spain, and also beyond.

54 Federación Ibérica de Juventudes Libertarias.

55 Dreyfus-Armand, L'Exil des Républicains Espagnols en France, p. 257.

56 Cited in M.-C. Rafaneau-Boj, *Odyssée pour la liberté. Les camps de prisonniers espagnols (1939–1945)* (Paris, 1993), p. 40.

57 Schor, *L'Opinion française et les étrangers*, p. 676. See also E. Salgas, 'Une Population face à l'Exil Espagnol: Représentation et Opinion. Le Cas des Pyrénées-Orientales', in *Españoles en Francia 1936–1946. Coloquio Internacional Salamanca, 2, 3 y 4 de mayo 1991* (Salamanca, 1991), p. 399.

58 Laborie, *L'Opinion française sous Vichy*, p. 136.

59 For more in-depth studies exploring the arrival of the Spanish refugees in the French press see: D. W. Pike, *Vae Victis! Los republicanos españoles refugiados en Francia 1939–1944* (Paris, 1969); Schor, *L'Opinion française et les étrangers*; M.-A. Blaizat, 'L'Opinion publique et les représentations des républicains espagnols dans la région toulousaine, 1936–1940' (Mémoire de maîtrise: Université de Toulouse-Le Mirail, 1987); J.-M. Ginesta, 'Les camps de réfugiés espagnols dans la presse française de 1939', in J.-C. Villegas (ed.) *Plages d'exil. Les camps de réfugiés espagnols en France – 1939* (Nanterre-Dijon, 1989); Salgas, 'Une Population face à l'Exil Espagnol'.

60 Cited in Rafaneau-Boj, *Odyssée pour la liberté*, p. 39.

61 Cited in Pike, *Vae Victis!*, p. 18.

62 *Gringoire* and *Je suis Partout* also excelled in this form of reporting. Ginesta, 'Les camps de réfugiés espagnols dans la presse française de 1939'.

63 Stein, *Beyond Death and Exile*, p. 21.

64 *Ibid.*, p. 27.

65 Rafaneau-Boj, *Odyssée pour la liberté*, p. 102.

66 Schor, *L'Opinion française et les étrangers*, p. 679.

67 'Food In Republican Spain: A Medical Memorandum', *British Medical Journal*, 1:4075 (1939), pp. 278–9.

68 AD Pyrénées-Orientales, 31W 274. Report, 'Plan de reception et d'évacuation'.

69 Stein, *Beyond Death and Exile*, p. 27.

70 FO 371/24154: Spanish Refugees in France. Report by Miss E. M PYE [sic] (Friends Service Council) 16 February 1939.

71 Pruja, *Premiers camps de l'exil espagnol*, pp. 35–6.

72 FO 371/24155: Spanish Refugees in France. Contained in a report by Sir J Kennedy, British Red Cross Society, 3 April 1939.

73 AD Pyrénées-Orientales, 31W 274. Report, 'Exode Espagnol', 6 March 1939.

74 *Ibid.*

75 FO 371/24154. Report by Dr Audrey Russell, International Commission for the Assistance of Child Refugees in Spain, 19 February 1939.

76 Rafaneau-Boj, *Odyssée pour la liberté*, p. 53. M. Fabréguet, 'Un groupe de réfugiés politiques: les républicains espagnols des camps d'internement français aux camps de concentration nationaux-socialistes', *Revue d'histoire de la Deuxième Guerre Mondiale*, 144 (1986), p. 20.

77 FO 371/24154. Report passed to Alexander Cadogan by Viscount Cecil of Chelwood on 2 March 1939.

78 D. Peschanski, *La France des camps. L'internement 1938–1946* (Paris, 2002), pp. 37–8.

79 In addition to raising these points, Peschanski suggests that the government policy of dividing the Spanish republican army units in the camps also contributed to an already difficult situation.

80 P. Izard, 'Argelès-sur-Mer. L'exode espagnol', in Villegas (ed.), *Plages d'exil*, pp. 214–15.

81 Salgas, 'Une Population face à l'Exil Espagnol', p. 398.

82 In 1932 the colony numbered 28,000 people. AD Gironde, 1M 444.

83 *La Petite Gironde* (7 February 1939).

84 AD Dordogne, 4M 161. Confidential circular to Préfets from Ministre de l'Intérieur, no. 38, 14 February 1939.

85 In accordance with article 25 of the 12 November 1938 decree.

86 A minority of refugees was able to avoid the restrictions. Those possessing valid identification papers and a visa could, with the Préfet's permission and with their own resources, reside outside the camps. In practice, this was usually limited to leading personalities of the Spanish Republic.

87 Schor, *L'Opinion française et les étrangers*, p. 682.

88 *Manchester Guardian* (2 February 1939).

89 Sharif Gemie has contrasted observers' perceptions of the exodus as chaotic with the organisational efforts of the refugees at the micro-level. S. Gemie, 'The Ballad of Bourg-Madame: Memory, Exile and the Spanish Republican Refugees of the *Retirada* of 1939', *International Review of Social History*, 51:1 (2006), p. 26.

90 Montseny, *El Éxodo*.

91 Interview with Elio Diaz, Bordeaux, 19 June 2002.

92 R. Duroux and R. Thiercelin, 'Los niños del exilio; Asignatura pendiente', in *Españoles en Francia 1936–1946*, p. 438.

93 Interview with Antonio Arias, Lormont, 4 July 2002.

94 N. MacMaster, *Spanish Fighters: An Oral History of Civil War and Exile* (Basingstoke, 1990), pp. 109–11.

95 A. Fernández, *Rebelde: Loco de amor por la libertad y la justicia* (Toulouse, 2000), pp. 66–7.

96 See the analysis of the memoirs of Michel del Castillo, Miguel Salabert and Jorge Semprùn by E. Younès, 'Les enfants de la débâcle: vision de la guerre et traumatismes', in *Enfants de la guerre civile espagnole. Vécus et représentations de la génération née entre 1925 et 1940* (Paris, 1999).

97 *Manchester Guardian* (30 January 1939).

98 *La Dépêche du Midi*, 'Espagne il y a soixante ans' (November 1996), p. 68.

99 Interview with Pura Arias, Lormont, 4 July 2002.

100 Interview with Eduardo Bernad, Bordeaux, 27 June 2002.

101 Duroux and Thiercelin, 'Los niños del exilio', p. 445.

102 Interview with Eduardo Bernad, Bordeaux, 27 June 2002.

103 D. Parkin, 'Mementoes as Transitional Objects in Human Displacement', *Journal of Material Culture*, 4:3 (1991), pp. 303–20.

104 J. Francisco Fuentes, *Luis Araquistáin y el socialismo español en el exilio (1939–1959)* (Madrid, 2002), p. 32.

105 A. Paz, *Entre la niebla* (Barcelona, 1993), p. 22.

106 Symbolising the dress of the working class, overalls became fashionable during the start of the conflict when social revolutions occurred throughout the country.

107 S. Berenguer, *Entre el Sol y la Tormenta: Treinta y dos meses de guerra (1936–1939)* (Calella, 1988), p. 293.

108 Interview with Maria-Pilar Lang, Villeneuve-sur-Lot, 27 September 2002.

109 A. Alted Vigil, 'El exilio republicano español de 1939 desde la perspectiva de las mujeres', *Arenal. Revista de historia de las mujeres*, 4:2 (1997), pp. 223–38.

110 Duroux and Thiercelin, 'Los niños del exilio', p. 438.

111 *Manchester Guardian* (3 February 1939).

112 MacMaster, *Spanish Fighters*, p. 108.

113 R. Moral i Querol, *Journal d'exil (1939–1945)* (Paris, 1982), pp. 26–7.

114 G. Regler, *The Owl of Minerva* (London, 1959), p. 321.

115 *La Dépêche du Midi*, 'Espagne il y a soixante ans' (November 1996), p. 69.

116 M. S. Alexander, 'France, the Collapse of Republican Spain and the Approach of General War: National Security, War Economics and the Spanish Refugees, 1938–1940', in C. Leitz and D. J. Dunthorn (eds), *Spain in an International Context, 1936–1959* (Oxford, 1999), p. 107.

117 A. Soriano, *Éxodos: Historia oral del exilio republicano en Francia 1939–1945* (Barcelona, 1989), p. 117.

118 Montseny, *Él Éxodo*, p. 27. E. Ferrer, *Derrière les Barbelés: Journal des Camps de Concentration en France (1939)*. (Limonest, 1993), p. 81.

119 Gemie, 'The Ballad of Bourg-Madame', p. 31.
120 FO 371/24154. Report by Miss E. M PYE [*sic*] (Friends Service Council) 16 February 1939. Memorandum on conditions in concentration camps by Miss Pye, 25 February 1939.
121 A. Paz, *Entre la niebla*, pp. 23–31.
122 Gemie, 'The Ballad of Bourg-Madame', p. 32.
123 Pruja, *Premiers camps de l'exil espagnol*, pp. 64–6.
124 C. Amalvi, 'Le 14-Juillet: Du Dies irae à Jour de fête', in P. Nora (ed.), *Les Lieux de Mémoire* (Paris, 1997), Vol. 1, p. 414.
125 G. Noiriel, *Le creuset français. Histoire de l'immigration, XIX–XX siècles* (Paris, 1988).
126 Cited in A. Téllez Solá, *La Red de Evasión del Grupo Ponzán: Anarquistas en la guerra secreta contra el franquismo y el nazismo (1936–1944)*, p. 132.

2

Reception, internment and repatriation, 1939–40

The Spanish republicans had their own name for the mass exodus of 1939: '*la retirada*'. Literally translated as 'the retreat', it refers to the Republican army's rearguard action and the civilians' flight from Catalonia. The term 'retreat' offers a different perspective to defeat. It embodies a transitory quality and the absence of conclusion: *la retirada* signalled an intention to return. In effect, both the refugees and French authorities perceived *la retirada* as the start of an intervening and temporary phase that would end with the return to Spain. However, this point of commonality should not be confused with consensus, for the aspirations of these two groups were more often in contrast than in harmony as the French government pushed forward its prime objective of repatriation.

The events surrounding repatriation emphasise how the most obvious border confronted by refugees, the Franco-Spanish geopolitical border, was only the first obstacle to overcome in exile. Once in France the Spanish republicans confronted a nexus of other borders, or more accurately, a series of boundaries relating less to the physical markers of national territory than to the legislative, metaphorical and cultural delineation of French national identity.[1] Less visible to the naked eye, these boundaries nonetheless exercised a tangible impact on the refugees' lives. Just as the Pyrenean border served to distinguish and separate the French nation-state from its Spanish neighbour, so the boundaries within the French nation-state functioned in order to differentiate French nationals from people without French nationality and the associated citizenship rights. Numerous mechanisms were at work in this respect. The press, as we saw in the last chapter, played a significant role in this process.

But so did local officials, whose reports reflect a will to differentiate and marginalise the Spanish republicans from French nationals and everyday life in France.

Much of this chapter explores the ways in which officials accentuated the refugees' liminal and marginal situation in order to precipitate repatriation. French officials and the public drew on a repertoire of pre-existing, as well as creating new, cultural and administrative boundaries in an attempt to secure the exclusion of refugees from French society. But while exclusion was a prominent characteristic, it was not the only response to the refugees' arrival. This chapter also recounts some of the numerous instances of support and solidarity from local French populations. In addition to organising material aid, some French nationals passed on propaganda to be distributed within the reception centres helping women refugees to contest the French policy of repatriation. Throughout the first year of exile various mechanisms of exclusion and inclusion were thus at work. It was a period when the refugees and French authorities created, negotiated and reaffirmed the structural conditions of exile, a process which was largely dominated by the French local and national authorities.

The most glaring form of exclusion lies in the physical expulsion of the body from society: the forced departure of refugees from Spain is one example; internment in French camps represents another. Some, though not all, influential Spanish republicans – politicians, intellectuals and professionals – only spent a short spell in the camps or avoided internment altogether. However, in line with instructions from the Ministry of the Interior, males of arms-bearing age were interned, and in practice some women, children, the elderly and the wounded also found themselves behind the barbed-wire enclosures on the Languedoc-Roussillon beaches. By mid-February, the authorities had interned an estimated 275,000 refugees.[2] Before the exodus, the small seaside villages of Argelès-sur-Mer, Saint-Cyprien and Barcarès had been largely unknown by the majority of French people, but soon featured in the national press for hosting the immense concentration camps. There is scarcely any more of a marginal and liminal space than a beach, and especially so when the beach in question is located in a frontier region and becomes a site of mass internment.

Other camps followed. The authorities opened two special, and particularly nasty, camps for people they considered to be particularly dangerous: one in the fort dominating the small Pyrenean port of Collioure; and further north, a second camp at Vernet d'Ariège where the

26th Division, formerly known as the Durutti column, was interned. To alleviate the pressure on the initial camps a number of smaller internment centres, each of which were supposed to hold between 15,000 and 18,000 internees, were also created: the elderly were sent to Bram (in the Aude), Catalan refugees were transferred to Agde (in the Hérault) and Rivesaltes (in the Pyrénées-Orientales); skilled workers were destined for Septfonds (in the Tarn-et-Garonne); and a camp at Gurs (in the Basses-Pyrénées) was initially planned for Basque refugees, but also held pilots from the Spanish Republican air force and members of the International Brigades.[3] Women considered as politically dangerous were interned in a camp at Rieucros (in the Lozère) and intellectuals were held at Montolieu (in the Aude).

Conditions on arrival: the camps

The Spanish republicans had fought or lived through several years of war against reactionary forces, endured a perilous trek over the Pyrenees and now struggled for the next moment's bare existence. Miguel Oviedo's concern for his very survival in Argelès camp (evoked in the introduction to this book) was no exaggeration. The border crossing had been a physically and mentally challenging journey during winter. Refugees needed shelter, food, drinkable water and in some cases medical attention. On entering Argelès they found literally nothing save the barbed wire. Some internees had managed to carry some items across the border and past the customs officials, and some military units had retained their field equipment. Members of the Reserva General de Artillería, for example, were lucky enough to have tents and provisions with them.[4] More generally, though, material provision was defined through absence rather than presence. The situation was not helped by the French military's reticence to accept help from aid organisations or even grant access to the camps.[5] Despite the restrictions, it did not take long for news about the abominable conditions to begin circulating beyond France's borders.[6]

In the UK, the International Commission for the Assistance of Child Refugees in Spain had already raised concerns on 8 February. A report from 19 February, by one of its representatives, Dr Audrey Russell, reveals that whilst conditions remained unchanged, the military authorities were at least starting to collaborate with aid agencies:

> Argeles [sic] camp is on a sandy expanse by the sea. There is no shelter of any sort from wind, sand or rain. A bitterly cold wind from the mountains

has produced a raging sandstorm for the past few days. There is a great deal of 'dysentery' probably from lack of good water and absence of sanitary arrangements. The refugees scoop hollows in the sand for protection against the wind, but if they go more than a few inches down it is wet. A number of women living in the camp and nearly 80 children nearly all of whom suffering conjunctivitis from the sand [sic]. Through the kindness of the Commandant a small house has been acquired by the International Commission as a day colony and bathhouse for the children where they are fed, bathed, reclothed and given medical attention.

Another relief worker, and husband of the aristocrat writer Nancy Mitford, Peter Rennell Rodd, reported similar conditions at nearby Saint-Cyprien camp, though he thought the possibilities for shelter were slightly better at Argelès: 'the presence of reeds enabled the prisoners to weave little kennels'.[7] Neither camp had adequate sanitary facilities, forcing the internees to dig holes in the sand or use the sea.

By 21 February the French authorities had succeeded in improving the supply of provisions, but it was obvious that fundamental problems remained. Although the internees appeared to receive two rations of dried vegetables or rice along with a little meat, they had to cook it themselves, which proved difficult due owing to inadequate fuel supplies and the strong winds. Given the scale of these internment centres, it was undoubtedly difficult to gain an overall sense of how much conditions had improved. A scene witnessed by Dr Audrey Russell and Peter Rodd, however, is a telling and troubling example of the continuing problems: 'It is very difficult to arrive at a true estimate of the food situation but it is disagreeable to see a stray mule slaughtered in an amateurish way with old lorry parts and then eaten raw by the sick men in an overcrowded hospital tent.'[8] There were a significant number of deaths during these first weeks in France, though the exact number is unknown.[9]

The French press continued to report on the Spanish republicans' plight, and as with reporting of the exodus, the tenor was still very much influenced by the political hue of the newspaper concerned.[10] The far-right press ignored the situation in the camps, instead demanding the refugees' repatriation. Less virulent in tone, the conservative press continued to depict the internees in a rather unfavourable light, focusing attention on the health and hygiene issues stemming from mass internment or distinguishing the internee soldiers from the 'international bandits'. The mainstream regional dailies of *La Dépêche* and *L'Indépendant des Pyrénées Orientales* continued to support government policy and rejected claims by French Communist and Socialist delegations to the camps about the appalling conditions, but adopted a slightly more compassionate tone towards the end of February. On the left, the press maintained a pro-refugee voice and placed concerted effort into reporting on the miserable environment of the camps with calls for government action.[11]

Despite the varied reporting, the French government faced burgeoning pressure and could not easily dismiss all of the demands for improvement. After a tour of the camps, a delegation of Communist deputies called for a series of measures that included the dismissal of Raoul Didkowski, the Prefect of the Pyrénées-Orientales. Another delegation, this time of Socialist deputies, toured the Pyrénées-Orientales from 9 to 14 February before issuing a set of recommendations. Further pressure came from several hundred deputies of the newly created French–Spanish friendship group, whose report by Dr Peloquin likened refugees' conditions in the camps to those suitable for livestock.[12] On 18 February, Daladier's cabinet met and, while dismissing many of the Socialist delegation's recommendations, agreed at least to improve conditions as well as appointing General Ménard, the head of the Toulouse military region, to oversee the growing network of internment camps throughout southern France.[13] To relieve overcrowding in Saint-Cyprien and Argelès, Ménard began transferring internees to the other newly created camps. Gradually conditions improved but not quickly enough: barrack construction in Argelès took months rather than weeks to complete.

The government's failure to implement an adequate reception strategy and its delay in improving conditions caused enormous physical suffering as well as mental anguish that accentuated an already existent sense of loss amongst the internee population. An extract from a letter written by one internee that appeared in the *Manchester Guardian* is telling:

> Am now in a concentration camp where we are treated just like infected dogs and by the Senegalese blacks . . . Obviously, they were ordered to be rough with us, so as to make us tired and oblige us, more or less, to go with Franco, which is what the authorities want . . . The food ration consists of: 8 a.m. a tin of hot dirty water, meaning to be coffee[*sic*]; 3 p.m. half a pound of bad bread and a tin of small and very bad sardines to be shared between three people. And that's all. . . . We'll die like flies soon. It would have been better to have been killed by bombs.[14]

The refugees' mistrust of the French colonial guards and the French authorities, as we have already seen, left a prominent trace in refugees' memories of the arrival.[15] Equally worth noting is the process of dehumanisation reflected by the reference to dogs and flies.

The articulation of dehumanisation through allusion to animals is a common theme in the memoirs of refugees. Eulalio Ferrer contrasted the organised food provision in April of 1939 to the 'Roman circus' of the previous two months when humiliating squabbles occurred over bread that was sometimes distributed on the end of a Senegalese soldier's bayonet.[16] Similarly, Dr José Pujol recounts how guards took pleasure in treating internees like animals when giving out food during the first weeks of the camps. One afternoon, a van full of bread discharged its contents onto the ground. A gendarme perched on a chair and proceeded to throw bread into a crowd of refugees who fought each other for a morsel. Other guards, he recalled, used to throw bread while seated on their horses, 'greatly enjoying the spectacle offered by men who fought each other like dogs for a piece of bread'.[17]

The lack of toilet facilities was equally debasing. The internees had to dig holes in the sand or use the sea, a situation made all the worse by the rampant diarrhoea caused by contaminated drinking water.[18] This was all the more inappropriate given that women and children were also present during the initial period of internment. The wind also compounded problems by blowing waste-encrusted sand into people's faces and into their makeshift shelters.[19] The base conditions and the abusive stance of some of the guards led one internee to conclude that this environment entailed 'a methodical destruction of all moral values, reducing the person to . . . a starving, dirty beast obsessed with the most elementary needs'.[20]

There is no element of hyperbole in the above statement. On the contrary, it not only stresses the dehumanising effects, but also points towards the darker side of internees' reactions to a challenging situation. Some internees understandably felt there had been a breakdown of social solidarity. Struggles over limited resources caused distrust. Eulalio Ferrer described the arguments over bread as based upon 'laws of force and guile, laws that exclude any moral scruple'.[21] Francisco Pons's bewilderment about how some refugees placed barbed wire around their makeshift shelters soon turned to comprehension when a friend's suitcase containing much-needed possessions was stolen while he slept.[22] Solidarity also existed, and increasingly so as internees and the authorities began organising life in the camps. But in the interim, the anomie of the early weeks reinforced a sense of personal loss, and was interpreted by some refugees as evidence of the degradation of the values of the Second Spanish Republic.

Making sense of concentration-camp life

Under these conditions it was essential for the refugees to find sources of distraction and re-create links with the outside world.[23] Searching for friends and relatives was not easy. Some internees did not even know in which country their friends and relatives were now located. Communication with Spain was initially out of the question, as postal services with France had ground to a halt.[24] In France, although the government was sympathetic to relatives contacting each other, granting refugees with a temporary postal franchise, it did not encourage family reunions other than as a prelude to returning.[25]

For the majority of people, the desire to re-establish familial networks was a major preoccupation.[26] The first step was to find out the whereabouts of friends and relatives. It was a task facilitated by the Spanish republicans' own press in France and some French newspapers which printed refugees' requests for information about particular individuals.[27] Noticeboards on the sides of barracks in the camps also contained similar lists.[28] Refugees could then take the next step of contacting each other through letters. This was not always a foregone conclusion since some refugees were illiterate, though help from a fellow internee who could read and write was normally solicited.

The re-establishment of networks through written correspondence provided an essential link between the camps and relatives and friends elsewhere in the country. It enabled internees to feel they had not been lost and forgotten, and was also a vector through which they could articulate identities associated with daily life on the other side of the barbed wire. Francisco Pons ensured he quickly passed on his new address to contacts on the outside as soon as he was transferred from one camp into Barcarès so as to minimise any disruption. He stated: 'This postal cordon which connects our world of concentration to the world outside is absolutely vital to the survival and to the maintenance of our moral health.'[29] Similarly for Eulalio Ferrer: 'To have news of family and friends, quite simply, has as much or more importance as food. It's the link which connects us with the world.'[30]

The feeling of being in a world apart could cause worrying symptoms. During the First World War the psychological effects of interning prisoners of war was described as 'barbed-wire disease'. The Second World War gave way to additional studies on a wider category of internees, including civilians and refugees.[31] Although the studies differed about the exact symptoms of mental disorder, there was agreement on one basic premise: internment caused psychological harm. In the absence of studies by contemporaries on the Spanish republican internees, it is difficult to assess the psychological effects with any precision. What is clear, however, is that a fear of mental illness prevailed in the camps on the French Mediterranean coast. The monotony of camp life and the singular conditions on the beaches led the refugees to coin their own term for a form of psychosis, '*la arentitis*', which translates as 'sanditis'.[32] The neologism stems from the Spanish word for sand (*arena*) and refers to an amalgam of the external discomforts of the sand and windy conditions, the torment stemming from being denied one's freedom and the despondency arising from the monotony of concentration-camp life.

In June 1939, the cultural review *Barraca*, produced by internees in Argelès camp, contained both humorous and tragic references to this phenomenon. In a spoof dictionary of words referring to life in the camp *arentitis* is defined as a 'mental illness for refugees with alarming symptoms of insomnia which causes illusions of future trans-Atlantic voyages'. The allusion to travelling reflects the refugees' hopes and frustrations of re-emigrating to Latin America, along with the controversial selection procedures of the Spanish republican aid agencies (a subject to which we shall return in the next chapter).[33] The review also contains a series of reflections by 'Amichatis' which end with a powerfully compelling comment on the effects of sand and internment: 'The sand has entered my soul and body. And I feel like crying to dry the ink with which I am writing, for my tears have turned to sand.'[34]

In refugees' memoirs fears about *arentitis* are articulated through stories of internees pushed over the brink of sanity. Ferrer wrote: 'what is certain, is that the illness spreads and spares nobody'. Amongst many cases cited, he refers to a man believing himself to be the best engineer from Spain, who spent his time throwing sand and pebbles into the sea to calculate the quantity and time needed to dry out the Mediterranean.[35] Another story which circulated amongst refugees was of a man who was desperate to regain his freedom. Dressed in his best clothes, he walked straight into the sea carrying two suitcases, stating he was off to Mexico. He was pulled out of the sea when onlookers realised he was about to drown himself.[36] What is of interest here is not so much whether these stories rested on actual events, but on their function as a warning against idleness and inactivity in the camps.

Rumours could serve another function. 'Every day a false rumour is born', noted Pons.[37] One story inferring that the internees would be shipped off to a faraway island was not as far-fetched as it might seem.[38] It echoed debates in French policy-making circles of the late 1930s about possible solutions to the country's perceived refugee problem.[39] Another and more fantastical story provided an alternative take on the notion of the *drôle de guerre*: some time after war had been declared between France and Germany, Parisians had apparently laughed themselves to death after the Germans had dropped laughing gas on the capital. Whether fictitious or factual, each rumour could provoke lengthy discussions, or make people laugh, thereby maintaining morale and offering momentary distraction from the daily banality of internment.[40]

The bleaker rumours about attempted suicide evoke the state of anomie and perceived degradation of moral values which was highlighted earlier in this chapter. The appearance of areas within the camps associated with wheeling and dealing was interpreted by some internees as further evidence of the erosion of values that had been at stake during the war in Spain. Refugees named these areas, where goods could be bought, sold and exchanged, after the *barrio chino*, or Chinese quarter, of Barcelona. There was nothing intrinsically Chinese about the so-called area of Barcelona, though it did evoke prostitution, the underworld and corruption. For Francisco Pons, the reappearance of the *barrio chino* in his camp led him to write: 'It was the offspring of the famous Chinese quarter in Barcelona that disappeared a certain Sunday of July 1936 when the Revolution had triumphed over the military uprising.'[41] Not all refugees interpreted the phenomenon in the same way. Eulalio Ferrer has left us with a more sanguine impression with details of barbers, bars, eateries, jewellery stalls and tailors, albeit in insalubrious conditions: it was 'an incredible universe in which everything goes on giving the impression that we are not living in confinement'.[42]

The *barrio chino* is one of many examples of refugees naming prominent places in the camps with familiar references from their country of origin. Catalans referred to the central passageways of the camps on the beaches of the Pyrénées-Orientales as 'Las Ramblas' in reference to the famous promenade which gently slopes towards the port in Barcelona. As in the Catalan city, the Spanish republicans congregated along these avenues to walk and exchange conversation or to distract themselves by the improvised shops and services which enterprising refugees had set up.[43] The Catalans' Ramblas may well have been the Madrileños' 'Gran Vía', named after the central Madrid thoroughfare. A description written at the time in the refugees' cultural review *Barraca* refers to a 'Wide promenade "asphalted" with moving sand' that began with a collection of improvised, ramshackle cabins where provisions could be bought, and even a 'bar' with a pretty waitress. 'The *Gran Via* of this large refugee city will pass into posterity, just like with the avenues of any other country, though without municipal backing or expenses running into the millions.'[44] The construction of spatial identities may seem an insignificant detail to highlight when evoking this singular world. It was not. The naming of camp areas in this way represented a means of reaffirming presence. It created an imagined and meaningful topography of homeland in a hostile environment that was predicated on both absence and the French repression of ideological and political identities.

Events in the Aquitaine

How did events develop elsewhere in the country? Although the greatest concentration of refugees remained in the Languedoc-Roussillon, the authorities transferred significant numbers of mainly women, children and the elderly to other regions. In the Aquitaine, the region's conservative and largest daily, *La Petite Gironde*, proved adept at peddling reductivist images of the refugees. On 29 January, just after the French government had reopened the border, an article entitled '1500 Spanish militia have been interned in Prats-de-Mollo' re-evoked the church desecrations that had gripped France back in the summer of 1936 through a report from just inside Spain: refugees rested 'at the foot of a burnt-out chapel, a sad vestige of anarchist domination'.[45] Perhaps as a half-hearted attempt to reassure the paper's readership, the report ended with the observation that combatants at Prats-de-Mollo had tried to conceal their weapons while being disarmed.

While *La Petite Gironde* devoted ample coverage to the exodus, it devoted less attention to the arrival of refugees in the *département* of the Gironde. The first article about arriving refugees referred to three Spanish republican pilots who landed their 'Russian-built' fighter planes at Illats on the morning of 5 February, the same day that the government had allowed combatants to seek refuge in France.[46] By this date women, children and elderly refugees had arrived at reception centres throughout the Gironde with at least 884 refugees in Bordeaux, Talence and Verdelais.[47] On 8 February, the number had risen to 1,112 refugees and then peaked on 25 February with 1,717 refugees in the Gironde accommodated at various locations. These included the Saint-André Hospital in Bordeaux, a makeshift hospital ship (the *Habana*) moored on the outskirts of Bordeaux in the port area of Bassens and the Boursier Hospital. These were supplemented by a hospital and reception centre at Langon, another at Blaye and others at Pessac, Pauillac, Gradignan, Cauderon, Cenon, Podensac, Preignac and Libourne.[48]

Despite the presence of refugees in the locality, the newspaper continued to direct public attention to the border and the subject of internment. On 12 February an article entitled 'What should be done with the 300,000 Spaniards who have crossed the border?' called for all 'prisoners of war' to be interned and deprived of all means of communication. As France was not at war with the Spanish Republic the reference to prisoners of war was resolutely incorrect, and illustrates once again how accuracy was neglected in the drive for exclusion. On this matter the newspaper's stance also matched government concerns. Five days beforehand, the newspaper *Le Temps* – the semi-official mouthpiece of the Ministry for Foreign Affairs which had been sympathetic to refugee issues earlier on in the 1930s – somewhat ambivalently depicted the majority of refugees as 'brave people worthy or respect' within an overall context of a military invasion which therefore required the government to prioritise questions of security.[49] Just over two weeks later, ministerial instructions to the Prefecture of the Gironde referred to 'an army under internment'. Under no pretext were internees authorised to reach the interior of the country.[50]

Only influential refugees and those classified as 'civilians' or wounded could avoid the internment camps. Even then, the authorities attempted to minimise the presence of the refugees in France's largest urban centres. In the Aquitaine, the *départements* of the Landes, Lot-et-Garonne and the Dordogne accommodated a comparatively larger number of refugees than the Gironde, where the region's administrative centre of Bordeaux was located. The Landes received over 4,000 refugees, mainly women and children.[51] Similarly, 4,249 refugees in the Lot-et-Garonne on 4 March were composed of 1,507 women, 2,295 children, 249 elderly people and 198 hospitalised combatants.[52] Just northwards in the Dordogne the number of refugees peaked on 20 February at 3,396, the majority of whom were, again, women and children.[53]

Local officials' reports reveal the appalling toll of war deprivation and the exodus. They contain frequent references to the terrible physical and psychological state of refugees, who were badly dressed and in some cases even without shoes.[54] After being transferred from the Pyrénées-Orientales to inland *départements*, the refugees were usually registered by the local authorities and given a medical check, accompanied by vaccinations. This was supposed to have occurred at the border, but the scale of

the exodus had completely overwhelmed the medical facilities and personnel of the Pyrénées-Orientales.[55] The Ministry for Public Health was
particularly concerned about the possible spread of typhus fever and
smallpox and instructed prefects to quarantine refugees for 14 days,
explaining that these measures were necessary out of humanitarian consideration for the refugees but also for the protection of the French
population.[56] Just over a week later, he reminded prefects that the Spanish
republicans should be kept apart from the local population.[57]

In the Lot-et-Garonne, a dossier of daily telegrams from the Prefect
to the Ministry of Public Health gives an indication of the range of the
refugees' medical ailments.[58] Between 1 February and 17 March a total of
185 individuals were hospitalised, of whom 75 were treated for war
wounds and 65 for various forms of contagious illness; a further 26
people were treated for lung complaints and frostbite brought on by the
conditions of the exodus and 19 suffered from a wide list of ailments
ranging from ear infections to appendicitis. Based on the total number
of refugees in the *département*, a total of 1.72 per cent of refugees were
diagnosed with a contagious illness (there were 12 diagnosed cases of
typhoid and one case of chicken pox). In the same period there were 11
registered deaths, 6 of whom were of combatants.[59]

'Civilian' refugees were housed in reception centres known as 'centres
d'accueil' or 'centres d'hébergement'. Orphans and children separated
from their parents were placed in colonies – holiday centres normally
used for French children. In the Aquitaine, as in other regions, conditions
very much varied between specific localities. In the Basses-Pyrénées some
centres lacked any toiletry facilities and straw was used for bedding.[60] In
the Dordogne, officials arranged accommodation in hospitals, and in a
range of public and private properties including two holiday camps,
two châteaux owned by the CGT, a former prison and some disused
buildings.

The refugees' arrival in the region provoked reactions amongst many
local officials and some members of the public which echoed images
from the conservative press (referred to in the previous chapter). Officials' correspondence from throughout south-west France suggests how
initial support, where shown, soon turned to ambivalence and in some
cases hostility. In this respect, the reports from the predominantly rural
Dordogne, with its population of around 161,000, provide a striking case
study of responses.

A report by the Secretary-General of the Prefecture, written at the
end of February, sets out his vision of how inhabitants throughout the

Dordogne had responded to the crisis. He referred to the public's willingness and generosity in providing refuge, and donations organised by primary-school teachers and reception committees. He then contrasted this public goodwill with the refugees' gratitude though lack of appreciation.[61] The public's charitable response was not in fact as uniform as suggested. During *la retirada*, the Sub-Prefect of Sarlat could only arrange accommodation for 450 out of the 700 places requested because buildings were unavailable either for health reasons or because owners refused to give their consent, despite the offer of state compensation.[62] The Prefect's request for information about refugees from around the *département* produced some interesting replies. On 24 February, just over a fortnight after the end of the exodus, the Sub-Prefect of Sarlat qualified the public's generosity with the words 'there is reason to believe that the local population will start to manifest some lassitude if the refugees have to remain here for a long time'.[63] Similarly, the Sub-Prefect of Bergerac referred to the public's kindness before reporting that some refugees were undeserving. He went on to claim that some Spanish women had only been prevented from 'debauched' activities through careful police surveillance, though what this actually meant was left unexplained.[64] The official at Nontron, on the other hand, depicted both local inhabitants and the refugees positively.[65]

Less than three months later, the Prefect sent a detailed report to the Minister of the Interior setting out the situation in the Dordogne.[66] The report offers a snapshot of the refugees living in the 19 reception centres. After four months of exile, many refugees were beginning to speak French well enough to be understood. Children in particular were adapting well to their new environment and the Prefecture seemed to be making efforts to maintain the children's morale and education by attempting to find personnel to teach Spanish, general schooling and French lessons.[67] In practice, as with living conditions, access to education varied according to locality and depended on the will of local officials, the availability of places in local schools and public reactions.[68]

The report is also revealing of officials' suspicions and prejudice towards the refugees. According to the Prefect a reversal in public opinion had occurred due to concerns about the financial and security implications of the refugees' presence. The local authorities were also worried about the lack of information relating to the refugees' backgrounds, and were particularly concerned with the activities of a 'small number of troublesome elements'. The Prefect mobilised cultural difference to justify discrimination. Despite the fleeting references to the refugees' adaptation to life in France, the official stressed they had 'a very different mentality from ours, belonging for the most part to a quite low level of the social ladder'. These cultural and class traits, he believed, explained the spirit of idleness and nonchalance which apparently prevailed in the reception centres.

The Prefect's comments are best understood in relation to his views on the possible participation of Spanish refugees in the local agricultural labour economy. He believed that any potential economic advantages were outweighed by the threat of refugees becoming incorporated into the working life of the *département*. The Prefect thus aimed to maintain refugees in a marginal and liminal situation in order to encourage repatriation. On the subject of work, he wrote:

> It would introduce a certain element of stability into a population whose stay in France must only be temporary. Public opinion in my *département* is starting to consider the refugees somewhat unfavourably notably because of the competition that these refugees could represent to the local labour market. . . . It is to be feared that if France offers them normal means of existence, in addition to a safe asylum, they will definitively lose any desire to return to their country.

A final justification for keeping Spanish refugees away from local jobs was raised in relation to security issues. The Prefect maintained it would be difficult to keep these refugees under surveillance if they were scattered around the agricultural exploitations of the Dordogne. Ungrateful, of a different mentality and class background, idle, nonchalant and finally potentially dangerous: these were some of the most repeated images used to differentiate refugees from local French inhabitants in the Dordogne.

In other parts of the Aquitaine and further afield, officials and local inhabitants also employed cultural difference to justify exclusion. In Pessac, on the outskirts of Bordeaux, a police superintendent described how the local population's initial sympathy for the refugees had begun to wane.[69] More specifically, he alluded to noise, dirtiness and the possibility of damaging the town's tourism as reasons for removing refugees from their accommodation in the hall of the local park.[70] Employees of the French railway, the SNCF, had also registered complaints from French passengers who found the Spanish refugees too dirty and therefore wished to be seated apart.[71] Moreover, concerns about women's behaviour, highlighted above, were not limited to the town of Bergerac. At the southern end of the Aquitaine some inhabitants of Laruns, in the Basses-Pyrénées, organised a petition against the 'deplorable moral behaviour' of 'licentious women' who apparently represented a danger to the moral and physical health of local adolescents. A subsequent enquiry concluded that the remarks were entirely without foundation.[72]

Local businessmen equally raised issues of morality and public hygiene. On 18 March 1939, the Chamber of Commerce in the Pyrénées-Orientales asked the Prefect to relay its concerns to the government about the risk of 'physical and moral contagion' posed by the refugees. The Chamber requested the government to evacuate refugees from the area, making an implicit link between the removal of the refugees and the fortunes of the tourist and agricultural industry.[73] Interestingly, some astute businesses saw an opportunity to profit from the refugees' arrival. Well aware of the lucrative gains to be made from the creation of large-scale internment camps, they were proactive in soliciting orders from the local authorities for services ranging from barrack construction to clothes provision.[74] The Chambers of Commerce, however, were uniformly against the refugees' presence in their vicinities. A statement by the Chamber in the Lot-et-Garonne is worth quoting in full to show how local business leaders politicised the refugee issue for economic motives:

> The Chamber of Commerce of Agen and the Lot-et-Garonne strongly insists on the danger posed to the French economy and to the country as a whole by the interference of Spanish elements, anarchists, revolutionaries, or criminals in our *départements*, and demands for these undesirable foreigners to be barred from the everyday social and economic life of our region.[75]

There is a comparison to be made with how Chambers of Commerce in north-eastern France had reacted to the arrival of German and East European refugees in the first half of the 1930s by seeking to bar them from local labour markets. There was a key difference, though, in the actual vocabulary of exclusion. In north-eastern France the Chambers of Commerce played on security fears about German refugees acting as spies for Nazi Germany and, as Vicki Caron points out, their calls also contained an anti-Semitic edge.[76] In the south-west, the Chambers' of Commerce discourse about the Spanish refugees was more ideological in character and echoed the wider sea change in debates about refugees which occurred in France towards the end of the 1930s. It also reproduced the reductive and scaremongering references to the Spanish Civil War which had featured in the French conservative and extreme right-wing reporting of the conflict.[77]

Alternatives

Discrimination was widespread but alternatives existed. A significant body of organisations and people countered the grid of administrative procedures and categories of exclusion through organised, or sometimes spontaneous, acts of solidarity. However small the gesture, it could make all the difference to weary and malnourished refugees who had endured distressful scenes at the border.

Ángel Granada, an officer in the Republican army, recalled his train journey to the *département* of the Cher where he was to be treated for war wounds. People gathered at station stops to hand out food packages: 'it was a party, a new experience'. Another combatant, Francisco Guzmán, framed his story of reception in terms of a dichotomy between the French authorities and French children:

> There were boys and girls, very young, who came towards us. I see them winding their way through the soldiers and gendarmes to offer us chocolate, bread, sweets. Things that couldn't nourish us much but which in reality would nourish us a lot: it warmed our hearts. We understood that the French people didn't have the one face of the hostile or indifferent gendarmes. That was what represented France, these children who were trying, in their own way, to alleviate our suffering.[78]

Spanish republicans who were children at the time have also retained vivid memories. Raquel Thiercelin described the animated setting of a large hall, decorated with different-coloured flags as if for a party, where hundreds of people sat eating. Although grateful for the first hot meal in days, she was baffled by the meaning of the 'celebration'.[79]

What type of organisation participated in the relief effort? Motivations varied and were frequently overlapping rather than mutually exclusive. They could involve a strong sense of anti-fascist conviction, class and professional solidarity, as well as ethnic and religious factors. The organisations were usually though not entirely associated with the Left, but some originated from traditionally Catholic and conservative circles.[80] An array of organisations which had appeared during the Spanish Civil War to raise material and moral support for the Spanish Republic redirected their efforts to refugee aid in France.[81] From the start, the French section of the International Anti-Fascist Solidarity (SIA) combined welfare work with a critique of successive French governments for their stance on the Non-Intervention treaty. It also dissimulated propaganda about the social revolution in Spain, and the CNT's contribution to the anti-nationalist struggle.[82] The French representatives of the SIA had originally created the Committee for a Free Spain (Comité de l'Espagne Libre), a libertarian-inspired organisation which also attracted interest and support from people outside libertarian circles. In 1937 the Committee became the French section of the SIA following the creation of the latter by the two largest trade unions in Spain, the CNT and UGT.[83] During *la retirada*, French representatives of the SIA organised fundraising and information campaigns in the two largest port cities of southern France. In Bordeaux, the SIA mounted a poster campaign requesting money, clothes and provisions while also lambasting the French government for continuing to deprive the Spanish Republic of arms. As part of the same campaign, a meeting in Marseilles attracted between 5,000 and 6,000 people.[84]

In another major urban centre of southern France, Toulouse, Dr Camille Soula spearheaded the University of Toulouse Committee for the Friends of Republican Spain (Comité Universitaire Toulousain des Amis de l'Espagne Républicaine).[85] The Committee secured funds from public donations, the Ministry of the Interior and other Spanish aid organisations to convert two former fire stations into reception centres for intellectuals, university staff and their respective families.[86] The centres were taken as a role model by two other organisations working with intellectuals, the Aid Committee for Catalan Intellectuals (Comité d'aide aux intellectuels Catalans) and the Ramon Llull Foundation, which opened a similar centre for Catalans in Montpellier.[87] From the first half of 1938, 'Fébriles', or intellectuals of Occitan culture, began creating committees along the major cities of the French Mediterranean coast in Marseilles, Montpellier and Perpignan to help Catalan intellectuals, personalities and their families.[88] Basque representatives had also developed links in France, and in particular, the French section of the International League of Friends of the Basques contained a number of influential figures.[89] Catholicism played a particular role in generating support for Basque refugees, reflecting how the Church in the Basque Country, unlike elsewhere in Spain, had opposed the nationalist uprising. The Basque government in exile was especially keen to portray Basque refugees through this Catholic lens in its paper, *Euzko Deya*, which was published in France.[90]

There could be no stronger sense of welcome than people allowing refugees into their own homes. The scale of this phenomenon is unknown, though unlikely to have been substantial as it was limited to women, children and the aged, but also dependent on the Prefect's permission. If not generalised, the shelter of refugees in people's homes should nonetheless be emphasised, given the qualitative difference compared to staying in a reception centre or internment camp. Why did some people accommodate refugees? In some cases, the authorities suspected profiteering. In the Dordogne, some inhabitants thought they had found a way to obtain free labour in return for board and lodging.[91] Fortunately for refugees, more altruistic factors were common. Family ties were important, as was the question of cultural kinship. The Federation of Spanish Emigrants of the Gironde Region had begun placing children with host families in and around Bordeaux during the Spanish Civil War, and notably in the commune of Floriac, with its density of Spanish immigrant families.[92] Perceptions of cultural kinship by French nationals also resulted in the shelter of Catalan and Basque refugees in the Catalan and Basque areas of southern France.[93]

The political hue of the hosts was a most relevant factor. This was the case throughout France, but particularly evident in Alain Léger's detailed study of a small Charentais town, Ruelle.[94] Some of Ruelle's population of 4,500 accepted a total of 311 refugees into 142 homes. Jean Antoine, the Mayor of Ruelle, who was from a Socialist and Communist background, set an example by inviting refugees into his own home. While the majority of hosts were indeed left-wing sympathisers, there were also two future Vichy municipal councillors and several people who became collaborators during the Occupation. Ruelle was rather unique in that it accepted nearly two-thirds of all Spanish refugees accommodated privately in the Charente. The explanation seems to lie in the stable and steady employment provided by local military contractors together with developed trade-union, co-operative, cultural and political networks, and significantly a municipality representing the left of French politics.

The correlation between hospitality and political background was repeated elsewhere. In the Lot-et-Garonne, the Communist Mayor of Port-Sainte-Marie, M. Laujol, participated in a reception committee that placed 104 refugees in French households.[95] Further southwards, in the Béarn, Spanish refugees wrote a letter to the local newspaper thanking local residents of Oloron-Sainte-Marie for their hospitality.[96] The town's Radical Socialist Mayor, Jean Mendiondou, also happened to be the only elected representative from a Popular Front background in the entire Basses-Pyrénées. Mendiondou campaigned vigorously for the reception of more Spanish republicans when the government sought to construct an internment centre in the region. The plans provoked a barrage of protest sustained by references to the now ubiquitous triptych of economic, health and security issues. Some local figures resorted to a sifted version of local history. At least two mayors dug deep into their local archives and cited ancient grazing rights as a reason for opposing the camp.[97] Similar treaties regulating the common pastoral interests of villages on both sides of the Pyrenean border, and which had a long tradition of intercultural co-operation, were not mentioned.[98] In counter-argument, Mendiondou cited both humanitarian and economic reasons for establishing the camp in his locality.[99] The economic argument was certainly convincing given that the region's firms would supply the timber for the construction of barracks, but his optimism for a humanitarian approach to refugee reception was overshadowed by subsequent events. On 15 March, the decision was finally taken to construct what was euphemistically referred to as a 'centre d'accueil' down the road from Oloron next to the village of Gurs. Initially designed to hold 18,000, the Gurs camp became the largest internment centre in the Aquitaine. During the Occupation, Jews were interned and deported from the camp.

As well as organising welfare, reception committees often provided the first opportunities for interaction between refugees and local inhabitants. They were also a potential channel through which politico-ideological affinities could develop, thus raising the Minister of the Interior's concern about the impact that Spanish revolutionary organisations might have on their French counterparts. As a consequence, prefects were to report any political activities.[100] The presence of confiscated publications in the *archives départementales* shed light on French inhabitants facilitating contacts between refugees in reception centres and elsewhere because of their shared ideological affinities. In the Lot-et-Garonne, officials thwarted an attempt to introduce 25 PSUC booklets into the refuge at Bon Encontre in April 1939. The information included details of the first meeting of the party's Central Committee and a speech by its secretary-general, Joan Comorera,[101] which criticised the British and French governments.[102] Numerous and similar incidents occurred in other localities. In the Dordogne, there were contacts between combatants recovering in the military hospital at Clairvivre, and Communist members of the local reception committee. The latter managed to pass brochures and written propaganda to refugees before the authorities stepped in and transferred the refugees in question to the Vernet punishment camp.[103] French Communists had also attempted, if not succeeded, in doing the same for Spanish refugees in Bergerac.[104]

Repatriation

The activities at Bon Encontre and Bergerac suggest that Spanish women, and/or adolescents and the aged, were implicated in the reconstruction of Spanish political and trade-union networks. From the available evidence it is impossible to know how many were involved or the nature of the activities. In part, the relative dearth of information may reflect a view by French officials that women refugees were not politically active. When women participated in, or organised collective forms of action, officials interpreted events as a problem of discipline rather than political activity. The domain in which women's agency is most visible relates to the anti-repatriation campaign.

The financial cost of sheltering the refugees sparked animated debates in the French parliament. The Daladier government's preferred solution had consistently been to return refugees to Spain. There can be no doubt that prefects, subordinates and local elected representatives pressurised and deceived refugees into returning, but it is not entirely clear whether the Ministry of the Interior ever issued instructions explicitly calling for the use of force.[105] The idea of mass forced repatriation had certainly been mooted at the national and local levels.[106] Moreover, Patrick Weil believes the French authorities were momentarily tempted to resort to 'forced repatriations' in April 1939.[107] But even if the Minister of the Interior never explicitly called for the use of force, his instructions were frequently suggestive of the need for strong measures and often interpreted by local officials in this sense.

Instructions and interpretations

In some cases, French pressure on refugees to return to Spain was almost instantaneous. At the border some officials incited male refugees to either return or to join the French Foreign Legion.[108] In the camps, relief workers and internees suspected the authorities of providing better conditions for those refugees opting to return.[109] On 3 February, less than a week into the exodus, Sarraut had ordered prefects to organise voluntary returns. One week later he sent out further instructions to identify all refugees likely to be returned and to use all possible means in this respect.[110] Another circular soon followed, with a demand for an acceleration of the rate of returns.[111] The Minister then reiterated his orders after a cabinet council meeting on 18 February.[112] Between 1 and 19 February more than 50,000 people crossed back over the border via the frontier towns of Hendaye and Irún.[113] But the numbers were insufficient to satisfy the French government.

The pace was hampered by the machinations of the embryonic dictatorship in Spain. On 20 February, the Francoist regime closed the border just before the start of formal negotiations with the French government on transferring Spanish republican assets in France to Spain and the terms for French recognition of Franco's government. The Radical senator, Léon Bérard, had in fact already visited nationalist Spain to discuss terms with General Gómez Jordana y Sousa on 2 February as part of the French government's strategy of keeping Francoist Spain neutral in the case of a French–German war. Despite the Second Spanish Republic being a legal entity with a democratically elected government – arguments that were raised by Léon Blum and the left more generally – the Bérard-Jordana agreement was signed on 25 February.[114] In addition to laying out the conditions for handing Spanish republican assets to the dictatorship, it included guidelines for bilateral relations between France and Francoist Spain that placed responsibility on the respective governments to prevent any activities which could destabilise the security of the neighbouring country. Two days later both the French and British governments recognised the nationalist Spanish government.

Recognition of Franco's regime represented a further step towards the delegitimisation of the Second Spanish Republic, a process which stretched back to the start of the Civil War with the sham of the Non-Intervention treaty (the international pact against involvement in the Civil War). It struck an enormous blow to the refugees' morale in France and to the remaining forces of the Spanish Republic still battling against the nationalist onslaught in Spain. For the French government, these issues were supplanted by foreign policy interests, along with the Ministry of the Interior's desire to rid the country of as many Spanish republicans as possible. Despite the agreement, however, the dictatorship blocked or facilitated repatriations depending on the vigour with which the French government organised the recuperation of the Spanish Republic's assets.[115]

How did refugees respond to the pressures and temptations of returning? They would certainly have considered the risks. Their judgements were predicated on existing knowledge about nationalist atrocities committed during the war, as well as on warnings from friends and relatives in Spain who used metaphors in their letters to outwit the dictatorship's censorship of post destined for France.[116] Counter-propaganda distributed by French sympathisers or Spanish migrants also informed refugees' decisions. Understandably, many showed little enthusiasm about going back to Spain. French officials throughout the Aquitaine signalled that Spanish republicans in the reception centres wished to postpone any decision about returning. In the first week of March, refugees in the Gironde responded negatively when asked if they wished to return.[117] The vast majority wanted to remain in France until the end of hostilities in Spain and a possible amnesty. Officials reported similar reactions in the Basses-Pyrénées.[118] News of Franco's Law of Responsibilities, which effectively rendered supporters of the Republic guilty of a crime, would have done little to change refugees' minds.[119]

On 14 March Sarraut gave assurances that the French government would uphold asylum for 'worthy' refugees.[120] Whether or not refugees in the reception centres were aware of Sarraut's assurances, they were manifestly anxious about the bloody and repressive context in Spain. On 17 March the Sub-Prefect at Blaye noted that the majority of women feared nationalist reprisals. Others who were unaware of the whereabouts of their husbands despaired at returning alone. Given this lack of enthusiasm, the official asked whether to proceed with compulsory repatriations. Ten days later, and without any response, he repeated his request but warned it could provoke unrest.[121] Most refugees remained resolutely determined. In the Gironde, only 209 departed between 4 February and 1 May 1939.[122] Meanwhile, in the Dordogne, 424 out of 2,108 refugees had reportedly taken the decision to return before 15 May.[123]

Anti-repatriation campaigns

Repatriation rates were regulated by a combination of the local authorities' determination, the degree of Francoist compliance at the border, the will of the refugees and often the solidarity of local authority figures. Some locally elected representatives, perhaps only a minority but a significant one nonetheless, acted positively on behalf of the Spanish republicans. What became known as 'the affair of Port-Sainte-Marie' in the Lot-et-Garonne is illustrative of how repatriations could be subverted through a combination of collective protest and local solidarity.

On 19 April, just over two weeks after Franco had proclaimed the 'official' end of the Spanish Civil War, the Prefecture summoned a group of refugees to the gendarmerie in the village of Port-Sainte-Marie. The Commandant informed them of their imminent repatriation to Spain and offered a choice of returning via Hendaye on the Atlantic coast or Cerbère on the Mediterranean coast. The refugees protested, resulting in a standoff with gendarmes and the subsequent intervention in the refugees' favour by the local councillor Robert Philippot, who was also a Communist *député* elected to represent Agen under the Popular Front.[124]

Events in Port-Sainte-Marie demonstrate how the presence of the Spanish republicans formed a screen onto which was projected the interplay of tensions at the local level between supporters of the Popular Front on the one hand, and conservative officials on the other. The Prefect subsequently ordered all refugees in the village to be dispersed across the whole of the Lot-et-Garonne, but deliberately kept the local Communist Mayor, Monsieur Laujol, in the dark. Laujol, who had previously been instrumental in organising the reception of the refugees, unsuccessfully tried to prevent the refugees' dispersion. With some tenacity, he then organised a poster campaign which thanked the local population for their generosity and remonstrated against the Prefect's decision. Local residents petitioned to have the refugees back, even guaranteeing to meet the accommodation costs. In coordination, Philippot published an article in *Le Travailleur* on 6 May criticising the Prefect's behaviour and the treatment of refugees more generally in this area of France.[125] But despite this energetic campaign and show of local support, the Prefect maintained his decision and banned any further refugees from residing in Port-Sainte-Marie.

The Prefect's reactions might well have been motivated by the prevailing wind of anti-communism in France but certainly reflected a preoccupation about the effects of counter-propaganda on the government's strategy of return. On 24 April, he ordered all Spanish and Catalan publications destined for the refugees to be censored.[126] A fortnight later, the head of the gendarmerie in the medieval walled town of Monflanquin warned that the secretary of the local branch of the PCF was distributing leaflets from a French coordinating committee for aid to Spanish republican civilians, the Comité Français de Coordination pour l'Aide aux Populations Civiles de l'Espagne Républicaine. The leaflets cited statements by the Minister of the Interior and the military head of the region, General Menard, that Spanish refugees were under no obligation to return. Unsurprisingly, the refugees became more strongly opposed to repatriation after the leaflets had been distributed. Further eastwards in Fumel, the mayor's office intercepted posters from another aid organisation, the Office Français Pour l'Aide Aux Réfugiés Espagnols. They described the repugnant conditions in the concentration camps, highlighted the French authorities' pressure on refugees to return and called for the right of asylum to be protected.[127]

Franco's declaration of the 'official' end of the Civil War on 1 April added urgency to the anti-repatriation campaign. The newspaper of the Spanish Republic's government in exile, *La Voz de Madrid*, was quick to react, arguing that sending refugees to Spain was as good as sending them to their death and calling for guarantees on the right to asylum.[128] At the same time, the pro-Spanish republican lobby in France continued to press for the refugees' rights.[129] The combination of local and national campaigns resulted in a clarification, albeit characteristically ambiguously, from the Minister of the Interior. On 5 May, Sarraut informed prefects that his previous instructions had actually insisted on the voluntary basis of repatriations but he also underlined how it was nonetheless the prefects' responsibility to convince the undecided to return. From this point onwards, reports from prefects and sub-prefects in the Gironde and Dordogne emphasised strategies of 'persuasion' and the refugees' free will in returning.[130] The term persuasion, though, seems to have been used liberally and we cannot, therefore, be sure of the exact circumstances surrounding refugees signing consent forms for repatriation.

The Prefect of the Lot responded to Sarraut's instructions by reassuring refugees that force had not, and would never be employed, but then outlined the advantages of returning: being reunited with relatives in Spain, rediscovering a 'normal way of life' and helping those compatriots unable to return by reducing numbers in France. He also reminded them that remaining in France carried the obligation of accepting any work offered by the local authorities.[131] Asylum in the Lot, as elsewhere, was evidently not unconditional, but clearly linked to work rather than the universal values on which it was supposedly based.

The lack of news about the health or whereabouts of relatives separated during the exodus was tremendously worrying for refugees. The French government was not completely insensitive to this problem, and various groups also helped refugees locate family members and friends. A Catholic association for Basques and Catalans, the Comité National Catholique Accueil aux Basques et de Secours à l'Enfance de Catalogne, established a central register of relatives trying to locate each other that had rapidly acquired several thousand names by the end of February. However, in the concentration camps some French officials wilfully manipulated the internees' sensibilities about their relatives as part of the persuasion to return.

At Argelès, officials displayed notices claiming that families could only be reunited by consenting to return.[132] Following the circulation of ministerial instructions in August, which advised that whole families could be repatriated on the sole consent of the head of the family, officials in Gurs camp used the same ploy. As a precaution some of the internees responded by writing to officials in charge of reception centres warning them not to repatriate their relatives.[133] Officials tried other means, circulating propaganda from nationalist Spain that called on refugees to return home,[134] or, as underlined earlier in this chapter, offering male refugees the choice of joining the Foreign Legion or returning to Spain. The latter strategy was not particularly successful. In Gurs camp, out of 11,814 refugees questioned, only 473 signed a repatriation agreement.[135]

The mass refusal of internees in Gurs, and in other camps such as Vernet and Agde, contrasts with the considerable number of refugees from the rest of France who did in fact risk the path of return.[136] Although there had been foot-dragging by refugees and the dictatorship alike during the spring months, the repatriations gathered steam over the summer. Once the French government had handed over nearly 5.5 million francs of the Spanish Republic's assets to Franco's regime, his government agreed to accelerate the pace of repatriations. By mid-June, the Spanish authorities had recorded a total of 121,284 returnees, though the actual number may have been higher as the total did not account for those who had returned clandestinely to avoid repression. Just over a month and a half later approximately 250,000 refugees had left France for Spain.[137]

Making room for French refugees and collective protest

The annual demand for seasonal agricultural workers and the growing threat of war with Germany turned the French government's attention towards using refugees as a cheap and flexible pool of labour.[138] However, it took some time before the French government recognised women refugees' potential for the labour economy.[139] In the meantime, the repatriation of women, children and the elderly remained a prime concern. More specifically, children with parents in Spain, women with children, and women without a partner in France or whose partner was unable to work were high on the list of desirable returnees.

There was renewed emphasis on the repatriation of Spanish republicans after the declaration of war with Germany as the French authorities proceeded with the evacuation of French nationals from north-eastern France. On 19 September Sarraut called for officials to exert 'heavy pressure' on non-economically active refugees to be repatriated and to intern remaining refugees whose behaviour had been any cause for concern. He explained that the humanitarian reasons which had led France to welcome the refugees had lost their value now the country was at war.[140]

In effect, local officials and the Ministry of the Interior were prepared to consider radical solutions for removing Spanish refugees from those areas designated as evacuation centres for French evacuees. Officials resorted to physical force at Mirepeix in order to ensure all refugees in the Basses-Pyrénées, save those with partners in work, were repatriated via Irún before the end of September. Jean Mendiondou failed in his efforts to incite refugees to remain, attracting criticism from the Prefect.[141] Further northwards the Prefect of the Dordogne complained that the task of receiving and sheltering French war evacuees from the Bas-Rhin was being complicated by the existing presence of Spanish republicans. As we saw earlier, this official had already expressed his desire for the Spaniards to return to Spain. He now seized the opportunity to rid his *département* of their presence by seeking permission to transfer all 1,934 out of the Dordogne to another area of France. The Minister of the Interior responded by advising him to press more women and children into returning to Spain and to contact the Prefect of the Pyrénées-Orientales with a view to accepting the rest.[142] It is most probable the Minister was envisaging the internment of these refugees until work could be found. But the transfer never materialised and by the end of November 1,041 Spanish republicans remained in the Dordogne.

Why and how so many Spanish republicans remained in the Dordogne is unclear. Elsewhere, however, there is evidence of refugee agency in contesting return. Back in August, a police superintendent in Talence, outside Bordeaux, requested the transfer of four women to a concentration camp without delay for having compromised the authority and discipline of the centre.[143] Women refugees also invented new forms of collective action. In one of a series of similar incidents, a train transporting 95 refugees, mostly women and children, from the Deux-Sèvres to the border never reached its destination.[144] As the train slowed to a stop in the station at Bordeaux, at 7.22 p.m. in the evening of 14 October, passengers in one carriage threw their luggage onto the platform, jumped off the train and resolutely refused to continue the onward journey. Officials promised to return the train to the Deux-Sèvres, but the women argued they had already been deceived into undertaking the trip in the first place. After an hour and a half of negotiations, the refugees eventually returned to the Deux-Sèvres.[145] Further south in the Landes, refugees forced another repatriation train to stop near to the station of Saubusse at 5.30 a.m. in the morning of 1 December. But this time the strategy failed. The authorities mobilised 13 gendarmes along with an army captain and 6 troops to ensure the refugees got back on the train so it could continue heading for the border.[146]

Refugees' motivations for returning

Women's collective actions on the repatriation trains sometimes produced positive results, but were not decisive in slowing down the overall rate of returns. Throughout 1939 a considerable number crossed back over the border, reducing the refugee population by two-thirds, leaving around 180,000 refugees, 45,000 of whom were women, children and the aged.[147] In the end, and despite the Minister of the Interior's fixation with returning refugees, the Ministry for Foreign Affairs became increasingly aware that the remaining refugees risked certain persecution if forced back to Spain.[148]

Why and how did so many refugees return to a country ravaged by war and bloody political repression? In addition to the French authorities' zeal for repatriation, we need to consider other motivating factors. There were (non-political) refugees who had left to escape the violence of the conflict, or who had found themselves in the republican camp due to their geographical location at the start of the Civil War, but who were not necessarily opposed to the nationalist regime. Some people returned out of acquiescence to, and even support for the new regime in Spain, notably the nationalist soldiers captured by the Spanish republicans and caught up in *la retirada*.[149] The desire to reconstitute families and pre-exilic life should also be taken into account. Orphans sent to children's colonies in France, and without relatives among the refugees were reclaimed by relatives and the regime in Spain, or simply returned by the French authorities. Mothers estranged from their relatives and partners faced the pressures of childcare in economically challenging circumstances divorced from their kinship networks. Having to find work was made even more difficult through childcare responsibilities. But irrespective of gender or age, the emotional turmoil provoked by the rupture of family networks was the same.[150] Discrimination in France and the harsh conditions of internment were equally influential. In the final balance, if we should note that many refugees freely consented to cross back over the border, then we should not forget that a considerable number, the exact extent of which will probably never be known, were coerced into leaving France.

As *la retirada* unfolded few people in February 1939 could have foreseen a dictatorship in Spain that would last for over thirty-five years. Most Spanish republicans, as well as their French hosts, hoped the stay in France would be transitory. However, the instability that can arise from the feeling of being in between destinations was amplified, perpetuated and exploited by government agencies and representatives in order to pressurise refugees into returning. Liminality formed one aspect of the perverse logic of exclusion. In the eyes of the Minister of the Interior, internment and separation were justified since these were temporary measures. Another legitimating factor lay in the plethora of pejorative images and categories that circulated in the pages of the press, in officials' correspondence and amongst the public. While reductive interpretations of the conflict in Spain legitimated the confinement of male refugees in concentration camps, cultural difference was evoked with a view to excluding Spanish women and adolescents from French public spaces.

Although public opinion was often ambivalent if not hostile to the presence of the Spanish refugees, local factors provided a certain degree of nuance. A relatively small but vocal minority of people expressed solidarity with the refugees by calling for the refugees' freedom and for the dire conditions of the camps to be improved. They also tried thwarting the local and national authorities' repatriation strategies. Despite the opposition campaigns a considerable number of refugees took to the path of return, some willingly, others under duress. The remaining refugees' determination to stay in France did not imply they wanted to remain indefinitely. They hoped one day to make the return journey not out of coercion, but out of choice and as part of the process of ridding Spain of the dictatorship. In order to do so, they embarked on reconstructing themselves in France through a diverse and often rich set of political, social and cultural activities; a process which, as the next chapter will explain, significantly developed from within the unlikely and barren landscape of the camps.

Notes

1 The terms 'border' and 'boundary' have often been used interchangeably. In the interests of clarity, I use 'border' to refer solely to the geopolitical line separating south-western France from the Iberian Peninsula.

2 J. Rubio, 'La politique française d'accueil: les camps d'internement', in P. Milza and D. Peschanski (eds), *Exils et Migration: Italiens et Espagnols en France 1938–1946* (Paris: L'Harmattan, 1994), p. 129. Around 12,000 people were also interned in French-controlled North Africa. For details concerning

the socio-professional composition of the Spanish male population of the concentration camps in June 1939 see Appendix.

3 D. Peschanski, *La France des camps. L'internement 1938–1946* (Paris, 2002), pp. 42–3.

4 J.-C. Villegas, 'La culture des sables: Presse et édition dans les camps de réfugiés', in J.-C. Villegas (ed.), *Plages d'exil. Les camps de réfugiés espagnols en France – 1939* (Nanterre-Dijon, 1989), p. 133.

5 FO 371/24154. Spanish Refugees in France. Report of 2 March 1939. On 14 February, Léon Groc of the daily *Le Petit Parisien* complained about the ban on journalists entering the camps. J.-M. Ginesta, 'Les camps de réfugiés espagnols dans la presse française de 1939', in Villegas (ed.) *Plages d'exil*, p. 155.

6 Vivid descriptions of the 1939 exodus and of the French concentration camps are contained in refugees' memoirs published soon after the event: R. Alberti, *Vida bilingüe de un refugiado español en Francia 1939–1940* (Buenos Aires, 1942); M. Andújar, *St Cyprien, plage: Campo de concentración* (Mexico, 1942); J. Espinar, *Argelès-sur-Mer: Campo de concentración para Españoles* (Caracas, 1940); M. García Gerpé, *Alambradas. Mis nueve meses por los campos de concentración de Francia* (Buenos Aires, 1941); S. Mistral, *Éxodo: diario de una refugiada española* (Mexico , 1941); F. Solano Palacio, *El éxodo: Por un refugiado español* (Valparaíso, 1939);. The titles and places of publication are interesting to note. In three out of the five titles, references to the concentration camps of the Pyrénées-Orientales are redolent of the refugees' sense of injustice about the reception in France. These books were also aimed at reminding the international community of the emerging dictatorship in Spain. Significantly, these were not published in France, but in Latin America, where most of the Spanish republican intellectuals in exile could be found. The lack of publishing activity in France is explained by the different socioeconomic and political factors heightened by the growing threat of war.

7 FO 371/24154. Report by Peter Rennell Rodd. Reg. No. W 3454/2694/41.

8 *Ibid.*

9 There are no accurate figures for the total number of deaths. For further details see G. Dreyfus-Armand, *L'Exil des Républicains Espagnols en France: De la Guerre Civile à la Mort de Franco* (Paris, 1999), p. 65.

10 *Ibid.*, p. 70.

11 Ginesta, 'Les camps de réfugiés espagnols dans la presse française de 1939', pp. 149–58.

12 D. W. Pike, *Vae Victis! Los republicanos españoles refugiados en Francia 1939–1944* (Paris, 1969), p. 48.

13 L. Stein, *Beyond Death and Exile: The Spanish Republicans in France, 1939–1955* (Cambridge, MA, 1979), pp. 58–63.

14 Letter from an interned Spanish soldier published in the *Manchester Guardian* (18 February 1939).

15 See the section on 'The Guards' in F. Cate-Arries, *Spanish Culture Behind Barbed Wire: Memory and Representation of the French Concentration Camps, 1939–1945* (Lewisburg, FL, 2004), pp. 57–62.

16 E. Ferrer, *Derrière les Barbelés: Journal des Camps de Concentration en France (1939)* (Limonest, 1993), p. 37.

17 Cited in F. Montseny, *El Éxodo: Pasión y muerte de españoles en el exilio* (Barcelona, 1977), pp. 27–8. One journalist from the *Midi socialiste* reported guards hitting internees with rifle butts as they rushed towards the bread lorry at Argelès. Other observers also reported trucks dumping bread directly onto the sand. M.-C. Rafaneau-Boj, *Odyssée pour la liberté. Les camps de prisonniers espagnols (1939–1945)* (Paris, 1993), p. 119, n. 1.

18 Ferrer, *Derrière les Barbelés*, p. 38.

19 *Ibid.*; F. Pons, *Barbelés à Argelès et autour d'autres camps* (Paris, 1993), p. 37.

20 L. Montagut, *J'étais deuxième classe dans l'armée républicaine espagnole (1936–1945)* (Paris, 2003).

21 Ferrer, *Derrière les Barbelés*, p. 32.

22 Pons, *Barbelés à Argelès et autour d'autres camps*, p. 41.

23 For an excellent account of refugees' everyday strategies and memories of internment see G. Dreyfus-Armand and É. Temime, *Les Camps sur la plage, un exil espagnol* (Paris, 1995).

24 A service was re-established in June 1939. AD Pyrénées-Orientales, 31W 274. Préfet to Ministre de l'Intérieur, 26 June 1939.

25 Rafaneau-Boj, *Odyssée pour la liberté*, p. 156.

26 Ferrer, *Derrière les Barbelés*, p. 100.

27 AD Pyrénées-Orientales, 31W 274. The Ministre de l'Intérieur asked the Préfet to pass on his gratitude to *l'Indépendant* for the newspaper's work. Letter of 12 April 1939. For *La Dépêche* see Stein, *Beyond Death and Exile*, p. 95. See also Dreyfus-Armand and Temime, *Les Camps sur la plage*, pp. 94–5.

28 Pons, *Barbelés à Argelès et autour d'autres camps*, p. 83.

29 *Ibid.*, p. 149.

30 Ferrer, *Derrière les Barbelés*, p. 100.

31 E. Vaughan, *Community Under Stress: An Internment Camp Culture* (Princeton, NJ, 1949), p. 102.

32 Dreyfus-Armand and Temime, *Les Camps sur la plage*, pp. 86–7.

33 For details of the controversy surrounding the re-emigration of refugees by the SERE and JARE see pp. 99–100.

34 Reproduced in J.-C. Villegas (ed.), *Écrits d'exil: Barraca et Desde el Rosellón. Albums d'art et de littérature Argelès-sur-Mer 1939* (Sète, 2007), pp. 84, 59.

35 Ferrer, *Derrière les Barbelés*, p.75.

36 R. Moral i Querol, *Journal d'exil (1939–1945)* (Paris, 1982), p. 90.

37 Cited in Dreyfus-Armand and Temime, *Les Camps sur la plage*, p. 88.

38 *Ibid.*, p. 89.

39 For more details on these debates see V. Caron, *Uneasy Asylum: France and the Jewish Refugee Crisis, 1933–1942* (Stanford, CA, 1999).

40 Dreyfus-Armand and Temime, *Les Camps sur la plage*, pp. 88–9.
41 Ferrer, *Derrière les Barbelés*, p. 39.
42 *Ibid.*
43 *Ibid.* Villegas (ed.), *Écrits d'exil*, p. 21.
44 *Barraca* (June 1939), p. 36. Reproduced in Villegas (ed.), *Écrits d'exil*, p. 83.
45 *La Petite Gironde* (29 January 1939).
46 *La Petite Gironde* (6 February 1939).
47 The authorities transferred around 170,000 refugees to 77 *départements* across metropolitan France. Dreyfus-Armand, *L'Exil des Républicains Espagnols en France*, p. 82.
48 AD Gironde, 4M 514.
49 Caron, *Uneasy Asylum*, p. 280.
50 Cited in C. Laharie, *Le Camp de Gurs, 1939–45: Un aspect méconnu de l'histoire du Béarn* (Biarritz, 1993), p. 30.
51 Dreyfus-Armand, *L'Exil des Républicains Espagnols en France*, p. 82.
52 AD Lot-et-Garonne, 4M 309.
53 AD Dordogne, 4M 161.
54 *Ibid.* C. Arnould, 'L'Accueil des réfugiés espagnols en Béarn et en Soule de 1936–1940', in M. Papy (ed.), *Les Espagnols et la Guerre Civile* (Biarritz, 1999), p. 342.
55 The medical facilities of the Pyrénées-Orientales were saturated. Complementary hospitals were created throughout southern France. Examples include the transformation of the ship *Habana* into a floating hospital in Bordeaux, the opening of an annexe to the hospital of Mézin in the Lot-et-Garonne and the establishment of a temporary hospital for 1,200 combatants at the centre of Clairvivre in the Dordogne. Despite the additional facilities, on 10 March the Préfet of the Gironde noted that all hospitals in the *département* were full. AD Gironde, 4M 514.
56 AD Dordogne, 4M 161. Ministre de la Santé Publique to Préfet of the Dordogne, 30 January 1939.
57 *Ibid.* Ministre de la Santé Publique to Préfet of the Dordogne, 8 February 1939.
58 AD Lot-et-Garonne, 4M 306. Dossier entitled 'Hospitalisations'. The information stems from medical examinations carried out immediately following the arrival of the refugees.
59 The number of deaths would certainly have been higher in the Pyrénées-Orientales, where conditions were particularly bad.
60 C. Arnould, 'L'Accueil des réfugiés espagnols en Béarn et en Soule de 1936–1940', in Papy (ed.), *Les Espagnols et la Guerre Civile*, p. 343.
61 AD Dordogne, 4M 161. Undated report but most likely written in February 1939 by the Secrétaire-général as a basis for a report to the Ministre de l'Intérieur.
62 *Ibid.* Sous-Préfet of Sarlat to Préfet, 2 February 1939.
63 *Ibid.* Sous-Préfet of Sarlat to Préfet, 24 February 1939.

64 *Ibid.* Sous-Préfet of Bergerac to Préfet, 24 February 1939.

65 *Ibid.* Sous-Préfet of Nontron to Préfet, 24 February 1939.

66 *Ibid.* Préfet to Ministre de l'Intérieur, 15 May 1939.

67 There is emerging research on the subject of centres housing Spanish republican orphans and children with missing parents. For an interesting study
see C. Keren, 'Autobiographies of Spanish Refugee Children at the Quaker
Home in La Rouvière (France, 1940): Humanitarian Communication and
Children's Writings', *Les Cahiers de Framespa*, 5 (2010), http://framespa.
revues.org/268 (accessed 1 June 2010). The Aquitaine region contained child
refugee centres in various places, such as at l'École de Plein Air d'Andernos,
at Andernos-les-Bains in the Gironde. The Comité Suédois pour l'aide aux
enfants d'Espagne cared for over 1,200 children in centres across France
including in the Basses-Pyrénées, the Pyrénées-Orientales and the Landes;
and a British association, Foster Parents Scheme, also operated a shelter in
the Basses-Pyrénées. AD Gironde, 4M 520.

68 The proportion of child refugees educated in France is unknown, though
some children arriving in 1939 between the ages of 10 and 12 reached adulthood in France without any formal education. National policy on the education of the refugee children had been subject to change, with sometimes
contradictory guidelines on the admission of Spanish refugee children to
French schools. See P. Marqués, 'Les colonies d'enfants espagnols réfugiés:
un regard singulier', in *Enfants de la guerre civile espagnole. Vécus et représentations de la génération née entre 1925 et 1940* (Paris, 1999), pp. 68–70.

69 AD Gironde, 4M 514. From Commissaire de Police de Pessac to Préfet, 12
June 1939.

70 The notion of noise as a signifier of cultural difference is analysed from the
perspective of the refugees in the section 'The personal and the social' in
Chapter 7.

71 AN SNCF report, 11 May 1939. R. Schor, *L'Opinion française et les étrangers,
1919–1939* (Paris, 1985), p. 689.

72 Arnould, 'L'Accueil des réfugiés espagnols en Béarn et en Soule de 1936–1940',
in Papy (ed.), *Les Espagnols et la Guerre Civile*, p. 345.

73 AD Pyrénées-Orientales, 31W 274. La Chambre de Commerce de Perpignan
et des Pyrénées-Orientales to Préfet, 18 March 1939.

74 A folder in the *archives départementales* of the Bouches-du-Rhône is packed
full of such letters. AD Bouches-du-Rhône, 4M 959.

75 AD Lot-et-Garonne, 4M 312.

76 Caron, *Uneasy Asylum*, pp. 26–7.

77 Schor, *L'Opinion française et les étrangers*, pp. 675–7.

78 R. Grando, J. Queralt and X. Febrés, *Camps du Mépris: des chemins de l'exil
à ceux de la résistance 1939–1945* (Canet, 1999), p.51.

79 R. Duroux and R. Thiercelin, 'Los niños del exilio; Asignatura pendiente', in
Españoles en Francia 1936–1946, p. 445.

80 Schor, *L'Opinion française et les étrangers*, pp. 694–6.

81 For further details see *Ibid.*; Rafaneau-Boj, *Odyssée pour la liberté*, pp. 138–9; and Dreyfus-Armand, *L'Exil des Républicains Espagnols en France*, pp. 31–3.

82 D. Berry, 'Solidarité internationale antifasciste: les anarchistes français et la guerre civile d'Espagne', in J. Sagnes and S. Caucanas (eds), *Les Français et la Guerre d'Espagne* (Perpignan: 2nd edn, 2004), pp. 73–88.

83 Dreyfus-Armand, *L'Exil des Républicains Espagnols en France*, p. 385, n. 125.

84 AN Fontainebleau, 20010216/170. Report from the head of Special Police to Préfet of the Bouches-du-Rhône, 6 February 1939. Report from the Préfet of the Gironde to Ministère de l'Intérieur, 3 February 1939. In 1938, the authorities estimated the number of SIA adherents in Bordeaux to be 79.

85 During the Vichy period Dr Soula participated in the 'Libérer et Fédérer' movement, which was composed of a mixture of Socialists, Communists and Christians. M. Goubet and P. Debauges, *Histoire de la Résistance dans la Haute-Garonne* (Toulouse, 1986), p. 39.

86 AD Haute-Garonne, 1960W 66. Dossier: 'Associations de secours aux réfugiés espagnols – SERE/JARE'.

87 P. Grau, 'L'aide des félibres aux intellectuels catalans', in Sagnes and Caucanas (eds), *Les Français et la Guerre d'Espagne*, pp. 206–7. Francoist officials followed the centre's activities, and those of refugee politicians with interest. AGA, caja 11287 06.

88 *Ibid.*, pp. 195–212.

89 The League in France included Cardinal Verdier; the Bishop of Dax; the Archbishop of Bordeaux; the intellectual François Mauriac; the President of the Chamber of Deputies, Édouard Herriot; the goverment minister, Auguste Champetier de Ribes and Louis Gillet, a member of the French Academy. AD Haute-Garonne, 1960W 64. Dossier entitled Oficina de Ayudos a los Bascos.

90 *Euzko Deya* was run by the Basque Delegation in Paris from November 1936. G. Dreyfus-Armand, 'L'Émigration Politique Espagnole en France au Travers de sa Presse 1939–1975'. (Thèse de Doctorat, Institut d'Études Politiques de Paris, 1994).

91 AD Dordogne, 4M 161.

92 AD Gironde, 4M 530. The Fédération Nationale des Émigrés Espagnols en France was created in September 1936, with its headquarters based in Paris. According to police reports, the association provided welfare and moral support to Spanish immigrants in France as well as facilitating relations between employers and Spanish workers. Republican in outlook, the association provided welfare for the families of volunteers who fought for the Spanish Republic. In the Gironde it was composed of 16 groups containing 2,757 adherents. Report from the Commissaire Divisionnaire de Police Spéciale to Préfet of the Gironde , 22 May 1939. AN Fontainebleau, 20010216/155.

93 Dreyfus-Armand and Temime, *Les Camps sur la plage*, p. 19.

94 A. Léger, *Les Indésirables: l'histoire oubliée des Espagnols en pays charentais* (Paris, 2000), pp. 73–5.

95 AD Lot-et-Garonne, 4M 312.

96 The letter, written in French and Spanish, appeared in the *Glaneur d'Oloron* on 16 February 1939. C. Arnould, 'L'Accueil des réfugiés espagnols en Béarn et en Soule de 1936–1940', in Papy (ed.), *Les Espagnols et la Guerre Civile*, p. 344.

97 Laharie, *Le Camp de Gurs*, pp. 21–9.

98 Agreements known as *lies et passeries* between villages on either side of the border had a long history containing episodes of mutual co-operation that transcended the ambitions of the French and Spanish states. See M. Lafourcade, 'La frontière franco-espagnole, lieu de conflits interétatiques et de collaboration interrégionale', in Lafourcade (ed.), *La Frontière Franco-Espagnole: Lieu de conflits interétatiques et de collaboration interrégionale* (Bordeaux, 1998).

99 Laharie, *Le Camp de Gurs*, p. 24.

100 The Prefecture of the Gironde kept a close eye on the activities of the Federation of Spanish Emigrants of the Gironde Region. AN Fontainebleau, 20010216/155. Report from the Commissaire Divisionnaire de Police Spéciale to Préfet of the Gironde, 22 May 1939.

101 Joan Comorera became secretary-general of the PSUC in 1936. Following his arrival in France, he went to the USSR, and then on to Mexico in 1940, returning to France following the war. He was expelled from the PSUC in November 1949 and led a rival PSUC. He entered Spain clandestinely in 1951 and was arrested three years later. He died in prison in 1957. Dreyfus-Armand, *L'Exil des Républicains Espagnols en France*, p. 411.

102 AD Lot-et-Garonne, 4M 312. The Préfet sent a copy of the booklet to the Ministre de l'Intérieur on 29 April 1939.

103 AD Dordogne, 4M 161. The Préfet to Ministre de l'Intérieur, 15 May 1939.

104 *Ibid.* Sous-Préfet of Bergerac to Préfet, 12 May 1939.

105 For a general overview of French policy and the statistics of return during 1939 see G. Dreyfus-Armand, 'Diversidad de Retornos del Exilio Republicano de la Guerra Civil Española', in J. Cuesta Bustillo (ed.), *Retornos (De exilios y migraciones)* (Madrid, 1999); see also Dreyfus-Armand, *L'Exil des Républicains Espagnols en France*, pp. 72–81. The refugees' narratives of return are discussed in R. Duroux, 'El Retorno y sus Retóricas', in Cuesta Bustillo (ed.), *Retornos*, pp. 129–48. For the existential dilemmas posed by return over the long duration see F. Guilhem, *L'obsession du retour* (Toulouse, 2005), and for the return of child refugees and high-profile figures see A. Alted Vigil, 'Repatriaciones y retornos', in *La voz de los vencidos: El exilio republicano de 1939* (Madrid, 2005), pp. 341–90.

106 Dreyfus-Armand and Temime, *Les Camps sur la Plage*, p. 32.

107 P. Weil, 'Espagnols et Italiens en France: la politique de la France', in Milza and Peschanski (eds), *Exils et Migration*, p. 92.

108 Dreyfus-Armand, *L'Exil des Républicains Espagnols en France*, p. 73.
109 FO 371/24154. Report by Peter Rennell Rodd on the measures taken by the French authorities for the reception of Spanish refugees.
110 AD Gironde 4M 538. Instructions to Préfets from the Ministre de l'Intérieur, 10 February 1939.
111 Cited in Arnould, 'L'Accueil des réfugiés espagnols en Béarn et en Soule de 1936–1940', in Papy (ed.), *Les Espagnols et la Guerre Civile*, p. 347.
112 Stein, *Beyond Death and Exile*, p. 63.
113 Dreyfus-Armand, 'Diversidad de Retornos del Exilio Republicano de la Guerra Civil Española', in Cuesta Bustillo (ed.), *Retornos*, p. 153.
114 Stein, *Beyond Death and Exile*, p. 80.
115 J. Rubio, *La emigración de la guerra civil de 1936–1939: Historia del éxodo que se produce con el fin de la II República española* (Madrid, 1977), Vol. 1, p. 117; Dreyfus-Armand, *L'Exil des Républicains Espagnols en France*, pp. 75–7.
116 A. Bachoud, 'L'État franquiste face aux camps de réfugiés (1939–1940): les archives du ministère des Affaires étrangères', in Villegas (ed.), *Plages d'exil*, p. 165. See also J. García Sanchez, 'La Correspondencia de los Españoles en Francia (1936–1946)', in *Españoles en Francia 1936–1946*.
117 AD Gironde, 4M 538.
118 C. Arnould, 'L'Accueil des réfugiés espagnols en Béarn et en Soule de 1936–1940', in Papy (ed.), *Les Espagnols et la Guerre Civile*, p. 347.
119 The law was published on 13 February 1939, P. Preston, *A Concise History of the Spanish Civil War* (London, 1996), p. 213.
120 Dreyfus-Armand, *L'Exil des Républicains Espagnols en France*, p. 73.
121 AD Gironde, 4M 538, Reports from Sous-Préfet de Blaye to Préfet, 17 and 27 March 1939.
122 AD Gironde, 4M 538, Commissionnaire de Police Spéciale to Préfet, 1 May 1939.
123 AD Dordogne, 4M 161. Préfet to Ministre de l'Intérieur, 15 May 1939. For information on the Hautes-Pyrénées see J. Cubero, *Les Républicains espagnols* (Pau, 2003), pp. 103–9.
124 AD Lot-et-Garonne, 4M 312.
125 *Ibid.*
126 *Ibid.* Letter from Préfet to Director of Postal Services, 24 April 1939. The Préfet referred to article 14 of the law of 29 July 1881 as providing the legal basis for this procedure. The decree of 6 May 1939 allowed the government to ban the circulation of papers in France that had been published abroad.
127 *Ibid.*
128 *Voz de Madrid*, no. 38 (1 April 1939). Cited in G. Dreyfus-Armand, 'La presse de l'émigration espagnole en France de 1939 à 1944. Contre vents et marées', in Villegas (ed.), *Plages d'exil*, p. 187.
129 *Le Midi socialiste* mounted a campaign during the first two weeks of April, and the French Committee for the Coordination of Aid to the Spanish

People appears to have lobbied Sarraut directly. See Stein, *Beyond Death and Exile*, p. 85 and Montseny, *El Éxodo*, p. 33.

130 AD Dordogne, 4M 161. Préfet to Ministre de l'Intérieur, 15 May 1939.
131 Guilhem, *L'obsession du retour*, p. 17.
132 Montseny, *El Éxodo*, p. 51.
133 Laharie, *Le Camp de Gurs*, p. 115.
134 Stein, *Beyond Death and Exile*, p. 85.
135 Laharie, *Le Camp de Gurs, 1939–45*, p. 114.
136 Guilhem, *L'obsession du retour*, pp. 23–34.
137 *Ibid.*, p. 23 and Dreyfus-Armand, *L'Exil des Républicains Espagnols en France*, p. 77.
138 The employment of refugees will be covered in more depth in Chapter 4.
139 For more information see the section 'Contrasting images: economic utility' in Chapter 4.
140 AN Fontainebleau, 19940500/138. Instructions from Ministre de l'Intérieur, 19 September 1939.
141 C. Arnould, 'L'Accueil des réfugiés espagnols en Béarn et en Soule de 1936–1940', in Papy (ed.), *Les Espagnols et la Guerre Civile*, p. 347.
142 AD Dordogne, 4M 161. Correspondence between Préfet and Ministre de l'Intérieur, 23 September 1939 and 12 October 1939.
143 AD Gironde, 4M 514. Commissaire de Police de Talence to Préfet, 11 August 1939.
144 For similar incidents see Rosa Laviñas's recollections in A. Soriano, *Éxodos: Historia oral del exilio republicano en Francia 1939–1945* (Barcelona, 1989), pp. 174–9; and A. Bachoud, 'L'État franquiste face aux camps de réfugiés (1939–1940): les archives du ministère des Affaires étrangères', in Villegas (ed.), *Plages d'exil*, p. 164.
145 AD Gironde, 4M 528. Commissaire Divisionnaire de Police Spéciale to Préfet, 14 October 1939.
146 AD Landes, 4M art. 314. Rapport du Commandant de la Compagnie de Gendarmerie des Landes, 1 December 1939.
147 Dreyfus-Armand, 'Diversidad de Retornos del Exilio Republicano de la Guerra Civil Española', in Cuesta Bustillo (ed.), *Retornos*, pp. 149–60, 155–6. An analysis of the statistics of returning refugees can be found in Rubio, *La emigración de la guerra civil de 1936–1939*, pp. 116–29.
148 Dreyfus-Armand, 'L'Émigration Politique Espagnole en France au Travers de sa Presse 1939–1975', p. 33.
149 Dreyfus-Armand, *L'Exil des Républicains Espagnols en France*, pp. 77–8.
150 During interviews informants often shed tears when recounting how they were reunited with their families.

3

Organisations, networks and identities, 1939–40

'We may have lost our freedom, but not our reason', affirmed Francisco Perez as he recounted how militants began reconstructing CNT networks in the Vernet d'Ariège concentration camp.[1] Although Francisco's statement was made in the context of libertarian identity reconstruction in exile, it is richly suggestive more generally of refugee agency in the face of internment. The monotonous life behind barbed wire intensified an already existent sense of loss, isolation and material deprivation. But as Perez's words imply, it would be misleading to entertain any idea of the Spanish republicans as passive victims of circumstance. They more frequently responded to exile with initiative, innovation and perseverance as they went about reconstructing organisations and politico-social networks.

The mobilisation of reason accompanied, if not legitimated, Spanish republican activities, exerting both centrifugal and centripetal pressure. It involved a search for the cause of the Republic's defeat, engendering divisions and, in the process, sharpening distinctions between the different organisations in exile. It was as if forced relocation and defeat released the final shackle of restraint from groups of militants whose uneasy alliance had been more cohesively defined in binary distinction to the rebels' nationalist campaign rather than through any other sense of commonality. But forces tending towards cohesion were also present. The looming spectre of a wider European conflict gave Spanish republicans the opportunity to remind their French hosts that the coalition of reactionary forces which had driven them out of Spain now threatened the rest of Europe. At certain junctures displays of Spanish republican solidarity crystallised around an imprecise but evocative mix of democratic values and a powerful sense of anti-fascism as refugees sought to challenge the reductive images which had accompanied their arrival in France.

As these opening paragraphs suggest, exile was not a unidirectional phenomenon, imposed by the French government and authorities, but a dialectical process involving the Spanish republicans' reactions, choices and strategies. Accordingly, this chapter switches from French responses and the processes of othering to a focus on the agency of the Spanish refugees.

Spanish republican organisations in exile

The process of reconstituting government, party and trade-union organisations began as soon as the refugees arrived in France. It was a difficult process owing to the precipitated exodus from Spain, the scattering of militants across France (and the rest of the world) and the Francoist victory. Individual initiative was necessary for this reconstructive drive, but could equally provoke indignant reactions from other refugees with competing visions of the Spanish republican exile. Underlying tensions between and within the different organisations re-emerged with vigour in exile.

Prime Minister Negrín, along with Spanish republican ministers, gathered in Toulouse before flying to Alicante on 8 February while the *reitrada* was in full flow. Negrín had gone to rally republican defences and obtain a public guarantee from Franco that there would be no reprisals after the end of hostilities. In the meantime, Negrín planned to evacuate compromised republicans from Spain and implant guerrilla units to destabilise the dictatorship in the event of a wider European war.[2]

Obtaining concessions from Franco had always been near impossible but was made even more improbable by President Azaña's refusal to return to Spain. His absence additionally facilitated British and French recognition of Franco's regime on 27 February. In poor health, the ailing president had moved from the Spanish republican embassy in Paris to convalesce in the Alpine village of Collognes-sous-Salève, from where he announced his resignation. Under the constitution, authority should have passed to the head of the Cortes, Diego Martínez Barrio, but he refused to accept the responsibility without first having full backing to end the war in Spain.

Negrín, on the other hand, was determined to continue the struggle until he met his objectives, but it was also a strategy which required unanimous backing. As the constitutional crisis demonstrated, the republican camp was terribly afflicted by the heavy and exhausting toll of three years of total war against insurmountable odds. The association of Negrín's government with the PCE continued to engender anti-communist sentiment amongst the non-communist organisations. And while Negrín was officially prime minister, he lacked the necessary state machinery and legitimacy to implement decisions. Crucially, he was also without the support of the commander of the Republican Army of the Centre, Colonel Segismundo Casado, who remained in Madrid.

While Casado shared Negrín's aim of obtaining a concession from Franco to guarantee the safety of republicans, he favoured a different tactic. Rather than bargaining from a position of resistance, Casado hoped to negotiate. He mounted an anti-Negrín coalition involving the repression of Communists, possibly hoping Franco would respond positively to this display of anti-communism. On 6 March, Negrín was forced out of Spain again, but this time by republican forces. Bitter fighting occurred between Communists and Casado's coalition, which included Socialists and anarcho-syndicalists, and similar conflicts broke out in other areas of republican Spain. Defeat followed, and on 1 April Franco announced an end to the war. There were no concessions. Instead, mass executions accompanied the start of Franco's rule.

The day before Franco's announcement, Spanish parliamentary deputies had met in Paris to decide who actually represented the government in exile. There were acrimonious exchanges about Casado's coup and mutual recriminations which served to emphasise the profound divisions among the Spanish republicans.[3] Although Negrín emerged as head of the government, he was opposed by many Spanish republicans in France. Given this disarray, the reconstruction of party and trade unions in exile was all the more important.

The CNT was by far the largest of the Spanish republican organisations in France.[4] Its general secretary, Mariano Rodríguez Vázquez, known more widely as 'Marianet', rapidly contacted other representatives of the CNT, FAI and FIJL who met in Paris on 25 February 1939. They agreed to amalgamate the leading committees of the three organisations to form a single General Council of the MLE which initially contained 13 members.[5] But as with the government in exile, and virtually every other organisation, the MLE experienced competing claims over the organisation's direction. A Co-ordination and Defence Committee appeared in Spain during March and contested the General Council's authority. During the same month, members from the national

committees of the CNT, FAI and FIJL in Spain met in Valencia and con-
stituted the National Committee of the Libertarian Movement, whose
status vis-à-vis the General Council was far from clear.[6] Following the
Casado coup, the members of this committee left for exile in London and
on 14 April met with Mariano Vázquez, the representative of the General
Council, to resolve the issue.[7] They decided that three members of the
'London group' – Avelino González Entrialgo, José Grunfeld and Isidoro
Pastor – would take up posts within the General Council in France. But
it was a fragile agreement, with militants in London frequently at odds
with the General Council over the MLE's relationship with the government in exile.[8]

The issue of the MLE's relations with the government was not a new
subject. It rearticulated a long-standing dilemma over libertarian ideology, practice and notably the extent, or not, to which libertarians should
be involved in government. Militants from one tendency attributed the
failure of the social revolution in Spain to the CNT's deviation from
anarchist principles and the participation of militants in the government
during the Civil War.[9] The opposing view considered that theoretical
dogmatism engendered isolation and thereby curtailed libertarian influence in the political arena.

To what extent did these divergences impinge on the reconstruction
of the organisation in France? There are several issues to consider. First
of all, it would be misleading to try and simply map these currents onto
the divergences between the General Council and militants in London,
for both groups contained militants of the two persuasions. Secondly,
given that these competing voices represented tensions reaching
back several decades, one could almost consider them as a semi-
permanent fixture in the CNT and MLE's decision-making structure, and
therefore an unsurprising element of reconstruction. General Council
members were already experienced in dealing with this point of contention. Furthermore, they were preoccupied with more pressing and external issues.

The Parisian police were following the General Council's activities
with interest, but drawing erroneous conclusions. The Prefect of Police
knew of the General Council's constitutive meeting but misreported it as
a gathering of the FAI. This may well have been a simple misunderstand-
ing but nonetheless evoked a different image of the General Council – the
FAI was created by militants wishing to boost anarchist ideals in Spain
and elsewhere during a period of CNT decline and, rightly or wrongly,
was perceived as the ideological overseer of the CNT.[10] Whatever the

reasons for the slip, the misinterpretation certainly lent added piquancy to the Prefect's remarks about the anarchists' intention to create a vast campaign of agitation in France.[11] Far from focusing on revolutionary activities in France, the General Council was actually concerned with far more urgent matters. In its first circular, the General Council declared it would never renounce returning to Spain.[12] The reference to return did not so much point to a tangible project, but rather served as a rallying call to bind militants together. The circular's real aim was to report on the creation of the General Council of the MLE while also highlighting the organisation's immediate priorities of saving militants from repression in Spain and from the camps in France, and the need to reconstruct militants' lives in exile.

Evacuating militants from Spain was complicated by communication problems and surveillance by the Francoist regime. But in June the General Council was spurred into action with the arrival of two *compañeros*. Antonio Aranda Gadea and Sebastián Vicente Esteban had crossed the border bearing information about militants interned in a concentration camp at Alicante only to end up behind French barbed wire. Their passage had been organised by the newly created National Committee of the clandestine CNT in Spain under the direction of Esteban Pallarols. Mariano Vázquez immediately contacted Juan Molina ('Juanel'), who was responsible for liaising between the General Council and militants in the French internment camps. He instructed Juanel to debrief the new arrivals and to ask Francisco Ponzán to cross into Spain to secure the release and safe passage of other militants. Ponzán was an obvious choice owing to his experience of behind-the-lines warfare during the Spanish Civil War, but he was also a reliable and determined libertarian with useful contacts. He had already been planning to return to Spain and had consequently prepared much of the necessary groundwork during his frequent absences from the Vernet camp.[13]

Twenty volunteers returned to Spain under the auspices of Ponzán's group and Pallarol's National Committee to organise the evacuation of the most compromised militants.[14] It was clearly a perilous and labour-intensive activity needing both nerve and financial backing. In September, Franco's authorities arrested and executed some of the original 20 volunteers. Raising money for the expeditions proved to be difficult. Juanel and Ponzán, along with militants in Spain, believed that the Spanish republican government, the Spanish republican aid agencies and even the MLE General Council could and should have allocated more money to the escape network.[15]

The untimely death of Mariano Vázquez from accidental drowning on 18 June may have led to a change in stance towards the evacuations. In October, Pallarol's National Committee in Spain sent Génesis López Claver to meet with the General Council and its new general secretary, Germinal Esgleas.[16] Before meeting Esgleas, López tried in vain to obtain financial support from the Spanish republican aid agencies. He obtained a marginally better result when Esgleas offered just 10,000 francs.[17] Esgleas was certainly more ideologically driven and in a different strand of the CNT compared to his predecessor Vázquez. But this in itself does not explain his apparent lack of will to fund the escape network and reconstruction of the CNT in Spain.

The exact reasons are difficult to elucidate, given that much of the literature surrounding this event stems from militants sympathetic to Pallarol's National Committee. Esgleas's subsequent rejection of Ponzán's activities with the British Secret Service in early 1940 is easier to explain. It was undoubtedly driven by a desire to avoid any compromise from working with the government of a country that had lamentably failed to lift a finger for the republican cause during the Civil War. For Ponzán and Juanel, British funding represented nothing more than a means to continue working with the CNT in Spain and in disgust, they broke relations with the General Council in late March 1940.

Esgleas's decisions should also be viewed in a financial context, and more specifically, the need to retain funds for the challenges confronted by an organisation in exile. In 1939, the MLE reserves appear to have been 4.5 million francs.[18] At first glance, this might seem considerable, but the sum takes on a more sobering dimension when compared to estimates of the reserves of the Spanish republican government aid agency, the Service for the Emigration of Spanish Republicans (SERE). According to one source, their monthly aid distribution amounted to 25 million francs from a reserve of 2 billion francs.[19] This differs from Louis Stein's reference to 100 million francs spent between March and December 1939, and to the total funds of 250 million francs cited by José María del Valle.[20] Irrespective of the exact figures, the MLE possessed a small share of the Spanish republicans' overall resources relative to the size of the organisation. Limited finances unquestionably posed obstacles to the MLE's priority of securing the release of militants from the French camps and facilitating the reconstruction of their lives. One ambitious solution involved plans for a series of agricultural co-operatives in France. Despite some difficulties, the MLE established two such co-operatives in the *département* of the Lot. The full potential of the project, however, was stymied by various factors (which will be detailed in the next chapter), which included the issue of funding.

The need for money and help in organising the re-emigration of militants to Latin America meant that the MLE had little choice but to work with the SERE. The Negrín government had created the SERE in March 1939 to organise aid distribution in France and re-emigration to Latin America (notably to Mexico following President Lazaro Cárdenas's offer of refuge for all Spanish republicans).[21] In theory, the SERE represented the interests of all Spanish republicans via an executive council composed of representatives from the various parties and trade unions.[22] But in practice the council's decisions were validated by a ministerial panel firmly under Negrín's control.[23] As such there was a widespread and well-founded suspicion amongst Spanish republicans (and the French government) that the SERE favoured Negrín's Socialist and Communist supporters. Demand far outstripped the availability of places on ships chartered to cross the Atlantic and controversy was rife.

The MLE General Council was well aware of the respectively low number of libertarians selected for re-emigration given their preponderance amongst Spanish republicans in France. In May 1939, it communicated to militants the statistics shown in Table 1.[24] The General Council's assurances that they were placing a great deal of effort into securing as many places as possible are telling of the disquiet amongst the grassroots in France and from the London group over the SERE affair.[25] However, as all applications for re-emigration were processed by the SERE and passed on to the Mexican embassy, the General Council had little choice but to pass through the aid organisation.

The MLE was not alone in its suspicions about the SERE. Anti-communism blurred with resentment against Negrín among many sectors of

Table 1   *The re-emigration of Spanish republicans from France according to political and trade union affiliation (%)*

Marxists (UGT, PSUC, PSOE, JSU*)	38
Republicans	33
Libertarians	24[26]
Without affiliation	5

Note: * United Socialist–Communist Youth Federation.
Source: AGA, Caja, 11287 06A. Circular 15 of the General Council of the MLE, 11 May 1939.

the Spanish republicans. Socialists were bitterly divided between two rival executive commissions of the PSOE.[27] The divisions dated back to the start of the 1930s but had steadily deepened throughout the war in Spain. In exile, militants coalesced around Negrín on the one hand, and his former Minster of Defence, Indalecio Prieto, on the other. The rivalry went far beyond the PSOE when Prieto cannily appropriated the republican funds which Negrín had sent to Mexico for safekeeping on the yacht *Vita*. The haul enabled Prieto to create a rival aid and emigration agency, the Aid Committee for Spanish Republicans (JARE), at the end of July.[28] The JARE was as similarly undemocratic as the SERE. Decisions were ostensibly the domain of a committee representing the various non-communist organisations in exile, but were actually taken by an executive headed by Prieto in Mexico.[29] Selection criteria favoured the (non-communist and non-Negrín) political elites of the Spanish and Catalan parliaments.[30] Despite these inadequacies the MLE was similarly constrained to work with the JARE, and especially after the French authorities disbanded the SERE along with all Communist organisations in the wake of the German–Soviet pact. The whole episode of re-emigration produced disappointing results for both the MLE and the Spanish republicans more widely. Between 1939 and 1940, the SERE and JARE managed 15,000 departures for Latin America, a number which contained a disproportionally high number of tertiary workers and intellectuals.[31]

Hardly any major Spanish republican organisation in France avoided division. The POUM was split over the issue of an alliance with the PCE. And while it is true that the Communists managed to reconstruct their organisations relatively quickly, this was facilitated by extensive help from their PCF counterparts.[32] Although the MLE benefited from the help of the SIA, the POUM from the Workers' and Peasants' Socialist Party (PSOP), and the PSOE from French Socialists, it was not on the same scale as the PCF support.[33] But even the more pronounced ideological cohesion of the Communists could not suppress the animosity between leading figures of the PCE and PSUC over the defeat of Catalonia and the subject of reconstructing party structures. The PSUC channelled efforts into maintaining autonomy from the PCE and created a commission in March 1939 to study and implement plans for the survival of the party in exile.[34] The efforts bore little fruit. Before the outbreak of the Second World War the committee re-emigrated to Mexico while the PSUC secretary, Joan Comorera, was summoned to Moscow. Once there, he announced that the PSUC would join the International as the Catalan section, thereby signalling the effective tutelage of the party to the PCE.[35]

Despite the divisions, tensions and bias of the re-emigration policies, leading representatives had few problems in settling in other countries. By June 1940, the majority of leading Communists had left for either Latin America or Russia as part of a strategy which dated back to at least September if not March 1939.[36] In isolation from the majority of exiles still in France, Negrín set up a provisional government of the Spanish Republic in London, though it lacked authority amongst the majority of Spanish republicans and the British government alike.[37] By contrast, either through will or circumstance, over half of the members of the MLE General Council remained in France.

Political–trade-union reorganisation in the concentration camps

The French authorities overseeing the camps took any sign of political/ trade-union activity or 'unruly' behaviour very seriously. Internees accused of infringing camp discipline could be punished with the 'hippodrome', an enclosed patch of the beach exposed to the elements with a post in the middle where the victim spent time running around to keep warm or even chained up. When the authorities judged a misdemeanour to be especially serious internees faced transfer to one of the disciplinary camps where conditions were infamously brutal.[38] In reality, the internees accused of 'political' or 'anti-French activities' could face punishment on the flimsiest of evidence.

The authorities were clearly intent on following Sarraut's obsession with national security, even if it meant taking the most incredible of stories seriously. Some police reports about activities in the camps of the Pyrénées-Orientales tell us as much about the pervasiveness of images from the conservative and extreme right-wing reporting of the Civil War as they do about what was actually occurring on the ground. In April 1939, the Special Police in Perpignan reported that the internees were ready to mount an uprising in the event of general mobilisation in France.[39] Around 100,000 men from the Saint-Cyprien and Argelès camps were apparently ready to march on Perpignan to carry out summary executions of people, including the Prefect and the bishop. A local magistrate added to the tension by claiming that nearly all internees in Argelès and Saint-Cyprien camps were armed with pistols and had buried stockpiles of grenades beneath the sand.

The hunt for escapees did nothing to ease the authorities' anxiety. In the last week of March, police in the Pyrénées-Orientales had apprehended around 300 refugees but complained about the difficulty in getting them back behind barbed wire: they simply leapt from the trucks en route to the camp. One guard was disturbed by a refugee's invitation to 'come along to the Spanish Centre for a cup of coffee'.[40] As for the question of pistols and grenades, there were indeed stories circulating at the time of arms being systematically hidden in the camps, but despite the authorities' best efforts they found no evidence of weapon stock-piles.[41] The origin and force of these rumours most likely stemmed from an image of the camps as a kind of no-man's land. With all the imagery of wildness, lawlessness and the absence of morality associated with indeterminate spaces, there was a clear impression that the refugees had not simply crossed the frontier: they had brought it with them.

In addition to fears that the capital of the Pyrénées-Orientales was under threat from the internees, the commander of Argelès camp reported on 27 April that refugees from the PSUC, PCE, POUM, CNT and FAI were busy trying to re-create the Popular Front.[42] Perhaps he had been struck by the refugees' commemoration of the Spanish Republic on 14 April (on which more follows later in this chapter). Even if this had been the case, the fact that refugees celebrated the same date in the Spanish republican calendar in no way amounted to the re-creation of the Spanish Popular Front. On the contrary, the myriad tensions of the Second Spanish Republic were being reproduced in the camps. Franscico Pons recalled: 'from our very first day of internment we were plunged into an atmosphere of war and politics, politics and war'.[43] Another refugee, the writer Ramon Moral i Querol, was fearful of tensions and the potential for violence between Catalans and centralists.[44] Given the mutual recrim-inations about the defeat in Spain, and the hostility felt by anarchists and quasi-Trotskyists towards the Communists, it is difficult to believe that any serious attempts to re-create the Popular Front were under way. Closer to the truth were officials' references to regular meetings, links between internees and the exterior and the use of cultural activities to disseminate political and union propaganda.

The French press played a facilitating role in reconstructing the refu-gees' trade-union and political networks. Abel Paz, alias Diego Camacho, and others interned in Saint-Cyprien camp managed to locate and join up with *compañeros* in Argelès camp through an advert placed in *Le Libertaire*, the newspaper of the French Anarchist Union.[45] It was partly for this reason that the authorities banned most of the French titles, as well as the Spanish republican press, from the camps. Apart from a handful of French newspapers supportive of the government line, everything had to be smuggled in. The authorities were especially wary of any Spanish republican literature, however innocuous, lest it encourage the reconstruction of organisations or anger the internees with news about the government's reception and repatriation strategy. In one incident, guards seized a PSOE leaflet from a boy at the gates to Saint-Cyprien that simply contained a speech by Sarraut about the Spanish refugees.[46]

As was the case with the reception centres, communication between the camps and the exterior was often possible because of a significant minority of French activists. Militants from the PCF and the Communist-linked Immigrant Workers' Movement (MOI), along with members of the aid organisation Friends of the Volunteers for Republican Spain, (AVER) had quickly contacted refugees from the International Brigades,[47] as well as Spanish Communists. One French Communist in the small town of Elne sheltered a Spanish official while he established contacts between the exterior and militants in nearby Saint-Cyprien camp. Internees were then able to pass party assets as well as PCE and PSUC documents out of the camp.[48] Further north-east it was a French gendarme who smuggled the French Communist newspaper *L'Humanité* into Septfonds camp.[49] If party evaluations are accurate, the Communists managed to distribute up to 75 per cent of their literature – relating to the Spanish and Catalan Communist parties, the Comintern and *L'Humanité* – to refugees in the camps and reception centres.[50]

French anarchists similarly passed correspondence between the MLE General Council in Paris and the camps. French intelligence sources believed that French citizens were acting as liaison agents across the south in Bordeaux, Marseilles, Narbonne and Perpignan.[51] In Narbonne, the person in question was an anarchist named Camille Boër, a mechanic whom the authorities had been interested in since the mid-1920s.[52] In Perpignan, Léon Surjus was suspected of cultivating links with Spanish libertarians, and Louis Montgon, a watchmaker and president of the Comité de défense de la révolution espagnole and of the Fédération des émigrés antifascistes espagnols, was thought to be aiding libertarians to escape from the nearby camps.[53] Not all French nationals aiding the MLE came from libertarian circles, though they were motivated by a humanist or anti-fascist conviction. From Vernet camp, Francisco Ponzán managed to contact Juan Molina, the MLE delegate responsible for liaising between the camp and the MLE leadership, with the help of a French Communist, Jean Bénazet, who lived in the nearby village of Varilhes. The relationship between Bénazet and Ponzán was formed when the former employed

Ponzán, enabling him to develop the network for evacuating libertarians from Spain.[54]

The exilic press

The Spanish republicans' press in exile was a significant vector through which information was exchanged, a sense of commonality produced and morale maintained. With more than forty titles circulating in France during 1939 alone, this was an impressive effort that additionally reflected the ideological and geographical labyrinthine quality of the Spanish republican exile.[55]

Some newspapers were in existence before the 1939 exodus. The Basque and Spanish republican government mouthpieces, *Euzko Deya* and *Voz de Madrid*, were created on 29 November 1936 and on 18 July 1938 (the second anniversary of the outbreak of the conflict), respectively. But the majority of publications appeared following the refugees' arrival in 1939. Another paper that characterised itself as above inter-party rivalry was the Catalan weekly *El Poble Català*. The newspaper's first issue claimed: 'THE CATALAN PEOPLE is not a party paper. Militants from various parties are combined in their efforts, and are united by the written word and art.'[56] It was actually close to Acció catalana, a Catalan nationalist republican party, and to Esquerra Republicana de Catalunya, the bourgeois Catalan Republican Party led by Lluis Companys, President of the Catalan government. But the newspaper was also open to other currents.[57]

Most newspapers were clearly associated with specific groups. In order to provide a flavour, rather than an exhaustive list, of the publications we could turn to *El Ramillete*, 'newspaper of the Spanish refugee children's centre at Orly', which was written in both French and Spanish with the help of Socialists from the French section of the Workers' International (SFIO), or the fortnightly paper *Anayak* of the Basque priests in exile.[58] Turning to the trade unions and political parties, the MLE initially received the support of the French Anarchist Union's newspaper *Le Libertaire* and the French section of the SIA. Refugees published a section in the French bulletin of the SIA entitled *España expatriada*, which became a weekly in its own right from the symbolic date of 14 July 1939.[59] The second largest trade union in exile, the UGT, produced the *Boletín de información sindical (UGT)* and also a version in Catalan, *Butlletí interior (UGT)*.[60] Socialists of the PSOE could read *España Libre*, although few issues seem to have been produced. Catalan Communists of the

PSUC printed *Treball.* The first issue of this newspaper appeared on 26 February 1939 carrying the headline 'Treat the refugees humanely' and a picture of one of the concentration camps.[61] The Spanish Communist Party, on the other hand, did not publish a paper in its own right, but influenced *la Voz de los Españoles* which was officially published by the *Federación de los Inmigrados españoles.*[62]

A newspaper's existence was partly determined by the refugees' resources but also by the French government's discretion. The government was sensitive to criticism and refused to allow the exilic press to hinder its repatriation strategy or to compromise its plans of maintaining Francoist Spain's neutrality in the event of war with Germany. It was consequently responsive to some of the Francoist demands for the Spanish republicans' press activities to be curtailed.[63] As the French ban of *Voz de Madrid* on 6 April 1939 reveals, not even the Spanish republican government's title was immune, though it was reincarnated as *Voz de España* with help from the CGT.[64] After six issues containing repeated calls for the French authorities to treat the Spanish republicans more humanely, *Treball* was closed down. It was re-created under the new name of *Solidarité* and pursued the same themes with equal determination. In the second and last issue of 7 April, the paper demanded that the Daladier government stop pressurising refugees into returning to Spain.[65] The difficulties in mounting and maintaining a publication, along with the relatively short period of exile before the outbreak of the Second World War, evidently limited what could be achieved. Some of the established newspapers from republican Spain, such as *El Socialista, Mundo Obrero* or *Solidaridad Obrera* of the PSOE, PCE and CNT, respectively, did not become a permanent feature of the exilic press until after the Liberation of France.[66]

At the same time as the French government was banning *Voz de Madrid* and *Solidarité* a range of bulletins and reviews began to flourish in the unlikely arena of the concentration camps. Some internees, usually in military units, had managed to cart typewriters into exile, allowing some bulletins to be typed, but much of what has become known as the 'presse/culture des sables' – sable being a reference to the sandy conditions of the coastal camps – was painstakingly written, drawn and reproduced by hand. Fortunately, copies of these astonishingly rich and colourful publications survive, affording us an insight into the internees' inventiveness, determination and aspirations.[67]

In April, the first issue of the *Boletín de los estudiantes*, produced by students of the Federation of University Students (FUE) and teachers of the Spanish Federation of Education Workers (FETE), appeared in Argelès camp. Antonio Gardó, who had been a FETE regional representative for Valencia (Valence), along with Miguel Monzó and Miguel Orts of the FUE and a young actress Adela Carreras, provided much of the impetus. As well as their union links, all four had served in an artillery outfit (Reserva General de Artillería) that had crossed the border with much of its equipment.[68] This modest beginning led to a veritable plethora of publications and activities at Argelès that was soon followed by refugees in other camps of southern France and also in the Algerian camp at Morand.[69]

The bulletins tended to share a similar format, starting with an editorial on the refugees' achievements in the camps and their future plans. This was followed by news features and details of the internees' activities. Practical advice was often given, such as with the article, 'Hygiene in the concentration camp', from the FUE bulletin, which offered information about medical facilities, showers, clean water and the camp toilets in Argelès.[70] Some of the longer publications also discussed the refugees' plight without criticism of the French authorities or reference to the refugees' organisations and rivalries. This censorship was partly imposed, given the French prohibition of political activities in the camps, but also a deliberate choice on the part of the editors whose aim was to forge a sense of commonality and purpose through cultural activities.

When a political issue was raised, it was usually in reference to Spain. The second issue of the FUE *Boletín de los estudiantes* (*Students' Bulletin*) on 17 April 1939 proclaimed: 'Students of the camp at Argelès-sur-Mer, we are continuing our task which began in Spain of increasing accessibility to culture.'[71] As well as expressing continuity with the past, the bulletin portrayed itself as representing the 'true' cultural values of Spain in contrast to the 'anti-Spain' of the 'Burgos Government', a reference to the Francoist regime which was based in Burgos. Another bulletin called on students to set an example of anti-fascist unity.[72] These examples are suggestive of how the press in the camps constructed a broad Spanish republican identity in opposition to the Spanish dictatorship.

Culture and education were mobilised for identity reconstruction but additionally served as a means of dealing with the internees' daily lives and future needs. Each bulletin listed the cultural programme of the camp. The activities included French lessons, literacy classes, poetry recitals, history and geography lessons, lectures on significant personalities from Spain and beyond and also sports events. According to one bulletin from Argelès, 34 French classes involving 850 students and 5 English classes for another 43, as well as literacy classes and sports events, occurred during the week leading up to 23 April.[73] The corresponding bulletin in Gurs camp explained how the French officials' reorganisation of the camp in May had hampered activities. Even so, the commission reported nine lectures, eight French classes, an English class and literacy classes, along with poetry recitals of works by Federico García Lorca, Antonio Machado and Juan Ramón Jiménez and an art exhibition which attracted thousands of internees.

The foundations for the place of Lorca and Machado in the Spanish republican exilic imaginary were laid within, and perhaps in reaction to, the camps. Both came to symbolise the plight of the martyred Republic but in different ways. In the case of Machado, the reference was as literal as metaphoric. The poet, who once wrote: 'Traveller, there is no path. The path is made by walking', died shortly after the exodus and was buried close to Argelès camp in the port of Collioure.[74] Lorca, on the other hand, was assassinated by rebel forces in Granada towards the start of the Civil War. Before his death, he had directed an itinerant university student theatre company which toured the Spanish countryside to bring culture to the masses through performances that espoused the themes of justice, freedom and transcendence through culture.[75] Lorca's body was never found, but the memory of his works and activities spurred the cultural drive in Argelès.

José Atienza and Efrén Hermida transformed their Barrack (no. 14) into a hub of artistic activity in Argelès camp. Their work on the cultural review *Barraca* (literally translated as barrack) articulated a determined sense of continuity with the past. The title of *Barraca* was pluri-vocal: it had been the name of Lorca's theatre company, it carried reference to the cottages of the Valencian region and also referred to the barrack where the review was painstakingly produced by hand.[76] As the meanings behind the title suggest, the Spanish republican exile engendered rupture, reconstruction, but also a sense of continuity that drew from symbolic references to the cultural achievements of the Second Republic. Militarily, the Spanish republicans were spent, but culture remained the one and universal field on which they could claim victory.

The importance of these activities should not be underestimated. Admittedly, most of the internees behind these accomplishments were students, teachers and intellectuals. Moreover, some caution is needed when interpreting the number of events and participants cited in the bulletins. Even so, these cultural activities took place in camps through-out southern France, were open to all and involved a sizeable proportion

of internees. They were a pragmatic response to exile through the anticipation of skills useful for life after internment in France.[77] Furthermore,
these events gave internees a sense of purpose by breaking the monotony
of imprisonment. In the words of Miguel Alama, 'knowledge helped us
to live'.[78]

The scale of publishing activity from within and beyond the camps
reflects the Spanish republicans' hardy dynamism and their high level of
politicisation. It is equally suggestive of the refugees' awareness of the role
of the press in forging group identities. There are parallels with Anderson's 'imagined communities', indicating that the processes for producing
national narratives of community are just as applicable for people
deprived of a national territory. It is a compelling point, but one which
must nonetheless be nuanced when considering the heterogeneous composition of the Spanish republicans. Even though some papers claimed
to speak for all Spanish republicans, they were almost always linked to
specific groups.

Stories and values

The press was one cog amongst many in the mechanism driving the
production of exilic identities. Another important aspect consisted of
everyday activities, stories and values. In a context of rupture from the
spaces and institutions central to political and trade-union activity in
Spain, internees drew on symbolic references and reaffirmed collective
values to forge a group consciousness in the camps through their everyday activities. Libertarians' life-history narratives place repeated emphasis on group solidarity and mutual aid amongst *compañeros* – even this
term functioned as a means of differentiation from other militants, and
especially Communists who described themselves as *camarada* – along
with incidents of conflict with other groups.

Scenes of libertarians regrouping in the camps frequently portray acts
of sharing. A salient example is Juan Giménez's recollection of being
reunited with friends in Vernet camp: 'they offered me what they had, a
tin of scrapings from potato skins that weren't so bad when boiled and
eaten warm. Each person gave me a little until the tin was full, but I told
them I wasn't hungry. I got out the sandwich the monk had given me
and shared it all around.'[79] The reference to the monk did not mean
Giménez had abandoned another central tenet of libertarianism, that of
anticlericalism.[80] On the contrary, earlier on in the memoir he explains
how he was forced to leave hospital to be interned after falling out with

the religious staff. His story of his arrival in the camp ends with the group putting their cigarettes in a kitty. Another militant in the same camp, José Borrás, explained how he shared the food he had earned through cutting the hair of the kitchen staff with other *compañeros*.[81] Abel Paz's description of reuniting with fellow members of the group 'Quijotes del Ideal' similarly evokes his libertarian identity through daily activities centring on solidarity and equality.[82] During the first months of internment, these types of activities were a necessary means of coping with material deficiencies but they also represented a form of sociability dating back to the development of the CNT into a mass workers' movement.[83]

The idea of direct action was also intimately linked with libertarian identity. Borrás's account of a food protest describes one internee knocking a French officer to the ground, which despite the threat of repression, resulted in the resolution of the problem.[84] Another quixotic illustration is provided by Francisco Perez and his recollection of another food dispute in the camp. A group of internees toured the camp banging on the containers used to collect rice from the kitchens as if they were drums.[85]

Collective identities were strengthened through opposition to the camp authorities but also through conflict between different groups. Antagonism was acutely evident between the libertarians and Communists. The former referred to Communists pejoratively as 'los chinos' or 'Chinese', and often contrasted their sense of democratic accountability to the Stalinist discipline of the Communists. News of the August Nazi–Soviet Pact fuelled existing tensions between Communists and non-communist groups. The organ of the MLE General Council, *Democracia*, claimed the agreement had caused an incompatible situation estranging the Communists from Spanish anti-fascists.[86]

Although there was generally little co-operation at a group level between the different parties and trade unions, certain forms of commonality existed. This was virtually unavoidable given the daily interaction, accompanying affinities and shared interests resulting from life within the confined spaces of the camps. Stories of confrontations with camp authorities could cut across political and trade-union boundaries. In doing so, these tales served to endow a general sense of agency amongst a population deprived of freedom. A Communist militant, Miguel Oviedo, described how internees of all ideological backgrounds in the Gurs camp disseminated a story about how the authorities' pressure on internees to choose between returning to Spain and the Foreign Legion ceased after one Spanish officer retorted that he would rather choose

Spain and potential death at the hands of the Francoists rather than become a mercenary.[87] While it is doubtful that an internee could influence the camp authorities in this way, the repetition of the story at the time would have been an empowering influence through the allusion to an internee influencing authority against all the odds.

Regional affinities could also cut across political and trade-union lines. Valeriano Espiga was a committed member of the CNT, and an ardent anti-communist, but was nevertheless friends with a Communist who came from the same region as himself.[88] For Eulalio Ferrer, an attachment to Santander was as at least as important as political allegiances.[89] And as was highlighted earlier in this chapter, another form of commonality consisted of cultural activities, with perhaps the most notable example being the 12 refugees of Barrack 14 in Argelès who transformed their shelter into the cultural and publishing hub of the camp.[90]

Celebrating the Republic(s)?

No survey of the camps would be complete without a tour of the commemorative events during the spring and summer of 1939. These celebrated a range of anniversaries: the Second Spanish Republic on 14 April, International Workers' Day on 1 May, Bastille Day on 14 July and the anniversary of the popular uprising in Spain on 19 July. Each of these dates were a catalyst for reflecting about past, present and future trajectories but were also a pretext for celebrating particular ideological affinities as well as Republican universalism.

On Friday 14 April, one group of refugees at Gurs camp marked the anniversary of the Second Spanish Republic by pledging their support to the French Republic in the event of war.[91] In Argelès camp, the day unfolded with a series of events including speeches, flamenco music and singing by an Asturian choir as well as by Ukranian and Polish choirs from the International Brigades in front of a reported audience of 7,000.[92] Internees' reactions to the festivities varied. Pons's memoir depicts a rather sombre day involving a meal and a toast to the Republic amid reflections on the Spanish Republic's defeat.[93] Ferrer's recollection, however, was of 'a joyful atmosphere' involving a gathering of people from the Cantabrian region of Spain.[94]

International Workers' Day provided another occasion for collective celebration but with more evident political overtones. The French commander of the camps in the Pyrénées-Orientales, Colonel Gauthier, warned the Minister of the Interior that political activity was under way in Argèles camp.[95] He may have been responding to the leaflets that Ferrer observed on the electricity poles and walls of the barracks which evoked solidarity, rights and remembrance: 'On this 1st of May 1939, we the Spanish refugees salute the French proletariat'; 'We demand the right to asylum, and a permit to work'; 'Let's honour the memory of the martyrs of Spain'.[96] While Ferrer also referred to altercations between Communists and anarchist internees, he emphasises an overly festive atmosphere. In his memoir, Pons recalls a sense of satisfaction at having celebrated the occasion despite the French authorities' surveillance. He participated in a sumptuous meal, at least by Argelès standards, which was followed by songs about the Civil War, the Second Republic, revolution and the Communist International. Revealingly, Pons states: 'in any other place we would have sung the Marseillaise'.[97]

Pons reminds us that the Marseillaise had in fact been widely sung in Spain because of its emphasis on the universal ideal of freedom and the battle against tyranny. It was not the only reference to (French) Republican universalism which had been appropriated in Spain. The Spanish republicans' representations of Hispania on posters calling for French solidarity during the Civil War were strikingly similar to the French Marianne. But now interned in France, the Spanish republicans viewed the French Republic, or rather its ruling elite, with a new-found mixture of irony and contempt. All the same, the internees celebrated the 150th anniversary of the French Revolution with some enthusiasm and thereby transformed the camps into one of the few places of energetic commemorative activity compared to an otherwise subdued atmosphere for the French left more widely.

Some Spanish republicans viewed Bastille Day as an occasion for manifesting their solidarity with the French Republic. The Prefect of the Pyrénées-Orientales sent the Minister of the Interior a selection of documents from the internees as evidence of 'the gratitude and loyalty of the Spanish refugees of my *département* towards France and the authorities of the Republic'. One letter from the Spanish Transport Corps read: 'On the 150th anniversary of the French Revolution the 6th and 7th Sections of the 4th Company of the Spanish Transport Corps send you our sincerest wishes and offer to place ourselves at your service, and at the side of the French people in the battle for peace and democracy.'[98] For some French guards the celebratory atmosphere created by the internees was clearly infectious. Gaston Ducournau, stationed at Gurs camp, recalled: '14 July 1939 was an unforgettable moment. The Spanish republicans, International Brigades and a large number of French soldiers all sang our revolutionary hymn of the Marseillaise together.'[99] In contrast to Pons, Ferrer recounts how the Marseillaise induced a feeling of commonality between the refugees and French nationals:

> Then in the agitated mass of people, we moved towards the main entrance where the French forces were parading. Inhabitants from the local villages surrounded us and the atmosphere transformed into one of utter human fraternity: from the other side cries of 'Vive la France!' from our side 'Vive la liberté!'[100]

While there were instances of fraternity, the different refrains of 'Vive la France!' and 'Vive la liberté!' alert us to the refugees' humour but also to a degree of ambivalence. In effect, there was a richly symbolic and substantively plural aspect to the Bastille Day celebrations in the camps. Some internees highlighted their solidarity with the French Republic or proletariat; others were highly critical of the French authorities. Refugees' speeches at Gurs camp referred to France in terms of 'democracy', 'nation' and 'people' while carefully avoiding any mention of state, government or the camp authorities.[101] For another refugee, Luis Bonet, universal values existed, but could no longer be associated with France. Bonet and his Communist comrades created a single edition of a newspaper which they gave as a gift to the Soviet Embassy in France. According to Bonet, the French authorities' attitudes towards the refugees were contrary to the principles on which the Republic had been established; the French people were the true inheritors of the Revolution.[102] According to another internee, David Granda, the event carried more significance for the Spanish republicans than for the French population.[103] He describes the poignant and multiple meanings attached to this anniversary in Septfonds camp. Refugees adorned the façades of several barracks with depictions of the storming of the Bastille, while another barrack was covered in cartoons containing satirical scenes of the refugees' liberation from the camp. A team of metalworkers re-created the insignia of their trade union and sculptors reproduced Goya's portrait, *La Maja desnuda*, in clay. Another impressive work consisted of a relief of Spain showing the insignia of the country's different trade unions.[104] Bastille Day was a significant moment for the expression of political and trade-union identities in an environment that was supposed to be devoid of such activity.

Less than a week later, the refugees transformed the camps once again into a hive of commemorative activity in memory of 19 July 1936, in many ways the Spanish equivalent of Bastille Day. Not to be confused with 18 July, the national holiday celebrated by the Francoist authorities in anniversary of their military uprising, 19 July represented above all the popular reaction to the *coup d'état*. It was the day when workers in Spain took up arms to counter the military uprising. One bulletin from Barcarès camp began its reporting of the commemoration with the opening lines: 'We celebrated the third anniversary of 19 July, a glorious date when the Spanish people, united within one powerful block, took up arms to oppose the criminal military rebellion which had opened the Spanish doors to the foreign fascist invader.'[105]

The political and social emancipation evoked by this anniversary was captured in the libertarian revolutionary anthem *A las Barricadas* (To the Barricades). Although a libertarian song *A las Barricadas*, with its spirit of revolt and the struggle for freedom, was sung by refugees from other tendencies. Irrespective of whether or not all refugees subscribed to the revolutionary surge which had been unleashed by the military uprising, the majority remembered 19 July as a day when a military putsch failed, against all odds, through popular opposition.

The level of frustration, disappointment and bitterness at having been interned by one Republic after battling for another may well explain the tendency in many refugees' memoirs to place more emphasis on the 1939 Bastille Day activities than on the celebration of 19 July. All the same, there were overlapping characteristics to the anniversary events. During the spring and summer of 1939, the refugees celebrated themselves as defenders of democracy in the context of an increasingly anti-democratic Europe. Some of their commemorative activities were imbued with a critique of the French Republic for not espousing the values on which it had been established. But there is also a sense that the celebration of 14 July consisted of an act of appropriation whereby the dominant and founding values of the French Republic were taken and transformed by the refugees to reflect their own experiences and future aspirations. This process was not the preserve of the Spanish refugees. The PCF was engaged in reviving the myth of 1789 and the recuperation of French Republican memory as part of its own struggle to reintegrate itself into the national community.[106] Here we see some overlap in intent. The refugees' displays of solidarity with the French people were also designed to secure reintegration: organisers hoped the celebrations would depict the internees in a favourable light and hence secure their release from the camps. In the process, the Spanish republicans tried to inverse their image in the French social imaginary from one which caricatured them as a threat to a portrayal of the refugees as supporters, if not defenders, of the French Republic.

It would be wrong to adopt a purely instrumental interpretation of these events, for many refugees were genuinely inspired by the French Republic's universal values. So were a significant minority of French nationals who endeavoured to ease the refugees' painful first months in exile. At the end of May, the Mayor of Argelès organised a fundraising event in the village based on the refugees' artistic works. Monsieur Cecchi, the owner of a garage on the beach of Argelès, began buying a copy of the *Barraca* review as well as several paintings from internee artists before organising a refugee art exhibition in his own home. The owner of the nearby château de Valmy became acquainted with the artists via *Barraca* and then obtained authorisation for all 12 to leave the camp on 28 June to set up a studio, from where they produced a new review, *Desde el Rosellón* (From the Roussillon).[107]

During the first months in exile, the task of reorganisation was hindered by the precipitated departure from Spain and the dispersion of militants across France. Important organisational documents were destroyed in the process. Some militants had destroyed archival material before leaving Catalonia to prevent information from falling into rebel hands. The PSUC managed to get militants' files past French border guards only to end up destroying them in Saint-Cyprien camp for fear they would be discovered by the authorities.[108] The MLE, on the other hand, managed to transport records into France where they were kept initially by the SIA office in Perpignan before being transferred to the General Council in Paris. But even with records, the task of tracing who had managed to cross into France and where they were situated was a complicated affair. French state repression was an additional obstacle to overcome.

Despite these pressures and under enormously difficult circumstances, the Spanish republicans engaged in a considerable degree of reorganisational activity, with some notable results. Suffering from internal fractures, the PSOE created a distribution network and organised the re-emigration of a small but significant number of refugees to Latin America through the auspices of the SERE and JARE. The Communists were notable in establishing a very effective clandestine press-distribution network. The MLE was no less innovative in reconstructing the movement from above and below. In the camps, traditional values of solidarity, anti-communism and anti-clericalism provided the symbolic glue for the nascent groups and networks. The MLE also re-established contact with militants in Spain.

The divisions between and within the organisations may well have hindered the reconstructive effort, but we can never know this for certain.

What can be underlined with certainty is that this was an exile involving many different groups, each pushing for its particular agenda. This raises the question of whether we should speak of exile in the plural. Would it be more apt to refer to 'routes to exiles' as opposed to 'the routes to exile'? The former certainly conveys the different aims and world-views of the various constituent groups of the Spanish republicans. Moreover there was no durable sense of an imagined community of Spanish republicans during the first year in France. In effect, if we look more closely at the dynamics of identity creation, we need to acknowledge the myriad ways through which group identities were re-created. In the camps this included the distribution and reading of the press, as well as regular interaction, whether through the form of meetings, informal discussions, the repetition of anecdotes and storytelling, conflict with the camp authorities or through rivalry between the different political and trade-union groups.

On the other hand, the structural conditions underlying daily life in France were the same for the vast majority of the refugees. The French government's reception strategy of segregation, return and the repression of political activity compromised the refugees' abilities to reorganise themselves. The commemorations of the spring and summer of 1939 are revealing of how the refugees responded to and negotiated the French authorities' suppression of political activities. The events were multi-vocal but nonetheless involved an admittedly fragile and nebulous set of common values, and above all took place within the shared experience of the concentration camps. The camps were not so much a site from which a national dominant narrative of the Spanish republic was reconstituted, for one had never existed amongst the Spanish republicans. But they were a space of considerable reconstructive activity and represent one of the major milestones of the routes to the Spanish republican exile as both lived experience and memory.

Notes

1 Interview with Francisco Perez, Bègles, 5 July 2003.
2 H. Graham, *The Spanish Republic at War 1936–1939* (Cambridge, 2002), p. 399.
3 J. M. del Valle, *Las Instituciones de la República española en exilio* (Paris, 1976), pp. 19–31.
4 Much of the literature on the Spanish Libertarian Movement in Exile has been written by militants or their relatives: J. Berruezo, *Contribución de la historia de la CNT de España en el exilio* (Mexico City, 1967); C. M. Lorenzo, *Les anarchistes espagnols et le pouvoir, 1868–1969* (Paris, 1969); J. M. Molina,

El movimiento clandestino en España 1939–1949 (Mexico City, 1976); Abel Paz, *CNT 1939–1951: el anarquismo contra el Estado franquista* (Madrid, 2001). An exception is the chapter by M. Torres, 'El exilio libertario y el movimiento obrero español', in M. F. Mancebo, M. Baldó and C. Alonso (eds), *L'Exili Cultural de 1939. Seixanta anys després*, Vol. 2, (Valencia, 2001).

5 The initial General Council included Mariano Vázquez (general secretary), Germinal Esgleas (deputy secretary), Roberto Alfonso, Serafín Aliaga, Juan Gallego Crespo, Juan García, Pedro Herrera, Rafael Íñigo, Francisco Isgleas, Horacio Martínez, Valerio Mas, Fidel Miró and Germinal de Sousa. CIRAS, Gestión MLE-CNT en Francia, 24 February 1939–14 May 1945. Carta Circular del exsecretario de relaciones exteriores de la CNT FAI, 25 February 1939. The Council expanded to 25 members, including Federica Montseny. M. Íñiguez, *Enciclopedia histórica del anarquismo español* (Vitoria, 2008), p. 437.

6 *Ibid.*

7 Marianet and Agustín Souchy met the following militants: Arturo García, José Cabañas, José Consuegra, José-María Jareño, Joaquín Delso de Miguel, Avelino González, José González, José Grunfeld, Manuel González Marín, Isidoro Pastor, Pablo Polgare (real name Paul Partos), Manuel Salgado and Edouardo Val. CIRAS, Gestión MLE-CNT en Francia, 24 February 1939–14 May 1945. Minutes, 14 April 1939.

8 CIRAS, Gestión MLE-CNT en Francia, 24 February 1939–14 May 1945. General Council minutes from 16 June, 28 June, 30 June and letter from J. G. Barberá to the General Council, 24 August 1939.

9 Four members of the CNT entered Largo Caballero's government in November 1936: Juan Peiró and Juan López accepted responsibility for industry and trade, Juan García Oliver was responsible for justice and Federica Montseny became minister for health.

10 For a discussion on the FAI's origins see J. Garner, 'Creating Unity or Division? The Origins of the Federación Anarquista Ibérica', *University of Sussex Journal of Contemporary History*, 6 (2003), pp. 1–14.

11 AN Fontainebleau, 20010216/170. Report by the Préfet de Police de Paris about relations between Spanish libertarians in France and London from the end of January to mid-March 1939.

12 CIRAS, Gestión MLE-CNT en Francia, 24 February 1939–14 May 1945. Circular no. 1, 25 February 1939 from the General Council of the Movimiento Libertario Español.

13 A. Téllez Solá, *La Red de Evasión del Grupo Ponzán: Anarquistas en la guerra secreta contra el franquismo y el nazismo (1936–1944)* (Barcelona, 1996), pp. 134–9.

14 Molina, *El movimiento clandestino en España*, p. 46. For the names of some of the people who escaped to France see Téllez Solá, *La Red de Evasión del Grupo Ponzán*, p. 139.

15 *Ibid.*, pp. 66–7.

16 López, along with Manuel Salas Blasco, had been asked to contact the General Council and outline the situation in Spain. They crossed the border with a number of other militants. Téllez Solá, *La Red de Evasión del Grupo Ponzán*, pp. 139–40.

17 *Ibid.*; Molina, *El movimiento clandestino en España*, p. 67.

18 Íñiguez, *Enciclopedia histórica del anarquismo español*, Vol. 2, p. 945.

19 D. Rolland, 'Extradition ou réémigration? Les vases communicants de la gestion xénophobe des réfugiés espagnols en France', in P. Milza and D. Peschanski (eds), *Exils et Migration: Italiens et Espagnols en France 1938– 1946* (Paris, 1994), p. 57.

20 L. Stein, *Beyond Death and Exile: The Spanish Republicans in France, 1939– 1955* (Cambridge, MA, 1979), p. 88. del Valle, *Las Instituciones de la República española en exilio*, p. 33.

21 The person responsible for getting the SERE aid to most of the camps in southern France was Ramon Peypoch Pich, former secretary-general of the Catalan Republican Party (Acción Catalana Républicana). But in August, he left to work for the rival JARE. Under the JARE, he organised distribution in the *départements* of the Ariège, Aude, Gers, Haute-Garonne and Basses-Pyrénées, visiting the camps of Gurs, Septfonds, Bram, Agde, Saint-Cyprien, Barcarès and Vernet d'Ariège. AD Haute-Garonne, 1960W 66. Statement by Ramon Peypoch Pich to the 8th Brigade of Mobile Police, 23 February 1940.

22 The Executive Council was composed of Pablo de Azcárate (former ambassador to London), Jaime Ayguadé Miró (Esquerra Catalana), Emilio Baeza Medina (Izquierda Republicana), Julio Jáuregui (Partido Nacionalista Vasco), Antonio Mije (PCE), Federica Montseny (FAI), Alejandro Otero (PSOE), Eduardo Ragasol (Acción Catalana), Manuel Rodríguez Vázquez (CNT), Amaro del Rosal (UGT) and Manuel Torres (Unión Republicana). J. Rubio, *La emigración de la guerra civil de 1936–1939. Historia del éxodo que se produce con el fin de la II República española*, Vol. 1 (Madrid, 1977), pp. 133–4.

23 The members of the Ministerial Panel were Juan Negrín (PSOE), Julio Alvarez del Vayo (PSOE), Tomás Bilbao (Acción Nacionalista Vasca), Segundo Blanco (CNT), Ramón González Peña (PSOE), Francisco Méndez (Izquierda Republicana) and José Moix-Regas (PSUC). *Ibid.*, p. 134.

24 For similar figures see G. Dreyfus-Armand, *L'Exil des Républicains Espagnols en France: De la Guerre Civile à la Mort de Franco* (Paris, 1999), p. 79.

25 CIRAS, Gestión MLE-CNT en Francia, 24 February 1939–14 May 1945. Minutes of the meetings of the General Council in London, 14 April 1939, and in Paris, 23 June and 30 June 1939.

26 On one ship, the anti-MLE bias was even more flagrant; Rolland, 'Extradition ou réémigration?', p. 56.

27 For the history of the PSOE see: C. Martínez Cobo and J. Martínez Cobo, *La Primera Renovación: Intrahistoria del PSOE Volumen 1 (1939–1945)* (Barcelona, 1989); R. Gillespie, *The Spanish Socialist Party: A History*

of Factionalism (Oxford, 1989), J. Martínez, 'Le PSOE à Toulouse et dans le midi de la France: 1939–1975', in L. Dormergue (ed.), *L'Exil Républicain espagnol à Toulouse 1939–1999* (Toulouse, 1999), pp. 79–95. On the UGT see: A. Mateos López, *Exilio y Clandestinidad. La Reconstrucción de UGT, 1939–1977* (Madrid, 2002); C. Tcach and C. Reyes, *Clandestinidad y exilio. Reorganización del sindicato socialista, 1939–1953* (Madrid, 1986).

28 For the controversy over re-emigration, see Rubio, *La emigración de la guerra civil de 1936–1939*, Vol. 1, pp. 129–49; del Valle, *Las Instituciones de la República española en exilio*, pp. 32–8; Rolland, 'Extradition ou réémigration?', pp. 56–7; F. Caudet, *Hipótesis sobre el exilio republicano de 1939* (Madrid, 1997), pp. 255–328; Dreyfus-Armand, *L'Exil des Républicains Espagnols en France*, pp. 79–80 and Stein, *Beyond Death and Exile*, pp. 87–91.

29 The following representatives sat on the JARE committee: Luis Nicolau d'Olwer (Acció Catala), Indalecio Prieto (PSOE), Carlos Esplá (Izquierda Republicana), José Andreu Abelló (Esquerra Catalana), Amador Fernández Montes (UGT), Emilio Palomo Aguado (Izquierda Republicana), Juan Peiró Bellis (CNT) and Faustino Valentín Torrejón (Unión Republicana).

30 Rubio, *La emigración de la guerra civil de 1936–1939*, Vol. 1, p. 147.

31 Dreyfus-Armand, *L'Exil des Républicains Espagnols en France*, p. 79.

32 J. Estruch Tobella, *El PCE en la clandestinidad 1939–1956* (Madrid, 1982); J. Estruch Tobella, *Historia Oculta del PCE* (Madrid, 2000); J. L. Martín Ramos, *Rojos contra Franco: Historia del PSUC, 1939–1947* (Barcelona, 2002); D. W. Pike, *Jours de gloire, jours de honte, Le PCE en France* (Paris, 1984).

33 There were a relatively small number of militants from the PCE and PSUC in exile. An internal report from July 1939 gives a total of 11,121 militants, plus a further 3,673 militants from the associated youth movement. D. Peschanski, *La France des camps. L'internement 1938–1946* (Paris, 2002), p. 51.

34 The last meeting of the PSUC in France also took place in March.

35 Martín Ramos, *Rojos contra Franco*, pp. 49–62.

36 Peschanski suggests the decision to evacuate leaders from France dates back to at least September 1939, and was probably motivated by André Marty's conviction that the French authorities intended to assassinate the Communist leadership in the camps; Peschanski, *La France des camps*, p. 70. Estruch Tobella believes the decision could have been taken during the first meeting of the political bureau in France on 12 March 1939. Estruch Tobella, *El PCE en la clandestinidad*, p. 11.

37 Stein, *Beyond Death and Exile*, p. 100.

38 G. Tuban, *Les séquestrés de Collioure: Un camp disciplinaire au Château royal en 1939* (Perpignan, 2003), p. 46.

39 AD Pyrénées-Orientales, 31W 274. Letter to Préfet, 13 April 1939.

40 Commissaire Central de Police to Préfet, 27 March 1939.

41 AD Pyrénées-Orientales, 31W 274. Report from Contrôleur Général in relation to Saint-Cyprien and Argelès camps, 9 March 1939.

42 *Ibid.* Report by Lieutenant-Colonel Tricottet, Commandant du camp d'Argelès-sur-Mer, 27 April 1939.

43 F. Pons, *Barbelés à Argelès et autour d'autres camps* (Paris, 1993), p. 63.

44 R. Moral i Querol, *Journal d'exil (1939–1945)* (Paris, 1982), pp. 31–2.

45 A. Paz, *Entre la niebla* (Barcelona, 1993), pp. 57–69.

46 AD Pyrénées-Orientales, 31W 274. Préfet to Ministre de l'Intérieur, 4 April 1939.

47 For further details of how the International Brigades reorganised see Peschanski, *La France des camps*, pp. 52–62. See also S. Courtois, D. Peschanski and A. Rayski (eds), *Le Sang de l'étranger. Les immigrés de la MOI dans la Résistance* (Paris, 1989), p. 53.

48 Martín Ramos, *Rojos contra Franco*, pp. 48–50.

49 Stein, *Beyond Death and Exile*, pp. 101–2.

50 G. Dreyfus-Armand and É. Temime, *Les Camps sur la plage, un exil espagnol* (Paris, 1995), p. 106.

51 AN Fontainebleau, 20010216/170. Report by Préfet de Police de Paris on FAI activities and relations between Spanish anarchists in France and in London between 25 January and 28 March 1939.

52 AN Fontainebleau, 20010216/170. J. Maitron and C. Pennetier, *Dictionnaire Biographique du Mouvement Ouvrier Français, 1914–1939*, Vol. 19 (Paris, 1983).

53 AN Fontainebleau, 20010216/170. AD Pyrénées-Orientales, 31W 274. Report no. 5549/5, undated in a dossier with information relating to the summer of 1939. For details of Louis Montgon's activities during the civil war, see D. Berry, 'Solidarité internationale antifasciste: les anarchistes français et la guerre civile d'Espagne,' in J. Sagnes and S. Caucanas (eds), *Les Français et la Guerre d'Espagne* (Perpignan, 2nd edn, 2004), p. 80.

54 For further details of Ponzán's network see P. Ponzán Vidal, *Lucha y muerte por la libertad. Memorias de nueve años de guerra: 1936–1945* (Barcelona, 1996) and Téllez Solá, *La red de evasión del grupo Ponzán*. Ponzán's activities during the Occupation of France are also detailed in V. Brome, *The Way Back: The Story of Lieut.-Commander Pat O'Leary, G.C., D.S.O., R.N.* (London, 1958) and L. H. Nouveau, *Des Capitaines par Milliers: Retour à Gibraltar des aviateurs alliés abattus (1941–43)* (Paris, 1958).

55 Although various examples survive, the collections are mostly incomplete and scattered around different public and private archives. For a comprehensive study of the exilic press see G. Dreyfus-Armand, 'L'Émigration Politique Espagnole en France au Travers de sa Presse 1939–1975' (Thèse de Doctorat, Institut d'Études Politiques de Paris, 1994).

56 *Poble Català* (27 October 1939).

57 Dreyfus-Armand, 'L'Émigration Politique Espagnole en France au Travers de sa Presse', p. 102.

58 G. Dreyfus-Armand, 'La presse de l'émigration espagnole en France de 1939 à 1944. Contre vents et marées', in J.-C. Villegas (ed.), *Plages d'exil. Les camps de réfugiés espagnols en France – 1939* (Nanterre-Dijon, 1989, pp. 188, 190).

59 Dreyfus-Armand, 'L'Émigration Politique Espagnole en France au Travers de sa Presse', p. 219.

60 *Ibid.*, pp. 82, 120.

61 *Treball* (26 February 1939).

62 Dreyfus-Armand, 'L'Émigration Politique Espagnole en France au Travers de sa Presse', p. 103.

63 Dreyfus-Armand, *L'Exil des Républicains Espagnols en France*, p. 92.

64 Dreyfus-Armand, 'L'Émigration Politique Espagnole en France au Travers de sa Presse', pp. 72, 564.

65 *Solidarité* (7 April 1939).

66 For example, there is only one known copy of the *Boletín de discusión* published by the POUM and the *Juventud Comunista Ibérica* (Iberian Communist Youth). Dreyfus-Armand, 'L'Émigration Politique Espagnole en France au Travers de sa Presse', pp. 72, 107.

67 Reproductions of some of these publications, some of which are in colour, can be found in J.-C. Villegas (ed.), *Écrits d'exil: Barraca et Desde el Rosellón. Albums d'art et de littérature Argelès-sur-Mer 1939* (Sète, 2007) and Villegas (ed.), *Plages d'exil*.

68 J.-C. Villegas, 'La culture des sables: Presse et édition dans les camps de réfugiés', in Villegas (ed.), *Plages d'exil*, p. 133.

69 Dreyfus-Armand and Temime, *Les Camps sur la plage*, p. 103.

70 *Boletín de los estudiantes* (FUE), no. 9, 1939. The *Hoja de los estudiantes* was produced in Saint-Cyprien, and the *Profesionales de la enseñanza* in all three camps.

71 Villegas (ed.), *Plages d'exil*, p.19.

72 *Boletín de Estudiantes*, no. 10, 25 May 1939. Cited in C. Boix, 'La notion de patrie dans le discours des réfugiés espagnols des camps d'Argelès et de St-Cyprien', in Villegas (ed.), *Plages d'exil*, p. 127.

73 *Boletín de los estudiantes* (FUE), no. 4 (23 April 1939). Villegas (ed.), *Plages d'exil*, p. 23.

74 A. Machado, *Campos de Castilla* (Madrid, 1912).

75 Villegas (ed.), *Écrits d'exil*, p. 330.

76 *Ibid.*

77 S. Salaün, 'Éducation et culture dans les camps de réfugiés', in Villegas (ed.), *Plages d'exil*, p. 118.

78 Interview with Miguel Alama, Bordeaux, 30 May 2002.

79 J. Giménez Arenas, *De la Unión a Banat: Itinerario de una rebeldía* (Madrid, 1996), p. 81.

80 For other examples of anticlerical incidents in exile see S. Soo, 'Exile, Identity and Memory: Spanish Republicans in the Southwest of France' (D.Phil. thesis, University of Sussex, 2005), pp. 74–6.

81 J. Borrás, *Del Radical-Socialismo al Socialismo Radical y Libertario: Memorias de un Libertario* (Madrid, 1998), p. 84.

82 Paz, *Entre la niebla*, pp. 66–9.

83 For an excellent study of this phenomenon see C. Ealham, 'Class and the City: Spatial Memories of Pleasure and Danger in Barcelona, 1914–23', *Oral History*, 29:1 (2001), pp. 40–1.

84 Borrás, *Del Radical-Socialismo al Socialismo Radical y Libertario*, pp. 84–5.

85 Interview with Francisco Perez, Bègles, 5 July 2003.

86 Cited in Dreyfus-Armand, 'La presse de l'émigration espagnole en France de 1939 à 1944', p. 189.

87 M. Oviedo, unpublished diary written in 1939. See also another recollection from the camp of Mazères: F. Guilhem, *L'obsession du retour* (Toulouse, 2005), p. 17.

88 Interview with Valeriano Espiga, Fargues-St-Hilaire, 21 May 2002.

89 E. Ferrer, *Derrière les Barbelés: Journal des Camps de Concentration en France (1939)* (Limonest, 1993).

90 For further details see Villegas, *Écrits d'exil*.

91 C. Laharie, *Le Camp de Gurs, 1939–45: Un aspect méconnu de l'histoire du Béarn* (Biarritz, 1993), p. 96.

92 *Boletin de los estudiantes* (FUE), no. 2 (17 April 1939). Villegas (ed.), *Plages d'exil*, p. 20.

93 Pons, *Barbelés à Argelès et autour d'autres camps*, p. 113.

94 Ferrer, *Derrière les Barbelés*, pp. 33–4.

95 AD Pyrénées-Orientales, 31W. Préfet to Ministre de l'Intérieur, 2 May 1939.

96 Ferrer, *Derrière les Barbelés*, p. 55.

97 Pons refers to 'Los Cuatro Muleros', 'Ay Carmela', El hymno a la XII brigada', 'Bandera Rosa', 'Els Segadors', 'La Comuna', 'A las Barricadas' and the 'Internationale'. Pons, *Barbelés à Argelès et autour d'autres camps*, pp. 114–15.

98 AD Pyrénées-Orientales, 31W 274. Préfet to Ministre de l'Intérieur, 18 July 1939.

99 *Gurs, souvenez-vous: lettre d'information de l'Amicale du camp de Gurs*, no. 97, p. 9.

100 Ferrer, *Derrière les Barbelés*, p. 107.

101 Laharie, *Le Camp de Gurs*, p. 102.

102 L. Bonet Lopez, *Mémoires d'exil d'un Espagnol* (Paris, 2002), p. 33.

103 N. MacMaster, *Spanish Fighters: An Oral History of Civil War and Exile* (Basingstoke, 1990), p. 130.

104 *Ibid.*, pp. 130–1.

105 *Hoja Estudiante FUE* (Barcarès, 27 July 1936).

106 C. Amalvi, 'Le 14-Juillet: Du Dies irae à Jour de fête', in P. Nora (ed.), *Les Lieux de Mémoire* (Paris, 1997), Vol. 1, pp. 383–423.

107 Villegas, 'La culture des sables', p. 139. See also Villegas, *Écrits d'exil*.

108 Martín Ramos, *Rojos contra Franco*, pp. 49–62.

PART II

Working in from the margins

4

Ambiguities at work: refugees and the French war economy, 1939–40

Throughout the 1930s officials and employers in south-western France had associated Spanish migrants primarily with their role in the economy. Whether in rural or urban areas, Spaniards were perceived as hard-working and exploitable but also effective workers. In Bordeaux, employers preferred to hire Spanish dockers rather than their French counterparts.[1] A similar picture emerged from a study conducted in the late 1930s involving interviews with French farmers in the south-west.[2] By 1939, a fundamental change occurred with the politicisation of the refugee issue by the Daladier government, and the accompanying fear that appeasement could be compromised by the presence of refugees in France and their alleged Communist allies.[3] In both government and public circles anti-refugee sentiment became embroiled with anti-communism (the extreme right meshed these themes together with anti-Semitism). This xenophobic turn began to affect all migrants, with the appearance in political and public circles of the idea of the 'undesirable' foreigner.[4]

The Spanish republicans had to contend with the xenophobia of the late 1930s as well as negative stereotypes from the Spanish Civil War. But despite this inauspicious context, there were pragmatic reasons for employing the Spanish refugees. Even though France was facing a challenging economic context, shortages in agricultural labour continued to afflict the southern part of the country. Furthermore, the French experience of the First World War suggested that immigrant labour would once more be required if war erupted between France and Germany. These were issues which the Spanish republicans' representatives and pro-refugee groups highlighted, and with some degree of success, in order to obtain the closure of the concentration camps.

This chapter begins with the various initiatives designed to secure the refugees' freedom from the camps. The Daladier government's eventual solution consisted of a dual system of labour where refugees were enrolled in paramilitary Foreign Labour Companies known as Compagnies de Travailleurs Étrangers (CTE), or as free workers (*travailleurs libres*). As we will see shortly, this strategy was accompanied by a dual discourse which portrayed the refugees as both a threat and an asset to the French Republic. The latter did not eradicate the former – many French officials and some employers stubbornly clung to preconceptions of the Spanish republicans as a danger to national security – but it did offer an alternative. Significantly, the discourse that depicted the refugees in terms of possibility is not only suggestive of the refugees' contribution to the French war economy, but also draws attention to a series of improvements to the Spanish refugees' living and working conditions. Admittedly, the wider situation of refugees was far from positive, and asylum was firmly linked to work rather than universal rights. However, as this chapter argues, even after the draconian legislation of November 1938 and the anti-communist crackdown of the following year, new opportunities arose for the improvement of the Spanish refugees' daily lives as a result of the labour demands of the war economy. This more inclusive stance opened up a new episode of the Spanish republican exile and furthers our understanding of refugee relations in France at the end of the Third Republic. In this way, this chapter contributes to the growing body of scholarship which eschews interpretations of the 1930s as a linear narrative of intensifying xenophobia, authoritarianism and the repression of foreigners by emphasising historical contingency.[5]

Initiatives and alternatives

Once the government allowed Spanish republicans to work in France the internee population began to drop steadily. By mid-June 1939, the number of internees had declined from 275,000 to 173,000; five months later the figure stood at 53,000; and at the end of April 1940 there were 3,000 people classified as unable to work.[6] Global statistics for the reception centres are unavailable, though it may be assumed that departures picked up pace during the summer months as repatriations to Spain peaked.

As we saw in the last two chapters, some refugees left the camps and centres for repatriation to Spain or re-emigration to another country.

There were also other alternatives. Escaping was initially very easy due to the improvisation and lack of organisation in the camps, and during the first months of internment quite a few internees tried their luck. For the majority of refugees, however, it was not a particularly viable option due to French surveillance and the difficulties of finding resources to live off in a foreign country.

At the start of the summer, the Prefecture in Perpignan believed that several hundred anarchists had left the camps via an escape network based in Paris with points of contact in Perpignan, Marseilles and Toulouse.[7] The MLE certainly had contacts in these cities but had in fact been trying to discourage militants from escaping since it could not guarantee them any means of subsistence.[8] Those who did so faced a challenging and discrete existence as their ability to remain free depended on resources and personal contacts. An idea of the difficulties can be gleaned from a letter written by the secretary of the FAI, José Grunfeld. The situation in Paris, he wrote, was 'very bad'. One *compañero* was beaten up for wearing the insignia of the FAI, and *compañeros* without the necessary French administrative documents had to live clandestinely. They were obliged to avoid the streets at night, use hotels which did not ask for identification, and last of all, refrain from speaking Spanish in public.[9] The problems of documentation and visibility in public spaces applied to all refugees, and so while many internees dreamt of escape, the actual number who did so remained relatively low. The case of one refugee is telling: having no resources, he asked the police services in Bordeaux to intern him.[10]

For the most part, Spanish republicans' representatives and pro-refugee groups campaigned for the closure of the camps, setting out proposals about the economic, social and military contribution that the internees could make to the French Republic. In anticipation, the MLE General Council began collating information during March on metal-workers, other militants with experience of work in war factories, and also those with agricultural labour skills.[11] A range of options was also discussed by prominent French personalities at a meeting in Paris on 3 May 1939, chaired by François Jourdain of the parliamentary French and Spanish Friendship Group. Maurice Viollette, who had been a Republican-Socialist Secretary of State under the Popular Front, called for the Spanish refugees to replace the seasonal workers recruited from abroad every year. Another proposition came from the Communist senator Eugène Hénaff. He had previously campaigned for German refugees in 1933, and now advocated using up to 40,000 Spaniards for defence-related work.[12] Albert Forcinal, a *député* from the Eure, suggested that Catalan workers with technical expertise could be employed in defence-related work, while troops from the International Brigades could be incorporated into the military, and other refugees used to repopulate central and southern France by taking over abandoned buildings.[13] Two months later, some of these ideas were reiterated during the July Conférence d'aide aux réfugiés espagnols, which was chaired by Professor Victor Basch from the League for the Rights of Man.[14]

Although humanitarian concerns lay behind the initiatives, they constituted a pragmatic response to some of France's problems. Military officers were worried about the country's low birth-rate and its correlative effect on troop numbers given Germany's larger population and army. The battle-experienced and ardently anti-fascist Spanish republicans, along with the International Brigades, represented an ideal opportunity to fill out the ranks of the French armed services. In February 1939, the French military ambassador to the Spanish Republic, Colonel Morel, had already discussed the valuable contribution that Spanish republican troops could make to the French armed forces.[15] The British were certainly keen enough to tap into the Spaniards' knowledge of modern warfare, which explains Squadron Leader Berkeley's trip to speak with Spanish pilots interned at Argelès.[16] But not everyone in France entertained the same idea. Although Pierre Dominique, editor of the Radical-orientated La République, was an advocate of using refugee soldiers, he excluded the Spanish republicans, whom he regarded as dangerous anarchists and Communists.[17] The head of the Montpellier military region, General Bresson, was dead against employing Spanish republicans for defence-related work. He suggested the benefits would be disproportionate to the number of security personnel required to monitor the refugees. The best option, he concluded, would be to repatriate as many refugees as possible.[18]

Agricultural co-operatives

Using refugees for agricultural work was less contentious than for defence-related work or enrolment in the military. France had a tradition of resorting to immigrant labour in southern France. Moreover, the prospect of using refugees to repopulate southern France had already been aired the year before. Philippe Serre was a Radical député who took up the new post of under-secretary of state for immigration under the Chautemps administration in January 1938. Aided by the ethnologist and immigration specialist, Georges Mauco, Serre proposed a plan to relocate all illegal Jewish immigrants from Paris and other urban centres to agricultural co-operatives in depopulated areas of south-western France.[19] The Serre plan aimed to appease a range of constituencies, from police concerns over public security, business preoccupations with economic competition and the demographic deficit in the rural south. The plan was definitely not based on humanitarian concerns, and neither was it devoid of anti-Semitic intent. But it did appear to offer a controlled, restricted method of incorporating refugees into the French economy without ruffling too many feathers amongst anti-refugee groups.

Interestingly, several Spanish republican organisations investigated the possibility of establishing their own agricultural co-operatives. The PSUC considered this in relation to Latin America, as did the former Republican chief of staff, General Rojo.[20] But it was the trade unions which pursued the idea furthest. The Executive Commission of the UGT Spanish Landworkers' Federation (FETT) circulated a document in July 1939 entitled 'The Labourer of the Land: Bulletin of the Spanish Refugee Farm Workers'.[21] The circular detailed discussions with the SERE about financing a series of co-operatives in France and Algeria. A subsequent circular announced that plans had been submitted to SERE representatives in Oran for a project involving 300 refugees and their families. But in the event, it seems the plans were never implemented. The MLE, on the other hand, managed to create two co-operatives in the *département* of the Lot: one near to Lamothe-Fénelon on a property named Grèze, and a larger project at Aymare near the town of Le Vigan.

Given the intentions behind the original Serre plan, it might seem surprising that Spanish republicans showed interest in a similar project. It is possible they were unaware of Serre's plan, given that it was discussed a year before *la retirada*. However, if they had heard of it they would have known about the French government's relatively favourable response to the idea as well as its eventual acceptance by Jewish associations. The Spanish republicans may also have been encouraged by the success of the agricultural co-operatives created by anti-fascist Italian migrants during the 1920s.[22] The prime impetus behind the Spanish republicans' plans, however, consisted of securing the release of internees by creating an opportunity for them to use their existing labour skills within a context which offered a certain degree of autonomy and ideological expression in France.

The co-operatives in France were evidently different from the revolutionary collectives created during the war in Spain. Notwithstanding the very different context, co-operatives offered libertarian refugees the nearest they could get to an ideal of communal work in France.[23] The authors of the MLE co-operative project were positively eager to frame it in relation to the collectives of the social revolution in Spain. An MLE circular from May 1939 reported details of an experiment in co-operative work in France, and more specifically referred to the acquisition of 125 hectares of land for a co-operative to enable militants from Aragon, Catalonia and the Levant to re-establish their lives.[24] The symbolic value of the project was unmistakable:

> The agricultural co-operative will be administered through statutes in agreement with the legal conventions currently in force. In addition, however, from the inside it will be impregnated with the spirit and solidarity that reigned in the glorious agricultural collectives in Spain.

The MLE hoped this modest start would eventually develop into a network of co-operatives for several thousand militants and their families. For this reason the MLE stressed the need for this first co-operative to succeed and attract a favourable reception amongst the local French populace.

Early developments were indeed promising. The MLE bought the property and terrain of Aymare from a Parisian lawyer and former communist *député*, André Berthon, on condition that he obtained all the necessary authorisations.[25] Contrary to officials' reactions to the presence of the Spanish refugees elsewhere in France, the Prefect of the Lot responded positively to Spanish refugees taking over abandoned farms in the area and requested a list of properties to be sold or rented out to refugee associations.[26]

During the summer of 1939, refugees began arriving at Aymare and by the end of the year, 171 men, women and children were registered at the address, as well as a reported 4 oxen, 20 cows, 53 sheep, 40 chickens and as many ducks.[27] There is no trace of local inhabitants' reactions towards the new arrivals in the French archives. But we do have an interesting anecdote about the libertarians' arrival from the memoir of a militant who lived at the property after the war and which continues to be recounted to this day by surviving libertarians.[28] A passage from the memoir entitled 'The End of Christ' recounts how refugees wasted no time in tearing down a three-metre effigy of Christ which stood at the property's boundary. According to the story the surrounding neighbours were critical of this act, but soon changed their opinions towards the new residents once the refugees began cultivating the land. It is not difficult to see the power of this story for libertarians. One of the first actions of the new arrivals was to affirm their libertarian identity through an outward display of anticlericalism. The libertarians then demonstrated their commitment to nature and hard work in order to achieve self-subsistence through mutual co-operation. Significantly, the story also conveys how the refugees were able to modify their French neighbours' perceptions through working the land.

The 'End of Christ' is a tale of initiative and aspiration that is entwined with libertarian symbolism and which portrays a determined and con-structive response to exile. It exists in the interstice between event and memory, telling us as much about what the property came to symbolise for some libertarians as to what happened on the refugees' arrival. There are no documents recounting how locals reacted to the disappearance of Christ's statue, but we do know that a good rapport between the libertar-ians and their French neighbours was rapidly achieved. Just months after the refugees arrived, one police official described relations between Aymare's inhabitants and the surrounding population in very positive terms. As well as doing a considerable amount of work on Aymare, the refugees had helped the surrounding neighbours with their harvest.[29] Many of the male refugees had the relevant experience of agricultural work, and the 17 from other backgrounds worked outside the co-operative and put their wages into a central fund.[30]

The co-operative's fortunes began to dip towards the end of the year as details of the refugees' background emerged. The MLE had bought the property under the cover of a couple of Marseilles-based industrialists acting as philanthropists: the official buyer of Aymare was Jean Roumil-hac, a textile industrialist,[31] while Félix Rambaud, also a company direc-tor, who had helped evacuate child refugees from Catalonia during *la retirada*, was registered as the head of the co-operative.[32] The Prefect was curious about the Marseilles industrialists' motivations and sought further information about their backgrounds and the refugees they were helping. Once he discovered the new residents were members of the CNT his initial enthusiasm for the project changed brusquely, and he asked the Minister of the Interior to block any more refugees with revolution-ary backgrounds from moving to the Lot.[33]

At the start of 1940, the Prefect limited the number of inhabitants at Aymare to 25 and dispersed the remainder around the *département*.[34] Aymare continued to exist, but it was a far cry from the original idea to create a series of agricultural co-operatives throughout France. But even if the Prefect had reacted otherwise, there were other obstacles. Federica Montseny suggested the wider project would have met with more success if the SERE had given the MLE the necessary finances and pursued the idea with the French authorities more vigorously.[35] Furthermore, by 1940 the French government had already implemented its own solution for putting refugees to work through its programme of paramilitary work companies.

The mass transformation of internees into workers

The FETT and MLE co-operative projects offered an alternative to internment and the possibility for refugees to work for themselves at no cost to the French state. The French government, however, chose to group Spanish republicans into paramilitary work companies or to use them individually to plug labour shortages in agriculture and industry. At the end of March, the Minister of the Interior asked prefects to establish a list of urgently needed public works. The legal framework for paramilitary work companies was then set out by the decree of 12 April 1939. The law applied to all stateless male persons between the ages of 20 and 48. They were henceforth subject to *prestations*: national-defence work for two years in peacetime; and the same obligations as French nationals in the event of war.[36]

The Ministry for National Defence and War ordered military commanders to create 53 companies at the end of April 1939, and a further 26 in mid-June.[37] These paramilitary work formations became known as the Foreign Labour Companies/Compagnies de Travailleurs Étrangers (CTE) and were used for defence-related projects such as fortifications, public-works programmes, and also to shore up labour shortages more generally. While the Labour Companies involved stateless persons from a range of nationalities (Members of the International Brigades were enrolled into the 251st and 252nd CTE), the vast majority of workers were Spanish refugees. This led the French authorities to refer interchangeably to Foreign Labour Companies (Compagnies de Travailleurs Étrangers) and Spanish Labour Companies (Compagnies de Travailleurs Espagnols). The CTE operated within a military context, with each company theoretically containing 250 men composed of 240 workers under the command of 10 French officers or non-commissioned officers.[38] There were no wages. Workers received a daily allowance of 50 centimes, together with a supplement for dangerous or hard labour. The rate could also be increased to 75 centimes in return for good conduct.

Not all the Spanish refugees worked in the CTE. In May, the Minister of Labour issued instructions for the employment of refugees in agricultural work instead of the habitual seasonal foreign workers. Moreover, the Minister stipulated that refugees' wages should be set according to the going rate for the profession in question.[39] It if appears as though personnel in the Ministry of Labour were attempting to secure favourable working conditions for the refugees, the Minister of the Interior's priority remained that of repatriation: employment was an interim solution.[40]

If they wanted to take up arms, Spanish republicans could also enlist in the French armed services. The April decree meant that refugees could now enrol in the French army during peacetime. Prior to this, their sole option had been the Foreign Legion. On 5 October 1939, further guidelines stipulated that refugees could join special foreign volunteer infantry regiments known as the Régiments de Marche de Volontaires Étrangers (RMVE). These regiments were linked to the Foreign Legion, but differed in command structure, personnel and length of service. Refugees could still sign up to for the Foreign Legion for a fixed duration of five years, but the RMVE enlistment lasted for the duration of the war. Nonetheless, prejudice against the Spanish refugees persisted. Unlike the Poles, Czechs and Slovakians, the Spanish republicans were not allowed to form units under the command of Spanish officers, which might explain their general lack of enthusiasm for the French army. By April 1940, there were only 6,000 in the ranks of the RMVE and the Legion, compared to 55,000 in the CTE and 40,000 (men and women) in agricultural and industrial work.[41]

The shift away from internment was accompanied by a change in administrative categorisations. The Ministry of Interior began classifying Spanish republicans employed in agriculture, and later in industry, as *étrangers ordinaires* or 'regular foreigners'. But this did not mean that refugee workers began to be treated in the same way as other immigrants in France. A May circular from the Ministry of the Interior contained a range of instructions aimed at monitoring and restricting the refugees. Local authorities had to report any absences from work, and in addition, a system of residence and work permits set temporal and spatial limits to the refugees' freedom of movement. For instance, agricultural workers were given provisional identification papers that were valid for three months, and which limited the range of jobs in which they could be employed as well as the particular *département* of residence. Any travel outside the designated *département* was forbidden without permission from the prefecture.

The category of 'regular foreigner' had nothing to do with rights. It merely signalled that the Spanish refugee in question was no longer dependent on state welfare. This was very much in line with the French administrative classificatory framework for refugees that had developed throughout the Third Republic. In daily practice, state officials frequently dealt with refugees within a paradigm of economic utility rather than human or social rights.

As had been the case with other refugee groups, the Spanish republicans' ability to remain free in France depended on employment: asylum went hand in hand with work rather than universal values. This was strikingly evident in ministerial guidelines about the status of asylum for the Spanish republicans. On 17 August 1939, prefects began listing Spanish refugees who wished to formally request asylum.[42] Two months later, the Ministry of the Interior asked prefects to ensure that those who had requested asylum were employed, and to transfer any refugees refusing offers of work to the border. Several months after the outbreak of war, the Ministry essentially wanted prefects to grant or force asylum status on refugees. Henceforth, all Spaniards applying for, or renewing a residence permit, had to provide a certificate of nationality or be classified as an asylum seeker, in which case he was subject to the CTE. It is possible that this was to avoid the problem of zealous local officials from forcing non-refugee Spanish immigrants into the Labour Companies.[43] Equally, if not more plausible, was the growing need for refugee labour. During the summer the government had recruited volunteers for the Labour Companies, but in December, military preparations for war entailed the creation of 40 new companies. This time around the workers were refugees with official asylum status and hence liable for enlistment in the CTE whether they liked it or not.[44]

Contrasting images: economic utility

The French declaration of war against Germany had profound and varied effects on refugees in France. For German anti-fascist refugees the consequences were disastrous, as the authorities set out interning all German migrants, anti-fascist or otherwise. Not only did this undermine asylum, it wasted a military and propaganda opportunity to mobilise some of the Third Reich's most vehement opponents. In contrast, France's transition to a war economy created a new context for a collective enterprise in which the Spanish refugees could participate. Representatives from several ministries had met at the Ministry of the Interior just before the declaration of war to discuss using Spanish refugees for the harvest in place of French workers called up for military service.[45] Issues regarding security were not entirely absent from the meeting, with concerns raised about the International Brigades and the continued surveillance of the Spanish refugees. But these were very much dominated by the subject of the refugees' role in alleviating France's labour needs.

The determination and initiative of one representative in particular was influential. Throughout the meeting, the director-general from the Ministry of Work, Alexandre Parodi, pushed for as favourable working conditions as possible.[46] He sought to prevent any further repatriation of the refugees, arguing that they represented an important source of labour. He also argued for refugees to receive proper wages as opposed to an allowance. Not all of his suggestions were immediately accepted. The Minister of the Interior's repatriation strategy remained practically unchanged, and Parodi's call for wages was rejected in favour of a daily indemnity of 5 francs. However, there was some progress, as this indemnity was used a benchmark, and in practice there was some leeway since the actual level varied according to the locality. The issue of local variance and individual recruitment was something Parodi wished to maintain.

The interest of individual, as opposed to collective, recruitment was that it could result in certain advantages for refugee workers. Giving employers some degree of freedom in setting indemnity levels could admittedly lead to exploitation. But it nonetheless enabled pro-refugee groups and individuals to find work for refugees with more promising conditions and an indemnity above the proposed flat-rate allowance. Parodi justified maintaining a more heterogeneous employment structure by once again stressing the importance of Spanish refugee labour to the French war economy.[47] Significant improvements for refugee workers followed with the decrees of 1 September and 6 November 1939. The decrees authorised prefects, military commanders and local representatives from the Ministry of Labour to set refugees' agricultural wages. As a guideline, this was based on 75 per cent of the national wage together with an additional payment of up to.50 centimes an hour for arduous working conditions and performance. For industrial workers, the decree of 10 November 1939 went further by setting salaries at the average national rate.[48]

Concessions went beyond questions of pay as ministers sought to encourage the loyalty and performance of Spanish workers. On 30 October, the Minister of the Interior encouraged prefects to permit workers and their families to be reunited. Beforehand, this had occurred but only according to strict criteria.[49] Parodi's views were reflected in a Ministry of Interior circular, dated 15 November 1939, in which Sarraut affirmed that he would henceforth allow Spanish workers' families to remain in France following advice from the Ministry of Labour. The circular also announced that relatives of CTE workers and soldiers of the RMVE could receive a family allowance.[50] In practice, much depended on the prefect's judgement, and in some cases, prefects would not agree to refugees' requests. In December 1939, Jean Moulin, the Prefect of the Eure-et-Loire and future resistance emissary of de Gaulle, refused requests, arguing that the refugees' wages were insufficient to support a family, and that the workers would be obliged to return to the internment camps from where they originated once the work contract ended.[51] The situation was additionally complicated for CTE workers based in remote areas, and also by the mobile nature of the Labour Companies. Once a particular project had been completed a CTE could be moved on to another locality.

Certain categories of Spanish republicans continued to be discriminated against. Women, children and elderly or disabled men who were all either unemployable or unrelated to Spanish refugees in work – in other words, those whose presence would not benefit the economy – faced repatriation. The costs of the reception centres continued to pre-occupy the Minister of the Interior. On 7 February 1940, he ordered prefects to repatriate: all children with relatives in Spain; orphans whose lives would not be at risk in Spain; women and children without a head of family in France; and lastly, the sick and disabled whose lives were not at risk in Spain (it was left to the prefect's initiative to ascertain this latter point). On the other hand, his instructions reiterated that those refugees entitled to stay in France could benefit from military family benefits and also reminded prefects of the advantages of family regroupings, using language redolent of Parodi's arguments from the 30 August meeting of the previous year. 'In the current circumstances this measure', Sarraut wrote, 'constitutes the best way of creating the stability of a workforce absolutely indispensable to the country's activity.'[52] Another sign of just how essential the Spanish republicans had become emerged before the month's end when Sarraut modified his previous instructions on repatriation. The implementation date for repatriations was rescheduled from March to May, and then to June. In the meantime the Prefect of the Gironde instructed local employers to recruit workers from Spanish women in the reception centres.[53] Then, in the month of May, the government ordered all Spanish refugee men, women, and children over the age of 14 who were suitable for manual work to be retained in France.[54]

Aid associations adapted to these changing conditions by seeking employment for women refugees. JARE representatives in Toulouse began trying to find work for the wives/partners of CTE workers.[55] While in the Gironde, the Comité National d'Aide aux Enfants Réfugiés and the Comité National Catholique de Secours aux Réfugiés d'Espagne liaised with the Ministry of Work. The Catholic association had created an agricultural school at Cadaujac capable of (re)training up to five hundred women and children.[56] The level of demand for Spanish agricultural workers was far from negligible, with the local labour office receiving around four hundred requests from farms in the surrounding area.[57]

Contrasting images: national security

Although officials had begun to perceive the Spanish republicans in terms of economic utility, a national security discourse continued to emanate from ministers, high-ranking officers and local officials. Much of the reason stemmed from the lingering and pejorative stereotypes from the Spanish Civil War rather than from the behaviour of the Spanish republicans. Even so, while the attitudes of many officials remained unchanged, the Spanish republicans' work effort led to a noticeable softening in the language of national government correspondence.

There was no shortage of will amongst Spanish republicans to work for French industry. Refugee representatives had raised the question as early as May 1939, and some internees had even taken the initiative of contacting local authorities directly with proposals for work.[58] Neither was there a shortage of experience, given that the Spanish republicans included a sizeable number of skilled workers from the industrially developed areas of Catalonia and the Basque country. However, the employment of the refugees in industry, and especially in the defence sector, had been a thorny subject. The refugees' case was not helped by the Nazi–Soviet Non-Aggression Pact of 23 August and the government's ensuing anti-communist witch-hunt. The Ministry of the Interior harboured suspicious that the Spanish refugees might be prone to acts of sabotage, and it was not until after the declaration of war that ministers gave the green light for employing them in defence-related factories.[59]

Not all factory owners and police officials were happy about the refugees working in sensitive factories. In the Hautes-Pyrénées, the Director of the Atelier de Construction de Tarbes had to be ordered by his superior to recruit refugees from the local camp at Gurs after he had tried to avoid the issue by citing regulations restricting the use of foreign workers.[60]

Even then he did his best to keep recruitment to a minimum, with some spurious comments:

> according to the Camp Commandant there can be no doubt that the Spanish militiamen currently in the camp, and who the French authorities have never been able to identify, have refused to go back to Spain because of a past of which they have every right to be worried about. *There can be no question of introducing these communist militants, who are also common criminals, into a centre such as l'Atelier de Construction de Tarbes* without the risk of contaminating the current and satisfactory workforce with ideas of dangerous sabotage, attacks, or even spying.[61]

There were similar signs of disquiet in the Bordeaux area. The Director of the gunpowder factory at Saint-Médard-en-Jalles, just outside Bordeaux, warned that the use of Spanish refugees risked causing profound discontent among the French workers. The CTE assigned to work in the factory were thus placed in barracks behind barbed wire and under armed guard.[62] Living conditions were better for Spanish workers in Bordeaux, but the city's police also had their suspicions. Theoretically, every potential worker was supposed to undergo a police check before leaving the concentration camp. However, the head of special police in Bordeaux had not been receiving the necessary reports from Septfonds camp. Moreover, he was alarmed that Spanish workers at a local aviation factory, the Société Nationale de Constructions Aéronautiques du Sud-Ouest, were living freely in the city's hotels.[63] Around the same time, the head of police in the other major urban centre of the south-west, Toulouse, argued that the Spanish refugees working in the local gunpowder factory and other establishments were a danger to national security.[64] David Pike suggests the official was reacting to Comintern instructions for workers in French defence factories to engage in go-slow tactics and even sabotage. Pike also refers to a Spanish Communist press report from Mexico which reported claims of sabotage in a Toulouse aluminium factory.

While it is difficult to ascertain levels of sabotage in French factories, we can emphasise the obsession among police services to identify and repress all forms of Communist activity following the Nazi–Soviet Pact. It is also important to distinguish between the claims of Spanish party leaders located outside the context of France and the practice of grassroots militants experiencing events in France. In the archives consulted for this study, there is no concrete evidence of Spanish workers being involved in such tactics. Moreover, even with the Nazi–Soviet Pact, it is difficult to believe that individuals forced into exile by Franco and his Axis allies would be readily prepared to hinder the production of materials aimed at defeating Nazi Germany. If Spanish workers were implicated in such activities at all, the number of people involved is likely to have been extremely small. In fact, refugees' life-history narratives tend to depict surprise and revulsion at French workers' adoption of go-slow tactics. Miguel Oviedo, a PCE militant, described his sense of incredulity when a French factory worker in Tarbes suggested that Miguel slowed down his work: he responded with a point-blank refusal.[65]

Officials also regarded the densely wooded *département* of the Landes as a sensitive location due to its timber stocks and the presence of military bases. At the end of 1939 and start of 1940, the Prefect of the Landes repeatedly warned the Minister of the Interior about concerns first raised by the head of a local paper-making firm by referring to the 'inconvenience and even the danger' of allowing Spanish refugees to work in the area. The Minister of Labour had already tried to reassure the Prefect in December by reiterating what he had told local officials across France just weeks beforehand: he was pleased with the Spanish refugees' work in both industry and agriculture. He also spelled out a wider issue at stake. The French government urgently needed to supply the British government with wood in exchange for anthracite and to achieve this 5,000–6,000 workers were needed. But the Prefect was, if nothing else, persistent, and raised objections throughout February and March 1940 about placing Spanish workers in the vicinity of firms working for the military.[66]

Suspicions about the refugees' backgrounds also affected the commanding officers of the Labour Companies. Despite recent advice to stop censoring workers' mail, the commander of the 150th CTE, based in the Landes south of Bordeaux, wished to maintain the procedure, given the absence of background information on the workers under his command.[67] Interestingly, he noted that the Spanish workers were generally well behaved. But where there had been tension, the commander interpreted events according to a pre-established framework of national security. Workers had staged several protests against working in bad weather and the quality of their food. The officer's remarks are revealing. As well as referring to the refugees as 'clearly of Communist tendency', he wrote:

> These demonstrations are undoubtedly not serious and can be suppressed quite easily with a little energy, but nonetheless prove that if our workers were to have too much freedom their ideas about independence would not fail to evolve.

> In short, and this is more serious in my opinion, there is without doubt
> some, perhaps even a large number – though as I've already said, we do
> not have the information – of people who would use their leave to go and
> propagate their extremist ideas to other refugees or even credulous French
> nationals.

The language deployed in the first paragraph resonates with the paternalism of military discourses. The rest of the quotation indicates that where details lacked, this official did not hesitate in conjuring up scenarios about the harmful influence the refugees could exercise on French nationals. The imagined threat appears to have been mobilised to give added weight to his initial argument for continuing with the postal surveillance, and also as justification for a range of restrictions: limiting visits to relatives, heightening surveillance and the suppression of all 2–5-day leave. These were not the isolated views of one officer. His superior also shared some of the concerns. Upon learning that workers of the 165th CTE in Captieux had been 'freely' visiting the administrative centre of the Landes, Mont-de-Marsan, he issued orders to prevent any further contact between the workers and local inhabitants.[68]

Even before the ban, the Landes offered the workers limited distraction with its sparsely populated and heavily wooded landscape. Refugees describe their experiences of working there in terms of isolation and boredom. Valeriano Espiga could not recall having had any contact whatsoever with the surrounding population.[69] For Ricardo Viscosillas the alienation was made even worse by not having access to either newspapers or radios.[70] For the refugees isolation engendered frustration and boredom, but for the officers in charge it was threatening. The Captain of the 138th CTE at Facture, close to where southern Gironde borders the Landes, requested a telephone line because his workers included 'a large enough proportion of anarchists'.[71]

These documents suggest that the officers' suspicions of the Spanish republicans in the Landes were fuelled by excessive military caution rather than fact. Severe restrictions on the workers' freedom of movement were imposed, even though there had been no incident involving a threat to public security.[72] Instead, the officers' anxieties were most likely grounded in the recent memory of the Spanish Civil War, and driven by the anti-communist sentiment which prevailed in France at this juncture. Several years earlier, clandestine networks of French officers had been created to eradicate communism from the French army and were undoubtedly motivated by the fear that war in Spain could be followed by a similar conflict in France.[73] There are also grounds to believe that the officers' concerns fed off memories of the 1917 mutinies. As during the First World War, the military authorities were cautious about contacts between military units and the home front.

Refugees' reactions

Spanish republicans had mixed reactions to working in France. For the internees it was foremost a means of regaining some freedom as well as a sense of esteem, even though the latter did not always follow the former. Miguel Oviedo's acute sense of anticipation and excitement about ending his 11-month period of internment is palpable in his diary entry for the day when he signed a contract for work in a Tarbes-based factory: 'I'm immensely happy because this time it's definite. I'm going to leave the barbed wire behind me. Until now, my only desire has been to know if we'll soon leave the camps.' His optimism immediately changed to despondency on learning he would not be working as a mechanic but with a pickaxe and shovel.[74]

A minority of refugees were fortunate to find employment which matched their skills. In Toulouse at least four medical specialists began working at the region's cancer unit based at the Hospice de la Grave. After the general mobilisation, the specialists were officially employed as assistants to Professor Ducuing with a monthly salary of 600 francs.[75] This was, however, exceptional. Although refugees from professional backgrounds and intellectuals could be theoretically exempted from manual work in the CTE, they were obliged, like the majority of refugees, to undertake whatever work they could find.[76] A loss of professional status or a complete change of employment was a common experience. This was as true for women as for men. For instance, out of fourteen women refugees in a reception centre at Libourne (near Bordeaux) considered for agricultural work, only two had any experience. The others originated from backgrounds in nursing, office work, tailoring, domestic service and factory work.[77]

In their desperation to leave the concentration camps, some Spanish republicans reinvented themselves according to job opportunities. Ramon Moral i Querol recalled how one internee artist disingenuously but energetically claimed he was from a farming family only for his suitcase to fall open revealing a set of drawings as he was being collected from the camp by his new farm employer.[78] José Berruezo, a militant who subsequently had a determining role in the reconstruction of the CNT during the Occupation, left Bram camp in December 1939 to work on a hydroelectric dam at l'Aigle in the Cantal. In his memoir he described the Spanish refugee workers with the words: 'everyone was specialist in something or other, for what mattered more than anything else was to regain freedom lost'.[79]

Working conditions, as we have already seen, varied widely. Accordingly Spanish republicans provide both negative and positive accounts of working. The CNT militant José Borras compared his job as a farm labourer with two different employers in the Loir-et-Cher. In his first job he slept in a barn and never received any wage, while in the second he had a bed, ate with his employers and received 400 francs a month.[80] Another CNT militant, Juan Giménez, had a more positive recollection about working for the Dewoitine aviation factory in Toulouse: his salary enabled him to dress well, and to rent a large room with his brother and a friend.[81] But even with a job, it was sometimes difficult to make ends meet. One group of refugee workers in Langon, *département* of the Gironde, received barely enough money to pay for their clothing needs.[82] Workers with families faced additional difficulties. Maria-Pilar Lang recounted how her father concealed his former career in education to be hired as a farmworker only to be forbidden to look his employers in the eyes when being addressed. She also remembered how her mother was forced to steal a chicken while the employer's family were at mass to feed her own family.[83]

There is also a recurring thread in refugees' recollections which likens their employment to slave labour. This is not limited to the Foreign Labour Companies, described by one refugee writer as an 'incarnation of modern slavery', but also to workers employed directly in agriculture and industry.[84] Francisco Pons gave an unflattering portrait of French farmers selecting workers from the mass of internees in his camp.[85] José Fortea similarly evoked an unsettling experience after getting off the train in Alès to go and work in the mines of the Gard. He depicted himself and the other refugees as 'merchandise' waiting to be shared out amongst the employers. The refugees left the station via the goods entrance before potential employers inspected the refugees' teeth and biceps.[86] Some employers in rural France, as well as Spain, did indeed use such debasing techniques to check the health and suitability of prospective manual workers.[87] Bearing in mind that many refugees came from urban areas, this practice would have appeared even more degrading and undoubtedly reinforced the refugees' self-perception as slave workers.

However, there was an additional factor driving this image. The brutal shock of internment, along with the insensitivity of transferring some refugee workers in cattle-train wagons, produced a matrix of discrimination and exclusion through which refugees internalised subsequent events. It could even make refugees suspicious of French food. Refugees' tales that are seemingly innocuous are often embedded within an overarching narrative of discrimination that is based on an interplay of memories of the past and interpretations of new experiences. 'A story of the Camembert' in Luis Bonet's memoir depicts CTE workers' mistrust when served the potent French cheese for the first time: 'Us Spaniards, the majority of whom had never seen this type of cheese and who were used to being very badly treated by the French administration, thought they had given it to us because it was filthy and rotten.'[88] The workers threw the cheese into a river. Similarly, Eduardo Bernad remembered his confusion as a child, when everything to him about the smell and consistency of the Camembert suggested it was rotten. In a previous incident, during a meal at a reception centre which took place just after the harrowing border crossing into France, he and his mother recoiled in horror when they were offered what they understood to be a slice of cat. The French word *gâteau*, cake, is similar in pronunciation to the Spanish word *gato*, cat.[89]

Despite the gradual introduction of a more liberal Spanish refugee labour policy from the spring of 1939, the overall picture was clouded by the loss of status experienced by most refugees, poor working conditions, the military discipline of the Labour Companies and, not least, by the instability resulting from a system of temporary work contracts with the threat of internment for those whose contracts were not renewed. Even with the improvements, the refugees were barred from the same employment rights as French nationals.

Spanish republicans had attempted to address some of these issues when the Foreign Labour Companies were initially created. On 10 June 1939, around 100 small posters appeared around Argelès camp calling for equality between Spanish and French workers.[90] The slogans were as revealing of the refugees' values as of their efforts to obtain better working conditions:

> We're workers and we want to work, but with the same rights and obligations as a French worker.
> We want to be of use to France but not treated like slaves.
> In the fight against fascism and for the defence of France we say 'Present'.
> In the Labour Companies we say 'Conditions'.
> Fellow refugees, by going to work without the same conditions as French workers we're dismissing the real character of our struggle.

We do not know anything about the people or organisation behind this poster campaign and therefore cannot say for certain if it was linked to political or syndical activities. Nor do the French documents contain many concrete details of political/syndical activities within the CTE. The reason may reflect the refugees' efforts to conceal their activities from the authorities, but more likely indicates a decrease in organisational activity as tens of thousands of refugees were relocated from the camps and dispersed across metropolitan France. Attempts were made to maintain political and syndical cohesion. One group of Socialists in Barcarès camp managed to be incorporated into the same Labour Company.[91] The MLE General Council advised militants to remain together within the CTE and obtain positions of responsibility.[92] There was a thus certain degree of continuity as small numbers of refugees grouped around their respective political/syndical affinities, but their activities were mainly limited to maintaining contact with their respective organisations. All the same, the refugees undoubtedly drew on their political and syndical experience when reacting to poor working conditions. As with the 150th CTE in the Landes, some refugees collectively organised work stoppages. Elsewhere, workers elected delegates to represent their interests. In the Alps, Luis de Lafuente López was interned for relaying complaints about the tented accommodation to the unit's commander. In the Aude, a similar tactic seems to have succeeded in improving the quality of food for workers in the 44th CTE.[93]

As the examples suggest, the precise modalities of work in the Foreign Labour Companies varied between *départements*, and further research is needed in this respect. It may well be that CTEs based in sensitive areas of France, and notably in the north-eastern part of the country, were subject to greater restrictions. The military certainly appear to have experienced more problems with Labour Companies located in the north-east and Alpine regions. Some refugees had asked to be repatriated only to change their mind on arrival at the border with Spain, while others simply escaped. One worker left his unit in the Moselle, returned to Septfonds camp and enrolled in the 218th CTE stationed at Saint-Médard-en-Jalles, close to Bordeaux. He refused to return to the Moselle and was interned in Vernet camp.[94]

Proximity to where hostilities were expected to erupt undoubtedly explains some of the workers' motivations for escaping from the north-eastern and Alpine regions. In the rest of France the most widespread reason for escaping, or in the French military's terminology, 'deserting', stemmed from the dual system of labour created by the French authorities. Free workers could earn higher wages and enjoy greater freedom of movement, better accommodation and the possibility of being closer to families. The authorities were well aware of the contradictions. The Ministry of Defence instructed regional military commanders to try and prevent CTE workers from being stationed at sites where Spanish 'free workers' were present. Differences in pay were clearly flagrant. At an armaments factory in Miramas, *département* of the Bouches-du-Rhône, workers in the 129th CTE earned 10 francs a day while Spanish refugees working for a nearby French company received 6 francs an hour.[95] In March 1940, local officials tried a carrot-and-stick approach by underlining how CTE workers received the same rates of pay, allowances, accommodation and leave as French military personnel, while also drawing attention to the obligations of *prestations*.[96] Recalcitrant workers faced repatriation as well as internment.[97]

Even the so-called 'free' workers faced internment if they broke the terms of their work contract. On 28 March 1940, three Spanish refugees employed by a forestry works at Saint-Jean-d'Illac in the Gironde were reported absent from work and subsequently found working for another company. They had quit after hearing it was easy to find better-paid factory work in Bordeaux.[98] The problem for the original firm seriously escalated. Two months later another 40 refugees disappeared. The police managed to find seven (they had become metalworkers for Motobloq in Bordeaux) and arrested two others, but could not find any trace of the remaining missing workers.[99]

The mass recruitment of Spanish republicans did not end the marginality and liminality of exile, but it did open up opportunities, albeit limited, for them to improve material circumstances, gain some freedom and to experience some degree of incorporation into French society. At the very least, departure from the concentration camps meant a qualitative improvement in an individual's living standards. By the end of 1939, the government began considering the refugees as a more lasting, though not permanent, presence in France. It is no coincidence that this occurred as the French government prepared the country for war and urgently needed to fill the places left in agriculture and industry by general mobilisation.

The context of war produced new possibilities for other migrants in France, especially those seeking to become French. The rate of naturalisations in 1939 was much higher than the previous year as the government sought to increase troop numbers.[100] For the Spanish republicans there were several opportunities: first, an acceleration in the rate of employment; the government also widened the categories of refugees authorised to remain and work in France; and thirdly, the government introduced improvements to refugees' working conditions as their role in the war economy became increasingly apparent.

While war with Germany created the context for a collective enterprise in France, and one which drew its strength from the participation of nationals and immigrants alike, it also stymied the viability of alternative projects such as the co-operative of Aymare. The diversity of refugees' experiences renders generalisation of this period a difficult task. The military ensured that a significant number of CTE workers were kept away from local populations. Refugees working directly for French employers were sometimes exploited. Moreover the threat of internment or expulsion was never far away. But it is also true that some workers began to earn comparable wages to their French counterparts. The appearance of a discourse within government that emphasised the Spanish republicans in terms of potential, as opposed to a threat, was a notable change. It did not herald a return to the more widely positive images of Spanish immigrants that had circulated France in the 1920s, but instead signalled a partial, though limited, depoliticisation of the Spanish republicans. Mass employment thus changed the dynamics of the Spanish republican exile. It also produced some surprising precedents for work practices and refugees' strategies during the dark years of Vichy and Occupied France.

Notes

1 AD Gironde, 1M 599. Commissaire Spécial to Préfet 15 April 1931. AD Gironde, 1M 601. Commissaire Divisionnaire de Police Spéciale to Préfet, 28 June 1937.

2 G. Hermet, *Les Espagnols en France: Immigration et Culture* (Paris, 1967), p. 104. For a useful overview of Spanish immigration in France see B. Vargas and D. Debord, *Les Espagnols en France. Une vie au-delà des Pyrénées* (Toulouse, 2010). For relations between Spanish women economic migrants and Spanish women exiles in France see the interesting article by A. Mira Abad and M. Moreno Seco, 'Españolas exiliadas y emigrantes: encuentros y desencuentros en Francia', *Les Cahiers de Framespa*, 5 (2010).

3 V. Caron, *Uneasy Asylum: France and the Jewish Refugee Crisis, 1933–1942* (Stanford, CA, 1999), p. 4.

4 P. Laborie, *L'Opinion française sous Vichy: Les Français et la crise d'identité nationale 1936–1944* (Paris, 2nd edn, 2001), p. 136.

5 Caron, *Uneasy Asylum*; M. D. Lewis, *The Boundaries of the Republic: Migrant Rights and the Limits of Universalism in France, 1918–1940* (Stanford, CA, 2007); and D. Peschanski, *La France des camps. L'internement 1938–1946* (Paris, 2002).

6 For further details: G. Dreyfus-Armand, *L'Exil des Républicains Espagnols en France: De la Guerre Civile à la Mort de Franco* (Paris, 1999), p. 72.

7 AD Pyrénées-Orientales, 31W 274. Préfet to Ministère de l'Intérieur, ref. P.A. no. 6816/5, and P.A. 6584/1, 28 June 1939.

8 AGA, Caja 11287 06A. Circular no. 13, General Council of the MLE, 25 April 1939.

9 CIRAS, Libro no. 1, Gestión MLE-CNT en Francia. Letter to Los Compañeros de Londres from Grunfeld, 4 May 1939.

10 AD Gironde, 4M 528. Le Commissaire chef de la Sûreté to Commissaire de Police, 31 March 1939.

11 AGA, IDD no. 97 Embajada de España en París 1939–71, Caja 11287 06. Circular 4, 12 March 1939, and Circular 5, 13 March 1939.

12 D. W. Pike, *Vae Victis! Los republicanos españoles refugiados en Francia 1939–1944* (Paris, 1969), pp. 58–9, 89–90; Caron, *Uneasy Asylum*, p. 86.

13 Pike, *Vae Victis!*, p. 90.

14 Peschanski, *La France des camps*, pp. 67–8.

15 J.-L. Crémieux-Brilhac, 'L'engagement militaire des Italiens et des Espagnols dans les armées françaises de 1939 à 1945', in P. Milza and D. Peschanski (eds), *Exils et Migration: Italiens et Espagnols en France 1938–1946* (Paris, 1994), p. 583.

16 FO 371/24156: Spanish Refugees in France.

17 Caron, *Uneasy Asylum*, p. 223.

18 Crémieux-Brilhac, 'L'engagement militaire des Italiens et des Espagnols dans les armées françaises de 1939 à 1945', p. 583.

19 For a detailed account of this plan see Caron, *Uneasy Asylum*, pp. 164–5. For details of Mauco's attitudes towards foreigners see K. Adler, *Jews and Gender in Liberation France* (Oxford, 2003), pp. 113–19.

20 J. L. Martín Ramos, *Rojos contra Franco: Historia del PSUC, 1939–1947* (Barcelona, 2002), pp. 51–2. AD Pyrénées-Orientales, 31W 274. Sous-Préfet de Prades to the Préfet des Pyrénées-Orientales, 15 December 1939.

21 AD Dordogne, 4M 167. *El Obrero de la Tierra: Bolletín de los campesinos españoles refugiados*, Circular 1, 1 July 1939.

22 See L. Teulières, *Immigrés d'Italie et paysans de France 1920–1944* (Toulouse, 2002), pp. 120–45 and M. Minardi, 'Les travailleurs des coopératives de la région de Parme à Toulouse. Des parcours individuels au destin d'une communauté', in Milza and Peschanski (eds), *Exils et Migration*, pp. 465–76.

23 On the subject of collectivisation and social revolution in Spain there is a brief historiography at the start of M. Seidman, 'Agrarian Collectives during the Spanish Revolution and Civil War', *European History Quarterly* 30:2

(2000), p. 209. See also H. Graham, *The Spanish Republic at War 1936–1939* (Cambridge, 2002), pp. 100–4, 230–3, 325–7, 353–4 and P. Preston, *A Concise History of the Spanish Civil War* (London, 1996), pp. 175–8.

24 AN CARAN, F7 14736. MLE Circular, 25 May 1939.

25 Berthon later helped the CNT representative Federica Montseny and her family to reach the Unoccupied Zone early on in the Occupation. F. Montseny, *Mis primeros cuarenta años* (Barcelona, 1987), pp. 191–213.

26 AD Lot, 4M 115. Instructions to Maires, 29 June 1939.

27 AN CARAN, F7 14736. Report, 'Coopérative d'Aymare, commune de VIGAN, Lot', 15 January 1940. AD Lot, 4M 115. Directeur Général de la Sûreté nationale to Préfecture, 19 September 1939.

28 J. Vergara, *Aymare: 1947–1963 (Colonia de los mutilados y ancianos de la revolución española del 1936 a 1939)* (La Rochelle, 1994), p. 9.

29 AD Lot, 4M 115. Report Directeur Général de la Sûreté nationale to Préfecture, 19 September 1939.

30 AN CARAN, F7 14736. Report, 15 January 1940.

31 Roumilhac became involved with anarchism as a porcelain worker in Limoges and then developed links with Spanish anarcho-syndicalists on business trips to Spain during the inter-war period.

32 AD Lot, 4M 115. Préfet to the Ministre de l'Intérieur, 15 November 1939, and intercepted letter from A. Berthon to Rambaud, 3 January 1940.

33 AD Lot, 4M 115. Préfet to Ministre de l'Intérieur, 15 November 1939, and 23 January 1940.

34 AD Lot, 4M 115. Instructions, 26 January 1940.

35 F. Montseny, *El Éxodo: Pasión y muerte de españoles en el exilio* (Barcelona, 1977), p. 83.

36 Caron, *Uneasy Asylum*, p. 224. Dreyfus-Armand, *L'Exil des Républicains Espagnols en France*, p. 104.

37 AN SHAT, 34N 375. Report, 20 April 1939 and 13 June 1939.

38 AN SHAT, 34N 375. Report ref. 1790 3/EAM-P, 20 April 1939. The 240 workers were supposed to be composed of 10 metalworkers, 10 carpenters, 10 stonemasons, 200 construction workers, 1 secretary/interpreter, 1 clerical assistant, 2 tailors, 2 cobblers and 3 cooks.

39 AD Landes, 4M 311. Ministre du Travail to Directeurs des Offices Départementaux de Placement, 25 May 1939.

40 Circular of 5 May 1939. Cited in J. Rubio, *La emigración de la guerra civil de 1936–1939*, Vol. 3 (Madrid, 1977), p. 859.

41 AN SHAT, 7N 2475/3.

42 AD Gironde, 4M 504. Circular, 17 August 1939.

43 AGA, Caja 11767. Letter from the Spanish Consulate in Hendaye concerning complaints by Spanish residents in Pau about being pressurised to become *prestataires*, 2 February 1940. Spanish Francoist Ambassador to France, José F. Lequerica to Consulate in Hendaye, 11 April 1940.

44 AN SHAT, 34N 375.
45 AN Fontainebleau, 19940500/138. M. Berthoin, Secrétaire Général du Minis-
    tère de l'Intérieur; M. Bussière, Directeur Général de la Sûreté Nationale; M.
    Combes, Directeur de la Police du Territoire et des Étrangers à la Sûreté
    Nationale; Général Menard, chargé de la coordination des camps de réfugiés;
    M. Parodi, Directeur Général au Ministère du Travail; M. Pages, Chef du
    Service de la main-d'œuvre étrangère au Ministère du Travail; M. Branchet,
    Directeur au Ministère de l'Agriculture.
46 Parodi's commitment to social rights is further substantiated by his attempts
    to maintain the State's commitment to asylum at the start of the Vichy
    regime. See P. Weil, 'Racisme et discrimination dans la politique française de
    l'immigration 1938–45/1974–95', *Vingtième Siècle: Revue d'Histoire*, 47 (1995),
    p. 82.
47 AN Fontainebleau. 19940500/138. Directeur Général du Travail et de la Main
    d'œuvre to Ministre de l'Intérieur, 15 September 1939. In April 1940, Parodi
    once again intervened using the same argument to prevent the families of
    Spanish workers in Toulouse from being repatriated. AN Fontainebleau,
    19940500/150. Directeur Général du Travail et de la Main d'œuvre to Secré-
    taire Général du Ministère de l'Intérieur, 3 April 1940.
48 In the case of semi-skilled workers, an additional performance-related
    payment of 75 centimes could be awarded. For skilled aviation workers this
    was set at 1.50 francs an hour. The maximum daily payment for miners was
    established at 15 francs. AN SHAT, 34N 375. Instruction sur l'organisation et
    l'utilisation des travailleurs étrangers (prestataires) en temps de guerre, 15
    May 1940.
49 AD Gironde, 4M 526. Ministère de l'Intérieur to Préfets, 30 October 1939.
50 AN Fontainebleau, 19940500/138. Circular, Ministre de l'Intérieur to Préfets,
    15 November 1939. The military allowances were set by the decrees of 1 Sep-
    tember and 6 November 1939.
51 É. Temime, 'Espagnols et Italiens en France', in Milza and Peschanski (eds),
    Exils et Migration, p. 26.
52 AN Fontainebleau, 199405001/138. Ministre de l'Intérieur, 7 February 1940.
53 AD Gironde, 4M 529. Préfet to Sous-Préfets and Maires of the Gironde, 10
    March 1940.
54 Dreyfus-Armand, *L'Exil des Républicains Espagnols en France*, p. 109.
55 AN Fontainebleau, 34N 375.
56 AD Gironde, 4M 515. Letter from the Comité National Catholique de Secours
    aux Réfugiés d'Espagne, 16 May 1940.
57 AD Gironde, 4M 515. Ministre du Travail to Préfet de la Gironde, 13 May
    1940.
58 AD Bouches-du-Rhône 4M 962. Letter from seven Spanish refugees in the
    Agde camp with experience of munitions work in Spain to the Maire of
    Marseilles requesting work in national defence factories, 7 April 1939.

59 Dreyfus-Armand, *L'Exil des Républicains Espagnols en France*, pp. 111–12. C. Laharie, *Le Camp de Gurs, 1939–45: Un aspect méconnu de l'histoire du Béarn* (Biarritz, 1993), pp. 116–17. M. L. Garde Etayo, 'El Primer Exilio del Sindicalismo Vasco: ELA/STV, 1936–1946', in *Españoles en Francia 1936–1946. Coloquio Internacional Salamanca, 2, 3 y 4 de mayo 1991* (Salamanca, 1991), p. 207. For Catalan refugees see Pike, *Vae Victis!*, p. 90.

60 A relatively high number of Basques did go on to work in the Tarbes factories and numbered 1,000 at the end of November. AD Haute-Garonne, 1960W 64. Commissaire Divisionnaire de la Police Spéciale to Colonel Commandant le BCR État-Major 17ème Région, 21 November 1939.

61 Emphasis in the original. AN SHAT, 31N 135. Directeur de l'Atelier de Construction de Tarbes to Ministre de l'Armement, 13 October 1939.

62 *Ibid.* Général Chauvin to Ministre de la Défense Nationale et de la Guerre, 8 November 1939.

63 AD Gironde, 4M 524. Commissaire Divisionnaire de Police Spéciale to Préfet, 20 December 1939.

64 D. W. Pike, *In the Service of Stalin: The Spanish Communists in Exile, 1939–1945* (Oxford, 1993), p. 27. Laffitte refers to an incident that occurred during the same month. At the Dewoitine factories refugees threatened to stop work unless their families were transferred to Toulouse. G. Laffitte, 'L'encadrement par le travail des étrangers dans le département du Gers 1939–1944: au cœur du dipositif GTE' (Mémoire de maîtrise: Université de Toulouse-Le Mirail, 2003), p. 24.

65 Interview with Miguel Oviedo, Fargues-Saint-Hilaire, 8 October 2002.

66 AN Landes, 4M 338. Main d'œuvre, demandes de travail forestier, 1939–40.

67 AN SHAT, 31N 135. Report, Chef de Bataillon, IV/182.

68 AN SHAT, 34N 378. Colonel Rogier to Lieutenant, Commandant le Détachement de Garde de la 165ème Compagnie de Travailleurs Espagnols, 27 January 1940.

69 Interview with Valeriano Espiga, Fargues-Saint-Hilaire, 21 May 2002.

70 Montseny, *El Éxodo*, p. 84.

71 AN SHAT, 34N 378.

72 The densely wooded Landes was admittedly a sensitive area of France with its important supply of wood. Any outbreak of fire would be potentially catastrophic. Nonetheless, this danger was not evoked in the officers' correspondence.

73 For further details of French military reactions to the war in Spain see T. Vivier, 'L'attitude des militaires français vis-à-vis de la guerre d'Espagne (1936–1939)', in M. Papy (ed.), *Les Espagnols et la Guerre Civile* (Biarritz, 1999).

74 Unpublished diary of Miguel Oviedo. The image of 'un pico y una pala' often appears in refugees' depictions of manual work in France.

75 AD Haute-Garonne, 1960W 66. Dossier: 'Associations de secours aux réfugiés espagnols – SERE/JARE'.

76 Guidelines exempting intellectuals from manual labour in the CTE were issued in May 1940. AN SHAT, 34N 375. Instruction sur l'organisation et l'utilisation des travailleurs étrangers (prestataires) en temps de guerre. Article 38, 13 May 1940.

77 AD Gironde, 4M 517. Fiches d'orientation, March 1940.

78 R. Moral i Querol, Journal d'exil (1939–1945) (Paris, 1982), pp. 98–9.

79 J. Berruezo, Contribución de la historia de la CNT de España en el exilio (Mexico City, 1967), p. 21.

80 J. Borrás, Del Radical-Socialismo al Socialismo Radical y Libertario: Memorias de un Libertario (Madrid, 1998), pp. 92–3.

81 J. Giménez Arenas, De la Unión a Banat: Itinerario de una rebeldía (Madrid, 1996), pp. 86–7.

82 AD Gironde, 4M 529. Sous-Préfet de Langon to Préfet, 11 March 1940.

83 Interview with Maria-Pilar Lang, Villeneuve-sur-Lot, 27 September 2002.

84 G. Dreyfus-Armand and É. Temime, Les Camps sur la plage, un exil espagnol (Paris, 1995), pp. 110–12.

85 F. Pons, Barbelés à Argelès et autour d'autres camps (Paris, 1993), pp. 65–6.

86 J. Fortea García, Tiempo de história: no hay más cera que la que arde (Badalona, 2002).

87 Dreyfus-Armand and Temime, Les Camps sur la plage, p. 112.

88 L. Bonet Lopez, Mémoires d'exil d'un Espagnol (Paris, 2002), p. 53.

89 Interview with Eduardo Bernad, Bordeaux, 27 June 2002.

90 AD Pyrénées-Orientales, 31W 274. Préfet to Ministre de l'Intérieur, 16 June 1939.

91 C. Martínez Cobo and J. Martínez Cobo, La Primera Renovación: Intrahistoria del PSOE Volumen 1 (1939–1945) (Barcelona, 1989), p. 74.

92 Circular 25 of the MLE, August 1939. Reproduced in Rubio, La emigración de la guerra civil de 1936–1939, Vol. 3, pp. 889–92.

93 L. Montagut, J'étais deuxième classe dans l'armée républicaine espagnole (1936–1945) (Paris, 2003), pp. 154–61.

94 AN SHAT, 34N 377. On 28 February 1940, the Ministry of Defence issued secret orders for commanders to intern all 'deserters' in the camp of Vernet.

95 AD Bouches-du-Rhône, 99W 78. Sous-Préfet d'Aix-en-Provence to Préfet, 23 May 1940.

96 AN SHAT, 34N 375. Ministère de la Défense Nationale et de la Guerre, 29 March 1940.

97 Ibid. Président du conseil, Ministre de la Défense et de la Guerre and the Ministre de l'Intérieur to Généraux Commandant de Régions, 19 March 1940.

98 AD Gironde, 4M 524. Commissaire Divisionnaire to Préfet, 2 April 1940.

99 Ibid. Préfet to Ministère de Travail, 4 May 1940.

100 Caron, Uneasy Asylum, p. 256.

5

Work, surveillance, refusal and revolt in
Vichy and German-occupied France,
1940–44

> The presence of the foreign labour force in our country poses an acute
> problem. Throughout the ages France has honoured itself as a welcoming
> land. One of the signs of its decadence, however, consisted of leaving the
> country's borders wide open for the ever pressing flood of foreigners.[1]

In August 1940, one of the largest newspapers in south-western France,
La Petite Gironde, greeted the agreement between the Vichy regime and
the Mexican government on the re-emigration of Spanish republicans to
Mexico with a mixture of relief and animosity. The article was written
barely three months after the defeat of France and the armistice which
divided the country into two zones: the Occupied Zone covering the
Atlantic coast and the northern half of the country; and the Unoccupied
or Southern Zone that was governed by Marshal Pétain's Vichy regime,
so called because it was based in the spa town of the same name. The
paper made no reference to the Spanish republicans' role in the defence
of France but rather associated them with unemployment, the so-called
decadence of the Third Republic and, by implication, the country's
defeat. All national identities engender introspection, but in this case, the
exclusion of refugees was elevated to the status of an ideological impera-
tive as part of Vichy's quest to redefine the nation and recast politics and
society through the National Revolution.

The repression of immigrants became a hallmark of Vichy's record
and has understandably attracted a good deal of historical attention. A
less widely known aspect of this history concerns how the Vichy and
German Occupying authorities' strategies for dealing with refugees

oscillated between exclusion and dependence. Given that the French countryside and peasantry were quintessential themes of the National Revolution, it is ironic that French officials came to associate Spanish refugees with the well-being of rural *départements* in south-western France. In the Occupied Zone the German Occupiers also staged a volte-face, replacing an initial inclination to rid the territory of Spanish republicans with an increasing need to use them for the construction of the Atlantic wall. The factors behind these changing attitudes and the accompanying implications for the Spanish republicans constitute the thrust of this chapter.

The Spanish refugees were a valuable workforce. They were a mobile and already displaced group of workers who the authorities would deploy, if not at will, then with great flexibility. However, even though the refugees became of great interest to the Vichy government and the German Occupying authorities, their use as a labour force was initially far from inevitable and the path was strewn with difficulties. There lay the challenges of deploying refugee workers in a xenophobic climate, the administrative complexities of their utilisation, and the fact that the Vichy authorities' labour needs gave refugees a certain degree of agency and bargaining power. This latter point is significant for it points towards an aspect of the Occupation that has yet to be fully explored.

The reason for this oversight is understandable, given the harrowing plight of refugees during the 'dark years' of the Occupation: unemployment carried the risk of internment; and to make matters worse, there was the threat of repatriation to Spain or of being sucked into the maelstrom of deportation and the German death camps. As harrowing as these fates were, they should not obscure the possibilities generated by a combination of the serious labour shortage and the contradictions in refugee work schemes across France. Refugee workers exploited differences between Vichy and German labour strategies while also realising that their workplaces could be nurseries for forging mutual interests between themselves and French nationals conducive for organising resistance. The workplace thus became the armature of the refugees' relationships with the Vichy regime and the German Occupying authorities. The official records enable us to reconstitute the range of constraints but also the opportunities which resulted.

The first half of this chapter sets out Vichy and German strategies for the Spanish republicans. I draw some parallels between the Third Republic and Vichy's use of mass foreign labour. As had been the case under the Third Republic, attempts to maintain the Spanish refugees on the margins of daily life in Vichy France through the use of paramilitary labour formations were compromised by a combination of the country's labour requirements and the employers' appreciation of their workers. The Janus-faced image of the Spanish republicans as a source of both economic potential and political instability also continued into the Occupation. Officials responsible for Vichy's Foreign Labour Groups (GTE) echoed Parodi in his interventions for the CTE – the subject of which was addressed in the previous chapter – when they presented pragmatic economic reasons for ameliorating refugees' working conditions. The refusal of some refugees to submit passively to poor working conditions nonetheless illustrates the limits to these officials' endeavours as well as a point of continuity concerning refugees' reactions to the paramilitary labour formations. Staging protests represented one refugee response; a second and increasingly more common form of refusal consisted of disappearing from work. While this had blighted CTE commanders, this time around, the presence of the German military in France produced an entirely different context. As a result of competition for Spanish refugee labour, the German military authorities and Vichy government became dialectically involved in the phenomenon of escaping refugees through a contradictory approach to foreign labour.

Given the crucial Nazi support for the nationalist cause during the Spanish Civil War, the Germans' use of Spanish republicans in the paramilitary Organisation Todt (OT) in Occupied France was bound to produce all sorts of frictions. The organisation took its name from Fritz Todt, who was originally the chief inspector for the maintenance and development of German highways in 1933. It was officially created in 1938, following Todt's involvement in constructing fortifications in West Germany, and developed into an essential service specialising in the provision of infrastructure and fortifications for the Wehrmacht in occupied territories and Germany. By 1943 the OT organisation controlled a million workers, the majority of whom were requisitioned or recruited throughout Occupied Europe.[2] In France, the German military relied heavily on Spanish republicans for the construction of the Atlantic coastal defences and submarine bases and for manpower in various German-controlled industries. In other areas of Occupied Europe, OT workers endured atrocious conditions.[3] What is not so widely known is that in south-western France the OT could offer certain, though limited, advantages over working in Vichy's Labour Groups. This appears to be particularly true of the situation in Bordeaux, where work patterns interacted with a unique blend of factors.

Working for the OT invariably evoked questions of collaboration, and yet the evidence suggests that resistance activities occurred. Even so, the complexity of relations between, on the one hand, the Spanish republicans and, on the other, the German and (to a lesser extent) French authorities cannot be understood simply in terms of the polarities of resistance and collaboration.[4] Instead, this chapter suggests that the experiences of the Spanish OT workers in Bordeaux unfolded within an indeterminate space that resonates with Primo Levi's notion of the 'grey zone'.[5] I highlight this comparison without wanting to overstate it, given the significant distance – both literally and conceptually – separating Levi's focus and that of this analysis. Nonetheless, if the categories of perpetrator/victim cannot account for the complexity of the system which Levi so poignantly analysed, the same applies to the collaborator/resister couplet and the specificities of having to work for the German military economy in the Gironde.

The second half of the chapter explores the dynamics of escape and subversion of Spanish workers on both sides of the demarcation line. Many of the escapes were driven through the desire, if not need, to improve living standards, or to avoid working for the German authorities. While the sheer volume of escapees ultimately undermined labour policy in France, the workers' refusal was driven by personal circumstances rather than an explicit intent to undermine the system. As such, this chapter argues for a distinction to be made between refusal and revolt. The number of refugees involved in refusal outnumbered those who resisted. But this should not divert attention from a highly significant minority whose resistance activities in Vichy France were facilitated by the very institution designed to minimise their influence in French society. The emphasis on both refusal and revolt demonstrates just how central Vichy's Labour Groups had become to the existence of rural *départements* of south-western France, and just how central the Labour Groups became to the existence and aims of Spanish resisters.

Asylum, Vichy and the Spanish refugees

Ministers of the Third Republic, and especially the Minister of the Interior, had already sullied the ideal of political asylum by linking it to paramilitary labour service and by pressurising refugees to return to Spain. Progress for the Spanish refugees had not been completely absent. The government had, after all, implemented measures to improve the refugees' material and familial circumstances. Vichy's replacement of the

'French Republic' with the 'French State' signalled a reversal of these gains, together with a certain negation of the status and responsibilities of asylum.

For the Spanish republicans, the first blow to asylum came very shortly after the end of hostilities, when German forces deported around 6,000 captured Spaniards from the CTE and RMVE. Less than a third of these men returned to France in 1945 after internment in the German concentration camp of Mauthausen.[6] In another incident several hundred refugees were deported from Angoulême, *département* of the Charente, in August 1940. The Germans sent the men to Mauthausen but returned the women and children from Germany to be repatriated to Spain.[7] A couple of months later, the German military issued orders for 'red Spaniards' to be sent to Germany from the Bordeaux area.[8] Although the Prefecture's archives show that the French authorities responded by collating statistics of Spanish republicans living in the vicinity, there is no indication as to whether the convoy went ahead.[9]

Could the Vichy administration have prevented the deportations of Spanish republicans? Admittedly, these incidents took place in Occupied France. However, the French state had formerly granted asylum, and hence protection, to the Spanish republicans. This point is all the more poignant if we consider that a government, albeit of the Third Republic, had not only linked asylum to service in the CTE and RMVE, but had also insisted that the refugee workers/soldiers were subject to equal conditions as French servicemen. And yet, Vichy made no effort with the German authorities for the Spanish republicans to be recognised as part of the French military, and hence subject to the same treatment as French prisoners of war in accordance with international law.

There is no doubting Vichy's desire to see the back of the Spanish refugees, hence the regime's interest in repatriation to Spain and re-emigration to Mexico.[10] However, neither strategy was particularly successful. The Francoist authorities were against the mass return of the Spanish republicans, and consequently there were only 20,000 returnees from metropolitan France and French-controlled North Africa for the entire Occupation period. However, the Spanish dictatorship was keen on extraditing key Spanish republican figures. Before dawn on 10 July, German agents, a police commissary from nationalist Spain and a representative of the Falange (Spain's Fascist organisation) raided a house named 'Villa Eden' in the Arcachon bay resort of Pyla-sur-Mer. They were hunting down the ailing and former President of the Second Spanish Republic, Manuel Azaña, but he was not there, having already left for the

Dordogne a month earlier.[11] Instead, the authorities arrested Azaña's brother-in-law, the playwright Cipriano de Rivas Chérif.[12]

Franco's regime displayed vindictive determination in tracking down and requesting the extradition of leading Spanish republican figures. Franco's Ministry for Foreign Affairs approached the German armistice commission to pressurise Vichy into slowing and preventing the refugees' re-emigration to Mexico. The effects of war on the availability and cost of maritime cross-Atlantic shipping meant that formidable hurdles already existed for refugees wishing to travel to Mexico. An already dire situation was thus further compounded. Between the signing of the Mexican–French accords and the rupture in diplomatic relations between these two countries in November 1942, just 5,900 refugees were able to leave France.[13]

One of the persons who Vichy barred from leaving the country was Julián Zugazagoitia, a former Minister of the Interior and leading member of the PSOE. German officials handed him over to the Francoist authorities following an extradition request. He faced the same fate as Lluís Companys, the former President of Catalonia; Joan Peiró Bellis of the CNT, who had been Minister for Industry in Largo Caballero's Cabinet; and Francisco Cruz Salido, who had worked at the Ministry of Defence: all were executed. Vichy officials also agreed to other extradition requests, but refused to authorise the majority of the several thousand people demanded by Franco's regime.[14] Thus while the Vichy regime did not completely abandon asylum for the Spanish refugees, the protection it was supposed to afford was extremely tenuous, to say the very least.

Vichy's Foreign Labour Groups, 1940–41

Vichy's slogan – '*Travail, Famille, Patrie*' – reflected the centrality of work to the new regime's preoccupations. And soon enough, policy makers began shaping the workplace along the anti-Semitic and xenophobic ideals of the envisaged new order. At the same time as legislators set out excluding Jews from French public life through the laws of August and October 1940, they sought to exploit Spanish refugee labour without compromising the French labour market. Their answer lay in the creation of the Foreign Labour Groups (GTE).[15] The law of 27 September stipulated that all stateless persons between the ages of 18 and 55, and surplus to the French economy, should be grouped into Foreign Labour Groups for an unlimited duration.[16] Conditions were basic with workers receiving board, lodging and a daily allowance of 10 francs.

The GTE were initially organised into five administrative regions, or *Groupements*, with headquarters in the cities of Clermont-Ferrand (*Groupement* 1), Toulouse (*Groupement* 2), Montpellier (*Groupement* 3), Marseilles (*Groupement* 4) and Lyons (*Groupement* 5). Each administrative region contained individual GTE units composed of anything between just over a hundred to several thousand workers. Some units were entirely composed of Jews, such as the 'Palestinian Groups' in the Dordogne,[17] but more frequently contained workers from different national backgrounds. By the summer of 1941, a total of 40,000 people of various nationalities were enrolled.[18] As with the CTE, the vast majority of the *travailleurs étrangers* (TE), or foreign workers, were Spanish republicans.[19]

There were clear continuities with the Foreign Labour Companies of the Third Republic. In fact, some officials failed to make any distinction referring to 'Companies' as opposed to the new designation of 'Groups'. There were similarities with the organisational structure and logic behind the CTE and Vichy's GTE. The Labour Groups were not meant to pose any competition to French workers and were thus designed to plug gaps in the labour economy, notably for work in agriculture, forestry and mining. There was one point of difference, namely that of the period of enrolment. For the CTE this had been clearly fixed, whereas the Vichy regime expected refugees to work in a GTE for as long as required. Generally, however, the aims behind paramilitary labour formations remained the same, as did the strategy for dealing with the unemployed. Unemployed refugees, as well as those considered to be a threat to national security, faced internment without trial in line with the law of 2 May 1938.[20]

Local officials were left in no doubt about keeping TE away from the labour market. In October 1940, the Commander of Land Forces pressed this point home to regional commanders with specific reference to rural labour.[21] Around the same time more precise guidelines emerged about the internment of Spanish republican men and women considered to be either surplus to the economy or a threat to public order.[22] And yet, the refugees' role in shoring up labour shortages in southern France had already become a reality. Back in the summer, just one week after the Ministry of the Interior had instructed prefects to begin regrouping CTE workers who had become dispersed across France during the debacle, the head of the 17th Military region announced that Spaniards working in either agriculture or industry could remain with their employers.[23] As the return of French prisoners of war failed to materialise and unemployment declined, the need for refugees in agriculture became ever more pressing.[24]

Vichy ministers soon began to accept the need to improve refugees' working conditions. By the end of 1940, representatives from the Ministries of the Interior, Industrial Production and Work, and Agriculture agreed on a series of measures. Families of TE would receive an allowance, and families would now be allowed to be reunited. Under the new guidelines relatives could request a transfer to the localities where their partners were based, or if that proved difficult, a worker could even apply to leave the GTE and move closer to his family if appropriate work could be found.[25]

The growing reliance on the TE was certainly a contributing factor, but cannot alone explain these concessions. A Commission dealing with unemployment, the Commissariat à la lutte contre le chômage (CLC), which was created within the Ministry of Labour and Industrial Production in October 1940, had taken over administrative responsibility for the Labour Groups. The Occupied Zone was under the direction of François Lehideux, but it was the head of the unoccupied zone, Henri-Clément Maux, who drove forward the progressive agenda.[26] Maux did not have any pro-refugee precedents, but was undoubtedly motivated by his Catholic faith and association with the journal *Esprit*, along with the inequalities he had witnessed as an engineer in French Indochina.[27] He was aided by Gilbert Lesage, the head of the organisation responsible for the welfare of TE and their families, the Social Service for Foreigners (SSE). Lesage was a Quaker who had actively supported refugees from Central Europe during the 1930s.[28] Under the leadership of Maux and Lesage, the CLC and SSE played a determining role in securing the best possible conditions for refugee workers.[29]

It took some time for the new measures to have some impact. In May 1941, prefects based workers' allowances on rates established by a February 1940 decree, the real value of which would have declined. To make matters worse, some families had not regularly received their entitlements.[30] But at the end of the year additional benefits were introduced, namely paid holidays and parity between the salaries of TE and French workers.[31] All the same conditions in the GTE varied considerably according to locality.

The shortage of labour in the Southern Zone was compounded by the issue of control and surveillance. It was an issue that had been central to the creation of the GTE but phenomenally difficult to achieve. Back in September 1940, the Commanding Officer of the 17th Military

Region remarked how the total number of Spanish TE was well below what it should have been and ordered local commanders to seek out the errant workers.[32] The police services also began publishing a list, the 'Bulletin de recherches des déserteurs et insoumis', but its impact was superficial: by the end of 1941, there had been just 635 arrests out of a total of 4,835 missing workers.[33]

The CLC had made it easier for refugees to disappear through undermining the paramilitary structure of the GTE. Rather than concentrating workers at the Labour Group base camps, the CLC began transferring as many TE as possible to local employers.[34] The Dordogne was typical of rural *départements* in the south-west. The dispersion of workers corresponded to the local labour needs of agricultural work, forestry and charcoal production, lignite mining, work on hydroelectric dams and public-works programmes. In October 1941, only 136 out of 1,497 workers were living at the base camp.[35] A similar scenario existed in the neighbouring Lot-et-Garonne, where just 80 of the 1,600 workers of the 536th GTE lodged at the GTE camp.[36] The CLC strategy was facilitated by a growing dependency on refugee workers. Throughout 1941, the GTE administration could only satisfy half of the overall demand for TE in the Dordogne, and similar problems were reported in the Gers.[37]

GTE commanders clearly had a difficult task in maintaining control and surveillance over the workers. One method consisted of a roll-call every Sunday at GTE headquarters, but this could not account for the refugees' activities during the rest of the week.[38] Material shortages made an existing problem even worse. The commander of the GTE at Fleurance in the Gers had just a couple of bicycles and a moped at his disposal to keep track of workers scattered over a wide rural area.[39] Work, surveillance and the Spanish republicans were insoluble problems for the Vichy regime.

Forced and voluntary labour in the Organisation Todt, 1940–42

An additional pressure on labour shortages in the Southern Zone came from the German Occupying authorities. In early November 1940, they asked the CLC to supply 2,940 French workers for construction sites at Brest, Lorient, Châtellerault and Saint-Nazaire.[40] The workers were needed by the Organisation Todt for the construction of Atlantic coastal defences and submarine bases, and also by German-controlled businesses. In response, François Lehideux, the head of the CLC for Occupied

France, offered to supply foreign workers, and notably Spanish refugees, from the camps and GTE of southern France.[41]

While around 26,000 Spanish republicans were enrolled in the OT during 1942–44, the figure for the whole of the Occupation is unknown, for several reasons.[42] It is partly because Spanish republicans began working for the OT in 1941, but is also due to a discrepancy between the number of workers requested by the OT and those actually accepted. German officials were initially interested in skilled workers only and consequently rejected up to 50 per cent of the Spanish republicans, though this declined to 10 per cent by the end of 1941 as demand for labour increased.[43] Moreover, the available figures tend to be based on the number of refugees transferred from the Unoccupied Zone and therefore do not include those who unofficially left the GTE for work in the OT.

Not all Vichy officials supported Lehideux's plan of using Spanish refugees. In the second half of 1941, the head of the 16th Military Division, General Altmayer, protested about the departure of half of all Spanish TE from the Montpellier region. At the same time, Maux used his position in the CLC to try and protect Spanish workers, arguing that they were crucial to the (French) national economy. His lobbying of the Vichy government's deputy premier, Admiral Darlan, and the Minister of the Interior, Pierre Pucheu, paid off with a six-month suspension of OT recruitment from the Southern Zone at the end of 1941.[44] Eight months before the introduction of the unpopular *Relève* scheme, which aimed to send French workers to Germany in exchange for the return of French prisoners of war, the first struggle over manpower, German recruitment and the well-being of Vichy France had been fought.

Throughout the Occupation the French and German authorities enrolled OT workers through a combination of forced recruitment and persuasion.[45] Initially, Spanish refugees had little say in the matter. On 20 August 1941 the Direction des Services de l'Armistice requested 3,000 Spanish refugees for the OT.[46] Little more than a week later French guards escorted Miguel Oviedo and other Spanish internees from Argelès camp to the local train station.[47] The authorities offered no reason for the transfer, sparking refugees' fears about being sent to work for the *moros blondes* in Germany.[48] It was not until German soldiers opened the wagon's doors in Bordeaux that Miguel discovered the final destination and that he was to work for the OT.

After the six-month pause in transferring Spanish workers to the OT, the German recruitment commission tried recruiting by persuasion in

1942. Without examining German archives it is not possible to clarify with any precision why the German authorities adopted this approach. Given the ramifications of the German invasion of Russia and the attacks on German officers during the autumn of 1941, it is curious that the Occupation authorities wanted to use Spanish refugee labour.[49] It is conceivable that the shortage and quality of available Spanish republicans outweighed potential security problems. A report detailing relations between the CLC and the Occupation authorities from August 1941 noted how the Germans appreciated the Spanish workers. Indeed, both French and German businesses attached to the OT had been demanding more.[50] However, some caution is required when interpreting these remarks since French officials at this time wanted to liberate French OT workers and also avoid the forced recruitment of more French nationals. Nevertheless, the Spanish republican population contained a relatively high number of skilled and semi-skilled workers who would have been invaluable for the German construction projects.[51] A further interrelated explanation was put forward by the OT recruitment commission, which included Karl Hack as head of propaganda and José María Otto Warnke (Otto), the head of OT workers in Bordeaux. Throughout 1942, recruitment agents stipulated that the German authorities had modified regulations following high numbers of Spanish workers deserting from the OT. Henceforth Spanish republicans would be treated as free workers, be permitted to work in uniquely Spanish teams and be consulted about their place of work.[52]

In 1942 there was a dual aspect to OT recruitment policy. Offering incentives formed one method; and a cynical portrayal of the French state's treatment of the Spanish republicans constituted the other. OT and German officials thus depicted themselves in stark contrast to the French authorities, with derogatory comments about France, and in the process provoked complaints from French officials. On 18 August 1942, 129 Spanish workers were convened to Rivesaltes town hall for a two-hour speech delivered in Spanish – most likely by Otto – which stressed how the refugees would be regarded as free workers, could return to Spain for holidays and would receive tobacco and a good salary. Three people volunteered.[53] Eight days later, at the 225th GTE stationed at Bram, only 7 out of 190 workers volunteered.[54] On 1 September, 60 Spaniards listened to a speech at Servian containing 'defamatory' language about France and the French government that resulted in two volunteers. One gendarme in the *département* of the Hérault recorded a speech which emphasised, among other things, how the French considered the refugees as animals rather than men. The same gendarme also reported only one volunteer out of the 277 Spanish republicans present.[55]

Elsewhere the rate fluctuated but, overall, only a minority of people volunteered to work for the OT during this recruitment campaign.[56] For those who did volunteer, their motivations appear to have been varied, ranging from Spanish Communists' disorientation over the Nazi–Soviet Pact to the need to improve material conditions.[57] But volunteers were never more than a minority, and therefore the German recruitment policy cannot be regarded as a success. All the same, whether by choice or force, a sizeable number of Spanish republicans found themselves in Bordeaux and the surrounding area.

Complicity at work: Otto and the Caserne Niel in Bordeaux

José María Otto Warnke, or 'Otto', as he was commonly referred to by Spanish republicans, is an intriguing character who epitomises the dislocation of cultural and political identity that figured in the German recruitment strategy.[58] He was born in Barcelona to German parents and frequently boasted to refugees that he had defended the Republic in Spain and had shared the misery of the French camps in 1939.[59] As well as having played a leading role in OT recruitment, he was also the liaison officer for the Spanish refugee workers based at the Caserne Niel, the military barracks in Bordeaux commandeered by the German authorities to accommodate Spanish workers.

Relations between the Spanish workers and the German authorities at the Caserne Niel were unstable and conditions were subject to change. The first workers to be lodged at the Caserne were initially confined to barracks, guarded at work, and could be subject to beatings.[60] By November 1941, however, French police began complaining about the relative freedom afforded to the Spanish OT workers and the ease with which they could circulate within the city and surrounding area.[61] By 1943, and most probably beforehand, OT workers who were married or had relatives working in Germany could live in privately rented accommodation.[62] It seems that Otto's influence, the German efforts to entice Spanish refugees to the OT, and the large number of companies supplying the German military in the surrounding area provided certain advantages over other OT centres.

OT officials in Bordeaux certainly put effort into portraying their appreciation of the Spanish workforce. A Christmas souvenir propaganda booklet given to Spanish workers by Otto in 1942 is a striking example. The first page of the booklet contains a poem that ostensibly recounts the pain and distress caused by exile, before ending on an optimistic note about the workers' role in a new beginning. Any doubt as to what the new era consisted of would have been dispelled with Otto's subsequent New Year greetings, which stated: 'Let us wish that this will be the beginning of the Year of Victory and let us feel honoured for having contributed through our work to the defence of the nascent New Europe.'[63]

The Christmas souvenir booklet contained a series of photographs representing different aspects of OT life across what appear to be three themes.[64] The first set of pictures emphasises the presence and responsibility of Otto. The initial photo depicts the man himself in his office. This is followed by a picture of a Spaniard playing a brass instrument and then by an image of the entrance to the Caserne Niel, both of which contain references to the role of Otto as head of the barracks and as the principal liaison officer for the Spanish Transport Workers.

The second theme is life and work in the OT. Workers are seen queuing for food in the courtyard of the Caserne or being ferried to work across the Garonne. There is also a scene of a worker receiving a medical inspection. The focus returns to a scene of Otto addressing Spanish workers, and finally there is an illustration of two Spaniards in a jocular mood in front of the building in which his office is located.

The final theme is the social life of the OT workers, illustrated in six photographs featuring bullfighting, a Spanish folklore event, a theatre production staged on 25 October 1942 and a football team. The prominence of leisure underlined the OT's apparent commitment to providing workers in Bordeaux with social activities that included the opportunity for expressing Spanish cultural identity in France.

The circulation of these photographs among Spanish refugees in Bordeaux would have done little to modify pejorative perceptions among them about the Caserne Niel. In this respect there was some overlap with the assumptions of the local French police. For these officials, who were wary of any large gathering of Spanish republicans, the Caserne Niel was an unwelcome site of refugee weekend sociability. It was a place where false ration tickets were bought and sold and which attracted people from as far away as the Landes.[65] Miguel Oviedo, who lived at the Caserne, recalled how a bar was created for the Spanish workers and how the Spanish permitted French women but not men to enter.[66] According to

Miguel the bar was a further example of German propaganda and a place to avoid. In his memoir, Juan Giménez comes to a similar conclusion.[67] Similar incidents and accusations of a more serious nature are found in Juan Carrasco's book, which describes how some Spaniards organised groups to expel and beat up French people they found in bars and other public places. Some Spanish resisters in the Gironde referred to these people as the 'Second Corps d'Occupation'.[68]

An additional piece to the mosaic of wartime Bordeaux consists of the existing Spanish immigrant population and the Spanish Church.[69] Even though some Spanish immigrants in Bordeaux participated in resistance activities, the Spanish republicans were generally wary of the other migrants and especially the church. The Spanish Church was financed by the Francoist dictatorship in Spain, and organised a summer youth camp at Toulenne where children had to sing the Falange (Spain's Fascist party) anthem, *Cara al Sol* (Facing the Sun).[70] As well as serving members of Bordeaux's long-standing Spanish immigrant community, the Spanish Church also appeared to participate in OT social events.[71]

Life histories suggest that while Spanish republicans did not regard OT work as a form of collaboration in itself, complicity with OT personnel could be perceived as such.[72] There was a difference of scale, however, between everyday complicity and connivance. Archival evidence clearly illustrates that some Spanish migrants (it is unclear whether these were Spanish republicans, migrants who came to France before the conflict or people sent by the Francoist authorities) became agents for the German and French police services responsible for counter-resistance activity in the OT. In light of the authorities' success in dismantling Spanish resistance in Bordeaux, the importance of these agents should not be underestimated, even if these collaborators were no more than a handful of individuals.[73]

The Occupied Zone: patterns of refusal, escape and subversion, 1941–42

Otto's propaganda booklet and greetings card evidently reflected a very specific version of work and life for OT workers in Bordeaux. The level of people abandoning the OT and other worksites in Occupied France paints an alternative picture. French and German reports show that the level of escaping Spanish workers had become a significant phenomenon by November 1941. Once refugees had been incorporated into the OT it was relatively easy to eschew French administrative controls. Moreover, the OT was effectively competing for Spanish refugee workers with businesses serving the German military labour economy. Labour demand was so acute that refugees were able to escape from the OT and obtain work with French and German businesses offering higher wages. Their new employers were not so much preoccupied with the refugees' backgrounds as with their work skills. The overall system of refugee labour was clearly faulty and dialectically involved in the escalation of disappearing workers.

Pierre Poinsot, the head of police in Bordeaux, was all too aware about the ease with which Spanish workers could elude his personnel. He was also convinced that the Gironde was overflowing with refugees.[74] The French administration had been collating statistics for the German authorities on the Spanish republicans since the start of the Occupation. Any Spaniard thought to be a Communist was classified as a 'Spanish red'. But in practice some French officials used the category for any Spaniard suspected of subversive activity, irrespective of his/her ideological hue. During the summer of 1940 the Prefecture believed that 9,100 Spanish republicans were present in the Gironde, of whom 7,160 were concentrated in the Bordeaux agglomeration.[75] The actual number in 1940 was very likely to have been higher, since French census data depended on the refugees declaring themselves to the authorities, and even higher still in November 1941, given the transfer of OT workers to the city. With this in mind, Poinsot tried beefing up surveillance as well as making it harder for Spanish workers to obtain identification papers and move from job to job.[76]

In December 1941, the Feldkommandantur also pressed for increased security. Recent acts of sabotage and attacks were behind a series of instructions that additionally sought to arrest the rising number of escaping refugee workers.[77] Officials were instructed to confiscate the identification papers of Spanish 'reds' and to pay the refugees only part of their salaries. Individuals arriving late for work faced punishment, and all escapes were to be immediately reported to prevent the culprits from seeking employment in other sectors of the OT. Furthermore, the authorities' interpretation of disturbances at work blurred any difference between refusal and revolt. Severe repression could result from the use of arms, 'illegal absences', 'political acts' such as the 'communist salute' or even a 'lack of discipline'.

Refugees' motivations for deserting were varied. The possibility of changing identity was seized upon by Spanish refugees engaged in clandestine activities. Jorge Pérez-Troya escaped from the submarine base at Brest and went to work in the Landes for a German-controlled firm where he was able to procure new identity papers. With his new identity he then moved to Bordeaux in June 1941, made contact with the PCE and began organising a group of resisters responsible for anti-Nazi propaganda, sabotage and an attack on German military personnel.[78] The desire to move closer to families and partners was also a good enough reason to abscond. In 1942 Francisco Perez, a member of the CNT, escaped from the OT at Bayonne with false papers in order to rejoin his family and *compañera* in the Unoccupied Zone. He was arrested in Dax, suspected of being involved in clandestine activities, and transferred to Bordeaux. There he was questioned by the infamous Otto, who subsequently arranged a pass for Francisco to visit his family on condition that he enrolled in the OT.[79]

Some escapees managed to cross the demarcation line and return to the GTE from where they had been recruited. Two refugees fled from the OT in La Pallice, next to La Rochelle, and rejoined their GTE in the Gers after suffering beatings from German OT guards over language problems and complaints about poor food.[80] Another example is provided by Calixto Casales, who left the OT in Brest for Bordeaux to avoid a transfer to Jersey where conditions were especially brutal. Following OT work at Royan, he returned to Bordeaux and in March 1942 headed for the Dordogne. After explaining to the police in Périgueux that he had escaped from the Germans, French officials simply enrolled him into the GTE at Chancelade.[81] In similar cases Vichy officials notified neither the German or French authorities in the Occupied Zone, thereby contributing to the administrative confusion about the whereabouts of missing workers.

Escapes from the OT were most commonly related to conditions. Sixteen refugees arrested for escaping made repeated references in their police statements to their desire to improve working conditions and to gain more freedom by working for French- and German-controlled firms in the vicinity of Bordeaux.[82] The issue of pay was also highly relevant. The inequality between wages offered by the GTE, the OT and local French- and German-controlled businesses was evidently staggering. One worker had initially received 7 francs a day at a GTE based in Rivesaltes. Shortly after arriving in Bordeaux for the OT, he abandoned his place of work and found a job with a daily salary of 200 francs and was then able to start sending money to his family.[83] The Spanish workers were clearly motivated to find work which was less physically demanding, offered more freedom and was better paid.

A claim that PCE militants organised the evasion of 2,000 Spanish republicans from Saint-Médard-en-Jalles, on the outskirts of Bordeaux, is exaggerated.[84] It nonetheless confirms a wider picture of growing numbers of Spanish republicans disappearing from the French and German administration's grasp in the Bordeaux area. At the start of 1942, the level of escaping workers was noticeably high and lends credence to the observation made earlier in this chapter that a change in OT recruitment strategy occurred in 1942. For January alone, 742 Spanish refugees were reported missing from the Caserne Niel and Saint-Médard camp. In February the number had risen to 984 and by April only 81 people had been apprehended.[85] The missing workers compounded French officials' concerns about controlling the whereabouts of the Spanish refugees. Two censuses conducted in December 1941 and January 1942 reported that 625 Spanish refugees were living without authorisation in Bordeaux and a further 312 in the rest of the Gironde. A round-up by French police in February found a further 11 refugees who had escaped from the OT.[86]

The scale of the phenomenon was sufficient to have clogged up the French judicial system in Bordeaux, leading one French official to call for the repatriation of refugees to Spain.[87] The nearby Mérignac internment camp was similarly showing signs of strain, with the Prefect warning that the internment of OT escapees was becoming increasingly difficult due to the existing level of internees. Vichy's delegate for the Ministry of the Interior in the Occupied Zone therefore agreed for Spanish internees to be returned to the OT, but with assurance from the Germans that the workers would be repatriated to Spain in the event of a second escape attempt.[88] The German authorities agreed, and warnings were issued to Spanish refugees from October.[89]

In the event, this assurance was not translated into practice. No expulsions or repatriations could occur without German permission, and this was given only in extreme cases due to the substantial labour force needed for the Atlantic wall. The scale of demand for Spanish labour and the stark differences in pay between different employers, together with the existence of two administrative authorities in the Gironde, offered Spanish republicans the means to improve their material circumstances and, if they wished, to change their identity. Escape constituted a 'weapon of the weak', a way of challenging the conditions of German- and French-controlled workplaces without incurring severe penalties.[90]

Subversion was a different matter. Incidents involving direct confrontation with the German authorities were dealt with harshly. During the second half of 1941, Spanish republicans had participated in two attacks in Bordeaux. In August, they mortally wounded a German officer, and two months later, Spanish Communists acted as bodyguards to Pierre Rebière (he had previously fought in Spain with the International Brigades) when he shot dead an officer of the Feldkommandantur. The German authorities responded by executing 48 hostages.[91] The French police had been assiduously gathering information on Spanish republicans and other Spanish migrants living in the Bordeaux area, and frequently conducted house searches. Whenever acts of sabotage occurred, French suspicions habitually fell on the city's Spanish population, and notably the refugees. The destruction of an electricity station at Pessac, just outside Bordeaux, resulted in 85 arrests, 44 of which involved Spanish 'reds', and yet the attack had actually been the work of the British Special Operations Executive (SOE).[92]

However spectacular these attacks were, examples of organised direct action during the first two years of the Occupation were as rare in Bordeaux as elsewhere. Generally, collective clandestine activity in Bordeaux during this period consisted of organisational matters and propaganda. Spanish republican reorganisation was fraught with obstacles. The disruption of the German invasion of France, along with the dispersal of refugees across the country in the GTE and OT, seriously compromised the fragile progress of organisational reconstruction which had begun with the refugees' arrival in 1939. Moreover, refugees had to deal with a triple form of surveillance from the French, German and Francoist intelligence services. From the very start of the Occupation the French police had assiduously tracked down leading militants from several organisations: the POUM in early 1941; anarcho-syndicalists towards the end of 1941;[93] and heavy repression of the Communists ensued in the spring of 1941, with the arrest of all leaders in the Occupied Zone and, as we will shortly see, wide-scale arrests on the other side of the demarcation line.[94]

Given these formidable challenges, the fact that any organised Spanish resistance appeared at all during the first two years of the Occupation is impressive, as is the range of propaganda produced and disseminated. Propaganda could take different forms, but the Spanish republicans were especially prolific with their clandestine papers, producing at least thirty titles.[95] Much of the Spanish literature initially concentrated on consolidating anti-fascist consciousness, which included discouraging people from working for the German authorities. One leaflet discovered by French police opposite an OT work yard in Bordeaux on 20 May 1942 warned refugees to ignore Otto's machinations; it was entitled 'Death to Traitors' and also contained a potted biography of Otto's dubious past.[96]

Who was behind the 'Death to Traitors' leaflet is unknown, though Spanish resisters in Bordeaux, and the rest of the Occupied Zone, were often linked to the French Communist-organised French Irregular Soldiers and Partisans (FTPF) or the attendant immigrant-based FTP–MOI (Immigrant Workers' Movement).[97] Communists were also keen to exploit opposition to Hitler and the Nazi regime amongst the German personnel in France. This was the aim of the 'German Work' (TA) section created by the PCF during the summer of 1941.[98] One of Miguel Oviedo's tasks in Bordeaux was to distribute leaflets written in German by shoving them through the canvas hauling of German military trucks. It was a high-risk strategy, as he did this in public spaces and could never be sure if any passengers were inside. Unsurprisingly, it was a task he disliked.[99]

While further research is needed to assess the extent to which Germans and Spanish refugees resisted together, there is some evidence of German guards advising Spanish OT workers in Bordeaux to be more discreet about their activities. Miguel Alama recounted how one soldier cautioned him about carrying a clandestine leaflet.[100] At the submarine base, Agustín Juan Diez's father sabotaged machinery by using concrete instead of oil as a lubricant. When a German guard told him that he was likely to be deported for sabotage he left for the Dordogne to join the maquis.[101] On at least two occasions, German reservists from the OT actually participated with Spanish refugees in subversive activities. In December 1941, one group obtained a stock of mercury from the Robert Piquet hospital and a month later they set fire to a wagon containing fodder in Bordeaux's central train station.[102]

Although Spanish Communist resistance in the Bordeaux region was well developed during this phase of the Occupation, anarcho-syndicalists of the CNT were not inactive. They were developing interpersonal mutual help networks for finding people (some of whom had escaped from the Unoccupied Zone) work and accommodation in the area. A formal CNT structure, though, did not emerge in this region until the second half of 1943 following the arrival of José Berruezo Romera, a militant who had been central to reorganising the CNT in the *département* of the Cantal.[103]

The Unoccupied Zone: patterns of refusal, escape and subversion, 1941–42

Officials in the Unoccupied Zone were just as ineffective in dealing with escapees. In the year leading up to October 1941, just 635 out of 4,835 missing Spanish refugees had been arrested. One official refused to believe that such a large number of people with limited French and without identification papers or ration cards could remain at large without support from a vast network of accomplices.[104] A subsequent investigation found no evidence of a refugee-organised escape network, but it did identify a number of characteristics concerning refugees escaping from Vichy's internment camps.[105]

Escapees from the camps of Vernet, Récébedou and Noé had found work in the region's farms, suggesting that a nebulous array of small-scale complicity networks were in operation. In the areas around the camps of Noé and Récébedou the police suspected that established Spanish immigrant families were acting as intermediaries. There was no explanation of how refugees from Vernet were finding work, though some suspicion surrounded the American Quaker centre in Montauban. But whatever the precise circumstances, the presence of Spanish refugee workers in small rural communes would have, at the very least, also required the tacit agreement of local French inhabitants. In the case of the Gurs and Barcarès camps, somewhat contradictory influences were apparent. Former Spanish internees had apparently written to fellow-refugees at Gurs with details of work opportunities in the region.[106] In addition to the possibility of earning decent wages at German firms in the nearby Occupied Zone, officials believed slack security at the Gurs camp to be a causal factor behind the escapes. However, internees were thought to be escaping from Barcarès, precisely to avoid the OT recruitment commission.[107]

The motivations and stakes surrounding escaping clearly differed according to the national and ethnic backgrounds of the refugees in question. Lesage and his SSE team tried to protect Jewish TE from the August 1942 round-up.[108] Whether it was due to an SSE agent or not, Peter Paisley and other workers in a GTE near Sainte- Livrade-sur-Lot in the Lot-et-Garonne were tipped off about the possibility of deportation and escaped to the nearby woods. After an unsuccessful attempt to cross the border into Switzerland, they eventually joined the Foreign Legion to escape persecution.[109]

More generally, the impecunious TE were driven to protest and escape by material circumstances. In April 1942, six Spaniards from the 554th GTE in the Lot who were working for a charcoal company in the commune of Cours downed their tools in protest about their living conditions, their daily allowance of 9 francs (initial GTE guidelines set a rate of 10 francs) and the company's refusal to allow workers to keep their ration cards.[110]

Perhaps even worse for morale was the knowledge that some employers deliberately allocated the most arduous and dangerous tasks to refugees rather than to French workers, as was the case for workers attached to the 518th GTE, based at Buzy in the Basses-Pyrénées.[111] Recalling conditions in the 160th GTE, Pascual Almudévar stated: 'badly dressed, badly nourished, and shamefully exploited by profiteers: that was the state we were in'.[112]

Inadequate wages also had implications for the workers' relatives. As the winter of 1942 approached, the local SSE representative of the Gers worried about how workers' families (Spanish but also Austrians, Belgians and Czechs) would cope with the weather: three-quarters of them were without shoes or woollen clothes.[113] To be sure, precise conditions varied according to the French commanding officers, employers, and the type of work involved, but they were often bleak, and in some cases dire.[114] Missing workers continued to be registered throughout 1942 in the Unoccupied Zone.[115]

Resistance activity was another, though less substantial, reason for escaping. In the Dordogne for example, Saturnin García Palacio, a Spanish refugee administrative assistant, and Eugène Degerman, the French deputy commanding officer of the 647th GTE, protected Spanish workers from the German authorities by directing them towards local resistance groups.[116] In this case, absence from the workplace was symptomatic of both the refugees' refusal to acquiesce and a decision to revolt through collective resistance. Refusal and revolt were nonetheless separate, though often overlapping, phenomena which echo Jackson's distinction between dissidence and resistance.[117] The latter involved a degree of intention to participate in overthrowing authority in a wider sense, whereas refusal constituted disobedience of a particular aspect of that authority, such as the poor working conditions of the GTE or being drafted into working for the German military.

While Spanish-organised resistance was developing in southern France, it was not at this stage dependent on large numbers of escaping TE. On the contrary, it was afoot within the Foreign Labour Groups. Frequently situated in remote rural areas, the GTE offered ideal conditions for clandestine activities. Even when the workers were dispersed around the countryside, communication between them was not difficult. Some Spanish republicans worked in the administrative office of the GTE, affording them access to all workers' records (and templates for forging documents).[118] In-between the weekly roll-calls at the base camp the TE could move around relatively unhindered as surveillance in rural areas continued to be severely compromised by poor policing resources. In the Basses-Pyrénées, for instance, the *Renseignements généraux* (the intelligence arm of the police service) clearly faced an uphill task regarding the 526th GTE. With only bicycles at their disposal, reaching the worksites in mountainous and wooded areas was unfeasible. And even if they had a moped, the monthly petrol allowance was insufficient for even a single agent to make a one-way trip.[119]

By 1942, anarcho-syndicalists and Communists in particular had managed to reorganise and, in some cases, start preparing the ground for resistance. Divergences over the direction of the CNT organisation occurred throughout the Occupation period. Until his arrest, Germinal Esgleas remained general secretary of the MLE General Council from his base in Salon, in the Dordogne, and was in contact with the Council's other members, most of whom were interned in Vernet camp. Esgleas and his supporters viewed armed struggle solely as a means for social revolution and therefore an inappropriate strategy in the context of Occupied/Vichy France. There were other currents of the CNT in France, with some militants even mooting the idea of creating a political arm of the CNT, to be called the Workers' Labour Party (POT). In February 1941, a circular, probably written by Esgleas, expelled the POT, along with the Friends of London (referred to in Chapter 3) from the MLE. Despite these internal conflicts, anarcho-syndicalists reorganised themselves across southern France, most notably in Lyons, Marseilles, the Montpellier area, Saint-Étienne and in Vernet camp. Perhaps the most significant resistance activity involving libertarian TE occurred around the l'Aigle dam in the Cantal under the representation of José Berruezo and José German González. The refugee workers teamed up with French resisters, and most notably André Decelle, to transform the GTE worksite into a safe haven for people on the run from the Occupied Zone. These activities were also a prelude for joining maquis groups in the surrounding area.[120]

The other Spanish organisation emerging as a resistance phenomenon within the GTE was the PCE. Contacts between Spanish republican and French freemasons led to the creation of forestry works to employ and protect both Spanish TE and French freemasons. From the end of 1941, Georges Thomas from Toulouse and Dr Delteil from Carcassonne were operating worksites in the Aude and Ariège. Dr Delteil even allowed the Spanish workers to use the proceeds from charcoal sales to finance their efforts.[121] These sites became central to the reconstruction of the PCE and the creation of groups of Spanish guerrilla fighters. Under cover of forestry work, the PCE militant Jesús Ríos set out to create an armed force which took its name from the 14th Guerrilla Corps of the Spanish Republican Army. The name was more than a reference to the Corps's experience of behind-the-line warfare during the Spanish Civil War; it also embodied a continuation of the refugees' struggle against fascism and Francoism and signalled an indomitable determination to return to Spain – a point which was articulated in the accompanying clandestine paper, *Reconquista de España*.

The political arm of the 14th Corps was the Spanish National Union (UNE), and was the Spanish equivalent of the French National Front strategy. PCE leaders in Moscow and Mexico had called for a 'National Union of all Spaniards' following the German invasion of the Soviet Union in June 1941. The call was taken up by some. In the Lot-et-Garonne area, refugees appear to have created 20 local UNE committees by the spring of 1942.[122] But it was not until a meeting in Toulouse at the start of November 1941 (it had been called the 'Grenoble' meeting to confuse the police services) that militants agreed on a definitive structure for the UNE. The organisation characterised itself as open to Spanish republicans of all ideological backgrounds, and did effectively attract people from different political and trade-union backgrounds. However, the PCE was the sole party officially represented in the UNE.

In many ways Spanish-organised resistance developed along the same trajectory as other immigrant organisations or purely French outfits: contacts were made, propaganda disseminated, groups organised and actions undertaken. The same applied to the gendering of roles. Women like Regina Arrieta, who formed part of the MOI leadership in Toulouse, or Teresa Gebellí de Sierra, who had a leadership position in the Montluçon maquis, were rare examples.[123] As with their French counterparts, Spanish women resisters often acted as liaison agents. For the most part, however, women were involved in tasks traditionally associated with femininity such as social care and domestic duties. They also had key responsibility in transforming homes into meeting places and refuges.

There were, however, certain traits specific to Spanish resisters. For one, they were inspired by a different cognitive map which was drawn from their experiences of the conflict in Spain. This applied to Spanish republicans from across the ideological spectrum. The rebirth of the 14th Guerrilla Corps illustrates how one legend could serve to create another. During the spring of 1942, the appearance of the first group of guerrilla fighters, the 234th Brigade under Jésus Ríos in the Aude, was already entwined with the image of the *guerrillero*, or guerrilla fighter, from Spain. This time around, though, the concept became the Spanish equivalent of the maquis conjuring up an image of doughty Spanish combatants operating from forestry, mine and other rural worksites from across southern France.[124] For most French nationals resistance was a phenomenon to be created, but for the Spanish republicans it was a form of continuation fuelled by their experiences and memories of the Spanish Civil War.

One of the earliest and most famous trans-Pyrenean escape networks, the Pat O'Leary network (named after the *nom de guerre* of a Belgian officer working for the SOE), owed much of its success to CNT militants under Francisco Ponzán. Ponzán had cut his teeth in clandestine activities by gathering military information and planning sabotage behind the Francoist enemy lines in Spain. He put the experience to good use shortly after the *retirada* by organising the passage into France of CNT militants in danger from Francoist persecution. He first came into contact with the British secret services in November 1939, and from autumn of the following year began helping allied pilots, Jews and resisters to escape from France via the Pyrenees.[125] While the idea of anarcho-syndicalists joining up with the British secret services caused friction within the CNT, Ponzán viewed it more pragmatically as a means of achieving Franco's downfall and the return to Spain.

The GTE's role as a vector for subversive activities was another specificity of the Spanish resisters. The point was not lost on Vichy's police services. In September 1942, Henri Cado from the general secretariat for police warned prefects and police officials across southern France of links between the GTE and subversion.[126] The warning followed numerous waves of arrests in the Lot-et-Garonne and the surrounding area of mainly TE, but also some Spanish women, for distributing propaganda and bomb-making. What Vichy officials termed as the *Affaire Reconquista de España* began on 6 July after a bicycle mechanic notified gendarmes that he had discovered copies of *Reconquista de España* hidden within the bicycle of José Ocino Torres. The lists of arrests indicate just how central the GTE had become to resistance. Amongst the first arrests in the Lot-et-Garonne, 16 out of the 25 people apprehended belonged to the 505th GTE at Fumel and the 536th GTE at Casseneuil.[127] Vichy police soon widened their net, arresting an even higher proportion of TE in the Cher, Corrèze, Dordogne, Haute-Garonne, Indre, Lot, Pyrénées-Orientales, Tarn-et-Garonne and the Vienne. By the end of 1942, TE from across the whole of southern France were becoming involved in resistance.

Localities and the dynamics of forced recruitment, acceptance and rejection, 1943–44

The Allied landings in North Africa and the extension of the German Occupation to the Southern Zone provoked mixed responses from Spanish TE in the Lot-et-Garonne. While they greeted news of the landings with certain joy, they were worried about the arrival of German forces.[128] The presence of German troops and the sharp increase in recruitment for the OT and Compulsory Work Service (STO) – the Compulsory Labour Scheme whereby predominantly French but also other nationals were sent to work in Germany – had a phenomenal impact on the levels of escaping workers from the GTE. The corresponding escalation of labour shortages also inspired prefects to complain about the loss of Spanish workers, with reports from some localities pointing towards a convergence of interests between Spanish republicans and some members of the local populations. The amorous and fictional relationship between a Spanish refugee and the woman employing him in Bernard Clavel's *l'Espagnol* was not a common experience, but it does highlight an experiential trait that began to emerge in French officials' reports in 1943: the increasing acceptance and dependence of local community structures on Spanish workers.[129]

Throughout 1942 officials in south-western France had expressed concern rather than alarm about escaping workers.[130] This changed with the New Year. In January 1943, the Prefect of the Tarn reported a sharp increase in disappearing GTE workers in response to German labour demands. Even areas of employment that once offered a degree of protection against recruitment – agriculture and forestry, to name but two – were now open to exploitation.[131] The 159th GTE at Castres had received orders to prepare 550 workers for transfer to the German authorities, but in the event an astonishingly low number of just 135 workers were available. Out of these, 14 were declared unfit, a further 31 were reportedly ill and a further 58 belonged to 'category e' – meaning they worked on farms of the wives or parents of French prisoners of war, single women and veterans, or had French family ties – and were therefore retained. There were 312 *défaillants*, or missing workers. The Prefect warned of serious consequences for the agriculture of the *département*, and more specifically stressed that the transfer of category e workers would lead to the abandonment of properties held by the elderly, wives and mothers of French prisoners of war. Some of the refugee workers had even been running these farms.

The Prefect of the Tarn was not alone in pressing for GTE workers to remain. During the spring and summer of 1943, the Regional Prefect in Toulouse received similar requests from employers. In April, the head of the Société Hydro-Méchanique in Toulouse requested exemption for Spanish workers from the 562nd and 513th GTE in order to prevent disruption to electricity supplies.[132] Two months later, the Prefect received another letter, this time from a forestry works owner in Arudy, Basses-Pyrénées, concerning the 526th GTE.[133] At the same time, the owner of a nearby forestry firm warned that the departure of skilled workers, some of whom had been with the business since 1939, threatened the business and also wood supplies to the SNCF.[134] This came after gravel production for the SNCF at Bagnères de Bigorre, in the neighbouring Hautes-Pyrénées, had ground to a halt for the same reason. The letters from these forestry firms were most probably a reaction to the mobilisation of 1,750 men from *Groupement no.* 2, the administrative region for the *départements* surrounding Toulouse.[135]

As the serious labour shortage deteriorated yet further, prefects began joining the chorus of complaints, providing echoes of the earlier remarks by the Prefect of the Tarn. In the Lot, departures had resulted in charcoal production plummeting by two-thirds. The Prefect unequivocally warned that any further departures 'would amount to a veritable suicide for both the government and country'.[136] In the Gers, some French locals had threatened to refrain from harvesting their crops in protest at departing TE.[137] Months later, the Prefect also showed some defiance by excluding 17 refugees from being transferred on the grounds they were indispensable to the local economy.[138] These warnings, however, carried little weight in the face of German labour demands on the Vichy government.

Complaints continued into 1944, with the Prefect of the Hautes-Pyrénees warning that the loss of trained forestry workers seriously threatened local wood and charcoal provision. More worryingly, disruption to the production and supply of bread and other foodstuffs had become a potential eventuality.[139] The loss of workers from *Groupement no.* 2 reached a nadir following December orders for the departure of a further 3,297 TE. The Ministry of Labour's regional representative was dismissive about meeting this demand, predicting that up to 30 per cent of workers were likely to abscond.[140] It proved to an optimistic estimation. French officials in the Gers managed to gather just 85 out of 250 workers, with gendarmes shooting one recalcitrant Spanish refugee in the thigh at Plaisance.[141] Further north-east in the Lot, 100 out of 262 workers were missing from the 554th GTE, and only 27 out of 145 could be gathered from the 508th GTE based in Carjac.[142] In the neighbouring Lot-et-Garonne, the rate of desertions ran as high as 50 per cent.[143] Out of a target of 33,000 for the whole of southern France, the administration managed to hand over just 5,920 workers to the German authorities.[144] The Vichy government's ability to assert its will on foreign workers was rapidly eroding.

What had happened to the missing workers? The Regional Prefect in Toulouse believed many had headed for the OT recruitment office in Toulouse in order to retain some choice over their place of work.[145] Not only did this strategy afford refugees some choice in their conditions and place of work, it represented the sole means of avoiding the STO without consequences from the French authorities.[146] Other refugees hid until the threat had passed and then returned to their GTE unit. For instance, at the start of 1944, 101 out of 136 escapees in the Lot-et-Garonne returned to the GTE once the threat of requisition was gone. They feared their departure would have deprived their families of the means to live.[147] The authorities suspected that other escaping workers were heading for the nearest maquis group.[148]

Refusing to comply with the requisition of labour was certainly not the preserve of refugee workers. The fact that so many workers happened to be missing at the right time raises the question of collusion from local officials. The Prefect of the Tarn's report on the difficulty in gathering workers for the OT at the start of 1943 alluded to this problem. Prefects elsewhere in south-western France were also questioning the desirability of the forced labour requisitions. In the Lot, the Prefect Antoine Loïc Petit may even have been implicated in actively hindering labour drafts.[149] Most prefects, though, remained within the parameters of Vichy legality; unlike some of their subordinates. The Prefect of the Gers believed an unidentified local official lay behind the recruitment problems of January 1944.[150] Several months later, in the Gers town of Vic-Fezensac, this proved to be the case when gendarmes warned Spanish refugees of imminent requisitions.[151]

The image of the Spanish refugees as troublemakers had not disappeared. In March, a police investigation partly attributed a spontaneous anti-STO demonstration in the Tarn town of Mazamet to Spaniards. However, the police report also implied that popular refusal to increasing STO demands was understandable.[152] It is difficult to know whether the January shortfall of Spanish workers in the Tarn reflected some degree of French officials' sympathy for the refugees, or alternatively for their employers and the wider agricultural health of the locality. But taken in conjunction with the March demonstration, there is every reason to believe that a convergence between the interests of refugee and French workers had emerged.

In contrast to the former Unoccupied Zone, French authorities of the Gironde remained uniformly and resolutely hostile to the presence of Spanish refugee workers. In November 1943, the *Rensignements généraux* in Bordeaux cited just about every reason possible – social, economic and political – for ridding the Gironde of the Spanish refugees. The French public, the report stated, would be only too happy to see the backs of them.[153] Although it is difficult to verify whether the remarks represented an accurate reflection of public opinion, they certainly found currency amongst other police services and local authority figures. One officer argued that a critical mass of refugees had been reached and supported his claim with well-established stereotypes of the refugees that conflated ideology with criminality.[154]

Officials in the Landes raised similar issues. Police reports in December 1943 reiterated remarks made in the previous year about Spaniards in the vicinity of Labouheyre, namely that recent Spanish arrivals had avoided French administrative controls by seeking work with German-controlled businesses. Surveillance was undermined even more by those refugees employed in forestry work who could literally roam the countryside at will.[155] Another police inspector alleged that the general public was worried that the refugees, with their experience of civil war in Spain, would readily team up with 'bad French elements'.[156] The official was not altogether wrong to stress the relationship between presence and revolt: Labouheyre was a significant area of maquis activity in the Landes. What the official did not know was that Spanish resisters had increasingly left Bordeaux to join the maquis in the Landes and other rural areas because of French and German counter-resistance activities. But even without this knowledge, the Prefect was sufficiently determined to rid the Landes of the 1,889 Spanish and 250 Italian workers by handing them over to the STO.[157]

In early 1944, the Prefect's proposal was rejected by the German authorities on the grounds that it would cause diplomatic problems with nationalist Spain. The most plausible reason, however, lay in the need for retaining Spanish workers in the OT and in the businesses working for the German military. The stiff competition for Spanish workers was reflected in the ongoing difference in salaries. In February 1944, a non-skilled worker for Schlotter, a German firm at Labouheyre, received food and 120 francs a day. The daily rate for an equivalent worker in the privately owned company Garbag, in Solférino, was between 300 and 400 francs, including food. In another privately owned but German-controlled business, workers earned between 600 and 800 francs. The local gendarmerie feared that high wages would attract even more Spanish refugees to the area.[158] But there was no way of knowing, since both German and French employers made little effort to help gendarmes with their enquiries. In the case of German firms, gendarmes had no authority to enter either the workplace or workers' living quarters. To make matters worse, these employers furnished very sketchy information about their personnel. Things were only marginally better in French-controlled firms. Although gendarmes could theoretically visit the worksites, this was complicated by the dispersion of the workers. Moreover, French employers' proved uncooperative, refusing to report the arrival and departure of workers while also hiring personnel illegally.[159] As in the Southern Zone, employers prioritised their economic interests over the state's security concerns.

Lehideux's proposal in 1940 to substitute Spanish for French workers seemed to offer Vichy two advantages. As well as reducing the German military's use of French workers and thus limiting the economic impact to French businesses, it raised the possibility of ridding the Southern Zone of Spanish republicans. This proved to be an all-round failure. The German authorities did indeed begin using Spanish refugees for the OT but without necessarily reducing the amount of French workers. Moreover, the transfer of Spaniards to the OT did nothing to alleviate the French administration's economic and security concerns in the Unoccupied Zone. If anything, the exact opposite occurred. The removal of Spanish workers from the depopulated rural *départements* of the southwest aggravated labour shortages and highlighted the Spanish republicans' invaluable contribution to the economy. This not only undermined Vichy's ideological project of refugee exclusion, but also encouraged some members of the public and local officials to transgress the law to prevent the German uptake of Spanish labour. The transfer of workers en masse to the Occupied Zone also created difficulties for French officials charged with the surveillance of refugees. The presence of two administrative authorities and the competition for labour made widescale surveillance in the Gironde and Landes manifestly unworkable.

What also emerges from the study of French officials' correspondence is a series of perceptions based on the presence and visibility of the Spanish republicans. Some of the most disparaging remarks occurred in *départements* where there was a particularly dense concentration of Spanish refugees. Throughout the Occupation, criticism was noticeably constant in the *départements* of the Gironde and the Landes. This contrasts with some of the rural *départements* in southern France, where refugee workers were less visible as a group apart. Whether enrolled in a GTE or employed directly by a local employer, the Spanish workers tended to be more dispersed and, significantly, their presence was linked to the French rather than the German economy.

The consensus in officials' observations in the rural Landes and the port city of Bordeaux problematizes any simplistic division between rural and urban contexts when examining the different images of Spanish workers in the northern and southern zones. Nonetheless, the urban and rural distinction should not be entirely dismissed. The refugees' contribution to local communities and their economies was more evident in *départements* where the labour market was dominated by agriculture and an accompanying shortage of manpower. In the Gironde and Landes, the arrival of Spanish workers coincided with the recruitment needs of the OT, thereby engendering fewer possibilities for Spanish republicans to create a positive image of themselves in the eyes of the French populace.

Employers, however, placed their economic interests before police concerns. By early 1944, employers on both sides of the demarcation line were willing to question and, in some cases, obstruct authority in order to retain Spanish refugee workers. In 1943, employers in the former Unoccupied Zone mainly expressed their discontent through written complaints to prefects. At the start of the following year, local authorities suspected employers and officials of colluding with the refugees to prevent the Germans' recruitment of labour. Refusal did not necessarily imply revolt, though the difference being the two is not always easily delineated.

The refugees' unwillingness to accept poor working conditions or forced requisition did not automatically amount to an intention to overthrow Vichy or German rule, even if this was sometimes interpreted by some French officials as evidence of rebellion. The most recurrent form of refusal consisted of abandoning the workplace, with many workers doing so to maintain some agency over their place of work or to improve their material circumstances. But even if revolt was restricted to a minority of Spanish republicans and French nationals, it is worth noting that a convergence of interests between refugees and some local inhabitants, along with a refusal to accept labour policy, increasingly called into question existing power relations. In some cases, refusal was a first step towards more active opposition. Other refugees were defiant from the start. But whatever the route into subversion, the workplace was often involved. At the start of the Occupation, employment structures in France seemed like a setback to the Spanish republicans' ambitions of returning to Spain: by early 1944, they had become central to achieving this goal.

Notes

1 'L'accord franco-mexicain va permettre un vaste mouvement de migration', *La Petite Gironde* (2 September 1940).

2 For an overview of the OT see F.W. Seidler, 'L'Organisation Todt', *Revue d'histoire de la Deuxième Guerre mondiale*, 134 (1984), pp. 33–58.

3 For a case study of the the Channel Islands see: M. Bunting, *The Model Occupation: The Channel Islands under German Rule* (London, 2004); P. King, *The Channel Islands War, 1940–1945* (London, 1991).

4 The problems with the typologies and definitions of collaboration and resistance are tackled in J. Jackson, *France: The Dark Years 1940–1944* (Oxford, 2001), pp. 166–70, 385–8.

5 P. Levi, *The Drowned and the Saved* (London, 1988). The use of the 'grey zone' to step beyond binary conceptualisation of actors as collaborators or resisters is referred to by K. Adler, 'Vichy Specificities: Repositioning the French Past', *Contemporary European History*, 9:3, pp. 475, 483, and Jackson, *France*, p. 243.

6 É. Temime, 'Espagnols et Italiens en France', in P. Milza and D. Peschanski (eds), *Exils et Migration: Italiens et Espagnols en France 1938–1946* (Paris, 1994), p. 27.

7 *Ibid.*, p. 28.

8 AD Gironde, SC 1908. Administration Militaire Régionale Allemande à la Feldkommandantur to the Préfecture. Objet: Livraison des Espagnols rouges, 8 October 1940.

9 There is some evidence suggesting that Spanish refugees may have been deported from the city. On 19 November 1940, the Préfecture asked the Feldkommandantur for details about where to assemble the Spanish 'reds' destined for Germany. Although there is no further reference in the French correspondence, René Terrisse states that a convoy of 115 people from the Gironde left for Hamburg on 29 November, and was followed by additional departures in early 1941. The source is not cited but the implication is that the convoy was composed solely of French workers. R. Terrisse, *Bordeaux, 1940–1944* (Paris, 1993), p. 61.

10 AD Gironde, Vrac 200. Général de Corps d'Armée, Délégué Général du Gouvernement Français dans les Territoires occupés to Préfets, 26 October 1940.

11 He then moved to Montauban, where he died on 3 November 1940.

12 SC 1075/79. Affaires d'Espagne 1940–44.

13 G. Dreyfus-Armand, *L'Exil des Républicains Espagnols en France: De la Guerre Civile à la Mort de Franco* (Paris, 1999), p. 142. Between 1943 and 1944 just over 1,000 refugees re-emigrated from metropolitan France and French-controlled North Africa. D. Rolland, 'Extradition ou réémigration? Les vases communicants de la gestion xénophobe des réfugiés espagnols en France', in Milza and Peschanski (eds), *Exils et Migration*, p. 60.

14 Dreyfus-Armand, *L'Exil des Républicains Espagnols en France*, pp. 143–5; Rolland, 'Extradition ou réémigration?', pp. 49–55.

15 For an overview of the GTE: V. Viet, 'Vichy dans l'histoire des politiques françaises de la main-d'œuvre', *Travail et Emploi* 98 (2004); M.-A. Maux-Robert, 'Le commissariat à la lutte contre le chômage en zone sud', *Guerres mondiales et conflits contemporains*, 2:206 (2002); M.-A. Maux-Robert, *La lutte contre le chômage à Vichy* (Panazol, 2002); D. Peschanski, *La France des camps. L'internement 1938–1946* (Paris, 2002). On the Spanish refugees in the GTE: Dreyfus-Armand, *L'Exil des Républicains Espagnols en France*. On Groupement no. 1 see J. F. Sweets, *Choices in Vichy France: The French under Nazi Occupation* (Oxford, 1986), and S. Farmer, 'Out of the Picture: Foreign Labour in Wartime France', in S. Fishman et al. (eds), *France at War: Vichy and the Historians* (Oxford, 2000). For the Dordogne, B. Reviriego, *Les Juifs en Dordogne 1939–1944* (Périgueux, 2003), and for the Gers, G. Laffitte, 'L'encadrement par le travail des étrangers dans le département du Gers 1939–1944: au cœur du dipositif GTE' (Mémoire de maîtrise, Université de Toulouse-Le Mirail, 2003).

16 AN SHAT, 34N 375. Loi relative à la situation des étrangers en surnombre dans l'économie nationale.

17 Notably the 664th and 665th Labour Groups in the Dordogne. Reviriego, *Les Juifs en Dordogne*, p. 121.

18 Estimates vary. This figure is from Maux-Robert, 'Le commissariat à la lutte contre le chômage en zone sud', p. 140. Sarah Farmer cites a total of 60,000 men in July 1941, a third of whom were Jews. Farmer, 'Out of the Picture: Foreign Labour in Wartime France', in Fishman et al. (eds) *France at War*, p. 252.

19 In August 1943, 31,000 out of a total of 37,000 workers were Spanish. Temime, 'Espagnols et Italiens en France', p. 29.

20 AD Haute-Garonne, 2517W 45, Secrétaire d'État à l'Intérieur to Préfets, 10 August 1940.

21 AD Haute-Garonne, 2517W 45. Le Général d'Armée Commandant en Chef des Forces Terrestres to Généraux commandant les 7° 9° 12° 13° 14° 15° 16° 17° 19° Régions, 3 October 1940.

22 C. Laharie, *Le Camp de Gurs, 1939–45: Un aspect méconnu de l'histoire du Béarn* (Biarritz, 1993), p. 142.

23 AD Haute-Garonne, 2517W 45. Note de Service, 17ème Région État-Major, 31 July 1940.

24 Of the prisoners of war, 36 per cent were farmers. R. O. Paxton, *Vichy France: Old Guard and New Order, 1940–1944* (New York, 1982), p. 209. A total of 30,000 unemployed in the southern zone at the end of 1940 is cited in P. Weil, 'Espagnols et Italiens en France: la politique de la France', in Milza and Peschanski (eds), *Exils et Migration*, p. 95.

25 AD Haute-Garonne, 2517W 45. Secrétaire d'État à l'Intérieur to Préfets, 31 December 1940.

26 The CLC was created on 11 October 1940 by René Belin, Minister of Labour. Lehideux was theoretically in charge of the CLC in both zones. He was replaced by Jean Terray on 3 December 1941.

27 Maux-Robert, *La lutte contre le chômage à Vichy*, pp. 8–9.

28 Maux-Robert, 'Le commissariat à la lutte contre le chômage en zone sud', p. 126.

29 Weil, 'Espagnols et Italiens en France', p. 95.

30 Daily payments to families of TE workers consisted of 7 francs in the Paris/ Seine area, 5 francs in towns with populations of more than 5,000 and 4 francs in villages. An additional sum of 4–5 francs was available for each child. AD Haute-Garonne, 2517W 46.

31 Maux-Robert, 'Le commissariat à la lutte contre le chômage en zone sud', p. 140.

32 AD Haute-Garonne, 2517W 45. Général de Corps d'Armée SCIARD, commandant le 17ème Région to Commandants des Subdivisions de Toulouse, Agen, Auch, Foix, Cahors, Montauban, Pau, Tarbes, Aire-sur-l'Adour, la Réole, 21 September 1940.

33 AN Fontainebleau 19890151/6. Note for the Inspecteur Général des Services de Police Judiciaire, 6 December 1941.

34 Weil, 'Espagnols et Italiens en France', p. 95.

35 AD Dordogne, 42W 60/2.

36 The 1,600 workers of the 536th GTE were mainly composed of Spaniards and were dispersed amongst 38 different employers in agriculture, forestry and various other industries. AD Lot-et-Garonne, 1W 92 and 2W 15.

37 AD Dordogne, 42W 60/2. Laffitte, 'L'encadrement par le travail des étrangers dans le département du Gers 1939–1944', p. 100.

38 AD Dordogne, 7 AV 19.

39 Laffitte, 'L'encadrement par le travail des étrangers dans le département du Gers 1939–1944', p. 100.

40 AN CARAN, AJ41 83.5.

41 AN CARAN, AJ41 344. Note sur l'envoi de travailleurs espagnols de zone libre à l'organisation todt, 20 November 1940.

42 Dreyfus-Armand, *L'Exil des Républicains Espagnols en France*, p. 131.

43 AN CARAN, AJ41 344. Note addressed to M. Lehideux, 16 November 1941.

44 Maux-Robert, *La lutte contre le chômage à Vichy*, pp. 116–18.

45 For more information on OT recruitment see S. Soo, 'Ambiguities at Work: Spanish Republican Exiles and the Organisation Todt in Occupied Bordeaux', *Modern and Contemporary France*, 15:4 (2007), pp. 642–3; Maux-Robert, *La lutte contre le chômage à Vichy*, pp. 116–19, 149–52; Dreyfus-Armand, *L'Exil des Républicains Espagnols en France*, pp. 132–3; L. Stein, *Beyond Death and Exile: The Spanish Republicans in France, 1939–1955* (Cambridge, MA, 1979), p. 136.

46 AN CARAN AJ41 344. The directive related to Spanish internees in Argelès, Rivesaltes and possibly Vernet camps, together with GTE workers from the Montpellier, Marseilles and Lyons areas.

47 Diary entry of 29 August 1941. For similar incidents elsewhere: J. Cubero, *Les Républicains espagnols* (Pau, 2003), pp. 103–9.

48 *Moros blondes*, literally translated as 'blond Moors', was a term used by Spanish republicans to describe the German soldiers fighting on the side of the rebel forces and their Moorish troops during the war in Spain.

49 Details of these attacks are provided later in this chapter, pp. 168–9.

50 AN CARAN, AJ41 344. Relations du Commissariat à la lutte contre le chômage avec les Autorités d'Occupation, 20 August 1941.

51 For socio-professional details of the refugees see Appendix.

52 Dreyfus-Armand, *L'Exil des Républicains Espagnols en France*, pp. 132–3.

53 AN CARAN, AJ41 344.

54 AN CARAN, AJ41 344. Chef des Renseignements généraux to the Préfet de l'Aude, 9 September 1942.

55 AN CARAN, AJ41 344. Report by Commandant de la section de Gendarmerie de Beziers, 9 September 1942.

56 For details about the benefits offered by agents to potential Spanish workers in the Lot and Cher see Dreyfus-Armand, *L'Exil des Républicains Espagnols en France*, pp. 132–3; for the Gers, Laffitte, 'L'encadrement par le travail des étrangers dans le département du Gers 1939–1944', p. 103; and for the Pyrénées-Orientales, Stein, *Beyond Death and Exile*, p. 136. See also Maux-Robert, *La lutte contre le chômage à Vichy*, pp. 116–19, 149–52.

57 Dreyfus-Armand, *L'Exil des Républicains Espagnols en France*, p. 134.

58 Although some historians cite Otto's full name as José María Otto, his name appears as José María Otto Warnke in archival documents, e.g. AD Gironde, SC 1918, 1949.

59 Dreyfus-Armand, *L'Exil des Républicains Espagnols en France*, p. 133.

60 G. Sanchis Martínez, 'Souvenir d'un Voyage Historique d'un Réfugié Espagnol' (unpublished manuscript, 2001).

61 AD Gironde D64. Commissaire Spécial to Commissaire Divisionnaire in Bordeaux, 4, 7 and 22 November 1941.

62 AD Gironde Vrac 365.

63 AD Gironde, SC 1918.

64 Some of these photographs are reproduced in Soo, 'Ambiguities at Work'.

65 AD Gironde, SC 308. Report by the Gendarmerie Nationale, Légion d'Aquitaine, Compagnie des Landes, Section de Labouheyre, 19 February 1944.

66 Interview with Miguel Oviedo, Fargues-Saint-Hilaire, 24 September 2002.

67 J. Giménez Arenas, De la Unión a Banat: Itinerario de una rebeldía (Madrid, 1996), p. 127.

68 J. Carrasco, La odisea de los republicanos españoles en Francia. Album-souvenir de l'exil républicain espagnol en France (1939–1945) (Perpignan, 1984), pp. 233–4.

69 A significant Spanish immigrant population existed in Bordeaux from the end of the nineteenth century. P. Guillaume (ed.), Étrangers en Aquitaine. Vol. 8, L'Aquitaine, Terre d'Immigration (Talence, 1990), p. 194.

70 The information about the youth camp stems from interviews with Claudio Castañeira del Cubillo, Bordeaux, 4 June 2002, and Gabriel Tapias, Bordeaux, 5 October 2002. They are both members of the Hogar Español, a federation of Spanish organisations in Bordeaux that is housed next to the Spanish Church. Photos of the youth camp are contained in the booklet Auxilio Social en Burdeos (November 1943), which can be consulted at the Spanish national archives: AGA IDD N° 97 Embajada de España en París 1939–71. Caja 11609 n° 89 (consulado en Burdeos 1941–45).

71 The head of the church, Vicente Garamendi, was in regular contact with the Francoist Spanish Consulate in Bordeaux during and after the Occupation. AD Gironde, Versement 1239/41.

72 Interviews with Agustín Juan Diez, Bordeaux, 20 June 2002 and Antonio Arias, Lormont, 8 July 2002.

73 The report 'Synthèse sur l'organisation et l'activité des services policiers allemands et de leurs satellites français dans le sud-ouest durant la période d'occcupation (1940–1944)' contains details of five Spanish agents of the German Police and SS Security Service (KPD). The KPD worked in conjunction with the French Section des affaires politiques (SAP) and the Section de répression des affaires judiciaires d'origine politique (SRAJOP). For an explanation of the different police services see the first two chapters in Terrisse, Bordeaux, 1940–44.

74 AD Gironde, D64, Commissaire Spécial to Commissaire Divisionnaire, 7 November 1941.

75 AD Gironde, SC 1908. Recensement des Espagnols Rouges.

76 AD Gironde, D64. Report to Commissaire Divisionnaire, 22 November 1941.

77 Ibid, Commissaire Divisionnaire de Police Spéciale to Préfet enclosing instructions from the Feldkommandantur to the OT, 5 December 1941.

78 N. Falguera, L. Figuéres and E. Mannevy Garcia, Guerrilleros en Terre de France: Les Républicains espagnols dans la Résistance française (Pantin, 2000), p. 64.

79 Interview with Francisco Perez, Bègles, 5 July 2003.

80 Laffitte, 'L'encadrement par le travail des étrangers dans le département du Gers 1939–1944', p. 106.

81 AD Dordogne, AV 6. Recording of an interview with Calixto Casales, 28 November 2000.

82 AD Gironde, SC 1905. A list of 16 *procès-verbaux*, 4 February 1942.

83 AD Gironde, SC 1906.

84 Falguera, Figuéres and Mannevy Garcia, *Guerrilleros en Terre de France*, p. 63.

85 AD Gironde, D64. Préfecture. An urgent request from the Feldkommandantur to search for 745 missing Spaniards, 23 January 1942.

86 AD Gironde SC 1905. Préfecture to Chef de Division, 23 February 1942.

87 AD Gironde SC 1905. Préfecture to Chef de Division, 'Recensement des espagnols rouges', 23 February 1942.

88 AD Gironde, SC 1906. Préfet Délégué du Ministre Secrétaire d'Etat à l'Intérieur to Préfet of the Gironde, 24 June 1942.

89 AD Gironde, SC 1906. Instructions to Directeur du Camp de Mérignac-Beaudésert, 24 October 1942.

90 J. C. Scott, *Weapons of the Weak: Everyday Forms of Peasant Resistance* (New Haven, CT, 1985).

91 Falguera, Figuéres and Mannevy Garcia, *Guerrilleros en Terre de France*, pp. 61–2 and Terrisse, *Bordeaux, 1940–1944*, p. 84.

92 M. R. D. Foot, *SOE in France: An Account of the Work of the British Special Operations Executive in France, 1940–1944* (London, 1966), pp. 157–8.

93 Federica Montseny managed to avoid arrest, but was nonetheless under close surveillance in the Dordogne.

94 G. Dreyfus-Armand, 'Les Espagnols dans la Résistance: incertitudes et spécificités', in J.-M. Guillon and P. Laborie (eds), *Mémoire et Histoire: La Résistance* (Toulouse, 1995), p. 224.

95 G. Dreyfus-Armand, 'L'Émigration Politique Espagnole en France au Travers de sa Presse 1939–1975' (Thèse de Doctorat, Institut d'Études Politiques de Paris, 1994), p. 222.

96 The leaflet claimed Otto had acted as a French police informer while interned in the Gurs camp. AD Gironde, Vrac 32. Intendant Régional de Police to Préfet, 26 May 1942.

97 The FTPF was also commonly referred to as Francs-Tireurs et Partisans (FTP). The FTP–MOI structure originated from the 1920s, when the MOI had been created to unionise foreign workers into sections based on their ethnic backgrounds.

98 S. Courtois, D. Peschanski and A. Rayski, *Le Sang de l'étranger. Les immigrés de la MOI dans la Résistance* (Paris, 1989), pp. 128–32.

99 Interview with Migel Oviedo, Fargues-Saint-Hilaire, 24 September 2002.

100 Interview with Miguel Alama, Bordeaux, 30 May 2002.

101 Interview with Agustín Juan Diez, Bordeaux, 20 June 2002.

102 Falguera, Figuéres and Mannevy Garcia, *Guerrilleros en Terre de France*, p. 63.

103 J. Berruezo, *Contribución de la historia de la CNT de España en el exilio* (Mexico City, 1967), pp. 136–7.

104 AN Fontainebleau 19890151/6. Note for Inspecteur Général des Services de Police Judiciaire, 6 December 1941.

105 *Ibid.* Commissaire de Police Judiciaire, 8 Brigade Régionale, 7 January 1942.

106 *Ibid.* Commissaire de Police Judiciaire, 17 Brigade Régionale, 19 December 1941.

107 *Ibid.* Chef Régional des Services de Police Judiciaire, 8 February 1941.

108 On attempts by Lesage and his team at the SSE to protect Jewish workers see Maux-Robert, *La lutte contre le chômage à Vichy*, pp. 169–72.

109 Correspondence with Peter Paisley, 4 August 2010.

110 AD Lot, 1W 646. Étrangers 1942–45.

111 AD Pyrénées-Atlantiques, 1031W 234. Travailleurs étrangers et espagnols postérieurs à 1940.

112 Cubero, *Les Républicains espagnols*, pp. 143–4. For examples elsewhere, Dreyfus-Armand, *L'Exil des Républicains Espagnols en France*, p. 130.

113 Laffitte, 'L'encadrement par le travail des étrangers dans le département du Gers 1939–1944', p. 88.

114 E.g. Cubero, *Les Républicains espagnols*, pp. 143–4.

115 AD Pyrénées-Atlantiques, 1031W 234. Travailleurs étrangers et espagnols postérieurs à 1940; AD Lot-et-Garonne, 2W 15. Commissaire Principal to Préfet, 21 April 1942; AD Lot-et-Garonne, 1W 92. Renseignements généraux in Agen to Renseignements généraux in Toulouse, 23 December 1942. For more details of Jewish workers who managed to escape the detentions in August 1942 see Reviriego, *Les Juifs en Dordogne*, pp. 194–5.

116 *Ibid.*, p. 137.

117 Jackson, *France*, p. 387.

118 For instance, Spanish Communists worked in the office of the 721st GTE at Saint-Jean-de-Verges in the Ariège.

119 AD PA, 1031W 234. Renseignements généraux , 26 August 1942.

120 Berruezo, *Contribución de la historia de la CNT de España en el exilio*, pp. 38, 97–125.

121 C. Delpla, *Les Guerilleros Espagnols dans la Zone Pyrénéenne* (published by the author, 2002), p. 8.

122 See the detailed local study by C. and H. Farreny del Bosque, *L'Affaire Reconquista de España 1942–1944: Résistance espagnole dans le Sud-Ouest* (Toulouse, 2nd edn, 2010).

123 N. Català, *Ces Femmes Espagnoles: de la Résistance à la Déportation* (Paris, 1994). For Spanish women and resistance see also: M. Moreno Seco, 'L'exil au feminine: républicaines et anti-franquistes en France', in B. Vargas (ed.), *La Seconde République Espagnole en Exil en France (1939–1977)* (Albi, 2008).

124 For details of the maquis legend see H. R. Kedward, *In Search of the Maquis: Rural Resistance in Southern France 1942–1944* (Oxford, 1993), p. 30.

125 Dreyfus-Armand, 'Les Espagnols dans la Résistance: incertitudes et spécificités', p. 221.

126 AD Lot-et-Garonne. Circulaire ref. POL.JUD.6.T, 1 September 1942.

127 Farreny del Bosque, *L'Affaire Reconquista de España 1942–1944*, p. 11.

128 AD Lot-et-Garonne, 1W 92. Inspecteur de Police Nationale in Fumel to Commissaire Principal des Renseignements généraux in Agen, 16 November 1942.

129 B. Clavel, *L'Espagnol* (Paris, 1981).

130 AD Pyrénées-Atlantiques, 1031W 234. Travailleurs étrangers et espagnols postérieurs à 1940; AD Lot-et-Garonne, 2W 15. Commissaire Principal to Préfet, 21 April 1942; AD Lot-et-Garonne, 1W 92. Renseignements généraux in Agen to Renseignements généraux in Toulouse, 23 December 1942.

131 AD Haute-Garonne, 1769W 1. Préfet of the Tarn to Préfet Régional in Toulouse, 7 January 1943.

132 *Ibid.* Président, Directeur Général de la Société Hydro-Mécanique to Préfet, 22 April 1943.

133 *Ibid.* Head of Blois Exploitations Forestières, 1 July 1943.

134 *Ibid.* Head of Scieries Mécaniques Exploitations Forestières to Préfet Régional and Ministère de la Production Industrielle, 3 July 1943.

135 *Ibid.* Chef du Groupement du T.E. N° 2 to Préfet of the Haute-Garonne, 1 July 1943.

136 AD Lot, 1W 5. Préfet rapport, 6 August 1943.

137 Laffitte, 'L'encadrement par le travail des étrangers dans le département du Gers 1939–1944', p. 83.

138 AD Haute-Garonne, 1769W 1. Préfet of Gers to Préfet Régional, 30 December 1943.

139 *Ibid.* Préfet of the Hautes-Pyrénées to Ministre de la Production Industrielle, 14 January 1944.

140 *Ibid.* Préfet of the Hautes-Pyrénées to Ministre de la Production Industrielle, 14 January 1944.

141 *Ibid.* Préfet to Préfet Régional, 6 January 1944.

142 AD Lot, 1W 953. Renseignements généraux , 7 and 16 January 1944.

143 AD Lot-et-Garonne, 2W 15. Préfet to the Secrétaire d'état de l'Intérieur, 27 January 1944.

144 Sweets, *Choices in Vichy France*, p. 28.

145 For an account of how one Spanish worker made his way from Toulouse to Bordeaux see J. Giménez Arenas, *De la Unión a Banat: Itinerario de una rebeldía* (Madrid, 1996), pp. 124–31.

146 In September 1943, Vichy agreed that deserters from the STO and GTE who worked for the OT could not be pursued by the French authorities. Kedward, *In Search of the Maquis*, p. 22.

147 AD Lot-et-Garonne, 2W15. Commissaire Principal to Commissaire Divisionnaire, Toulouse, 16 February 1944.

148 AD Lot, 1W 646. Renseignements généraux, 'Propagande en faveur de la
Résistance au sein des milieux espagnols', 29 December 1943.

149 L. Yagîl, *Chrétiens et Juifs sous Vichy, 1940–1944: Sauvetage et désobéissance
civile* (Paris, 2005), p. 393.

150 AD Haute-Garonne, 1769W 1. Préfet of Gers to Préfet Régional, 6 January
1944.

151 Laffitte, 'L'encadrement par le travail des étrangers dans le département du
Gers 1939–1944', p. 83.

152 Kedward, *In Search of the Maquis*, pp. 21–2.

153 AD Gironde, SC 755. Bulletin hebdomadaire des Renseignements généraux.

154 AD Gironde, SC 308. Intendance de Police of Bordeaux to Préfet, 24 December 1943.

155 AN CARAN, AJ 41 344. Préfet of the Landes, reports 2 October–2 December
1943.

156 AD Gironde, SC 308. Inspecteur de Police to Commissaire Principal des
Renseignements généraux in Mont-de-Marsan, 11 December 1943.

157 AD Gironde SC 953. Préfet to Ministre de l'Intérieur, 23 February 1944. Préfet
to Feldkommandantur, 29 March 1944.

158 Police in the Lot-et-Garonne believed that most Spanish refugees deserting
the GTE had headed for either Bordeaux or Mont-de-Marsan. Commissaire
Principal in Agen to Commissaire Divisionnaire in Toulouse, no. 562, 16
February 1944. AD Lot-et-Garonne, 2W 15.

159 AD Gironde, SC 308. Commandant de la Section de Gendarmerie de
Labouheyre, 19 February 1944.

PART III

Aspirations of return, commemoration and home

6

~~~~~~~~

Mobilisation, commemoration and return, 1944–55

In the *département* of the Lot stands a tree with an inscription carved into its trunk: 'MAQUIS DE LA RÉSISTANCE DE LIBERTÉ'. This non-official monument was created by Spanish refugee maquisards from the 'Liberté' group as they passed through the area following the battle of Larnagol.[1] Further west, in Bordeaux, another trace can be found in the form of a plaque that was unveiled in the post-Liberation period in memory of Pablo Sanchez, 'shot by German troops on 27 August 1944'. These memorials – one rural, the other urban – draw attention to the participation of the Spanish republicans in liberations across France whilst also demonstrating that the commemoration of the Spanish republican exile is no recent phenomenon.

During and after the Liberation of France, the Spanish refugees engaged in a flurry of public meetings and memorial services. They were energised by an infectious optimism that spread to swathes of the French public about the prospects for a liberated Spain. There were good reasons to be optimistic. At the international level, despite the lack of coherence in the Western democracies' positions on the Spanish dictatorship, there had been sufficient public statements to fuel belief in some form of Allied support for regime change.[2] In France, the press ran articles systematically throughout the summer months and autumn of 1944 on the subject of Franco's removal and the return of the Republic in Spain.[3] Amongst Spanish republicans themselves, there could be no mistaking the vitality of the anti-Francoist cause: activism was inseparable from return.

The strategies adopted by the refugees to legitimate their actions and, more specifically, the role of memory in this process constitute the main focus of this chapter. In the first place, this chapter outlines the context surrounding the refugees' reconstructed sense of self and the reactions of the French national and local authorities. Whilst the resistance had created new opportunities for the Spanish republicans, a combination of national interests and deeply ingrained prejudice continued to shape the perceptions of some French officials. But at the same time, French local officials and organisations demonstrated significant support for the Spanish republican cause. The refugees legitimated their actions by mobilising the past, and the second part of this chapter analyses exactly how and why a socio-political framework of Spanish republican exilic memory emerged, its constituent narratives, and the reason for its disappearance from French public spaces at the start of the 1950s. The final part of this chapter further contextualises the decline of Spanish republican exilic memory with a discussion on the membership figures of the various organisations.

There has been some pioneering work on Spanish republican remembrance. Scholars have discussed how specific associations have recalled the past, as well as accounting for both the absence of the internment camps from the French national memory cadre and the corresponding importance of internment for the Spanish republicans in forging a collective sense of self in exile.[4] The important role of the exilic press in disseminating a mythologised recollection of the Spanish Civil War has also been explored, whilst historians at the University of Toulouse have emphasised the fragmented aspect of Spanish republican memory.[5]

The heterogeneity of the Spanish republicans certainly needs acknowledging when investigating their commemorative activities, but there were junctures when Spanish refugees from across the ideological spectrum invested in a common set of memory narratives. The liberation and post-liberation period was one such occasion and therefore merits close attention. Never before had the refugees organised and participated in a series of public meetings and remembrance ceremonies that so explicitly centred on the organised commemoration of the Spanish republican *exile in France*. They had celebrated the past before, notably behind barbed wire during the spring and summer of 1939, but this was the first time that their presence in France featured as a memory narrative. It is also important to underline that this was not a unilateral phenomenon. In some localities, both the refugees and their French hosts invested in a Spanish republican resistance liturgy. Their activities offer us a reminder of the plurality of commemorative discourses surrounding the Liberation in France and, in some localities, the limited impact of the nascent

Gaullist and (French) Communist myths of the Resistance in framing resistance as a purely French affair. By accounting for these nuances, this chapter contributes to a fuller picture of how the Occupation was remembered in France.

The analysis of these activities also contributes to memory studies of exile and the development of the memorial landscape in France. At a heightened moment of anticipated return, the remembrance practices contained none of the paralysing nostalgia commonly associated with Spanish republican exilic literature. On the contrary, the refugees mobilised the past in order to secure an end to exile, thereby using memory as one of the weapons in their armoury for combating the regime in Spain. This explains why the socio-political framework of exilic memory began to wane as prospects of western intervention in ridding Spain of the dictatorship declined. Even though this memory work had petered out by the end of the 1940s, it laid the foundations for a subsequent commemorative culture of exile which gathered momentum towards the end of the twentieth century (more of which follows in the next chapter). For this reason we can refer to these early memory practices as constituting a 'proto-commemorative' culture of (the Spanish republican) exile.

From vanquished to victors

On 24 August 1944, among the advance guard of General Leclerc's 2nd Armoured French Division as it entered the French capital were Spanish republicans of the Ninth Company. These foreign liberators might well have gone unnoticed were it not for the slogans on the side of their half-track armoured vehicles evoking past battles and icons from the Spanish republican imaginary: 'Madrid', 'Guadalajara', 'Brunete', 'Guernica' and 'Don Quixote'. After a short stay in Paris they went on to see action in Eastern France and Germany. But it was in the southern half of France where Spanish republicans were most widely involved in liberating the country through their participation in a wide variety of resistance organisations.

Not all localities were liberated through fighting, but rather through the unopposed departure of German troops. However, where combat occurred Spanish refugees were frequently involved, and increasingly so as German forces headed for northern France or the Spanish border after the Allied landings in Provence on 15 August. In the Basses-Pyrénées, Spanish republicans saw action in the Ossau and Aspe valleys.[6] In the Gers they could be found in the ranks of the 35th Spanish Guerrilla

Brigade under Tomas Guerrero, in the Secret Army 'Armagnac battalion' led by Maurice Parisot or in the Resistance Organisation of the Army.[7] All of these groups operated in conjunction with the SOE agent George Reginald Starr ('Hilaire') to tie down potential German reinforcements for the D-Day landings.[8] Further eastwards, the Tarn was also a hive of Spanish republican activity. For a while the headquarters of the Spanish Guerrilla Group (AGE), formerly the 14th (Spanish) Guerrilla Corps, was based around Gaillac.[9] Spaniards could also be found in the French and anti-communist Corps Franc de la Montagne Noire, or in the Vendôme group, which gathered together Spanish and Polish miners along with anti-fascists from other central and Eastern European backgrounds who had previously fought in the Spanish Civil War. On 12 August a battle on the Lagupie road was followed by a series of engagements to liberate the Tarn over the next ten days.[10] In the Occupied Zone of the Dordogne, the Spanish republicans were in the ranks of the FTPF, while in the Southern Zone they organised a warfare training centre. In the south-east of the same *département* CNT militants grouped around José Cervera, and operated in close contact with the French group 'Soleil'.

Spanish republicans were active in other areas of southern France. They fought around Rodez in the Aveyron, and were involved in actions further south in the Pyrénées-Orientales. At the battle of La Madeleine in the Gard, guerrilla fighters under Cristino García and Miguel Arcas joined forces with the FTPF to attack a substantial German column heading northwards.[11] But perhaps more than any other *département*, it is the Ariège which epitomises the role of the Spanish *guerrilleros*. On 19 August, Spanish fighters of the 3rd Brigade of the 26th Division of Spanish Guerilleros, in liaison with two inter-allied commanders (Bigeard with the nom de guerre 'Aube', and a British operative, Major William Probert), set out to dislodge German forces from Foix, and by the evening had secured the city. To the west, along the axis of Saint-Girons, Prayols and Castelnau-Durban, more Spaniards and an FTP group harangued German forces, the Milice and members of the Parti populaire français for two days before taking 1,600 prisoners on the evening of 22 August.[12]

The summer of 1944 was a far cry from 1939 when the same *départements* in southern France had been synonymous with the mass internment of Spanish refugees. New contacts and relations between the refugees and French nationals had developed over the intervening period in workplaces and resistance groups at various levels. In the upper echelons of organisations, the UNE had relations with the MOI, PCF and French Forces of the Interior (FFI), while the CGT had assisted the MLE in its search for a safe haven, provisions and arms towards the end of the Occupation. At the grass-roots level, Spanish republicans could be found alongside French nationals in various resistance outfits, or even as military training instructors. One French *maquisard* from the Dordogne recalled: 'our instructors were veterans from the Spanish Civil War and had all the necessary skills and experience for the job'.[13]

Although the Spanish republicans' motivations and strategies for resisting had varied, one identity above all served as an ideological cohesive: anti-fascism. As such, different organisations and groups drew on anti-fascist consciousness to legitimate their own interests.[14] As with most forms of identification, there are issues to do with definition. The refugees often conflated anti-fascism with anti-Francoism, even though the two were slightly different, albeit overlapping, phenomena. While General Franco's regime contained fascist elements, it was more characteristic of an extreme nationalist and authoritarian Catholicism. Moreover, there were limits to the emotive draw of anti-fascism. Even if the PCE-dominated UNE managed to unite militants of various ideological tendencies under an anti-fascist umbrella, this was not a powerful enough centripetal force to bring the CNT and the PCE-dominated organisations together. Nevertheless, irrespective of these issues, anti-fascism represented a notable frame of reference that mobilised and galvanised grass-roots militants from various ideological and national backgrounds.[15] There was a steadfast belief among the refugees that they, and their fellow international combatants from the Spanish Civil War, were pioneers in the global fight against fascism.[16] As such, resistance in France represented another, and perhaps closing, stage of a conflict that had erupted on the other side of the Pyrenees in July 1936. As the National Committee of the CNT declared at the start of 1945, 'France is only the means and Spain is our immediate goal.'[17]

Border politics

French views of the Spanish republican resisters in France were not uniformly positive. Individual French resisters could be critical, associating Spanish resisters with banditry, indiscipline or reckless behaviour.[18] The PCE–UNE strategy of concentrating guerrilla fighters in the frontier *départements* along the Pyrenees had also been a source of friction. The MOI accused the UNE of compromising the aim of liberating the whole of France through its focus on the border and Spain.[19] More spectacularly, the policing role adopted by Spanish resisters – with their UNE armbands featuring the colours of the Spanish Republic, the Cross of Lorraine and the acronym UNE–FFI – generated concern amongst the national and some local authorities.

The infrastructure problems caused by the liberation fighting and the relative isolation of the Pyrenean *départements* meant that policing the French side of the border was largely dependent on the FFI. In many areas this included a substantial, if not predominant, number of Spanish resisters. In the Pyrénées-Orientales, the Ariège and the Basses-Pyrénées they could even be found manning the French border posts. Although sympathetic to the Spanish republicans, the French provisional government was keen to marginalise Spanish republican influence in the region for two reasons. First, the government was worried that its authority could be undermined by the new moral currency of the Spanish republicans in France and their relationships with French local authorities. Secondly, it believed that cross-border conflicts between the refugees and Spanish nationalist forces risked destabilising the region and compromising French relations with Franco's regime.[20]

From mid-1944, small armed groups had in fact been crossing into Spain to try and link up with guerrilla units to prepare the population for a mass uprising. An infraction of French national sovereignty had also occurred on 8 September, when Francoist border guards fired upon Spanish republican resisters and even breached the border near Perthus in the Pyrénées-Orientales to take prisoners.[21] Although aware of significant Spanish republican movements in this region, there was actually very little the French government and local authorities could do to assert their influence. General Bertin tried without success to assert the government's authority by ordering all FFI troops, including the guerrilla fighters, to evacuate the border area on 6 September.[22] A month later, the Prefect of the Basses-Pyrénées admitted he had little authority over the 1,500 *guerrilleros* in his locality.[23] In fact, from the first week in October Spanish republicans had begun crossing into Spain at various points virtually on a daily basis, in preparation for a mass incursion that became known as the Val d'Aran expedition.[24]

The French government hoped to rein in the UNE when it charged General Caille with responsibility for the Pyrenean region in early October.[25] But difficulties in establishing authority persisted. Spanish republicans retained control over border crossings and customs posts for as long as possible. Even after relinquishing this responsibility they continued to intervene in the policing process by reproaching the French authorities over contacts with Francoist officials.[26] By mid-November, though, the Spanish republicans agreed to French requests to withdraw behind a 50-km border-exclusion zone. Towards the end of the month, a report by one *commissaire de la République* expressed satisfaction at the situation and, interestingly, suggested that regional stability depended more on the French commanding officer than on the *guerrilleros'* behaviour. A leading general had been referring to the refugees, the FFI and FTP as *rouges*, and one of his underlings apparently had monarchist and pro-Franco sympathies. The report recommended removing the two officers from the region.[27]

These reports from along the frontier contain echoes of the two very different French approaches to Spanish foreign policy outlined by David Messenger: a 'realpolitik' vision based on French national interests; and a 'justice' model inspired by universalism and an accompanying belief that France should aid the Spanish republicans in overthrowing Franco to restore republican democracy.[28] The complaints of local officials and the creation of an exclusion area along the border reflected French national interests. Yet this contrasts with some local French responses to the border crossings and the Val d'Aran expedition. The fact that approximately 7,000 Spanish republicans were able to cross into Spain during October and November – and sometimes by the lorryload – not only illustrates the lack of government authority in the region, but also the overlapping issue of local complicity by French nationals who supported the refugees' cause.

Another characteristic of local officials' perceptions and actions towards the Spanish refugees was the continuity in pejorative labelling that dated back to the refugees' arrival in 1939. The Mayor of Pauillac in the Gironde referred to the Spanish refugees in his locality, left unemployed after the departure of the German authorities, as 'a problem of surveillance, subsistence, and of potential trouble'.[29] Elsewhere in the Gironde, the burglars of a house in Verdelais were 'presumed to be Spanish'.[30] More serious allegations occurred further southwards towards the border. In the Basses-Pyrénées, the *Renseignements généraux* claimed the majority of residents in Pau attributed a series of bomb explosions to the *guerrilleros*.[31] In reality, the bombs were the work of French nationals frustrated about the slow pace of trials against former collaborators.[32]

In the neighbouring *département* of the Landes, the complaints of a lawyer and member of the 'Ceux de la Libération' resistance movement (founded in late 1940 by Maurice Ripoche, an engineer with extreme right-wing views) provoked an investigation into claims that *guerrilleros* had been involved in searches, pillaging and insurrectionary behaviour.[33] An ensuing report by the Prefect depicted an uneasy relationship between French locals and the 500 *guerrilleros* grouped around the town of Dax.[34] Several people had referred to a mass grave of 15 bodies, 9 of which were German, but a judicial investigation could not proceed because of apparent threats to the local population. Friction was also noted elsewhere in the vicinity. At the start of November, a request by Spanish republicans to the village council of Josse for 350 men to be accommodated in the locality sparked a lively protest. Furthermore, the Prefect suspected the refugees were forcing farmers to sell produce. It is the end of the report, though, that highlights what was really at stake, namely the Prefect's unease about local power relations. While the UNE was theoretically subject to the FFI commander's authority, in practice this was ineffective, given the dispersion of the Spaniards around the countryside (an observation which echoed officials' concerns about Spanish workers in the Landes during the Occupation). The Prefect ultimately desired to disband or confine the *guerrilleros* to barracks, but this was unrealistic, given the absence of state-controlled forces.

Relations between French nationals and the *guerrilleros* in the Landes were in reality less black and white than the image sketched by the Prefect. If there was unease amongst some French nationals about the continued armed presence of the Spanish *guerrilleros* in the Landes, it is indicative that French officers of the 18th Military Region showed no immediate concern. Moreover, the participation of the UNE in two ceremonies commemorating French victims of the Occupation of Dax in the same month as the investigation was conducted suggests some level of French support.[35]

Re-establishing Spanish republican legitimacy in France

Whilst the situation at the border was largely resolved by the end of November 1944, a significant issue remained with the refugees' appropriation of Spanish consulates across France. These actions had started during the Liberation. As German troops surrendered in Paris, the PSOE militant and member of the UNE, Julio Hernández, took over the Spanish Embassy with a group of men, replacing the rebel flag with the tricolour of the Spanish Republic.[36] Similar events occurred elsewhere and especially throughout south-western France, where the UNE had concentrated its forces. In Bordeaux, 200 Spanish republicans overran the Spanish consulate and invited the consul to switch allegiance. He declined and on 18 September had to be escorted by the French authorities to the border for his own security. In the meantime, the refugees mounted a UNE banner and reopened the building for Spanish nationals in France. They also confiscated secret archives, money and official stamps.[37]

Further south, the consulate in Pau was able to avoid the same fate through the Prefect's intervention. But Spanish republicans transformed the Bayonne consulate into the UNE local headquarters decorated with the flags of the French and Spanish Republics. The action was repeated at the Hendaye consulate.[38] At another consulate, close to the Gurs camp, Spanish (nationalist) officials were forced to give documents, archives and consular stamps to the French Sub-Prefect for safekeeping.[39] In the Lot-et-Garonne, the honorary Spanish consul responded to threats by leaving Agen but later returned to try and recuperate the archives seized by the UNE.[40]

Many refugees saw this reaffirmation of Spanish republican legitimacy in France as a prelude to returning to Spain. For the French provisional government, however, it presented an additional obstacle to developing relations with nationalist Spain. While mindful of the Spanish refugees' participation in the Liberation of France, the French state had recognised Franco's dictatorship as the legitimate government of Spain in 1939 and was consequently obliged under international law to protect Spanish (nationalist) consular staff and buildings. The Minister of the Interior outlined the government's dilemma to prefects across the country in late October.[41] He drew attention to the importance of maintaining positive relations with the regime in Spain as well as explaining how relations between the French Committee of National Liberation (Comité Français de Libération) and the Francoist authorities during the latter stages of the Occupation had secured the protection of French resisters in Spain. He also cited international conventions surrounding diplomatic relations and thus instructed prefects to evacuate the UNE from the consulates.

Perhaps mindful of the Spanish republicans' moral currency with the French public, the Minister omitted to mention that foodstuffs imported from Spain were playing a role in the reconstruction of France. However, he was keen to express the provisional government's sympathy for the refugees, reminding prefects they should afford the refugees the same treatment as Spanish nationals. In fact, the French government went even further by formally granting the Spanish republicans formal refugee status in March 1945. The refugee statute was, all the same, a perfect example of the government's stance towards appeasing Spanish republicans and their French supporters: it offered an important concession whilst having minimal impact on Francoist Spain.[42]

Even when a consulate reopened under the Spanish nationalist banner, it remained a site of contestation. Throughout February and March 1945, the Spanish nationalist consul in Pau noted the equivocations of the French authorities who were trying to prevent attacks against the consulate without wishing to be seen as openly protective. He was also concerned about the Departmental Liberation Committee's (CDL) lack of assurances about guaranteeing his personal safety.[43] A demonstration of 5,000 people in Pau on 18 February did nothing to placate the consul's fears. The protest was directed against the return of Francoist representatives to consulates in the Basses-Pyrénées, but additionally criticised Spain's support for the Axis troops dug in on the Atlantic coast north of Bordeaux. The day began with a meeting and calls for the government to expel the consuls from Pau, Hendaye and Bayonne and to cut diplomatic relations with Spain.[44] Speeches were given by representatives from the League of the Rights of Man, the Front National, the CGT and Spanish republican representatives. During the march through the city centre police simply observed as one individual climbed up the consular building to tear down the nationalist insignia. By the end of the day, a French–Spanish committee had been created with the aim of liberating Spain. It was supported by the Prefect, Mayor, local newspaper editors, members of the Departmental Liberation Committee and a high-ranking military officer.[45]

The extent of support in Pau was not unique: Prefects of the Aveyron, Hérault and the Pyrénées-Orientales also openly voiced opposition to Franco's regime.[46] At the national level, politicians from leading parties and some Catholics also adhered to the same cause.[47] But the opportunity to take a national stance towards Spain did not occur until a year later when de Gaulle resigned in January 1946 as head of government. He was replaced by Félix Gouin, a Socialist and staunch supporter of the Spanish Republic, at the helm of a coalition of the PCF, SFIO and the Christian Democrats of the Mouvement Républicain Populaire. A month later, there was popular indignation at news that Franco's regime had sentenced 12 captured guerrilla fighters to death. Among the condemned was Cristino García, who was known for having played a leading role in the Resistance in the *départements* of the Gard, Lozère and the Ardèche before being captured during a clandestine mission in Spain. Anger at the execution was noticeably robust in south-western France, with renewed focus on the consulates and a series of strikes by the French CGT and its affiliate unions.[48] Despite the reticence of the Foreign Affairs Minister, Georges Bidault, who favoured a realpolitik stance towards Spain, pressure from the rest of the governing coalition and the National Assembly led the government to close the border with Spain on 1 March 1946.

The politics of remembering

Each of the rival Spanish republican organisations strove to affirm its hegemony as the most appropriate body to administer a post-Francoist Spain. In some areas of liberated France the UNE managed to portray itself as the sole representative of the Spanish republicans, and the consular occupations had been part of this strategy. However, the UNE's standing amongst the refugees and some French local authorities began to wane after the disastrous Val d'Aran episode and as stories circulated about the organisation's nefarious recruitment methods.[49]

The two largest trade unions, the CNT and UGT, had publicly challenged the UNE back in August 1944. Their joint circular addressed to 'all Spanish anti-fascists' criticised the UNE's tactics and its claim of embodying cross-party/syndical interests.[50] A sustained anti-UNE campaign followed. Similar concerns were reiterated months later by anti-Negrín militants of the PSOE and UGT during the first congresses of their respective organisations in France. During the MLE's national plenary in Toulouse, delegates from across France reported UNE threats to libertarians and discussed the viability of an opposing cross-party/syndical body.[51] This alternative was the Spanish Democratic Alliance (ADE), which grouped together all of the non-communist parties and trade unions.[52] On 23 October, the Alliance became the French section of the Spanish Liberation Committee (JEL).[53] Its strategy soon began to bear fruit as the JEL surpassed the UNE in members and became the preferred umbrella organisation of some local French authorities because of its less confrontational approach.[54]

The government of the Spanish Republic in exile was conspicuous for its lack of involvement with the refugees. It had ceased to function during the first years of the Second World War and was reconstituted during August 1943 in Mexico. Unsurprisingly, it was rather removed from Spanish republicans' daily preoccupations in France. While it continued to focus on diplomatic initiatives with the French and Allied governments, the refugees' daily concerns and discussions about returning were threshed out within the various political parties and trade unions. Even when the Giral government took up residence in Paris in February 1946, along with the Basque and Catalan governments, the focal point of Spanish republican activity remained the south-west of France.

Commemoration was inseparable from the conflicts between, and within, the Spanish republican organisations. It was a vector through which power relations were played out with each organisation seeking to legitimate itself, both to refugees and the French authorities, as the most representative and responsible body. But irrespective of political/syndical creed, public memorial narratives possessed a range of shared characteristics including opposition to the Francoist dictatorship, the role of Spanish republicans in liberating France and the enthusiastic representation of the French Republic.

Refugees organised meetings around a cluster of themes. These included rallies around symbolic dates from the Spanish and French republican calendars, commemorations of French and Spanish people killed during the Occupation, protests against the imprisonment and execution of anti-Francoists in Spain, demands for the rupture of diplomatic relations between France and Spain and general fund-raising events. There was also a pronounced ritualistic aspect to these occasions. The cinemas and halls tended to be decorated with the French and Spanish republican flags, and sometimes with those of the USA, Great Britain and the USSR. French representatives of local authorities, political parties, trade unions and other associations sympathetic to the Spanish republicans were also invited to attend and give speeches. Finally, the events usually ended with the singing of French and Spanish republican anthems.

The narratives and rituals of a proto-commemorative culture of exilic memory

Celebrating the past was not a new phenomenon for the refugees. There were some similarities with the activities from the spring and summer of 1939 when refugee internees across southern France had celebrated key dates from the Spanish and French republican calendars.[55] However, the form, context and role of Spanish republican commemoration in Liberated France were substantively different. For the first time since their arrival, the refugees began celebrating a collective memory of their exilic past.

There was a selective aspect to remembrance that was mostly designed to avoid compromising French–Spanish (republican) relations. For instance, the refugees abstained from recalling the saga of the French reception and internment policy of 1939. This absence was not entirely instrumental as it partly stemmed from the recognition that however poorly the French authorities had treated the refugees, asylum had nonetheless been offered. But the prime reason lay in the relationship which the Spanish republicans hoped to forge with the post-Vichy governments. There was much at stake. Refugees believed there was a good chance of ending Franco's dictatorship and returning to Spain. They were also aware this could not be achieved alone and regarded the support of the French – as well as the other Allied – authorities as crucial. The refugees were consequently wary of harming relations by recalling episodes from their past that might offend French sensibilities.

The memory of the camps was not entirely obliterated.[56] The *Espagne républicaine* newspaper called on the Spanish government in exile to write the history of the camps, the CTE and maquis, but significantly without reproach to the French state.[57] Generally, though, whenever the concentration camps of 1939 were cited, it was for an exclusively Spanish audience. For instance, a CNT leaflet marking the anniversary of the social revolution described the refugees' arrival in France as having occurred 'at the point of a bayonet'. It also implied that the German prisoners of war taken at the Liberation were interned under better conditions than had been the case for the Spanish refugees in 1939.[58]

The CNT leaflet is equally telling of how Spanish libertarians viewed their situation in France as part of a long-term pan-national struggle. It located the various episodes when libertarians had fought against German troops in exile – for the French military during the battle of France, then for the Resistance in France and for Allied forces elsewhere – as part of an ongoing struggle against Franco's regime that stretched back to 1936. This narrative strategy was also employed for commemorative events. To mark the same anniversary, the local branch of the CNT in Périgueux, the Dordogne, organised a meeting of French–Spanish fraternity during which they laid a wreath at a monument commemorating local resisters killed during the Occupation.[59]

Participation in memorial ceremonies linked to the Occupation represents an early example of Spanish republicans affirming relations with French local authorities and organisations. On 1 November 1944, UNE representatives in Dax laid a wreath of flowers depicting the colours of the French and Spanish Republics on the graves of French locals killed by German troops.[60] Similar scenes were repeated in Armistice Day ceremonies across the Aquitaine region.[61] In the region's administrative centre, Bordeaux, the UNE also distributed leaflets written in both French and Spanish recalling the eighth anniversary of the battle for Madrid, thereby establishing a link between November 1936 and November 1944. The French leaflet recalled French participation in the defence of Madrid, whilst the Spanish leaflet drew on La Pasionaria's celebrated maxim, calling on refugees to unite and transform the 'they shall not pass of yesterday to we will pass to crush Franco and his Falange'.[62]

Fundraising also formed part of the remembrance practices. On 19 November the UNE organised a social event in the Mérignac area of Bordeaux in support of French and Spaniards shot during the Occupation. The following week, the Front National and UNE held another fundraising evening at Oloron in the Basses-Pyrénées with funds destined for the FFI. On 26 November, militants decorated a hall in Dax with the French tricolour alongside a number of banners, one of which read 'L'Union nationale espagnole rend homage à ses Frères Français' ('The Spanish National Union pays homage to its French brothers').[63] Back northwards to Langon, in the Gironde, participants at another event took part in a Spanish–French cultural event. The walls of the hall were covered with a scene representing three fatally wounded Spanish refugee soldiers expressing satisfaction at having liberated France and calling for the liberation of Spain.[64]

The extent of French public support for commemorative events involving the Spanish republicans varied from place to place. In some localities, a French nationalist interpretation of the Resistance was apparent early on. The level of public support of the local authorities in Pau, discussed earlier in this chapter, was certainly not reciprocated in the region's administrative centre of Bordeaux. In this city, Spanish refugees soon discovered they were extraneous to the dominant resistance narratives so central to the reconstruction of post-war French national identity. A meeting between the JEL and the CDL in August 1945 was cancelled when the CDL's head, Dr Marcade, failed to turn up. Three days later, on 28 August, frustration turned to exasperation as the JEL was excluded from the city's commemoration of the Liberation. Despite an invite from former resisters of Libération Nord for the JEL to attend the ceremony, the *commissaire de la République* rejected the latter's request to make a speech on behalf of the 'Spanish anti-fascist refugees of Bordeaux'. The French official alleged that 'the commemoration was really a French affair and consequently no speeches could be made by any Spanish group.'

A JEL report into the organisation's relationship with the city's authorities concluded pessimistically: 'we do not hold any great hope, for the near or far future, of being able to form a friendly anti-fascist relationship, which should exist between the French and Spanish refugees to overthrow Franco and his regime'.[65] Shortly afterwards, the JEL committee decided to restrict the participation of French representatives at JEL meetings.[66] Although it is unclear if the organisation minimised the presence of French representatives at future events, the JEL nonetheless continued to try and rally French support for their cause through commemorative activities. After three years of planning, the JEL inaugurated a plaque recalling the place where German troops had shot dead Pablo Sanchez while they evacuated Bordeaux during the liberation. The format of the ceremony was familiar. Representatives laid wreaths representing the French and Spanish Republics and a former maquisard evoked the circumstances surrounding Pablo Sanchez's death before underlining the need for a French–Spanish union and a free Spain.[67]

Shattered hopes

Following the dissolution of the UNE in June 1945, the PCE continued its remembrance activities, and greeted the French closure of the French–Spanish border with enthusiasm. But by 1947, there was a more subdued emphasis on the French Republic as the PCE prioritised a more obviously Communist interpretation of events, past and present. The PCF deputy of the Gironde attended a ceremony which the police services described as hostile in tone towards the French government. In departure from previous events, the past was evoked exclusively in ideological terms through references to the International Brigades of the Spanish Civil War and Spanish participation in the FTPF during the Occupation.[68]

The change in emphasis was partly linked to the specificity of growing anti-communism in France. But it also probably reflected a resurgence of anti-Spanish refugee sentiment amongst local authorities. In 1947, officials from the Gironde produced a synthesis of the previous year's police reports which suggested that an important number of Spanish refugees were involved in common crime. There was no evidence to support this claim. But as had often been the case with the Spanish republicans in France, there was an underlying desire to see the back of the refugees. Accordingly, the report concluded that the actual scope of the problem would only be ascertained once the refugees returned to Spain.[69]

The French municipal elections in late October 1947 and the strikes of the following month proved to be a catalyst for a recrudescence of French officials' anxieties about refugees and public order issues across the country. The *Renseignements généraux* in Toulouse produced unflattering reports about the presence of Spanish Communists at various political meetings in the Haute-Garonne for the Minister of the Interior.[70] The latter reacted by declaring that any foreigners apprehended for work stoppages or for participating in pickets, violence and sabotage would face immediate expulsion.[71]

Between the end of November 1947 and January 1948 few immigrants were actually arrested. In the whole of France, a total of four Spaniards received an expulsion order, and in the south-west, apart from one Russian in Toulouse, there were no reported arrests. But even so, officials in the south-west were quick to identify Spanish republicans as a problem. Admittedly, their concerns were partly linked to clandestine migrants crossing the border from Spain.[72] But this negative perception also reflected a broader and longer-term tendency of linking the refugees with public order issues. Accordingly, prefects from across southern France met in Toulouse on 3 March 1948 to discuss the Spanish republicans.[73] The Minister of the Interior responded to the prefects' deliberations with circulars on 26 and 31 March containing instructions about residence restrictions for 'undesirable' refugees and newly arriving clandestine immigrants.

With the reopening of the French–Spanish border in February 1948, the French government became more responsive to Francoist calls to suppress the refugees' activities.[74] But as we have seen, the French government's receptiveness to such demands was also linked to a resurgence of anti-communism, and a renewed emphasis on the Spanish republicans as a public order issue. The modified international and domestic context did not bode well for Spanish republican hopes of returning to Spain. As this aspiration began to look increasingly untenable there was a noticeable change in the refugees' memory activities.

Until 1950, Spanish republicans from across the political and ideological spectrum mobilised a memory of exile by recalling their participation in the Liberation of France as part of a long-term struggle against fascism. The realisation that the national interests of the Western democracies would be the prime driving force behind international diplomacy rendered an anti-fascist discourse increasingly redundant as a way of generating French and international support. Paradoxically, the memory of exile had featured prominently when refugees' expectations about returning to Spain ran high. But as the realisation sank in that they could expect little or no help from France and the Allies, the political function of Spanish republican exilic memory no longer served the purpose of securing a return to Spain. Although the refugees continued to celebrate the past, the focus of remembrance shifted entirely from their exploits in exile to a constellation of symbolic events and personalities from pre-exile.

With the onset of the Cold War, the French government was very sensitive to the presence of Spanish Communists in France. The discovery of an arms cache linked to the *guerrilleros* in the south-west fuelled French concerns even further. In September 1950, the government launched operation 'Boléro-Paprika' and banned all Spanish Communist organisations in France. To the delight of Franco's regime, French police arrested several hundred militants and forced them into a second exile with the choice of leaving France for an East European country or for a life of surveillance in Corsica or southern Algeria.[75] The ban included a veterans' association of former FFI and Spanish resisters, l'Amicale des anciens FFI et résistants espagnols, thereby suppressing memorial as well as political activities.

The repercussions of this repressive climate also stretched to the Socialist organisations in exile. A year later, the leading UGT militant, Pascual Tomás, told colleagues that he was pessimistic about the restoration of a Republic in Spain given that Franco was taking full advantage of American fears about Communism in Europe.[76] It was around this time that references to the social revolution, which had occurred at the start of the Civil War in Spain, began to fade from the discourses of the PSOE and UGT.[77] The Spanish republicans' exilic memory narratives had positioned the refugees' struggle as part of a wider ideological conflict that affected all of Europe. But by 1950, the vocabulary of anti-fascism and anti-Francoism was ill-shaped for an international arena now dominated by the confrontation between capitalism and Soviet Communism.

Membership, work, welfare and solidarity

How did the changing climate in France affect the refugees' organisations in exile? In terms of membership levels, a case study of the Gironde shows a drop in fully paid-up members after an initially high level of activity between 1945 and 1948. In the aftermath of the Liberation, there were around 24,000 Spanish immigrants in the Gironde, of whom around 6,000 were refugees. By 1952, the number of refugees had increased slightly to 6,145, while the overall Spanish population had decreased to 19,238.[78] Throughout this period, the French police services consistently distinguished the refugees from other immigrants – and from their French counterparts – through the intensity of their organisational activity. This was a striking characteristic considering that Spanish immigrants accounted for just 2.8 per cent of the population of the Gironde, with Spanish refugees making up an even smaller figure.[79]

Out of all the Spanish refugees' organisations, the most representative was without doubt the CNT. At the end of 1945, the Prefecture believed CNT membership in the Aquitaine to be 2,500, with 800 in Bordeaux. In 1947, membership in the Gironde was estimated at 1,000, with 700 belonging to the 'apolitical' wing and 300 in the group that had supported CNT participation in the Giral government. It is unclear how many of the *cenetistas* also belonged to the FIJL and FAI, though the membership of the SIA was around 250.[80]

Communists were less numerous. In March 1947, the police estimated there were 500 militants of the PCE and 300 of the PSUC in the Gironde, though it should be noted that PSUC militants also tended to belong to the PCE. As with their French counterparts, the Spanish and Catalan Communists were most prolific in creating satellite associations mirroring the PCF strategy of '*la présence partout*'. Thus in parallel to the Front National, refugees created La Solidaridad Española. In 1947 the reported membership of the latter stood at 1,200, and included the support of non-communist French personalities such as Mgr Saliège, the Archbishop of Toulouse whose initial support for Pétain turned to open condemnation due to the regime's persecution of Jews.[81] In counterpart to the French Women's Union (Union des Femmes Françaises) was the Spanish Women's Union (Union des Femmes Espagnols), which had a reported 400 adherents who mostly came from the PCE and PSUC.[82] Finally, a Spanish federation of deportees and political internees (the Fédération Espagnole des Déportés et Internés Politiques Victimes du Fascisme), with its 60 members, mirrored the National Federation of Deportees, Internees and Resisters (Fédération Nationale des Déportés, Internés et Résistants).[83]

As for the Socialists, the various tendencies of the PSOE were thought to contain 600 adherents in the Gironde. According to the *Renseignements généraux*, PSOE activity was far more limited in comparison with the Communist and libertarian organisations. The Socialist grouping of the UGT amounted to 800, most of whom also belonged to the PSOE. A further 560 were thought to belong to the Negrínist faction of the UGT, some of whom were also members of the Communist parties. The various Republican parties were even less active. The largest was l'Esquerra

Republicana de Catalunya, with a membership of 500. The other Republican parties had a very small number of adherents: 60 for Izquierda Republicana; 50 for Unión Republicana; a dozen people for the Estat Català and the Partido Republicano Federal, both of which the police described as 'practically insignificant'. The POUM had a membership of 60.[84]

Although these statistics must be treated with caution, the level of activism by refugees between 1945 and the start of 1948 was arguably high. In 1949, the Spanish republicans were still characterised by a high degree of politicisation, even as membership statistics decreased. The CNT, PCE, PSOE and Izquierda Repúblicana maintained an organisational presence, but some of the smaller organisations no longer showed any sign of activity.[85] At the start of the 1950s, the Gironde authorities estimated that around 2,000 out of the 6,000 Spanish refugees continued to adhere to parties and trade unions.

The pattern of declining membership numbers was reflected in the waning proto-commemorative culture of exile and shrinking circulation of the exilic press towards the end of the 1940s.[86] The impossibility of returning to a Francoist-free Spain was the prime reason, but there were also other factors at work. Miguel Oviedo stopped attending the three PCF meetings a week due to a mixture of family and work commitments, whilst Valeriano Espiga's absence from the CNT was driven by the split in the organisation.[87] All the same, it would be misleading to evaluate the vitality of the refugees' commitment to their various organisations solely on the basis of membership statistics and attendance at party/syndical meetings. For this would preclude other significant activities such as welfare, work, sociability and education.

The MLE co-operative at Aymare, *département* of the Lot, which had initially been created to secure the release of militants from the concentration camps in 1939, was temporarily transformed into a libertarian radio station for disseminating anti-Francoist propaganda in Spain. Libertarians installed a pair of hefty long-range broadcasting masts and surprisingly, attracted a favourable response from the local authorities and police services.[88] However, perhaps under pressure from Francoist Spain, the French Minister of the Interior banned the station.[89] In its stead, the libertarians developed the co-operative into a centre for sick and disabled refugees.

The aim was to provide welfare but also a sense of agency for the refugees by encouraging them to participate in the running and organisation of the agricultural co-operative. For this purpose, the MLE sought finance from the International Rescue Relief Committee, the Intergovernmental Committee on Refugees, and the International Refugee Organisation (IRO) to build a new wing.[90] With the finance in place, the MLE mobilised its network of militants for the building work. The call was taken up by militants in Bordeaux who had established a construction co-operative, the 'Pessaquese du Bâtiment', named after the commune of Pessac in the Bordeaux agglomeration. One founding member, Valeriano Espiga, underlined how the 'Pessaquese du Bâtiment' was inspired by the memory of the 1936 social revolution in Spain.[91] During its two-year existence, the 24 workers shared the same status and salary, while using profits to build houses for themselves and to fund the anti-Francoist resistance in Spain. Their work at Aymare was successfully completed and the new wing was inaugurated by an IRO representative on 22 January 1950.

CNT militants were also busy in two other welfare projects in Bordeaux. The Fédération Espagnole des malades chroniques et invalides victimes de la guerre d'Espagne en exile sought help from international aid organisations, such as the IRO and the International Relief Committee, to cater for seriously ill or disabled refugees.[92] Another project concerned refugees with less severe disabilities. From June 1946, disabled refugees worked as part of a sandal-making co-operative.[93] By October 1947, the co-operative was sustaining 26 workers and their families. It had close ties to an association responsible for refugees with war injuries from the Spanish Civil War, the Ligue des Mutilés et Invalides de la Guerre d'Espagne, which appears to have been influenced by the CNT.[94] The Spanish republican government in exile was particularly interested in the co-operative and explored the possibilities for expansion as well as granting loans in May and December of 1947.

The PCE also ran its own welfare and employment concerns. The Varsovie hospital in Toulouse had initially served to treat *guerrilleros*. Staffed mainly by Communist medical personnel, it went on to treat Spanish refugees more widely.[95] One of the largest refugee employment enterprises in southern France was a forestry firm, the 'Société FERNAN-DEZ-VALLEDOR', which took its name from the founders General Luis Fernández Juan and Colonel José Valledor. Both had played a leading role in the *guerrillero* outfits of the Pyrenean region. By the time it was renamed the Société Forestière Française du Midi (French Forestry Company of Southern France) in 1948, the business had become the main supplier of railway sleepers to the SNCF. There were 250 full-time personnel, all but five of whom were Spanish, located in four major worksites in the Aude, Ariège, Gers and the Tarn, as well as 'seasonal' workers who were effectively militants en route or on return from resistance activities in Spain.[96] In addition, the company appears to have run a vehicle-repair yard along with a convalescence centre near Toulouse at Fenouillet and St-Simon, respectively.[97]

By grouping together militants from the same ideological backgrounds these projects offered refugees a sense of continuity whilst presenting a solution to the pressing issue of employment. At the same time, these activities encouraged militants to maintain a vision of a future life in Spain, either through the prospect of continued resistance or through the implementation of working practices which could represent a viable alternative to the Francoist policy of autarky. This latter point was one of the reasons why Manuel Torres Campañá from the Ministry of Emigration and Work in exile was so keen to develop the sandal-making co-operative in Bordeaux and the idea of a co-operative-driven economy more generally.[98]

Another aspect ignored by membership statistics is the issue of gender. Even if women such as Federica Montseny of the CNT and Dolores Ibárruri of the PCE were prominent figures, at the local level women were mostly absent from meetings dealing with organisational business. The reason reflected dominant gender patterns regarding domestic responsibilities, though oral-history evidence demonstrates that women were not entirely missing. Feliciana Espiga, who was born in France to Spanish parents, remembered 1945 as the year when she married both Valeriano Espiga and the revolution. She accompanied Valeriano to a four-day congress of the libertarian Juventudes Libertarias in Toulouse, describing it as 'a kind of honeymoon'.[99] Young women were notably present in the youth movements of the various Spanish republican organisations. Pura Arias participated in a Communist youth-performance group which organised folklore, theatre and choral events in the Bordeaux area.[100] As a young woman, Maria-Pilar Lang attended the 1947 JSU congress in Paris as a member of the delegation from the Lot-et-Garonne. She was also actively involved in organising social events. Her motivations were not always driven by ideology or the return to Spain, important though they may have been. As a young woman, unfettered by domestic demands of family life, these events enabled her to enact a sense of Spanishness and to socialise beyond the watchful eyes of her parents.[101]

Cultural and social events were often dependent on political and syndical networks of people whose names are often missing from the membership statistics. The involvement of children was an additional activity unrecognised by membership details. Gloria Gargallo recalled how her father started taking her to the local CNT branch in Bordeaux at the end of the 1940s. He took this decision on realising she had been bullied at school after she asked: 'What's a filthy race?' She also began attending plays organised by the CNT-influenced 'Cultura Popular'.[102] As an adolescent, Eduardo Bernad began learning about his Spanish republican heritage through the JSU. He was originally from Catalonia and had not made any progress in Castilian since his arrival in France. He referred to the Bourse du Travail, or Trades Council, as 'my university', for it was the place where the JSU organised classes on Castilian and introduced him to the poetry of Federico García Lorca and Miguel Hernández.[103]

The refugees' organisations were clearly a hub for wider activities which re-created and sustained political-ideological group boundaries by retaining an exilic gaze on Spain. This did not necessarily entail elaborating a nostalgic imaginary of a pre-exilic or even contemporary utopia concerning daily life over the Pyrenees. On the contrary, all of the organisations regularly updated their members on the political repression and economic deprivation which prevailed in Spain. With the drop in membership and the interdiction of Spanish Communist activities in France, informal social-based networks of people with the same ideological affiliation continued to exist and largely explain the absence of either a mass return to Spain or mass adoption of French nationality.

For the Spanish republicans and their supporters in France, the postwar years opened with a formidable sense of expectation about returning to Spain. By the start of the 1950s, this anticipation seemed out of kilter with the foreign policy interests of France and the Western democracies. On 2 July 1955, a bridge spanning a river and the Franco-Spanish border on the outskirts of Bourg-Madame was inaugurated. A plaque on the bridge recalls how the ceremony took place in the presence of the French and Spanish civilian, military and religious authorities. The memorial is a far cry from the monuments of the Liberation period outlined at the start of this chapter and the ensuing proto-commemorative culture of the Spanish republican exile. In effect, by 1955, the optimism driving the refugees' actions during the Liberation and immediate post-war years must have seemed like water under a bridge.

In the polarised context of the Cold War the Spanish republicans had very little room for manoeuvre as the popular aspirations behind the creation and subsequent defence of the Second Spanish Republic had no place in Western post-visions of Spain. And yet, a steadfast refusal to gratify the Francoist regime by resettling in Spain remained as Spanish republicans opted to maintain their refugee status and thereby endure ongoing discrimination and an uncertain exile in France.

Notes

1 I would like to thank M. Pierre Combes, Président Fondateur du Musée de la Résistance du Lot, for this information.

2 For an excellent recent study of the French government's relations with Francoist Spain see D. A. Messenger, *L'Espagne Républicaine: French Policy and Spanish Republicanism in Liberated France* (Brighton, 2008). See also: P. Brundu, 'L'Espagne franquiste et la politique étrangère de la France au lendemain de la Deuxième Guerre mondiale', *Relations Internationales*, 50 (1987); G. Dreyfus-Armand, 'Les réfugiés républicains au cœur des relations franco-espagnoles, 1945–1962', *Relations Internationales*, 74 (1993); A. Dulphy, 'La Politique Espagnol de la France 1945–1955', *Vingtième Siècle: Revue d'histoire*, 68 (2000); A. Dulphy, 'La politique de la France à l'égard de l'Espagne franquiste, 1945–1949', *Revue d'histoire moderne et contemporaine*, 35:1 (1988). In respect of Great Britain see: D. J. Dunthorn, 'The Prieto–Robles Meeting of October 1947: Britain and the Failure of the Spanish anti-Franco Coalition, 1945–1950', *European History Quarterly*, 30:1 (2000); P. Preston, *Franco* (London, 1995), chs 21–2. For the USA see A. Viñas, *Los pactos secretos de Franco con Estados Unidos: bases, ayuda económica, recortes de soberanía* (Barcelona, 1981).

3 A. Bechelloni, 'Italiens et Espagnols dans la presse française de septembre 1944 à décembre 1946', in P. Milza and D. Peschanski (eds), *Exils et Migration: Italiens et Espagnols en France 1938–1946* (Paris, 1994), p. 285.

4 F. Hernando Villacampa, *Historia de la Amical de antiguos guerrilleros españoles en Francia (F.F.I.), 1947–1984* (Toulouse, 1992); H. Mauran, *Espagnols rouges: un maquis de républicains espagnols dans les Cévennes* (Nîmes, 1995); G. Dreyfus-Armand and É. Temime, *Les Camps sur la plage, un exil espagnol* (Paris, 1995); F. Cate-Arries, *Spanish Culture behind Barbed Wire: Memory and Representation of the French Concentration Camps, 1939–1945* (Lewisburg, FL, 2004).

5 P. Laborie and J.-P. Amalric, 'Mémoires en devenir. La construction des sens de l'exil', in L. Domergue (ed.), *L'Exil Républicain espagnol à Toulouse 1939–1999* (Toulouse, 1999).

6 J. Ortiz, 'La résistance espagnole en Béarn', in M. Papy (ed.), *Les Espagnols et la Guerre Civile* (Biarritz, 1999), pp. 405–6.

7 The Secret Army (*Armée secrète*) was a coalition of paramilitary forces from different resistance organisations which took its orders from General de Gaulle. The Resistance Organisation of the Army (*Organisation de Résistance de l'armée*) evolved from the clandestine activities of disbanded French military officers who began organising themselves at the start of 1943.

8 N. Falguera, L. Figuéres and E. Mannevy Garcia, *Guerrilleros en Terre de France: Les Républicains espagnols dans la Résistance française* (Pantin, 2000), pp. 131–4; J. Cubero, *La Résistance à Toulouse et dans la Région 4* (Toulouse, 2005), pp. 316–23.

9 The UNE reorganised the 14th Guerrilla Corps into the AGE in December 1943. For more information see G. Dreyfus-Armand, *L'Exil des Républicains Espagnols en France: De la Guerre Civile à la Mort de Franco* (Paris, 1999), p. 171.

10 E. Pons Prades, *Republicanos españoles en la 2a Guerra Mundial* (Barcelona, 1975), pp. 89–91; H. R. Kedward, *In Search of the Maquis: Rural Resistance in Southern France 1942–1944* (Oxford, 1993), pp. 183, 216; Falguera, Figuéres and Mannevy Garcia, *Guerrilleros en Terre de France*, pp. 158–61.

11 *Ibid.*, pp. 145–8.

12 J. Cubero, *Les Républicains espagnols* (Pau, 2003) pp. 232–5; Falguera, Figuéres and Mannevy Garcia, *Guerrilleros en Terre de France*, pp. 112–22.

13 Pons Prades, *Republicanos españoles en la 2a Guerra Mundial*, p. 136.

14 R. Trempé, 'Le rôle des étrangers: MOI et guérilleros', in *La Libération dans le Midi de la France* (Toulouse, 1986), pp. 63–78.

15 S. Gemie and S. Schrafstetter, 'Reassessing Anti-fascism', *European History Quarterly*, 32:3 (2002).

16 S. Carlos, 'La guerre d'Espagne et l'antifascisme en question', in Papy (ed.) *Les Espagnols et la Guerre Civile*, p. 332.

17 CIRAS, Gestión MLE-CNT en Francia. Circular no. 22, 20 January 1945.

18 Kedward, *In Search of the Maquis*, pp. 259, 266.

19 S. Courtois, D. Peschanski and A. Rayski (eds), *Le Sang de l'étranger. Les immigrés de la MOI dans la Résistance* (Paris, 1989), p. 392.

20 Messenger, *L'Espagne Républicaine*, pp. 44–5.

21 AN CARAN, F1A 3346.

22 Messenger, *L'Espagne Républicaine*, p. 45.

23 AN CARAN, F1A 3346. Préfet of the Basses-Pyrénées to Commissaire de la République in Bordeaux, 10 October 1944.

24 *Ibid.* Report by Directeur Général des Études et Recherches, 22 November 1944. For an overview of the expedition see J.-L. Dufour and R. Trempé, 'La France, base arrière d'une reconquête républicaine de l'Espagne: l'affaire du Val d'Aran', in J. Sagnes and S. Caucanas (eds), *Les Français et la Guerre d'Espagne* (Perpignan, 2nd edn, 2004), pp. 261–84; A. Cowan, 'The Guerrilla War Against Franco', *European History Quarterly*, 20:2 (1990).

25 AN CARAN, F1A 3346. Ministre de l'Intérieur to Commissaires de la République in Toulouse, Montpellier, Bordeaux, 8 October 1944.

26 *Ibid.* Services des Commissariats de la République to Ministre de l'Intérieur, 8 November 1944.

27 *Ibid.* Report for Ministre de l'Intérieur, 20 November 1944.

28 Messenger, *L'Espagne Républicaine*, pp. 1–8.

29 AD Gironde, SC 1949. Mairie de Pauillac to Préfecture, 11 September 1944.

30 AD Gironde, SC 569.

31 *Ibid.*

32 For an intricate account of the trials of collaborators in Pau see S. Ott, 'The Enemy as Insider: German POWs as Trial Witnesses in the Basses-Pyrénées,

1944–1946', in S. Ott (ed.), *War, Exile, Justice and Everyday Life 1936–1946* (Reno, NV, 2011), pp. 309–34.

33 AN Fontainebleau, 19980221/13. Letter to Ministère de l'Intérieur, 10 November 1944. Ministère de l'Intérieur to Commissaire Régional de la République in Bordeaux, 24 November 1944.

34 AN Fontainebleau 19980221, art. 13 no. 132B.

35 *La IV République* (1 November 1944); *La Victoire* (17 November 1945).

36 R. Gillespie, *The Spanish Socialist Party: A History of Factionalism* (Oxford, 1989), p. 70.

37 AD Gironde, SC 308. Renseignements généraux, 19 September 1944. The report's wording is revealing, with its references to 'extremist Spanish elements'. An inventory of missing objects occurred in April 1945. Secrétariat Général de Police to Commissaire de la République, 10 April 1945.

38 AN CARAN, F1A 3346. Préfet of the Basses-Pyrénées to Commissaire de la République in Bordeaux, 10 October 1944.

39 AGA, Caja 11774. Report by Spanish Vice-Consulate in Mauléon, 4 November 1944.

40 AD Gironde, SC 308.

41 *Ibid.* Circular, 26 October 1944.

42 For a detailed discussion of the refugee statute see Messenger, *L'Espagne Républicaine*, pp. 54–5.

43 AGA, 11453. Spanish Consulate in Pau to Spanish Embassy in Paris, 15 February 1945.

44 *Ibid.* Spanish Consulate in Pau to Spanish Embassy in Paris, 18 February 1945.

45 *Ibid.* Spanish Consulate in Pau to Spanish Embassy in Paris, 19 February and 3 March 1945.

46 Dreyfus-Armand, *L'Exil des Républicains Espagnols en France*, p. 178.

47 L. Stein, *Beyond Death and Exile: The Spanish Republicans in France, 1939–1955* (Cambridge, MA, 1979), p. 186.

48 Messenger, *L'Espagne Républicaine*, pp. 91–3.

49 For references to UNE assassinations of refugees refusing to join the organisation see: J. Borrás, *Políticas de los exiliados españoles, 1944–1950* (Paris, 1976), pp. 20–3; *Les Dossiers noirs d'une certaine résistance: trajectoire d'un fascisme rouge* (Perpignan, 1984), pp. 169–71; *Les Anarchistes espagnols dans la tourmente (1939–1945)* (Marseilles, 1989), pp. 163–5; J. Berruezo, *Contribución de la historia de la CNT de España en el exilio* (Mexico City, 1967), pp. 121–5; J. Martínez Cobo, 'Le PSOE à Toulouse et dans le midi de la France: 1939–1975', in Dormergue (ed.), *L'Exil Républicain Espagnol à Toulouse 1939–1999*, p. 83.

50 Gillespie, *The Spanish Socialist Party*, p. 68.

51 CIRAS, Gestión MLE-CNT en Francia, libro 2, 1940–45. Minutes of the National Plenary Meeting, Toulouse, 8–13 October 1944.

52 *CNT*, no. 2 (21 September 1944).

53 The JEL was founded by Spanish republicans in Mexico in 1943.

54 AD Gironde, SC 569. Renseignements généraux, 19 November 1944. AN CARAN, F7 14936, Rapport d'Information Générale, 5 January 1945.

55 These activities are discussed in the section 'Celebrating the Republic(s)?' in Chapter 3.

56 Some refugees began publishing memoirs which echoed the resistance narrative while also recalling internment. For an overview of the refugees' memoirs see S. Gemie, 'The Ballad of Bourg-Madame: Memory, Exile and the Spanish Republican Refugees of the *Retirada* of 1939', *International Review of Social History*, 51:1 (2006).

57 G. Dreyfus-Armand, 'L'Émigration Politique Espagnole en France au Travers de sa Presse 1939–1975' (Thèse de Doctorat , Institut d'Etudes Politiques de Paris, 1994), p. 118.

58 CIRAS, Gestión MLE-CNT en Francia, libro 1, 1945–46. CNT-AIT leaflet, 19 July 1945.

59 *CNT*, no. 17, 26 July 1945.

60 *La IVº République (Organe Landaise d'Informations)* (1 January 1944).

61 *La Victoire* (17 November 1945).

62 AD Gironde, SC 569. Renseignements généraux, 11 November 1944.

63 *Ibid.* Daily reports by the Renseignements généraux.

64 *Ibid.* Renseignements généraux, 28 November 1944.

65 CIRAS, JEL report, 1 September 1945.

66 CIRAS, minutes of 30 September 1945.

67 AD Gironde, Versement 1239/42.

68 *Ibid.*

69 AD Gironde, Versement 1239/42. Renseignements généraux, 23 January 1948.

70 AN Fontainebleau, 199000353/19. Direction des Renseignements généraux, 14 November 1947.

71 *Ibid. Journal Officiel*, 2 December 1947.

72 The border authorities did not always uphold the principles of asylum. In 1950, the authorities in the Basses-Pyrénées tried to force a group of anti-Francoist fighters seeking asylum to join the Foreign Legion. AD Pyrénées-Atlantiques, 1031W, 237. For a first-hand account of this incident see F. Martínez-Lopez, *Guérillero contre Franco: La guérilla antifranquiste du León (1936–1951)* (Paris, 2000).

73 The prefects represented the *départements* of the Gironde, Landes, Basses-Pyrénées, Hautes-Pyrénées, Ariège, Pyrénées-Orientales, Aude, Hérault, Bouches-du-Rhône, Gard, Tarn, Tarn-et-Garonne, Gers, Lot-et-Garonne and Aveyron.

74 For further details see Dreyfus-Armand, 'Les réfugiés républicains au cœur des relations franco-espagnoles, 1945–1962'.

75 Dreyfus-Armand, *L'Exil des Républicains Espagnols en France*, pp. 265–6.

76 AD Gironde, Versement 1239/43. Renseignements généraux, 22 September 1951.

77 A. Mateos López, *Exilio y Clandestinidad. La Reconstrucción de UGT, 1939–1977* (Madrid, 2002), p. 50.

78 AD Gironde, Versement 1239/42.

79 *Ibid.* Renseignements généraux, 23 July 1949.

80 *Ibid.* Renseignements généraux, 'Les Étrangers en Gironde', 23 January 1948.

81 M. Goubet and P. Debauges, *Histoire de la Résistance dans la Haute-Garonne* (Toulouse, 1986).

82 AD Gironde, Versement 1239/42. 'Les Étrangers en Gironde', 23 January 1948.

83 *Ibid.* Note de renseignements, 2 July 1948.

84 *Ibid.* 'Les Étrangers en Gironde', 23 January 1948.

85 *Ibid.* Renseignements généraux, 17 September 1949.

86 For the press see Dreyfus-Armand, 'L'Émigration Politique Espagnole en France au Travers de sa Presse 1939–1975', p. 144.

87 Interviews with Miguel Oviedo, Fargues-Saint-Hilaire, 9 December 2002 and Valeriano Espiga, Fargues-Saint-Hilaire, 21 May 2002.

88 AD Lot, 1W 923.

89 *Ibid.* Ministre de l'Intérieur to Préfet, 28 September 1948.

90 AN CARAN, AJ 43 306. Reports by the director of the IRRC, undated.

91 Interview with Valeriano Espiga, Fargues-St-Hilaire, 21 May 2002. Details of the co-operative are also contained in the memoirs of two other participants: F. Gargallo Edo, *La raison douloureuse* (Madrid, 1999), pp. 132–43 and J. Giménez Arenas, *De la Unión a Banat: Itinerario de una rebeldía* (Madrid, 1996), pp. 153–9.

92 AD Gironde, Versement 1239, liasse 42. Report 'Les Associations Espagnoles en Gironde', June 1950.

93 Fundación Universitaria Española: Archivo del Gobierno de la II República en Exilio: 872–4/1947–48. Report by a representative of the Spanish Republican Government in exile, 31 October 1947.

94 AD Gironde, Versement 1239, liasse 42. Report 'Les Associations Espagnoles en Gironde', June 1950.

95 Dreyfus-Armand, *L'Exil des Républicains Espagnols en France*, pp. 360–1.

96 P. Pigenet, 'La protection des étrangers à l'épreuve de la «guerre froide»: L'opération «boléro-paprika»', Revue d'histoire moderne et contemporaine, 46:2 (1999), p. 303.

97 AN CARAN, F7 15589.

98 Fundación Universitaria Española: Archivo del Gobierno de la II República en Exilio: 872–4/1947–48. Report, 31 October 1947.

99 Interview with Feliciana Espiga, Fargues-Saint-Hilaire, 16 November 2002.

100 Interview with Pura Arias, Lormont, 8 July 2002.

101 Interview with Maria-Pilar Lang, Villeneuve-sur-Lot, 23 July 2003.

102 Interview with Gloria Gargallo, Latresne, 23 April 2002.

103 Interview with Eduardo Bernad, Bordeaux, 11 July 2002.

7

Moving memories, 1970–2009

'Remembrance Tour: Toulouse the capital of [*sic*] Spanish Republican Exile', read the caption of a tourist map leaflet produced by Toulouse City Council in 2009. In June of the same year, the seventieth anniversary celebrations of the *Retirada* included the inauguration of a plaque reciprocating the map's slogan and the dedication of a stretch of river as 'The Spanish Republican Exile Quay'. The following day the local newspaper reported: 'the City of Toulouse has made a symbolic and powerful gesture towards the former Spanish exiles, their children and grandchildren by offering a true realm of memory'.[1]

The celebration was very much recognition but also partly constitutive of the position that Spanish republican exilic memory had come to occupy in relation to the city's heritage and France's memorial topography more widely. It was undoubtedly a moving occasion for many of the former refugees and their descendants who participated. But there was also evidence of a sanitised image of the past emanating from this officially sanctioned heritage. The local newspaper's report of the events ended with a quote by a 93-year-old Spanish republican, Francisco Folch: 'I think that had I worked in Spain I would never have made such a good living as here in Toulouse.'[2] Did this commemoration reflect a transformation of the Spanish republican exile itself into a realm of memory, welded to France's national memorial framework, and imbued with an accent on the successful integration of these former refugees?

To answer the above question the various modes through which remembrance has occurred and the accompanying contexts in which this has taken place need to be considered. This chapter consequently explores public forms of commemoration as well as remembrance in former refugees' homes. In doing so, it raises two significant issues: first, the interrelationship between the different spaces of remembrance involving the public/private and national/transnational domains; and secondly, the long-term impact of exile on individuals' lives and their strategies for dealing with the past.

Memory, refugees and the French nation-state

'There are realms of memory because there are no more memory environments', states Pierre Nora in the introduction to his encyclopaedic *Les Lieux de mémoire*.[3] It follows that while memory used to be an integral facet of everyday actions, it has since become externalised and substituted by the phenomenon of the realm of memory. Although this process may be relevant to the memory dynamics of the French nation-state, it is not altogether accurate for Spanish republicans. The loss and marginalisation associated with the Spanish republican exile, along with the long and difficult development of a public memorial culture, generated new meanings in relation to everyday actions, prompting what we may consider as a return of the 'memory environment'. Given that a fully developed commemorative culture of the Spanish republican exile in France has been a relatively recent phenomenon, do we need to reverse Nora's maxim to 'there are memory environments because there are no realms of memory'?[4] The answer to this question will be addressed through a discussion of the most salient aspects of Nora's work in relation to migrant groups and the empirical evidence of the Spanish republicans' memory activities.

Nora's edited collection of 130 essays offers a historical analysis of the major nodal points of memory constituting contemporary French identity.[5] He refers to these nodes as 'lieux de mémoire', a notion that has been translated variously as 'place of memory', 'site of memory' and 'realm of memory'. Although the difference between these translations may appear slight, I believe 'realm' is a more apt term for refugees' memories. 'Realm' tends to place less stress on a physical location than the notions of 'site' or 'place' and more on the geographical notion of 'space'. It additionally conveys a greater sense of diffusion while also more effectively capturing the immaterial and abstract aspect of Nora's concept.[6] Accordingly, a realm of memory describes a material or abstract object or event that possesses a material, symbolic and functional framework of an enduring presence either through the will to remember or through the effects of time.[7]

By the end of the project, Nora was pessimistic about the state of memory in contemporary France. In the concluding chapter, 'The era of commemoration', he outlined concerns about the exclusionary dangers of patrimonial or heritage culture.[8] Rather than operating as a collective and all-inclusive ensemble, Nora viewed heritage as a vehicle that could be used for enacting 'sectoral identities' and exclusion. It is worth noting that he was writing during a period when the xenophobic and far-right National Front party was enjoying increasing influence in the country. Notwithstanding the virulently introspective vision of France held by the National Front, Nora's point merits full consideration, especially as heritage can be linked to the exercise of power and can mobilise criteria for belonging and, by implication, exclusion.[9] There can be no doubting the introspective and power-serving potential of heritage, or the capacity for this type of remembrance to deflect attention from present-day problems by offering a nostalgic, comfortable and ultimately reductive vision of the past.[10] But there are grounds for optimism. Raphael Samuel's work in the UK, for instance, stressed the democratic possibilities of ordinary people constructing their own forms of heritage and accompanying sense of the past.[11]

Heritage is evidently an ambiguous process. Its appeal can be both inherently exclusive and anti-democratic, and fundamentally inclusive and participatory. Much, if not all, depends on context. Spanish republican exilic memory in France, as with the memory practices of all groups, has involved issues of identification. On occasion, this has involved a strong emphasis on Spanishness. At the same time, there has been a discernible tendency amongst some of the memory associations to create and reinforce networks of solidarity that transcend sectoral identities at the local and indeed national levels.

Although the pan- or trans-national potential of remembrance is not discussed in Les Lieux de mémoire there are two chapters that tackle the questions of ethnic and cultural diversity. Pierre Birnbaum's important contribution drew attention to the issue of Jewish memory by tracing the relationship between France and its Jewish population. Birnbaum discussed the difficulties in finding Jewish realms of memory by referring to the absence of the internment camps from France's memorial topography. Unfortunately, the author inadvertently elides the memory of the Spanish refugees and men of the International Brigades by describing how foreign Jews and then French nationals were interned in the camps of Argelès and Saint-Cyprien from 1939 onwards.[12] The minimal details about how these camps were created to intern refugees from the conflict in Spain is understandable given the chapter's focus on Jews in France. Nevertheless, the omission concerning the camps' origins, however unintentional, can run the risk of privileging a particular version of history to the exclusion of others.[13] This was undoubtedly not Birnbaum's aim, but the overall impetus of the chapter underplayed the idea of the camps as representing an inter-ethnic realm of memory.

Gérard Noiriel explores ethnic diversity in his contribution to Nora's collection on 'French and foreigners'. At the time of writing he observed a growing tendency of immigrants to render their histories public with reference to the associations of Spanish migrants and their descendants in south-west France. A most interesting point, which merited further attention, relates to the correlation between the absence of public remembrance and the role of the home as a memory depository.[14] Despite the appearance of immigrant associations, the essential traces of refugee history were to be found more modestly in the form of personal archives, furniture and photographs.

Birnbaum and Noiriel's essays represented a much-needed foray into the subject of ethnic and cultural diversity on the memorial landscape. Since their work was published, there have been significant developments in the commemoration of the Holocaust and the Spanish republican exile which have responded to the issue of memorial absence. Important questions nonetheless remain about how we characterise realms of memory which intersect the national framework, and secondly about the relationship between the ways in which memory is produced in the home and in public spaces.

Nora identifies a fundamental link between a minority group's memory and a realm of memory. He suggests the latter have appeared because there are no longer spontaneous, organic memory processes. There is little reflection on the length of time involved here, or on what might happen before a realm of memory is created. Where the private space is evoked, it is in terms of a memory depository which eventually becomes the basis from which a realm of memory is launched: 'This is why the defence of minorities of a privileged and jealously guarded memory in the refuge of their homes only served to show the burning truth of all realms of memory. Without a commemorative vigilance, history would soon brush them under the carpet.'[15] There is recognition that in the absence of realms of memory, groups such as refugees invest in memory-work behind closed doors. The activities might be of a different scale, but the principle is the same.

As we will shortly see, ethnographic oral-history interviews confirm that memory production does indeed occur within homes. But the evidence also reveals that Nora's argument may only be accepted if the meanings surrounding human–object relations and daily rituals are ignored. The implication is that the relationship between realms of memory and memory environments must be reconsidered. Given that refugees were barely able to cross the border with anything more than their memories, and were then confronted with obstacles to creating a fully-fledged commemorative culture of exile, there is a compelling argument for taking into account the creation of memory environments as a responsive strategy to exile.

My reference to 'Moving memories' in this chapter's title aims to capture the shifting spatial arena of memory activities and builds on Alistair Thomson's notion of 'moving stories'.[16] Immigrants' oral histories tend to be characterised by movement in three ways: the stories are about people who have experienced movement from one country to another; the narratives are often emotionally moving; and finally, what is recounted can often change over time. This latter point refers mainly to the performative aspect of oral histories, but retains some currency in respect of organised commemoration. As the last chapter explained, during the proto-commemorative phase of exilic remembrance during the late 1940s, the issue of internment did not feature in the refugees' public remembrance narratives for political reasons. It did, however, as we will shortly discover, feature in the commemorative culture of exile which began to emerge two decades later.

A commemorative culture of exile

After the demise of the proto-commemorative culture of exile, the refugees did not cease recalling their past in France. Whenever they gathered – for a *jira* or outing to the countryside, on Sundays at the Place de Victoire in Bordeaux where the exilic press was sold, or at the local party or trade-union office – they recounted stories.[17] But there was no organised commemoration of exile. While some memorial and historiographical activity occurred in the 1960s, an overall feeling of having been excluded from history prevailed among refugees.[18] This explains the title of Antonio Vilanova's collection of refugees' stories: *Los Olvidados*, 'the forgotten'.[19] The 1970s, on the other hand, proved to be a decade which favoured a gradual emergence of the Spanish republicans' exilic past in French public spaces.

Historians have identified the generational revolt of the 1960s and reawakening of Jewish self-consciousness as causal factors behind the fragmentation of the Gaullist and Communist myths of the Resistance at the start of the 1970s.[20] Frank Cassenti's film on the Manouchian group of the FTP-MOI in Paris, *L'Affiche rouge*, challenged the Franco-centric cinema of the Resistance with its focus on foreign resisters. Nonetheless, although a stress on plurality was emerging, national interpretations of the past remained dominant. The mirror through which the national past was viewed had been shattered but the cadre holding the pieces together remained in place.[21] Thus while the idea of the nation as a unitary framework for remembrance had not been fully dismantled, the possibility now existed for alternative narratives to (re)emerge.

It is difficult to ascertain if the development of Spanish republican exilic memory was a result of, or partly constitutive of, this deconstruction of national memory in France. The same observation also holds for other migrant memories and signals the need for more research about the relationship between local and national memorial processes. Furthermore, in lieu of an in-depth comparative study of European countries and beyond, or of the Spanish republican diaspora, the extent of international factors and trends remains unknown.[22] In Spain, the relatively less repressive censorship that accompanied Franco's demise certainly facilitated publications on the republican exile, but the impact of these events in France is less clear.[23] What can be emphasised with certainty is that Spanish republicans in France began rehabilitating their memory at the local level in two main ways.

The concentration/internment camps became, if not the subject, the context for remembering as former internees began restoring camp cemeteries. In several localities the former camps were virtually unrecognisable: in the case of Vernet d'Ariège and Septfonds, farmland had replaced the wooden barracks; and at Gurs the area had been covered by woodland. Even if the cemeteries were still visible, they had fallen into neglect. In 1959, a Frenchman complained after he had taken an American friend to the Gurs cemetery so the latter could visit his father's grave. It was 'a place of complete desolation and utterly abandoned'.[24] Just over a decade later, a similar state of degradation prevailed at the Vernet cemetery. Though there was a monument, one former internee who visited the camp commented:

On the monument, there is an inscription, laconic, cold and empty of meaning: 'To the foreigners who died far from their country'. . . . Curiosity is fulfilled and forgetting is all the more complete. . . . The cemetery bears no resemblance to normal cemeteries. Here there are no cypress trees, monumental graves, crosses made from stone, granite, marble, plaster or metal. Nor is there a protective wall topped with broken bottles to prevent any acts of profanation, or a gate, one can enter at one's free will. But one aspect made me shiver . . . in place of a wall is barbed wire, rusting through old age, and held by crumbling concrete posts.[25]

Renovating camp cemeteries was the initiative of former internees, who were often but not uniquely Spanish republicans. At Vernet d'Ariège, the Amicale des anciens internés du Camp du Vernet d'Ariège was founded for this purpose in 1972. They spent the ensuing three years working on the cemetery, with the help of the former Prefect of the Ariège and finance from the local council. The monument was rededicated 'To the memory of anti-fascist combatants, known and unknown, who died for the freedom of all people'.[26] In the case of the Septfonds camp, a Spanish former internee and deportee began the process in 1973 by contacting a veterans' association for former resister internees and deportees, the Fédération nationale des déportés et internés résistants patriots. It eventually liaised with the local authorities to organise the inauguration of a monument in October 1978.[27]

Several points can be observed from the examples of Vernet and Septfonds. First, the concentration camps became focal points of organised commemoration through an initial focus on those who died in internment, irrespective of their nationality. Secondly, there was a contradictory emphasis on the universal, with anti-fascists linked to the general on the one hand, whilst on the other, the very regime that created the camps, and which was itself founded on universal values, was sidelined through a focus on the Vichy period. Finally, although the impetus came from former internees, it would be misleading to interpret this as an example of commemoration organised solely from the bottom up, given the participation of the local authorities.

The origins of a memorial culture at the Gurs camp differ with its early and dominant focus on the internment and deportation of Jews.[28] Throughout the late 1940s and 1950s, the French Federation of Jewish Societies (Fédération des sociétés juives), and then a German-Jewish association, the Oberrat der Israeliten Badens (representing an area in Germany from where Jews were transferred to Gurs prior to deportation), corresponded with the local authorities over the restoration of the cemetery and erection of a monument. In 1963, a ceremony finally took place to commemorate the newly named 'Deportees' Cemetery'.[29] Whilst it is not clear if Spanish republicans participated in the inauguration, subsequent commemorations included both German and Spanish representatives, and in June 1982 the Amicale du camp de Gurs (for a more detailed discussion of this association see the next section) inaugurated a stele dedicated to the Spanish republicans and volunteers of the International Brigades.[30]

During the same period as the camp cemeteries were restored, Spanish republicans requested recognition from the French state for their participation in the struggle against Nazism during the Battle of France and the ensuing Occupation period. In 1973, the head of one association that represented foreign veterans, the Amicale des Prestataires Militaires Étrangers (AMPE), approached the French military and Ministry of Defence to obtain official recognition for Spaniards who had served in the Foreign Labour Companies. The tone of his letter reflected an accumulation of frustration and bitterness shared by other Spanish refugees at the time:

> We're thinking about dissolving our association. On the one hand, we are 'foreigners who volunteered or were mobilised for the army', and on the other hand, looked down upon. The Ministry of Defence refuses to recognise us. We were therefore illegally armed at the Loire, as at Dunkirk, and at La Sarre, we wore your uniform illegally. . . . I am a former Spanish republican soldier, French citizen, non-communist, obliged to hide from my 'civilian bosses' the wounds from my time in a German prison in the service of your army. We are 'filthy foreigners' who are eating your bread.[31]

Calls for recognition from former Spanish *guerrillero* resisters had also been gathering steam since the 1960s. As part of their campaign they solicited the support of local French veterans' associations, while Luis Bermejo, a former commander of the *guerrilleros*, produced a report and corresponded with the French military about the Spanish guerrilla fighters' resistance activities during the Occupation.[32] Bermejo pointed out how the government's interdiction of the Amicale des anciens FFI et résistants espagnols in 1950 had resulted in the confiscation of archives detailing Spanish resistance activities and consequently hindered the task of providing evidence. The report was consequently compiled from oral sources. Nevertheless, he hoped the French state would be able to extend official recognition to Spanish resisters, especially since only 1 per cent of former Spanish resisters carried a veteran combatants' card in the mid-1960s.[33]

In July 1976, the government finally authorised the creation of the Association of Veteran Spanish Guerrilla Fighters (Amicale des anciens guérilleros espagnols, or FFI) en France, with Bermejo at its head. Two years later, 400 veterans' cards were issued and the Amicale then constructed a monument to Spanish guerrilla fighters at Prayols in the Ariège. The hardy granite statue of a partisan purposefully clutching his rifle was inaugurated in June 1982 in the presence of civilian, military and state representatives, along with other veterans' associations. It has since become an annual focus of commemoration.[34] Indicative of the cross-border emphasis which refugee-based commemoration can encompass, this association also collaborated with counterparts in Spain to construct a memorial at Santa Cruz de la Moya.[35] Revealingly, it was dedicated to partisans who died in Spain and beyond from 1936 to 1950: the war in Spain was neither entirely national in emphasis or over by 1939.

Consolidating a commemorative culture

During the 1970s, Spanish republican exilic memory emerged in a partial and limited fashion. It was in a different context from the short burst of proto-commemorative culture during the late 1940s when memory had served to secure the return to a Francoist-free Spain. Remembrance in the 1970s surrounded two main issues: the memory of those who died in French camps; and a wish to be recognised for having played a role in the Battle for France and in the Liberation of the country from Vichy and German Nazi domination. While these narratives remained integral aspects of commemoration over the following decades, other issued emerged.

Two associations at the vanguard of remembrance practices have been the Amicale du camp de Gurs based in the Pyrénées-Orientales, and the Fils et Filles de Républicains Espagnols et Enfants de l'Exode ('Sons and Daughters of the Spanish Republicans and Children of the Exodus', FFREEE) in the Pyrénées-Orientales. There are other associations which have also been instrumental to the commemorative process since the 1980s. However, the aim here is not so much to provide an all-encompassing account of all memorial activity, but rather to illustrate some interesting aspects of the commemorative process through a focus on two associations which have received little attention from scholars of the Spanish republican exile.[36]

In 1979, the Maison des Jeunes et de la Culture d'Oloron organised a series of events for the fortieth anniversary of the Gurs camp. In June 1980, the Amicale du camp de Gurs held a constitutive meeting that attracted more than a hundred former internees from across Europe, including Spanish republicans, former volunteers of the International Brigades and French nationals, along with German, Austrian, French, Yugoslav and Czechoslovakian Jews.[37] This international emphasis was reflected in the Amicale's aims outlined in June 1980, and which consisted of transmitting the memory of those who died or passed through the camp, and mobilising memory for contemporary concerns, notably the rise of racism in Europe and nuclear disarmament.[38]

The Amicale's activities have principally focused on the rediscovery of the camp within France and overseas. Its bulletin, *Gurs, souvenez-vous: lettre d'information de l'Amicale du camp de Gurs*, is sent to members in France and overseas. The association's website provides a similar, though more public, function with details on the camp and the recollections of former internees.[39] Much work has centred on three annual commemorations in the camp cemetery. The April event recalls the opening of the camp in 1939 for Spanish refugees and members of the International Brigades, as well as the national day to remember deportees. A July commemoration coincides with the national day of commemoration of the persecution of the Jews, and the anniversary of the arrival of German Jews is recalled in October. The Amicale's representatives have equally participated in other associations' commemorations of the Occupation period as well as those dealing more specifically with the Spanish republican exile. In addition, alongside the organisation of exhibitions, the Amicale has worked in partnership with schools and the educational authorities. By April 2002, it had distributed a video on the camp to the region's schools and organised school visits to the camp, as well as a training day for teachers. A further achievement was the opening of a visitor centre in the summer of 2007 and the development of guided walkways through the former camp.[40]

The Amicale's bulletin has reflected awareness of some of the pitfalls that can result from an overly retrospective focus on remembrance. The editorial of the December 2003 issue discussed the challenge of making the memory of Gurs relevant to younger generations in contrast to commemorations which have been 'ritualistic and therefore emptied of meaning'.[41] The discussion continued into the following year, with additional emphasis on how memory should be mobilised for contemporary and future concerns which echoed, or perhaps responded to, similar concerns raised by Henri Rousso:[42]

> The 'duty to remember' is far from a theoretical subject. . . . It's what allows us to understand the present in relation to the past, and more effectively

to envisage the future. The values which have motivated men and women to battle in order to safeguard the Rights of Man and democracy are as relevant as ever in dealing with contemporary problems. . . . The meaning of the Gurs internment camp stretches beyond a simple invitation to commemorate the past. More than 60 years after the events, the memory of Gurs leads us to reflection and action.[43]

Much effort has thus focused on the production and transmission of the memory of the camp and its internee population (during both the Third Republic and Vichy eras) with a view to countering racism and anti-Semitism. From amongst its initial aims, the issue of nuclear disarmament has not been a prominent focus, probably due to the end of the Cold War. But the organisational prowess of the association has been remarkable.

At the same time, there has been a constant reminder of the international background of the camp's internees.[44] In remembrance of the internment of German Jews, French and German state officials have delivered speeches, with Jewish religious rituals performed by a German rabbi in front of the monument to Jewish internees. During the same event, attention has then moved to the monument for the Spanish republicans and International Brigaders, with speeches in French and Spanish by representatives of the Amicale and the Spanish consulate. Moreover, for the first time, on 24 April 2005, a representative of two veterans' associations concerning volunteers who had fought in the Spanish Civil War (L'Association des Combattants en Espagne Républicaine and l'Association des Volontaires en Espagne Républicaine) unfurled the flag of the French section of the International Brigades.[45]

Accommodating the memory interests of different groups has not been entirely without its problems. The two monuments in the Gurs cemetery are redolent of the different, if overlapping, layers of memory. While the specific historical conditions and causal factors surrounding the internment of different groups are recalled, there is also a sense of overlapping histories owing to the shared space of the monuments. During oral-history interviews conducted in 2002, some Spanish republicans believed their past had been overshadowed through the predominance of references to Jewish internees and deportees in the former camp and its cemetery. The challenge of negotiating different but overlapping memories within the same memorial space was a prime motivating factor behind the Amicale's creation and has continued to characterise the association's memory work. For instance, the bulletin contained a lengthy discussion about one of the 2004 annual commemorations when a lack of time potentially compromised the Spanish republican and International Brigade aspect of the event.[46] This issue may have been addressed through the inauguration in 2005 of a plaque at the cemetery's entrance indicating the presence of Spanish republican and International Brigade graves.[47]

There are clear historical reasons behind the emphasis on the Jewish internees and deportees. This partly relates to the sheer magnitude of the Holocaust, and the predominance of Jewish graves in the cemetery, but also stems from how the cemetery initially developed into a realm of memory through the initiative of the German – Jewish association, Oberrat der Israeliten Badens. Even so, the Amicale has successfully managed to embody, and mediate between, the various interests and identities linked to the shared inter-ethnic memorial space of the Gurs camp through a commemorative narrative which stretches from the Spanish Civil War to the Holocaust.

Based near the former Argelès camp, FFREEE is another association which has dealt with the issue of national boundaries in its memory work. Even if one of its listed aims is to bring together descendants of the Spanish republicans, membership is open to everyone and its commemorative events have regularly included reflection on other ethnic groups and nationalities. María-Amparo Sánchez-Monroy created the association in July 1999 and elaborated its guiding principles with Sonia Marzo. Both are daughters of Spanish republicans. In addition to Spanish republican memory, FFREEE set out to cultivate humanistic values; to be vigilant about the defence of republican consciousness and the application of democratic values for all; and to provide help and support to all victims of forced displacement.[48] The acronym used by the association undoubtedly reflects its preoccupation with universal values.

As with the Gurs association, FFREEE has developed a wide range of activities. Much time is devoted to an annual weekend-long event in February which commemorates the arrival and internment of the Spanish republicans.[49] The first of these anniversaries took place over an entire week in February 1999, generating wide interest and acting as a catalyst for a surge of Spanish republican exile commemorative activity in the region and beyond. FFREEE has also produced a bulletin and maintains a website detailing its work.[50] Since its inception, it has adopted a steadily significant pedagogical, archival and research role. This has consisted of presentations in local schools, libraries and conferences; showing (French and Spanish) schoolchildren around places of historical interest; collecting life-history narratives and objects of historical interest; acting as a point of contact and facilitator for academics, students and notably relatives (of the Spanish refugees) wishing to research the Spanish republican exile; identifying all of the refugees' points of entry into France; and the construction of an inventory of the Spanish republican exilic realms of memory in France. Finally, it has links with a solid range of organisations within France and Catalonia.[51]

This association's agenda has frequently been 'routed' in present-day concerns with a corresponding will to work memory in a dynamic and radical fashion. As part of the 2003 anniversary, it organised a symposium on the Palestinian exodus and exile. The following year's topic was entitled 'In solidarity with "Today's Undesirables"' and featured a paper by Catherine Withol de Wenden, a researcher from the French National Centre for Scientific Research (CNRS) on 'Crisis of Asylum, Crisis of the Rights of Man'. The accompanying leaflet linked the experiences of the Spanish republicans in 1939 to immigrants in contemporary France and drew the readers' attention to the state's immigration detention centre located close to the former camp of Rivesaltes in the Pyrénées-Orientales.[52] Two years later, they dedicated part of the commemoration to comparing the war in Spain of 1936 with present-day conflicts.

Not all members have agreed with this wider remit of Spanish republican remembrance. The vice-president's discussion of the association's future objectives in November 2003 called on the membership to honour the past by engaging with social and political issues of the present:

> to be attentive to events which, in the brutal light of the present, is redolent of our painful past. In response to the hunt for clandestine immigrants in the new market-led Europe, FFREEE must show solidarity, not only in principle, but through action, by actually meeting these men and women who flee the countries that deny them their most basic rights – working to feed oneself, the freedom of expression – and which endure a colonising influence that denies existence. Such was the intention behind our symposium ... in support of the Palestinian people and also behind our opposition to the American offensive in Iraq. The same applies to our categorical opposition to the erection of a memorial at Rivesaltes barely metres away from the detention centre for immigrants awaiting expulsion.[53]

As with any social groups, FFREEE cannot be characterised as a homogenous whole and the specific characteristics of its activities at any one moment reflect the balance of power in the steering committee. Nonetheless, the association has repeatedly manifested a progressive approach to the task of remembering.

The symbiosis of cultural identity and memory has not, however, been neglected. The annual commemoration involves speeches in French and Spanish along with Spanish cultural entertainment. Representatives of FFREEE have also campaigned on behalf of the Spanish republicans and their descendants. In June 2004, the association's president raised a complaint with the Prefect of the Pyrénées-Orientales and the Ministers of the Interior and Armed Forces, after the government responded to the desecration of a memorial portrait depicting child internees in the Rivesaltes camp by referring uniquely to the memory of Jewish children. FFREEE's president not only pointed out the elision of Spanish republican exilic memory but drew on universal values to stress the multi-ethnic character of the memorial: 'Where the present authorities can only see Jewish children, Friedel Bohny-Reiter, the camp nurse and artist of the portrait, only saw child internees without distinction of religion or origin. They were Jewish, but also gypsies, Spanish and other children.'[54] In the same year, the president also lobbied the Spanish government to grant dual nationality to Spanish republican children born in France.[55] All the same, some of FFREEE's members have sought to limit the association's focus more strictly on remembering the Spanish republican exile and organising (Spanish) cultural activities.[56]

Another distinguishing characteristic of FFREEE has been its commitment to inclusivity. While the ideological heterogeneity of the association has provoked tensions, the steering committee has maintained a commitment to the freedom of expression of various political/syndical identities. At the 2001 remembrance ceremony, members of the CNT installed a book table, and at the 2003 event one member unfurled the Communist flag during speeches in front of the monument marking the former Argelès camp. Diversity was particularly evident during the border crossing in February 2006, with participants carrying flags of the CNT, POUM Second Spanish Republic, and the French tricolour.

This inclusive approach to memory work has also encompassed less well-known aspects of the Spanish republican exile as well as refugees from other national origins. The experiences of women marked the February 2001 commemoration. In front of the stele in the cemetery of the Argelès camp, one of the people invited to speak was Neus Català, a former resister and deportee who passionately recalled the women of the Spanish republican exile, 'the forgotten of the forgotten'.[57] The afternoon's event concentrated on the Spanish and Jewish women and their children interned at Rivesaltes camp. It included homage to two Swiss women: Friedel Bohny-Reiter, a nurse who worked in the Rivesaltes camp; and Elisabeth Eidenbenz who created a maternity hospital at nearby Elne.

One of the most innovative aspects of FFREEE's remembrance practices has been the annual symbolic walk across the Pyrenean border known as the 'marche symbole'. The original idea was, according to one of the association's founders, Sonia Marzo, to go against the grain of commemorations that typically involve a static approach to memory.[58] It is also a practice which, by its very nature, transcends the national framework of remembrance characteristic of traditional realms of memory. It was instituted in 2002 when participants gathered to listen to a speech at a monument to the exodus in the Catalan village of La Vajol. They then hiked over the border along the path taken by refugees, including the Presidents of the Second Spanish Republic, Catalonia and the Basque country. A second set of speeches were delivered on arrival at the French village of Las Illas, and the hardiest of walkers then hiked back across the border via a different route, traversing the Coll de Manrella and passing a memorial to Lluis Companys. This return journey recalled those refugees who returned to Spain to combat Franco's dictatorship, together with French nationals who left France during the Occupation to join the Free French Forces. Subsequent commemorative walks have served to identify and remember the other paths taken by refugees across the Pyrenees with the accompanying inauguration of new memorials. In 2004, the focus was on the passage between Portbou and Cerbère, and in 2006 a sculpture was unveiled at Le Perthus after a walk from La Junquera.

National and transnational contexts

Both the examples of the Amicale de Gurs and FFREEE show how migrant forms of commemoration can shift out of, and across, national contexts. This is not to say that the national context in France can be entirely dismissed. The associations have invited various state representatives from ministers, to prefects and sub-prefects, as well as locally elected figures such as mayors, to the commemorative events. Their participation gives legitimacy, national recognition and often financial support to the associations' initiatives. But there have also been constraints. In return for support, compromises have sometimes been made.[59] The presence of (French) government ministers at the 1999 inauguration of the Argelès camp monument was subject to some wrangling about the wording of the epitaph. Instead of featuring the label, 'camp de concentration', the association compromised with the words 'camp d'Argelès'.[60] The ceremony went without hitch but left a problematic legacy for some of FFREEE's members. At the 2003 ceremony, the polemic became public when one member jostled with the local mayor as the former covered the official epitaph with an improvised plaque which was identical save for the reference to 'concentration camp'.

But just as the national context cannot be completely sidelined, neither can the transnational dimension. Numerous aspects of the Amicale de Gurs and FFREEE point towards a significant transnational emphasis to their commemorative spaces.[61] Both associations recognise the multi-ethnic histories of the camps and consequently the different layers of memory to be acknowledged through commemoration. The most clearly transnational characteristic stems from the role of the associations as hubs for sets of practices which regularly transcend France's borders. The Gurs association represents a point of contact from former internees and their descendants from across the world and also sends representatives to commemorations in other countries, whilst receiving representatives from abroad for the annual ceremonies in the camp cemetery. Furthermore, it was a Jewish–German association which created the first monument after leasing the Gurs cemetery. With its emphasis on the Spanish republicans and their descendants, FFREEE admittedly has a more focused membership. However, its activities and relationships involve frequent and regular cross-border communications. The annual symbolic border crossing is the most graphic example, not only because of the physical act of moving from one national territory to another, but because of the participation of organisations and representatives from each side of the border. Contact with organisations from Catalonia and other territories in Spain has become an increasingly important aspect of FFREEE's work.

With their progressive approaches towards memory, the two associations studied here offer a more optimistic vision than Nora's pessimistic, though understandable, prognosis about the relationship between heritage and sectoral identities. Paradoxically, perhaps it is their commitment to universal values which, in their aspirations and their everyday reality, sets refugee realms of memory apart from the range of examples in Nora's seven-volume collection. The links between identity and memory cannot be reduced to a single national framework, nor can they be tied to one specific time or place. In some respects, the space of refugee commemoration seen here hovers between a 'here and now' and a 'there and then'. Further studies will undoubtedly demonstrate the extent to which this applies to other remembrance practices surrounding refugees and their descendants. There will likely be shared characteristics but also significant differences. Consequently this interpretation of the Amicale de Gurs and FFREEE cannot be deterministically ascribed to all forms of such commemoration.

The personal and the social

At the individual level, Spanish republicans' memories emphasise a central experiential trait of exile: discrimination. It is a characteristic affecting the three elements – of time, space and social interaction – which collectively constitute the 'routes' to the Spanish republican exile in France. In addition to state-sanctioned forms of discrimination, the refugees confronted daily forms of prejudice. Some refugees recount how French nationals regarded Spain as a backward country lagging behind France in the process of modernisation. Refugees originating from urban areas in Spain were particularly irritated when asked: 'Have you ever been in a lift?' or 'Is there any electricity in Spain?' During the post-war years and into the 1960s, they also dealt with virulent remarks stemming from their political backgrounds and association with Spanish immigration more widely. Spanish republicans could thus be depicted as people who 'ate priests' or as 'filthy Spaniards', a 'filthy race' or accused of 'being here to take the bread from our mouths'.

As this book has frequently asserted, the 'normative' effects of exile were exacerbated by state and public responses in France. The heightened state of sensitivity forged from the reception in France could produce an overstated awareness of cultural difference. The absence of people and an accompanying silence is one way in which refugees characterised public spaces in France. Images of deserted streets with windows and shutters resolutely closed permeate recollections of arriving in towns and cities for the first time. Rosa Laviña's memory of when she left the reception centre for the first time stresses the sound of windows shutting along her path.[62] Sometimes, the depictions convey an accompanying narrative of agency that underlines the refugees' ability to reverse their status among local inhabitants. Francesc Parramón's depiction of Armistice Day in 1939, when refugees laid a wreath at a town's war memorial in the Hérault, emphasises how they initially formed up and marched towards the memorial in perfect order: 'on the way in, all of the windows and patio doors were shut, but on returning they were all opened to celebrate our gesture'.[63]

Stories of this kind are not restricted to the first years of exile. Ramon Falomir, a second-generation refugee who came to France in 1947 to rejoin his exiled father, described his early feelings of Bordeaux rather bleakly.[64] Unlike the small Valencian village from where he originated, the front door in Bordeaux had to remain shut and noise kept to a minimum. In Valencia, early-evening street life was vibrant, whereas in France there was disquieting silence. A similar picture is drawn by another second-generation refugee, Agustín Juan Diez, who arrived in France to be reunited with his father in 1949.[65]

A post-war article by the Spanish intellectual León Felip, which appeared in the anarchist youth review *Inquietudes* in October 1947, parodies the 'noisiness' associated with Spaniards as part of a narrative strategy to produce a positive sense of exilic identity.[66] Felip initially asserts: 'The loudness of the Spaniard is an old racial defect, old and incurable. It is a chronic illness.' He then identifies thee moments when 'the Spaniard' has had to scream himself hoarse: the discovery of the South American continent; the anguished cry of Don Quixote for justice; and thirdly in Madrid in June 1936. According to Felip, the anguished cry from Madrid served to warn the world about the spread of fascism and the coming of the Second World War, but it was a warning which fell on 'ears wrapped in concrete'. The final sentences conclude: 'The Spaniard does not speak loudly. I have just demonstrated so, and I will repeat it again. The Spaniard speaks at the exact level for mankind. He who thinks that the Spaniard speaks too loudly must be listening from the depths of a well.' Spanish republicans mobilised narratives of the past to buffer the blows on selfhood that exclusion engendered.

There is also a wider conceptual point to be made. The refugees came to France devoid of the resources usually associated with commemorative infrastructure. One consequence of this was the use of literature as an early vector for Spanish republican exilic memory. Francie Cate-Arries's perceptive analysis on how the camps became a *lieu de mémoire* and part of the foundational myth of exile in the literary works of Spanish republicans in Mexico during the 1940s is fascinating in this respect.[67] The camps also featured widely in the memoirs of those Spanish republicans who remained in France.[68] The second early form of memory activity to emerge was less obvious but as equally significant. The absence of resources and all things familiar to the refugees augmented the symbolic aspect of memory in their daily lives. Everything associated with a refugee's *habitus*, and which was normally taken for granted, involved a certain degree of reconstruction in the new context of France. In short, memory environments emerged as a coping strategy for exile.

Remembering was a salient and symbolic feature of daily practices due to the instability engendered by forced displacement, separation and repression. As a young girl, Antonia Illazque used to dream of her grand-mother's *tortillas* (omelettes) to offset the hunger and monotony of internment in the Argèles camp.[69] Antonio Arias recalled his family's celebration of their first New Year's Eve in France, and notably their fruit-less efforts to re-create a 'Spanish' dish of bread, olive oil and sugar. The substitute of vegetable oil produced a nasty taste that epitomised not only the daily struggle to feed themselves, but also to do so in a familiar and meaningful manner.[70] Studies of the Spanish refugees in Latin America also suggest that the rituals of food preparation and eating have played a role in generating and transmitting memories throughout the course of exile.[71] For Gloria Gargallo, a gathering of family and friends around paella was synonymous with stories about Spain, the social revolution, and the struggle for equality.[72]

Making it home

One of the most prominent spaces associated with rituals surrounding food was the home, though the sentiment of being at home has been a relatively recent phenomenon for Spanish republicans. Up until 1945, they experienced multiple displacements as they were forced to move around France because of the country's labour demands. After the war, refugees could also regularly change accommodation in the search for better living conditions. Furthermore, the anticipation of returning to Spain could also defer the production of a sense of home. It is difficult to ascertain with precision when this began to occur, as it most likely corresponded with generational factors: marriage, having children and retirement. Nonetheless, the 1970s were a turning point in refugees' reflections about the location and significance of home. Many Spanish republicans had retired or were approaching retirement and, in addition, Franco's death provoked reflection among refugees about where they were likely to spend the rest of their lives.

What exactly constitutes home? Some clarification is needed, since it is a term that has been criticised and even called into question as a useful category of analysis.[73] Part of the reason is because of a tendency to conflate 'home' with 'homeland'. In effect, some interviewees for this study spoke about not feeling at home as France was not their country.

At the same time, however, they endowed the space within which they lived with symbolic meanings with accompanying references to 'mi casita' or 'chez moi'. In this context, I understand home as a socially constructed space where individuals are able to enact roles of belonging and foreignness.

The interviews occurred in four households during the spring and summer of 2002 in the Gironde and Lot-et-Garonne. There was no aim to generalise on the basis of these findings. At this point in time, even if it were desirable, it would have been impossible to attempt any meaningful sample since most of the first-generation Spanish republican population had died. Neither was there an attempt to study the influence of ideological background on how people recount their pasts, though this would make for a fascinating study. The rich and qualitative data from these interviews provide an insight into how some Spanish republicans have responded to exile through the perspective of material culture and daily rituals of the home.[74] The resulting narratives disrupt teleological perspectives that portray the Spanish republicans as a group of refugees who, irrespective of the hardships endured in France, successfully 'integrated' into French society.

Antonia Illazque was born in 1925 in Tarrasa, Catalonia.[75] Both her parents were libertarians and she continued to adhere to the same values. After the *Retirada* she spent several months in the Argelès camp and then, later during the Occupation, Antonia met and married her husband while working as a wet nurse. She lived in rural areas of south-west France before moving to Bordeaux in 1952. Two years later, her husband returned to Spain with a serious illness and died in 1962. When recalling her life in France, Antonia frequently referred to the fear, discrimination and constraints of raising seven children virtually by herself. Despite speaking impeccable French she described herself as completely Spanish and not integrated into French society, stressing that she had refused to adopt French customs because of racism. Her working life, she stated, had prevented her from leading a 'Spanish' lifestyle. Retirement, on the other hand, had given her the freedom and opportunity to adopt the lifestyle of her choice. The Spanish imaginary for Antonia represented the freedom to live life as she wished, including the lack of restriction or inhibition regarding the volume at which people spoke and sang.[76]

Antonia described home in the following words: 'Home is where I can feel as though I'm in my own country. It makes me proud since we were regarded as an insignificant people who didn't amount to much.'[77] The material culture of Antonia's apartment reflected some of the prominent themes in her narrative of exile. The front and dining rooms, a corridor leading to the kitchen and the kitchen itself were decorated with objects reminiscent of Antonia's cultural imaginary. Items included figurines, jugs, a sombrero and a decorative plate depicting Don Quixote and Sancho Panza. The corridor wall was decorated with articles from tourist magazines on Spain and its regions which Antonia had begun to collect in the 1970s. This emphasis on regional diversity was also reproduced on the fridge with stickers from Spanish oranges. The most revealing of the objects, however, was a set of spoons which she had bought on a trip to Spain. She recalled buying the spoons because she had never seen any-thing like them in France. According to Antonia, the spoons were evi-dence that Spanish culture was capable of producing innovative items lacking in France. Moreover, as they originated from Málaga, they were testament to the diversity and richness of culture in Spain. The reason for emphasising diversity was to offset the stereotyping of the Spanish repub-licans as having come from a homogenous and underdeveloped country.

Maria-Pilar Lang also drew on home furnishings to assuage memories of discrimination.[78] Maria-Pilar was born in the province of Lérida in 1931. Her father was a Socialist, and as a young woman, she belonged to the PSUC. Her family was able to avoid internment thanks to the friends of a relative. But all the same, she recalled her parents being humiliated by a French employer during the first year of exile. Whilst having positive memories about primary school in France, she confronted discrimina-tion from other pupils at secondary school. Outwardly, Maria-Pilar had successfully acculturated to life in France and spoke French without a trace of an accent, which she explained was because of her father's mantra: 'when you're in another country, you need to be the best'. Reveal-ingly, she also described her educational and cultural achievements in terms of 'an account to settle'.[79] Later on Maria-Pilar married a French national from a distinguished family in Villeneuve-sur-Lot. Once again, home represented a safe space: 'I need to surround myself with objects, Spanish things . . . It's perhaps my secret garden . . . At the end of the day, I feel well in France thanks to this house. I owe much to this house . . . it's a refuge, you understand, a refuge . . . and nothing gives me more plea-sure than when there are people who come and say, "Ooh, it feels like Spain in here."'[80]

Amongst the numerous references to her country of birth were wooden trunks on various landings of the house, a picture of Don Quixote next to the cellar door and a model of Christopher Columbus's ship in a spare bedroom. As with Antonia, Maria-Pilar had invested objects with meanings to contest the reification she had personally encountered when younger. The display of objects often evoked the Spanish discovery of Latin America, projecting a different period of history when Spanish culture was exported across the world. A commentary about a sixteenth-century heirloom was notably indicative of the strength of feelings generated by memories of exile. In words charged with emotion, she explained the meanings attached to this item:

> Now, I'm going to tell you what that represents for me . . . the power of Spain, because I need to, because we were far too humiliated . . . do you understand? You see, because I have much more need of a reference like that in order to say that we exist, that we were really a great people . . . that we used to be practically masters of the world . . . than the family aspect. I don't give two hoots about that. Do you understand? I don't feel strongly about that, but the rest is more important.[81]

The accent on cultural as opposed to familial identity is revealing of the intensely ambivalent reactions resulting from a personal and collective sense of humiliation endured in exile. It is not a subject which Spanish republican families readily passed on to their children,[82] but one which some of the people interviewed for this study broached after their children had reached adulthood.

On the outskirts of Bordeaux in Lormont, the past was also present in Antonio and Pura Arias's daily lives.[83] Both were born in Madrid in 1925. After the exodus, the French authorities placed Antonio and his mother in a reception centre in the Loir-et-Cher whilst his father was interned at Argelès. During the Occupation, Antonio joined the Spanish Communist resistance whilst working for the OT in Bordeaux, and continued activities with the PCE in the post-war period. His wife, Pura, also arrived in France as a teenager. She followed the exodus with her mother and then stayed in a reception centre, whilst her father remained in Madrid. She dealt with confinement in the reception centre by remembering the family life she had led in Spain. The memory of the arrival and first months in France was still vivid enough to keep Pura awake at night, 63 years later. During the Occupation, Pura worked for the German military and then as a nanny for a French family, who she believes (wrongly) denounced her for resistance activities. She only escaped deportation due to the intervention of a German officer who had been her previous employer. In the post-war period, she participated in a cultural group linked to the PCE. According to Pura, 'The house, it's home as my Mum used to say, it's my little home, my little home. When we're away on a trip, for example, as happy as we may feel, we do like to return to our little home. We have our tranquillity ... the life we both want to lead and that counts for a lot, doesn't it?'[84]

The reference to 'the life we both want to leave' alludes to the role of daily practices in enacting a Spanish imaginary. While both Antonio and Pura underlined that they were internationalists, their memories of being separated from relatives and marginalised in France has had a correlative effect on their views about acculturation. More specifically, the disappointment about their first years in France and the belief that their history had been occluded was reflected in a rejection of daily practices considered to be French. The degree of rejection varied through time, given that the demands of life and work evidently obliged them to adhere to French customs, such as eating at French mealtimes and being overly respectful with neighbours about noise at home. Having children led them to consider life in France from a longer-term perspective and was the catalyst for furnishing their home. Beforehand, they refused to invest in any furniture in case it hindered their returning to Spain. A significant event shaping the memory environment of their home, however, was retirement, and the corresponding realisation that they would never return to the Spain they remembered.[85]

Retirement enabled Antonio and Pura to revert to eating at Spanish mealtimes. While the preparation and ingredients of their meals remained unchanged, the ability to eat later than is the norm in France had created a symbolic emphasis. In addition, being able to stay up later and watch Spanish satellite television generated another opportunity of re-creating a sense of Spain within the home as opposed to the previous intention of re-creating home in Spain. And yet, despite these strategies, the couple still professed to a feeling of being in a foreign country.

The issue of noise remained a notable signifier of difference between French and Spanish cultural identity. The couple demonstrated how they each plugged a pair of headphones into the television to watch their favourite programmes – usually weekly entertainment shows featuring Spanish music and songs – late into the night/early morning without disturbing their neighbours. The placement of objects within the living room also reflected a preoccupation with Spain. On the wall opposite the television there were two pictures: a reproduction of Velázquez's *Las Meninas*, with its interrogation about reality and more specifically about what or who is precisely the subject of the artist's work; and secondly, a picture of the coastal town of Sitges situated south-west of Barcelona. Pura spent two years in the town during the war in Spain and her sister was later buried there.[86] Were these pictures reminiscent of Spain deliberately placed opposite the couple's photographs of their children and grandchildren who were born in France? In another home, objects representing Spain and family photos were organised in the same way. Whatever the intention, it is worth drawing attention to a tendency for some of the former refugees to end their interviews by talking about the achievements of their children and grandchildren born in France. As much as children can remind parents of one of the reasons why they never retuned to Spain, they also allay the discomfort through family support and the parental pride generated by the children's achievements in France.

As with all oral histories, the emphasis of the stories, or the stories themselves, may have differed had the interviews occurred in another place at another time. Would the reactions have been the same with Spanish republicans interviewed in Toulouse following the celebrations of the seventieth anniversary of the Spanish republican exile? Would the interviewees have spoken so ambivalently about acculturation in France with a French – as opposed to a British – interviewer? In lieu of a full-scale longitudinal oral-history project involving Spanish republicans from different regions of France, these are questions easier asked than answered. All the same, these interviews illustrate a noteworthy consequence of cultural othering.

The fourth oral-history interview, with Miguel Oviedo, is equally revealing of the role of memory in constructing home, though for different reasons.[87] Miguel was born in Madrid in 1915. He fought for the Spanish Republic and after the exodus he was interned in Argelès and other camps in France. Once free, he worked in an armaments factory and in agriculture, but was once again interned in the early Vichy period. He subsequently worked in a GTE near the Pyrenean border before the French authorities transferred him to Bordeaux for work with the OT. While working for the German military, he entered into urban resistance activities with the PCE and joined a maquis group in the *département* of the Landes towards the end of the Occupation. After the Liberation Miguel married twice and continued to be active with the PCE up until 1959. At the time of the interview he lived with his French wife in Fargues-Saint-Hilaire, not far from Bordeaux.

In Miguel's words, 'at home I feel at home. I don't have any nostalgia for Spain. While Franco was there it meant nothing to me.'[88] While there is admittedly some conflation of 'home' with 'homeland', Miguel's words hints at a different symbolic space of home to that of the previous three households. This is not evident to the naked eye, for the house also exhibited objects reflective of Spanish culture, including a figurine of Don Quixote and Sancho Panza. But these represented nothing more than souvenirs, a record of the holidays that Miguel had taken with his wife.

Yet Miguel was keen to talk about the most quintessential signifiers of displacement: a suitcase. The case, which is stored in his garage, was imbued with symbolic significance, though this had nothing to with his journey to France. Miguel bought it on 22 February 1940, with his first wages in exile.[89] It symbolised the start of the life he had reconstructed in France and a series of personal achievements that included participation in the Liberation, marriage to a Frenchwoman and establishing a family. Miguel's favourite item relating to home was in fact a set of trees he had planted to provide shade for family gatherings in the garden. In this case, home was neither a refuge nor was it a space for a Spanish cultural imaginary: it represented the construction of his life and family in France.

The question of cultural identity was not entirely absent. Miguel retained his Spanish nationality but also claimed to be a good Frenchman in that he abided by the laws in France. What entitled him to this dual form of belonging, he stated, was his activity in the Resistance and maquis. The combatant era of his life was clearly displayed in a corner of the front room decorated with photographs of him in the Spanish Republic's Army, the camps of 1939 and his comrades from the maquis. Significantly, there was also a photograph of Miguel receiving a decoration from a French official for his resistance work hanging next to the accompanying framed certificate. Moreover, another photo showed Miguel standing and gazing with contemplation at the collection of photographs. Finally, above the photographs, there was a picture of an imaginary house which Miguel drew when he was younger. This memorial corner reflected, and was also constitutive of, a person whose history and memory had been officially recognised in France.

Feelings of disappointment, humiliation and bitterness stem from the shared historical experience of exclusion. The stories behind the material culture and rituals in these homes are suggestive of both the long-term effects of discrimination but also the redemptive possibilities of being officially reincorporated into a nation's commemorative narrative. Some of these issues have finally begun to be addressed through public commemoration, but for many, if not the majority of Spanish republicans, this should have occurred much sooner. As Nancy Wood has observed, resentment is a common symptom when painful aspects of a group's past has not been dealt with publicly.[90] Moreover, given that a male-dominated narrative of the Spanish republican resistance often, though not exclusively, prevails at commemorative events, it remains to be seen if and how a more gender-balanced narrative of Spanish republican exilic memory can be achieved on the memorial landscape.

In the meantime, as a response to their painful memories some of the former refugees have constructed a sense of self in opposition to perceptions of what is French. This process has not been without traces of essentialism and an over-emphasised sense of Spanish identity. All the same, this should be noted but not exaggerated. As with all identities, the performative element to identification produces other subjectivities. Having children and grandchildren of French nationality has most visibly stimulated acceptance of, and a certain attachment to, France. However, the history and political outlook of the Spanish exile must also be considered. Spanish republicans believed the conflict in Spain, and participation in the Resistance in France, had been fought for ideals that transcended national interests. All of the interviewees underlined they were internationalists. For some, a new relationship to Spain and France has been forged from the experience of exile. Maria-Pilar Lang belonged to an association in Villeneuve-sur-Lot which receives schoolchildren from other countries. In 2002, the association organised the reception of Spanish schoolchildren with excursions to places of local interest. Antonia Illazque recounted how being in exile had enabled her to regard Spain, and for that matter all countries, with more objectivity. She was keen to underline that 'by leaving a country we become more human'.[91]

During the first decade of the millennium, the Spanish republican exile became a distinct feature on France's memorial landscape. In 2002, a statute dedicated to *La Retirada* and financed by the Toulouse municipal authorities was inaugurated in the Minimes area of the city. It was the first of a series of engagements by both the city and regional council with the memory of the Spanish republican exile. Two years later, a plethora of commemorations occurred across the country with financial help from local, regional and national authorities. The enthusiasm was partly shaped by the overlapping memory of the 60th anniversary of the Liberation of France and the accompanying interest in the role played by immigrants.[92] The role of Spanish refugees in the Resistance was a dominant theme, but other aspects emerged. For the first time, former refugees in the CNT devoted part of the annual commemoration of the social revolution to the memory of exile and produced a calendar recalling the libertarian co-operative of Aymare.

Even if some of the social actors involved have pushed for a representative memory of the Spanish republican exile, the input of local or regional council funding invariably poses questions about what precisely is being celebrated.[93] On 19 November 2004, over a thousand people attended a commemoration of the Spanish republicans in Toulouse organised by the Regional Council.[94] There were interventions by the head of the Midi-Pyrénées region, Martin Malvy (Socialist Party), and the leader of the Catalan Generalitat, Pasqual Maragall, but there was no speech by any Spanish republican. It may have been difficult to invite representatives from all the different groups of the Spanish exile; it may also have been controversial since some aspects of their history remain contested between the various groups. Political diversity was nevertheless a historical trait of the Spanish exiles and should be adequately reflected if the aim is to produce a form of commemoration in which all tendencies feel recognised. Some former refugees from the CNT who had come from the Pyrénées-Orientales to attend the event were disgruntled.[95] The next day other first-generation exiles expressed similar reservations at the office of the CNT in rue Belfort, Toulouse.[96]

The intervention of local representatives and politicians has invariably provided opportunities for the reappropriation of Spanish republican exilic memory. However, the accompanying and increasing public awareness of this memory has prevented any single present-day concern from being stitched onto the memorial fabric. In 2006, the right-wing-dominated Toulouse municipal council celebrated the 75th anniversary of the Second Spanish Republic. Towards the end of the ceremony in the city's main square, Place du Capitole, a group of young adults with anti-fascist salutes protested against the French government's unpopular temporary work contract for French youths (Le Contrat Première Embauche). There are all the signs that the Spanish republican exile has become a realm of memory, albeit one which has been mobilised by very different social actors for varying reasons.

Perhaps it is the centrality of universal values, which the refugees held so dear, to Spanish republican memorial narratives that has enabled such disparate groups to identify with this memory. Perhaps it is the diversity of actors and associations which has prevented this collective memory from being transformed into a form of heritage devoid of a progressive memory politics. In 2009, a range of celebrations across France indicated the widespread interest in the Spanish republican exile. A sample from the many events provides a glimpse of the phenomenon. They included an exhibition in Bédarieux, and another in Bordeaux. Further northwards, homage was paid to Spanish republicans in Alençon, and numerous commemorations took place in Paris. Back in the south of the country, a conference in Montbeton was organised for the end of the year in December 2009. What is clear is that the participation of first-generation Spanish republicans had noticeably diminished. Given that FFREEE's secretariat has spent a lot of time responding to queries from descendants of refugees eager to trace their (often deceased) parents' trajectories, perhaps Nora's maxim now characterises this memory. As the first generation passes away and their descendants become commemorative participants, perhaps after all, 'there are realms of memory because there are no more memory environments'.

Notes

1 *La Dépêche* (28 June 2009).

2 *Ibid.*

3 P. Nora, 'Entre mémoire et histoire: La problématique des lieux', in Nora (ed.), *Les Lieux de Mémoire*, Vol. 1 (Paris, 1997), p. 23.

4 The initial evidence seemed to point in this direction. See S. Soo, 'Between Borders: The Remembrance Practices of Spanish Exiles in the Southwest of France', in S. Gemie and H. Altink (eds), *At the Border: Margins and Peripheries in Modern France* (Cardiff, 2008), p. 97. I am grateful to the University of Wales Press for allowing me to reproduce short extracts of the aforementioned text in this section.

5 The essays were originally published in seven volumes between 1984 and 1992. All references here are taken from the 1997 edition.

6 See Nora, 'Entre Mémoire et Histoire'.

7 *Ibid.*, pp. 23–43.

8 P. Nora, 'L'ère de la commémoration', in Nora (ed.), *Les Lieux de Mémoire*,Vol. 3, pp. 4687–719.

9 B. Graham, G. J. Ashworth and J. E. Tunbridge, *A Geography of Heritage: Power, Culture and Economy* (London, 2000), p. 34.

10 This has notably been the case during the era of industrial decline in France and Great Britain. See H.-P. Jeudy, *La Machine patrimoniale* (Belval, 2008) and R. Hewison, 'The Heritage Industry Revisited', *Museums Journal*, 91:4 (1991).

11 R. Samuel, *Theatres of Memory: Past and Present in Contemporary Culture*, Vol. 1 (London, 1994).

12 P. Birnbaum, 'Grégoire, Dreyfus et Copernic', in Nora (ed.), *Les Lieux de mémoire*, Vol. 2, p. 2680.

13 See Henri Rousso's caveat about the potential problems of mythmaking and the exclusion of other important aspects of Vichy history by solely focusing on Jewish experiences. E. Conan and H. Rousso, *Un passé qui ne passe pas* (Paris, 1994), pp. 9–30, 267–86.

14 G. Noiriel, 'Français et étrangers', in Nora (ed.), *Les Lieux de mémoire*, Vol. 2, p. 2447.

15 Nora (ed.), *Les Lieux de mémoire*, Vol. 1, p. 29.

16 A. Thomson, 'Moving Stories: Oral History and Migration Studies', *Oral History*, 27:1 (1999).

17 A *jira* literally refers to an excursion to the countryside organised by friends, families, an association or all three.

18 J. Semprún, *Le Grand Voyage* (Paris, 1963); G. Laroche, *On les nommait des étrangers: les immigrés dans la résistance* (Paris, 1965); J. Berruezo, *Contribución de la historia de la CNT de España en el exilio* (Mexico City, 1967); M. Constante, *Le Triangle bleu. Les républicains espagnols à Mauthausen* (Paris, 1969); C. M. Lorenzo, *Les anarchistes espagnols et le pouvoir, 1868–1969* (Paris, 1969); D. W. Pike, *Vae Victis! Los republicanos españoles refugiados en Francia 1939–1944* (Paris, 1969).

19 A. Vilanova, *Los Olvidados: los exilados españoles en la segunda guerra mundial* (Paris, 1969).

20 J. Jackson, *France: The Dark Years 1940–1944* (Oxford, 2001), p. 613.

21 For an in-depth analysis see Chapter 3, 'Le miroir brisé (1971–1974)', in H. Rousso, *Le Syndrome de Vichy de 1944 à nos jours* (Paris, 1990).

22 For an insight into memory and the Spanish republican exiles in Uruguay see: E. Allier Montaño, 'Memoria: una lenta y sinuosa recuperación', in S. Dutrénit Bielous, E. Allier Montaño and E. Coraza de los Santos, *Tiempos de exilios. Memoria e historia de españoles y uruguayos* (Montevideo, 2008), pp. 236–52.

23 A. Bartra, *Pere Vives i Clavé: Cartes des dels camps de concentració* (Barcelona, 1972); A. Fernández, *Emigración republicana española (1939–1945)* (Algorta, 1972); S. Iniesta, *Flon-Flon: Los republicanos españoles en la Legión Extranjera francesa* (Barcelona, 1972); A. Fernández, *Españoles en la resistencia* (Bilbao, 1973); E. Pons Prades, *Los que sí hicimos la guerra* (Barcelona, 1973); A. A. Bravo-Tellado, *El peso de la derrota 1939–1944: La tragedia de medio millón de españoles en el exilio* (Madrid, 1974); J. Rubio, *La emigración española a Francia* (Barcelona, 1974); A. Artís-Gener, *La diáspora republicana* (Barcelona, 1975); T. Pàmies, *Quan érem refugiats. Memories d'un exili* (Barcelona, 1975); E. Pons Prades, *Republicanos españoles en la 2a Guerra Mundial* (Barcelona, 1975); J. L. Abellán (ed.), *El Exilio español de 1939* (Madrid, 1976); T. Pàmies, *Los que se fueron* (Barcelona, 1976); E. Pons Prades, *Españoles en los «maquis» franceses (verano de 1944)* (Barcelona, 1976); A. Ros, *Diario de un refugiado republicano* (Barcelona, 1976); M. Ferrer, *La Generalitat de Catalunya a l'exili* (Barcelona, 1977); F. Giral, *La República en el exilio* (Madrid, 1977); F. Montseny, *El Éxodo: Pasión y muerte de españoles en el exilio*

(Barcelona, 1977); E. Pons Prades, *Los derrotados y el exilio* (Barcelona, 1977); J. Rubio, *La emigración de la guerra civil de 1936–1939*, Vols. 1–3 (Madrid, 1977); J. Tusell, *La oposición democrática al franquismo (1939–1962)* (Barcelona, 1977); J. A. de Aguirre, *Veinte años de gestión del Gobierno vasco (1936–1956)* (Durango, 1978); F. Montseny, *Seis años de mi vida (1939–1945)* (Barcelona, 1978); J. Peiró, *Trayectoria de la CNT* (Madrid, 1979); A. del Rosal, *Historia de la UGT de España en la emigración (Tomo I)* (Barcelona, 1979).

24 AD Pyrénées-Atlantiques, 72W 53. Letter to Préfet of the Basses-Pyrénées, 29 August 1959.

25 J. Carrasco, *La odisea de los republicanos españoles en Francia. Album-souvenir de l'exil républicain espagnol en France (1939–1945)* (Perpignan, 1984), pp. 177–8.

26 Information obtained from the museum of Vernet d'Ariège.

27 S. Zorzin, 'Le Camp de Septfonds (Tarn-et-Garonne): soixante ans d'histoire et de mémoires' (Mémoire de recherche, Institut d'Études Politiques de Bordeaux, 2000).

28 During the Occupation, 3,907 internees were deported, of whom 95.2 per cent were Jewish. C. Laharie, *Le Camp de Gurs, 1939–45: Un aspect méconnu de l'histoire du Béarn* (Biarritz, 1993), p. 242.

29 AD Pyrénées-Atlantiques, 72W 53.

30 Laharie, *Le Camp de Gurs, 1939–45*, p. 360.

31 AN SHAT, 34N 375. Letter from A. J. Escoriguel to Ministre des Armes, 29 September 1973.

32 For the campaign see H. Mauran, *Espagnols rouges: un maquis de républicains espagnols dans les Cévennes* (Nîmes, 1995), p. 92. For Bermejo's correspondence see AN CARAN 72 AJ 73: Archive of Luis Bermejo.

33 *Ibid.* Letter to head of the 5th Military Region, 17 January 1966.

34 President François Mitterrand and the Spanish Premier Felipe González participated in the 1994 remembrance ceremony at Prayols.

35 *Bulletin d'Information de l'Amicale des Anciens Guérilleros en France (F.F.I.)*, no. 103, September 2006.

36 For details of a Spanish republican memory association in the Lot-et-Garonne see S. Soo, 'Putting Memory to Work: A Comparative Study of Three Associations Dedicated to the Memory of the Spanish Republican Exile in France', *Diasporas. Histoires et sociétés*, 6 (2005), pp. 110, 117–20.

37 Memory activities in this region of France have not always been inclusive. The chapter 'Uneasy Commemorations' in S. Ott, *War, Judgement, and Memory in the Basque Borderlands, 1914–1945* (Reno, NV, 2008), pp. 172–86 offers a fascinating and nuanced insight into the mediation of memory at the local level.

38 The aims or 'Appel de Gurs' appear in Laharie, *Le Camp de Gurs, 1939–45*, p. 370.

39 www.campgurs.com (accessed 1 September 2010).

40 *Gurs, souvenez-vous*, no. 106, March 2007.

41 *Ibid.*, no. 89, December 2003.

42 Conan and Rousso, *Un passé qui ne passe pas*, pp. 9–30.

43 *Gurs, souvenez-vous*, no. 94, March 2004.

44 The German prisoners of war, people suspected of collaboration or refugees arriving from Spain who passed through Gurs between September 1944 and December 1945 do not appear to have been remembered.

45 *Gurs, souvenez-vous*, no. 99, June 2005.

46 *Ibid.*, no. 95, June 2004.

47 *Ibid.*, no. 98, March 2005.

48 Commemorative leaflet produced by FFREEE in 1999.

49 The association produced videos of the earliest commemorative events: *Argelès-sur-Mer se souvient ... La Retirada, le camp* (1999) and *100,000 lumières pour 100,000 réfugiés: Argelès-sur-Mer* (2001).

50 http://ffreee.typepad.fr/fils_et_filles_de_rpublic/ (accessed 2 September 2010).

51 One of the aims of the 2001 commemoration was to build a network with 15 associations from both sides of the Pyrenean border. The following associations and organisations participated in the 2008 commemoration: Prats Endavant, Les Amis du Musée de Céret, Les Amis du Monde Diplomatique, La ligue de Droits de l'Homme, Le Musée Mémorial du Camp de Rivesaltes, La Fondation Machado and the Museu d'Exili de la Jonquera. *FFREEE*, no. 14, March 2008.

52 Author's personal archive.

53 *FFREEE*, no. 5, December 2003.

54 FFREEE Information letter, June 2003.

55 *Ibid.*, June 2004. The Spanish Cortes passed a law in 2008 offering citizenship to the descendants of Spanish republicans and former members of the International Brigades.

56 Interview with Sonia Marzo, Argelès-sur-Mer, 23 November 2002.

57 N. Català, *Ces Femmes Espagnoles: de la Résistance à la Déportation* (Paris, 1994).

58 Interview with Sonia Marzo, Argelès-sur-Mer, 23 November 2002.

59 William Kidd's comparative research into commemoration in two of France's frontier regions illustrates how the interaction between different agencies, from the local and the national, or national and the sectional, produces a double-bind to the commemorative process. W. Kidd, 'From the Moselle to the Pyrenees: Commemoration, Cultural Memory and the "Debatable Lands"', *Journal of European Studies*, 35:1 (2005).

60 Interview with Sonia Marzo, Argelès-sur-Mer, 23 November 2002. Informal discussions with other members of the association, November 2002.

61 For a definition of transnational social space see T. Faist, 'The Border-Crossing Expansion of Social Space: Concepts, Questions and Topics', in T. Faist and E. Özveren, *Transnational Social Spaces: Agents, Networks and*

Institutions (Aldershot, 2004). For a discussion of transnationalism amongst historians see 'AHR Conversation: On Transnational History', *American Historical Review*, 111:5 (2006), pp. 1441–64; and, for an overview charting the development of this concept within migration studies, see P. Levitt and B. N. Jaworsky, 'Transnational Migration Studies: Past Developments and Future Trends', *Annual Review of Sociology*, 33:129 (2007).

62 The centre was in Brûlon, *département* of the Sarthe. E. Pons Prades, *Las guerras de los niños republicanos (1936–1995)* (Madrid, 1997), p. 227.

63 A. Soriano, *Éxodos: historia oral del exilio republicano en Francia 1939–1945* (Barcelona, 1989), p. 111.

64 Interview with Ramon Falomir, Floirac, 22 May 2002.

65 Interview with Agustín Juan Diez, Bordeaux, 20 June 2002.

66 AD Gironde, Versement 1239/42. *Inquietudes: Revista de la Juventudes Libertarias* (5 October 1947).

67 F. Cate-Arries, *Spanish Culture behind Barbed Wire: Memory and Representation of the French Concentration Camps, 1939–1945* (Lewisburg, FL, 2004).

68 For an overview of the Spanish republicans' memoirs see S. Gemie, 'The Ballad of Bourg-Madame: Memory, Exile and the Spanish Republican Refugees of the *Retirada* of 1939', *International Review of Social History*, 51:1 (2006).

69 Interview with Antonia Illazque, Bordeaux, 7 May 2002.

70 Interview with Antonio Arias, Lormont, 7 April 2002.

71 A. Alted Vigil, 'El exilio republicano español de 1939 desde la perspectiva de las mujeres', *Arenal. Revista de historia de las mujeres*, 4:2 (1997).

72 Interview with Gloria Gargallo, Latresne, 23 April 2002.

73 A. Bammer, 'The Question of "Home"', *New Formations*, 17 (1992), p. xi.

74 During the interviews, I encouraged the informants to talk about how the past was represented in their homes. Consequently, they identified what objects and practices were meaningful to them.

75 When referring to cultural identity Antonia used the term 'Spanish' far more frequently than that of 'Catalan'.

76 Interviews with Antonia Illazque, Bordeaux , 7 May, 14 August and 13 September 2002.

77 Interview with Antonia Illazque, Bordeaux, 13 September 2002.

78 Interviews with Maria-Pilar Lang, Villeneuve-sur-Lot, 27 September, 29 November 2002 and 23 July 2003.

79 Interview with Maria-Pilar Lang, Villeneuve-sur-Lot, 27 September 2002.

80 *Ibid.*, Villeneuve-sur-Lot, 23 July 2003.

81 *Ibid.*

82 See J. Forné, '"Familles, je vous aime!": L'Intégration des Réfugiés Politiques Espagnols à Toulouse et dans sa Région', in L. Domergue (ed.), *L'exil Républicain espagnol à Toulouse 1939–1999* (Toulouse, 1999), pp. 251–76.

83 Interviews with Antonio and Pura Arias, Lormont, 4, 8 and 16 July 2002.

84 *Ibid.*

85 For an analysis of how Spanish republicans have compared returning to Spain with the Spain of their pre-exilic past see F. Guilhem, *L'obsession du retour* (Toulouse, 2005).

86 Interview with Antonio and Pura Arias, Lormont, 16 July 2002.

87 Interviews with Miguel Oviedo, Fargues-Saint-Hilaire, 24 September, 8 October, and 9 December 2002.

88 Interview with Miguel Oviedo, Fargues-Saint-Hilaire, 8 October 2002.

89 Miguel narrated this story from his unpublished diary written at the time of events.

90 N. Wood, *Vectors of Memory: Legacies of Trauma in Postwar Europe* (Oxford and New York: Berg, 1999), p. 199.

91 Antonia Illazque, Bordeaux, 5 July 2002.

92 During the summer of 2004, the television channels TF1 and France 2 reported on the participation of colonial troops in the Allied landing in Provence, together with the presence of Spanish refugees in the vanguard of the 2nd Armoured Division that entered Paris on the evening of 24 August 1944.

93 J. Jornet, "'Il était une fois la République espagnole...': Un projet d'hommage officiel développé par la Région Midi-Pyrénées', *Les Cahiers de Framespa: Nouveaux champs de l'histoire sociale*, 3 (2007), http://framespa.revues.org/442 (accessed 1 July 2011).

94 The publication of a book accompanied the event: *Républicains espagnols en Midi-Pyrénées: Exil histoire et mémoire* (Toulouse, 2004).

95 Informal discussions, Toulouse, 19 November 2004.

96 Informal discussion, Toulouse, 20 November 2004.

Conclusion: trajectories and legacies

In periods of crisis, societies and smaller-scale groups have often searched for answers, if not a panacea, by focusing on the past. This retrospective gaze has often turned towards the notion of origins and roots in order to resolve contemporary problems, though in practice this type of soul-searching has frequently achieved little more than to distract attention away from the issues at stake. The temptation to engage in this specific relationship with the past has been even greater for refugees, given the sense of rupture, loss and insecurity which accompanies forced displacement and exile.

Although the Spanish republicans often dwelled on their pre-exilic past, or wrote about their nostalgia for Spain, their daily lives were characterised by more immediate and pressing needs. In seeking to understand how refugees adapted to exile, this book has explored the relationship and responses of the Spanish republicans to their environment over the long duration. Exile was, above all, a composite of interactions between the refugees on the one hand, and the populations, authorities and organisations they encountered in France. But it also involved the Spanish republicans responding to new social spaces in France and mobilising memory as a resource for dealing with contemporary issues. The 'routes' to the Spanish republican exile thus emerge as an amalgam of refugees' reactions to the interactive, spatial and temporal dynamics of daily life in France.

With its symbiotic approach to history and memory, this book reveals just how deeply refugees were affected by their arrival in France. The sense of loss, instability and vulnerability that afflicted Spanish refugees in 1939 was considerably intensified by the French authorities' reception strategies, pejorative press reporting and the circulation of stereotypes. Once over the French–Spanish border, the refugees had to contend with a grid of both material and discursive boundaries that acted to differentiate and exclude them from French society. Before the exodus was even over, a host of national fears and prejudices were seemingly legitimated through the mass internment of the refugees. Xenophobia became meshed with anti-communism, which in turn was linked to concern over internal unrest and the looming conflict with Germany. The Spanish republicans formed a canvas onto which national fears and anxieties could be projected: they were held up to be all that France was not.

There were certainly acts of generosity and solidarity at the popular and elite levels. While reception committees raised funds, parliamentary committees endeavoured to ameliorate the conditions in the camps. Moreover, some representatives worked against the grain of government policy. The examples of the *député* at Port-Sainte-Marie, Lot et Garonne, and the Deputy Mayor of Oloron-Sainte-Marie in the Basses-Pyrénées attest to how government policy could be contested at the local level, albeit with limited success. The fact that the refugees in Port-Sainte-Marie were eventually permitted to remain in France points to the grey area surrounding the legitimacy of the repatriation policy. Similar actions were most likely reciprocated in other regions of the country, and further research would shed additional light on this subject. What can be affirmed, however, are the Popular Front backgrounds of the French representatives involved. Their actions made a difference. But more widely, there was severe incomprehension and disappointment among the Spanish refugees who had expected, at the very least, a more generally compassionate reception.

The sense of rejection that refugees internalised during the arrival in France affected their subsequent and early interpretations of French cultural practices. As such they interpreted certain events as an extension of a dehumanising process that had begun at the border. Life-history analysis suggests that refugees paid considerable attention to creating a positive image in the localities where they were present. It also offers a striking insight into the long-standing effects of exile on perceptions of cultural difference. In this sense, there is substance to Noël Valis's claim that it is not possible to 'separate the historico-political fact of exile from the feelings which emerge from it'.[1]

The second contribution of this book centres on the relationship between asylum and the economy. Officials continually linked asylum to the country's labour needs, often quite literally interpreting asylum as a right to be earned. More particularly, we discovered why and how governments of the Third Republic and Vichy eras reversed policies concerning refugee employment according to labour-economy demands.

Following the outbreak of war with Germany in 1939, the government introduced improvements to the Spanish republicans' working conditions – in both the CTE and other labour sectors – as their contribution to the war economy became ever more apparent. This did not occur across the board for all refugees in France. The government chose to intern refugees from Central and Eastern Europe, irrespective of whether they were anti-fascist or not. Conditions and rights during the last year of the Third Republic were thus variable according to the particular group of refugees. The example of the Spanish republicans is a reminder that refugee policy in the latter years of the Third Republic varied according to the origins of the refugees and was, furthermore, characterised by nuances, twists and turns, rather than by a linear narrative of steadily declining rights.

Despite the changing circumstances, the representation of the Spanish republicans as a threat to public security did not disappear. During the period of the Second World War, from the Third Republic through to Vichy and the Liberation, two prominent and conflicting discourses can be discerned: officials perceived the refugees in terms of a threat and as potential workers. The initial reactions of Vichy to the Spanish republicans unfolded in a similar fashion to the Third Republic's response. An emphasis on exclusion and the desire to see the departure of the refugees was accompanied by Vichy's consideration of the GTE as a method of exploiting a cheap and flexible pool of labour that could, in theory, be kept under surveillance.

In practice, the dual aim of exclusion and control was soon compromised by necessary changes to working conditions and the daily realities of the Foreign Labour Groups. As had been the case with the CTE, some workers abandoned their workplaces in search of better working conditions, or to retain an element of choice over their place of work. There were evidently clear differences between the Third Republic and the Vichy period. All the same, the contradictions shaping refugee employment policy during the CTE era were unresolved and in some cases accentuated. As such, both the Vichy regime and the German Occupying Forces unwittingly produced conditions favourable for the refugees to change their type and location of work. This undoubtedly facilitated subversion and, during the latter half of the Occupation period, many Spanish republican workplaces became associated with refusal, revolt and resistance. The stakes of such actions were high: overthrowing the German and Vichy authorities represented a step towards returning to Spain but carried potentially deadly consequences for those refugees suspected of resistance activities.

The evidence also shows that despite the pronounced xenophobia of the Vichy regime, the presence of Spanish republicans in some rural areas of the south-west became not only tolerated but even desirable. Employers and officials in both zones began willingly to subvert French government policy concerning recruitment for the OT and German firms. Ultimately, though, labour provision in Vichy France was irrevocably compromised by the unworkable contradictions shaping the OT and Vichy employment policy in the two zones.

Finally, this study has provided the first account of Spanish republican remembrance practices over the long duration, together with insight into the relationship between different memorial frameworks: from the public to the private, as well as from the national to the transnational. The refugees were astutely aware of the socio-political function of commemoration when they celebrated a range of anniversaries behind barbed wire during the spring and summer of 1939. However, it was during the Liberation of France that the basis for a collective memory of exile emerged. From the mid-1940s to the end of the 1950s, refugees developed a proto-commemorative culture of the Spanish republican exile as part of their strategy for returning to Spain. For a brief but significant period, the refugees created a space for themselves in post-war resistance narratives as they participated with local French organisations in joint remembrance ceremonies. The (French) national Gaullist and Communist discourses of the Resistance certainly became dominant prisms concerning the memory of the Occupation, but the process was neither immediate nor uniform at the local level.

It was not until the 1970s that a veritable commemorative culture of exile began gradually to emerge, becoming a more widely visible presence on France's memorial topography over the turn of the millennium. A salient characteristic of the associations' work has been the play between national and transnational memory spaces. In the meantime, the memory environments of the homes of some Spanish republicans have mediated between the past and present, playing a crucially enabling role for those whose histories and memories have been absent from public remembrance.

On the cusp of the 70th anniversary of the *Retirada*, local authorities publicly honoured the Spanish republicans' participation in the Resistance in the Aquitaine region. On 21 November 2008, the Mayor of Bordeaux awarded 12 Spanish republicans the 'Médaille de la Ville', the French equivalent of the keys to the city.[2] A week later, a similar ceremony occurred close to the former Gurs camp at Oloron-Sainte-Marie in honour of two former resisters: Luis Alberto Quesada, who was now living in Argentina, and the memory of his wife, Asun, who had died earlier that year. Their son collected the awards on behalf of his parents, declaring to the local paper, 'After 68 years we had lost hope that France would one day recognise the Spanish republicans' part in the fight against the fascist axis.'[3]

By 2009, it was no longer possible to view the Spanish republican exile as a neglected memory. The extent of commemoration that year was partly reflective of the gradual disappearance of first-generation Spanish republicans and the corresponding commemoration of their lives by their descendants and other French nationals. It also took place within the wider context of fascination with commemoration in contemporary France and the growing awareness of the country's ethnic plurality. But, while 2009 was an auspicious year, and arguably one of the busiest on record for commemorating the Spanish republican exile, it was also when Eric Besson, the Minister for Immigration, Integration and National Identity, began organising controversial public debates on 'national identity' and what it meant to be French. Introspection of this kind rarely encourages a positive and celebratory acceptance of foreigners, but can engender a chimerical and retrospective search for answers in the past.

This book has charted the complexities surrounding the relationship between the Spanish republicans and their French hosts through a symbiotic approach to history and memory. An interpretative framework of this kind, in which the perspectives of refugees and hosts are integrated, is all the more necessary given the (national) identity-politics at stake in officially sponsored commemorations of refugees in France. Antonia Illazque was one of the Spanish republicans in France who generously allowed her life-determining experiences and memories to be the subject of our investigation. She felt that she had learnt to become more human through exile. If so, it was at a very considerable human cost.

Notes

1 N. Valis, 'Nostalgia and Exile', *Journal of Spanish Cultural Studies*, 1:2 (2000), p. 117.
2 http://mer47.free.fr/spip.php?article215&debut_articles_rubrique=45 (accessed 1 October 2010).
3 *Sud Ouest* (Pyrénées-Atlantiques) (28 November 2008).

Appendix
Details concerning the socio-professional composition
of the Spanish male population of the concentration
camps in June 1939[1]

Agricultural sector

Unskilled workers	45,918	28.9%
Skilled workers	2,451	1.5%
Total	48,369	30.4%

Industrial sector

Textile and leather industry	3,645	2.3%
Wood trade	5,922	3.7%
Mines and quarries	6,810	4.3%
Metalwork, electricity, mechanics	18,894	11.9%
Construction and public works	15,628	9.8%
Food industry	4,926	3.1%
Transport	9,558	6.0%
Others	6,919	4.3%
Total	72,302	45.4%

Service sector

Commerce	6,325	4.0%
Administration	5,679	3.6%
Military (professional)	2,372	1.5%
Liberal professions	2,202	1.5%
Total	16,578	10.5% [*sic*]
Classifications believed to be false	21,900	13.7%
Overall total	159,149	100% [*sic*]

Note

1 J. Rubio, *La emigración de la guerra civil de* 1936–1939, Vol. 1 (Madrid, 1977), p. 216.

Bibliography

Archival sources

FRANCE

AN Fontainebleau
19890151   Ministre de l'Intérieur
19890158   Ministre de l'Intérieur
19900353   Ministre de l'Intérieur
19940500   Direction Générale de la Sûreté Nationale
19980221   Ministre de l'Intérieur
20010216   Direction Générale de la Sûreté Générale

Centre d'accueil et de recherche des Archives nationales (AN CARAN)
72AJ   Papiers du Comité d'histoire de la Deuxième Guerre mondiale et fonds
       privés relatifs à la période 1939–45
AJ41   Organismes issus de l'armistice de 1940
AJ43   Organisation internationale pour les réfugiés (OIR)
BB   Ministère de la Justice
F1a   Inspection Générale des Services Administratifs
F7   Ministère de l'Intérieur

Service historique de l'armée de Terre (AN SHAT)
7N 2475/2–3   Programme d'utilisation des matériels
7N 2478   Travailleurs étrangers
34N 135   Compagnies de travailleurs et miliciens espagnols du camp de
              Gurs, 1939–40
34N 375   Travailleurs espagnols et divers, 1939–40
34N 377–8   Compagnies de travailleurs espagnols

Archives Départementales des Bouches-du-Rhône (AD Bouches-du-Rhône)
99W 78   Réfugiés espagnols, 1940–41
4M 962   Lettres adressées aux réfugiés

Archives Départementales de la Dordogne (AD Dordogne)
7 AV 19–20   Oral-history interview, Annick Garcia Palacio
4M 161   Espagnols hébergement, 1939–40
4M 170   Préfecture, Police
42W 60/2   Ressortissants espagnols
AV 6   Oral-history interview, Calixto Casales

Archives Départementales de la Gironde (AD Gironde)
D64   Surveillance des étrangers
SC 308   Fonds du Commissaire régional de la République
SC 460   Action communiste
SC 569–70   Rapports journaliers des Renseignements Généraux, 1944
SC 755   Rapports des Renseignements Généraux, 1943
SC 784   Rapports concernant la situation générale
SC 952–3   TODT recherches réfractaires, 1943–44
SC 1906   Arrestations d'espagnols évadés des chantiers d'organisation TODT, 1942
SC 1908   Recensement des espagnols 'rouges', 1940–46
SC 1909   Arrestations d'espagnols évadés des chantiers d'organisation TODT, 1942
SC 1916   Étrangers, 1941–42
SC 1918   Étrangers, 1940–45
SC 1949   Travailleurs Étrangers
Série 1M   Administration Générale du Département
Série 4M   Police

Versements:
1239/41–43   Groupements Étrangers
Vrac 32   Affaires pendant l'occupation: tracts communistes et journaux clandestins, 1940–42
Vrac 200   Recherches d'individus étrangers évadés des camps de travail, 1940–42

Archives Départementales de la Haute-Garonne (AD Haute-Garonne)
1769W 1   STO, organisation Todt, travailleurs étrangers, 1943–44
1960W 64   Oficina de Ayudos a los Vascos
1960W 66   Associations de secours aux réfugiés espagnols
2517W 45   Instructions étrangers deuxième semestre, 1940
2517W 46   Instructions étrangers, 1941–42
2517W 47   Instructions étrangers, 1943

Archives Départementales du Lot (AD Lot)
1W 5   Rapports mensuels du Préfet
1W 646   Étrangers, 1942–45
1W 923   Étrangers
1W 953   Étrangers
4M 115   Rapports de police
4M 117   Réfugiés politiques espagnols, centres d'hébergement du département
1180W/1   Rapports des Renseignements Généraux, 1942–44

Archives Départementales de Lot-et-Garonne (AD Lot-et-Garonne)
1W 92   Rapports des Renseignements Généraux
2W 11   Instructions, listes, assignations à résidence, internements
2W 15   Groupements des Travailleurs Étrangers
4M 299   Enfants espagnols, 1937–40
4M 306   Hospitalisations, 1937–49
4M 309   Situations journalières et hebdomadaires, 1937–40
4M 312   Rapports de police, 1939
4M 316   Réfugiés espagnols employés dans l'agriculture, 1939–40

Archives Départementales des Pyrénées-Atlantiques (AD Pyrénées-Atlantiques)
72W 53   Cimetière: entretien, plan et cérémonies, 1945–72
77W 33   Recrutement de la main d'œuvre au camp de Gurs
1031W 232   Résistance intérieure espagnole
1031W 234   Travailleurs étrangers et espagnols postérieur à 1940
1031W 235   Frontière franco-espagnole

Archives Départementales des Pyrénées-Orientales (AD Pyrénées-Orientales)
31W 274   Guerre civile, exode. Rapport du Préfet, 1939–40
1287W 1   Camps provisoires d'hébergement

Centre International de Recherches et d'Archives Sociales, Bègles (CIRAS)
Gestión MLE–CNT en Francia libros 1–2, 1945–46
Minutes of the Junte Espagnole de Libération in Bordeaux 1945–46
Origen y Gestiones, CIR, 1945–47

GREAT BRITAIN
British National Archives (FO)
FO 371/24154: Spanish Refugees in France
FO 371/24155: Spanish Refugees in France

SPAIN

Archivo General de la Administración, Alcalá de Henares (AGA)
IDD No. 30   *Consulado de España en Hendaya, 1849–1960:*
Caja 11765/7   Consulado de España en Hendaya, 1849–1960
Caja 11771   Repatriados españoles, 1941
Caja 11774/6   Consulado de España en Hendaya, 1849–1960
IDD No. 97   *Embajada de España en París, 1939–71:*
Caja 11287   Actividades de los rojos
Caja 11453   Actividades rojos en Francia
Caja 11517   Actividades de Vascos españoles rojos en Francia
Caja 11597   Consulado en Burdeos, 1946–55
Caja 11609   Consulado en Burdeos, 1941–45

Fundación Universitaria Española: Archivo del Gobierno de la II República en Exilio
872–4/1947–8   Documentación sobre la cooperativa alpargatera de Burdeos creada por mutilados españoles

Internet sources

http://campgurs.com
http://ffreee.typepad.fr/fils_et_filles_de_rpublic/

Life-history sources

MEMOIRS AND DIARIES

Alberti, R. *Vida bilingüe de un refugiado español en Francia 1939–1940* (Buenos Aires: editorial Bajel, 1942).

Andujar, M. *St Cyprien, Plage: Campo de concentración* (Mexico: Cuadernos del Destierro, 1942).

Berenguer, S. *Entre el Sol y la Tormenta: Treinta y dos meses de guerra (1936–1939)* (Calella: Seuba Ediciones, 1988).

Bonet Lopez, L. *Mémoires d'exil d'un Espagnol (Deux-Sèvres, Charente-Maritime, Gironde)* (Paris: Le Croît vif, 2002).

Bonet, L. *Une Auberge Espagnole* (Paris: Éditions Gallimard, 1994).

Borrás, J. *Del Radical-Socialismo al Socialismo Radical y Libertario: Memorias de un Libertario* (Madrid: FSS Ediciones, 1998).

Castillo, M. del *Tanguy* (Paris: Éditions René Julliard, 1957).

Català, N. *Ces Femmes Espagnoles: de la Résistance à la Déportation*, trans. C. Langlois (Paris: Éditions Tirésias, 1994).

Espinar, J. *Argelès-sur-Mer: Campo de concentración para Españoles* (Caracas: Editorial Elite, 1940).

Fernández, A. *Rebelde: Loco de amor por la libertad y la justicia* (published by the author, 2000).

Ferrer, E. *Derrière les Barbelés: Journal des Camps de Concentration en France (1939)* (Limonest: L'Interdisciplinaire, 1993).

Fortea García, J. *Tiempo de história: no hay más cera que la que arde* (Badalona: Fundació d'Estudis Llibertaris Federica Montseny, 2002).

García Gerpé, M. *Alambradas. Mis nueve meses por los campos de concentración de Francia* (Buenos Aires: Editorial Costa, 1941).

Gargallo Edo, F. *La raison douloureuse* (Madrid: Fundación de Estudios Libertarios Anselmo Lorenzo, 1999).

Giménez Arenas, J. *De la Unión a Banat: Itinerario de una rebeldía* (Madrid: Fundación de Estudios Libertarios Anselmo Lorenzo, 1996).

Kent, V. *Quatre ans à Paris* (Paris: Éditions le Livre du Jour, 1947).

Levi, P. *The Drowned and the Saved* (London: Penguin, 1988).

Martínez-López, F. *Guérillero contre Franco: La guérilla antifranquiste du León (1936–1951)* (Paris: Éditions Syllepse, 2000).

Mistral, S. *Éxodo: diario de una refugiada española* (Mexico City: Editorial Minerva, 1941).

Montagut, L. *J'étais deuxième classe dans l'armée républicaine espagnole (1936–1945)* (Paris: Découverte, 2003).

Montseny, F. *El Éxodo: Pasión y muerte de españoles en el exilio* (Barcelona: Galba, 1977).

Montseny, F. *Seis años de mi vida (1939–1945)* (Barcelona: Barcelona, 1978).

Montseny, F. *Mis primeros cuarenta años* (Barcelona: Plaza y Janes, 1987).

Moral i Querol, R. *Journal d'exil (1939–1945)* (Paris: Éditions Éole, 1982).

Nouveau, L. H. *Des Capitaines par Milliers: Retour à Gibraltar des aviateurs alliés abattus (1941–43)* (Paris: Calmann-Lévy, 1958).

Paz, A. *Entre la niebla* (Barcelona: Editorial Medusa, 1993).

Pons, F. *Barbelés à Argelès et autour d'autres camps* (Paris: L'Harmattan, 1993).

Ponzán Vidal, P. *Lucha y muerte por la libertad. Memorias de nueve años de guerra: 1936–1945* (Barcelona: Tot Editorial, 1996).

Regler, G. *The Owl of Minerva* (London: Rupert Hart-Davis, 1959).

Ros, A. *Diario de un refugiado republicano* (Barcelona: Grijalbo, 1976).

Sanchis Martínez, G. 'Souvenir d'un Voyage Historique d'un Réfugié Espagnol' (unpublished manuscript, 2001).

Sans Sicart, J. *Comisario en el exilio. La esperanza frustrada de un luchador por la libertad* (Lleida: Editorial Milenio, 2004).

Semprún, J. *Le Grand Voyage* (Paris: Gallimard, 1963).

Solano Palacio, F. *El éxodo: Por un refugiado español* (Valparaíso: Editorial Más Allá, 1939).

Vergara, J. *Aymare: 1947–1963 (Colonia de los mutilados y ancianos de la revolución española del 1936 a 1939)* (published by the author, La Rochelle, 1994).

ORAL EVIDENCE

Manuel Alama, Bordeaux, 30 May 2002
Antonio and Pura Arias, Lormont, 4, 8 and 16 July 2002
Eduardo Bernad, Bordeaux, 27 June and 11 July 2002
Elio Diaz Leon, Bordeaux, 19 June 2002
Agustín and Ignacia Juan Diez, Bordeaux, 19, 20 June and 25 September 2002
Valeriano and Feliciana Espiga, Fargues-Saint-Hilaire, 21 May 2002
Ramon Falomir, Floirac, 22 May 2002
Gloria Gargallo, Latresne, 23 April 2002
Antonia Illazque, Bordeaux, 7 May, 5 July, 14 August and 13 September 2002
Maria-Pilar Lang, Villeneuve-sur-Lot, 27 September and 29 November 2002 and
    23 July 2003
Sonia Marzo, Argelès-sur-Mer, 23 November 2002
Miguel Oviedo, Fargues-Saint-Hilaire, 24 September, 8 October and 9 December
    2002
Francisco Perez, Bègles, 5 July 2003

NEWSPAPERS AND BULLETINS

Boletín de los estudiantes (FUE), Argelès (17 April and 18 May 1939)
Boletín de los estudiantes (FUE), Barcarès (27 July 1939)
Bulletin d'Information de l'Amicale des Anciens Guérilleros en France (FFI) (Sep-
    tember 2006)
CNT (5 September 1944–3 February 1945/17 March 1945–9 January 1946)
FFREEE (March 2002–March 2008)
Gurs, souvenez-vous: lettre d'information de l'Amicale du camp de Gurs (April
    2002–January 2010)
Hoja Estudiante FUE, Barcarès (27 July 1936)
Inquietudes: Revista de las Juventudes Libertaria (5 October 1947)
La IV° République (Organe Landaise d'Informations) (1 January 1944)
La Dépêche du Midi, 'Espagne il y a soixante ans' (Novembre 1996)
La Petite Gironde (January–February 1939)
La Victoire (17 November 1945)
Manchester Guardian (30 January and 2, 3 and 18 February 1939)
Poble Català (27 October 1939)
Solidarité (7 April 1939)
The Times (16 January and 1 February 1939)
Treball (26 February and 6 March 1939)

Secondary sources

BOOKS AND ARTICLES

Abellán, J. L. (ed.), *El Exilio español de* 1939 (Madrid: Taurus, 1976).
Adler, K. *Jews and Gender in Liberation France* (Oxford: Oxford University Press,
    2003).

Aguirre, J. A. de, *Veinte años de gestión del Gobierno vasco (1936–1956)* (Durango: Leopoldo Zugaza, 1978).

'AHR Conversation: On Transnational History', *American Historical Review*, 111:5 (December 2006), 1140–64.

Alexander, M. S. and H. Graham (eds), *The French and Spanish Popular Fronts: Comparative Perspectives* (Cambridge: Cambridge University Press, 2002).

Alted Vigil, A. 'El exilio republicano español de 1939 desde la perspectiva de las mujeres', *Arenal. Revista de historia de las mujeres*, 4:2 (1997), 223–38.

Alted Vigil, A. *La voz de los vencidos: El exilio republicano de 1939* (Madrid: Aguilar, 2005).

Alted Vigil, A. and M. Aznar Soler, *Literatura y Cultura del Exilio Español de 1939 en Francia* (Salamanca: Aemic-Gexel, 1998).

Amar, M. and P. Milza, *L'Immigration en France au XX Siècle* (Paris: Armand Colin, 1990).

Les Anarchistes espagnols dans la tourmente (1939–1945) (Marseilles: Centre international de recherches sur l'anarchisme, 1989).

Anderson, B. *Imagined Communities: Reflections on the Origin and Spread of Nationalism* (New York: Verso, 1991 edn).

Angoustures, A. 'Les Réfugiés Espagnols en France de 1945 à 1981', *Revue d'histoire moderne et contemporaine*, 44:3 (1997), 457–529.

Arasa, D. *Años 40: los maquis y el PCE* (Barcelona: Argos Vergara, 1984).

Artís-Gener, A. *La diáspora republicana* (Barcelona: Editorial Euros, 1975).

Augé, M. *Les Formes de l'oubli* (Paris: Rivages poche, 1998).

Bammer, A. 'The Question of "Home"', *New Formations*, 17 (1992), vii–xi.

Barth, F. (ed.), *Ethnic Groups and Boundaries: The Social Organisation of Culture Difference* (London: George Allen & Unwin, 1969).

Bartra, A. *Pere Vives i Clavé: Cartes des dels camps de concentració* (Barcelona: Antologia Catalana, 1972).

Berruezo, J. *Contribución de la historia de la CNT de España en el exilio* (Mexico City: Editores Mexicanos Unidos, 1967).

Bonnet, J.-C. *Les pouvoirs publics français et l'immigration dans l'entre-deux-guerres* (Lyon: Presse Université de Lyon, 1976).

Borrás, J. *Políticas de los exiliados españoles, 1944–1950* (Paris: Ruedo Ibérico, 1976).

Bravo-Tellado, A. *El peso de la derrota 1939–1944: La tragedia de medio millón de españoles en el exilio* (Madrid: Edifrans, 1974).

Brenan, G. *The Spanish Labyrinth* (Cambridge: Cambridge University Press, 1986).

Brome, V. *The Way Back: The Story of Lieut.-Commander Pat O' Leary, G.C., D.S.O., R.N.* (London: Companion Book Club, 1958).

Brundu, P. 'L'Espagne franquiste et la politique étrangère de la France au lendemain de la Deuxième Guerre mondiale', *Relations Internationales*, 50 (1987), 165–81.

Bunting, M. *The Model Occupation: The Channel Islands under German Rule* (London: Pimlico, 2004).

Burgess, G. *Refuge in the Land of Liberty: France and its Refugees, from the Revolution to the End of Asylum* (Basingstoke and New York: Palgrave Macmillan, 2008).

Camino, L. A. and R. N. Krulfeld (eds), *Reconstructing Lives, Recapturing Meaning: Refugee Identity, Gender, and Cultural Change* (Basle: Gordon & Breach, 1994).

Caron, V. *Uneasy Asylum: France and the Jewish Refugee Crisis, 1933–1942* (Stanford, CA: Stanford University Press, 1999).

Carrasco, J. *La odisea de los republicanos españoles en Francia. Album-souvenir de l'exil républicain espagnol en France (1939–1945)* (Perpignan: Imprimerie Saint-André, 1984).

Català, N. *Ces Femmes Espagnoles: de la Résistance à la Déportation*, trans. C. Langlois (Paris: Éditions Tirésias, 1994).

Cate-Arries, F. *Spanish Culture Behind Barbed Wire: Memory and Representation of the French Concentration Camps, 1939–1945* (Lewisburg, FL: Bucknell University Press, 2004).

Caudet, F. *Hipótesis sobre el exilio republicano de 1939* (Madrid: Fundación Universitaria Española, 1997).

Clavel, B. *L'Espagnol* (Paris: France Loisirs, 1981).

Cobo Martínez, C. and J. Cobo Martínez, *La Primera Renovación: Intrahistoria del PSOE Volumen 1 (1939–1945)* (Barcelona: Plaza y Janes, 1989).

Conan, E. and H. Rousso, *Un passé qui ne passé pas* (Paris: Fayard, 1994).

Constante, M. *Le Triangle bleu. Les républicains espagnols à Mauthausen* (Paris: Gallimard, 1969).

Constante, M. *Les années rouges. De Guernica à Mauthausen* (Paris: Mercure de France, 1971).

Coser, A. L. *Maurice Halbwachs on Collective Memory* (Chicago: University of Chicago Press, 1992).

Courau, C. *Les Poudriers dans la Résistance: Saint-Médard-en-Jalles (1940–1944)* (Pau: Princi Néguer, 2001).

Courtois, S., D. Peschanski and A. Rayski (eds), *Le Sang de l'étranger. Les immigrés de la MOI dans la Résistance* (Paris: Fayard, 1989).

Cowan, A. 'The Guerrilla War Against Franco', *European History Quarterly*, 20:2 (1990), 227–53.

Cubero, J. *Les Républicains espagnols* (Pau: Éditions Cairn, 2003).

Cubero, J. *La Résistance à Toulouse et dans la Région 4* (Toulouse: Éditions Sud Ouest, 2005).

Cuesta Bustillo, J. (ed.), *Retornos (De exilios y migraciones)* (Madrid: Fundación F. Largo Caballero, 1999).

Delpla, C. *Les Guérilleros Espagnols dans la Zone Pyrénéenne* (published by the author, 2002).

Domergue, L. (ed.), *L'Exil Républicain espagnol à Toulouse 1939–1999* (Toulouse: Presses Universitaires du Mirail, 1999).

Dreyfus-Armand, G. *L'Exil des Républicains Espagnols en France: De la Guerre Civile à la Mort de Franco* (Paris: Albin Michel, 1999).

Dreyfus-Armand, G. 'Les réfugiés républicains au cœur des relations franco-espagnoles, 1945–1962', *Relations Internationales*, 74 (1993), 153–69.

Dreyfus-Armand, G. and É. Temime, *Les Camps sur la plage, un exil espagnol* (Paris: Éditions Autrement, 1995).

Dulphy, A, 'La politique de la France à l'égard de l'Espagne franquiste, 1945–1949', *Revue d'histoire moderne et contemporaine*, 35:1 (1988), 123–40.

Dulphy, A. 'La politique espagnol de la France 1945–1955', *Vingtième Siècle: Revue d'histoire*, 68 (2000), 29–42.

Dunthorn, D. J. 'The Prieto–Robles Meeting of October 1947: Britain and the Failure of the Spanish Anti-Franco Coalition, 1945–1950', *European History Quarterly*, 30:1 (2000), 49–75.

Dutrénit Bielous, S., E. Allier Montaño and E. Coraza de los Santos, *Tiempos de exilios: Memoria e historia de Españoles y Uruguayos* (Uruguay: Textual, Fundación Carolina, Instituto Mora, 2008).

Ealham, C. 'Class and the City: Spatial Memories of Pleasure and Danger in Barcelona, 1914–23', *Oral History*, 29:1 (2001), 33–47.

Enfants de la guerre civile espagnole. Vécus et représentations de la génération née entre 1925 et 1940 (Paris: L'Harmattan, 1999).

Españoles en Francia 1936–1946. Coloquio Internacional Salamanca, 2, 3 y 4 de mayo 1991 (Salamanca: University of Salamanca, 1991).

Estruch Tobella, J. *El PCE en la clandestinidad 1939–1956* (Madrid: Siglo Veintiuno de España Editores, 1982).

Estruch Tobella, J. *Historia Oculta del PCE* (Madrid: Ediciones Temas de Hoy, 2000).

Fabréguet, M. 'Un groupe de réfugiés politiques: les républicains espagnols des camps d'internement français aux camps de concentration nationaux-socialistes', *Revue d'histoire de la Deuxième Guerre Mondiale*, 144 (1986), 19–38.

Faist, T. and E. Özveren, *Transnational Social Spaces: Agents, Networks and Institutions* (Aldershot: Ashgate, 2004).

Falguera, N., L. Figuéres and E. Mannevy Garcia, *Guerrilleros en Terre de France: Les Républicains espagnols dans la Résistance française* (Pantin: Le Temps des Cerises, 2000).

Farreny del Bosque, C. and H. *L'Affaire Reconquista de España 1942–1944: Résistance espagnole dans le Sud-Ouest* (Toulouse: Éditions Espagne au Cœur, 2nd edn, 2010).

Fernández, A. *Emigración republicana española (1939–1945)* (Algorta: Zero, 1972).

Fernández, A. *Españoles en la resistencia* (Bilbao: Zero, 1973).

Ferrer, M. *La Generalitat de Catalunya a l'exili* (Barcelona: Aymà, 1977).

Fishman, S. et al. (eds) *France at War: Vichy and the Historians* (Oxford: Berg, 2000).

'Food In Republican Spain: A Medical Memorandum', *British Medical Journal*, 1:4075 (1939), 278–9.

Foot, M. R. D. *SOE in France: An Account of the Work of the British Special Operations Executive in France, 1940–1944* (London: HMSO, 1966).

Fuentes, J. Francisco, *Luis Araquistáin y el socialismo español en el exilio (1939–1959)* (Madrid: Biblioteca Nueva, 2002).

Garner, J. 'Creating Unity or Division? The Origins of the Federación Anarquista Ibèrica', *University of Sussex Journal of Contemporary History*, 6 (2003), 1–14.

Gedi, N. and Y. Elam, 'Collective Memory – What Is It?', *History and Memory*, 8:1 (1996), 30–50.

Gemie, S. 'The Ballad of Bourg-Madame: Memory, Exile and the Spanish Republican Refugees of the *Retirada* of 1939', *International Review of Social History*, 51:1 (2006), 1–40.

Gemie, S. and H. Altink (eds), *At the Border: Margins and Peripheries in Modern France* (Cardiff: University of Wales Press, 2008).

Gemie, S. and S. Schrafstetter, 'Reassessing Anti-Fascism', *European History Quarterly*, 32:3 (2002), 413–19.

Gillespie, R., *The Spanish Socialist Party: A History of Factionalism* (Oxford: Clarendon Press, 1989).

Giral, F. *La República en el exilio* (Madrid: Ediciones 99, 1977).

Gilroy, P. *The Black Atlantic: Modernity and Double Consciousness* (London: Verso, 1993).

Goubet, M. and P. Debauges, *Histoire de la Résistance dans la Haute-Garonne* (Toulouse: Éditions Milan, 1986).

Graham, B., G. J. Ashworth and J. E. Tunbridge, *A Geography of Heritage: Power, Culture and Economy* (London: Arnold, 2000).

Graham, H. *The Spanish Republic at War 1936–1939* (Cambridge: Cambridge University Press, 2002).

Graham, H. *The Spanish Civil War: A Very Short Introduction* (Oxford University Press: Oxford, 2005).

Grando, R., J. Queralt and X. Febrés, *Camps du Mépris: des chemins de l'exil à ceux de la résistance 1939–1945* (Canet: Editorial del Trabucaire, 1999).

Grele, R. J. *Envelopes of Sound: The Art of Oral History* (Chicago: Precedent Publishing: 1985).

Guilhem, F. *L'obsession du retour* (Toulouse: Presses Universitaires du Mirail, 2005).

Guillaume, P. (ed.), *Étrangers en Aquitaine*. Vol. 8, *L'Aquitaine, Terre d'Immigration* (Talence: Maison des Sciences de l'Homme d'Aquitaine, 1990).

Guillon, J.-M. and P. Laborie (eds), *Mémoire et Histoire: La Résistance* (Toulouse: Éditions Privat, 1995).

Halbwachs, M. *La mémoire collective* (Paris: Presses Universitaires de France, 1950).

Hall, S. and P. du Gay (eds), *Questions of Cultural Identity* (London: Sage, 1996).

Hermet, G. *Les Espagnols en France: Immigration et Culture* (Paris: Éditions Ouvrières, 1967).

Hernando Villacampa, F. *Historia de la Amical de antiguos guerrilleros españoles en Francia (F.F.I.), 1947–1984* (Toulouse: Imprimerie SGI, 1992).

Hewison, R. 'The Heritage Industry Revisited', *Museums Journal*, 91:4 (1991), 23–6.

Iniesta, S. *Flon-Flon: Los republicanos españoles en la Legión Extranjera francesa* (Barcelona: Editorial Bruguera, 1972).

Íñiguez, M. *Enciclopedia histórica del anarquismo español* (Vitoria: Asociación Issac Puente, 2008).

Jackson, J. *France: The Dark Years, 1940–1944* (Oxford: Oxford University Press, 2001).

Jeudy, H.-P. *La Machine patrimoniale* (Belval: Éditions Circé, 2008).

Jornet, J. '"Il était une fois la République espagnole . . .": Un projet d'hommage officiel développé par la Région Midi-Pyrénées', *Les Cahiers de Framespa: Nouveaux champs de l'histoire sociale 3 (2007)*, http://framespa.revues.org/442 (accessed 1 July 2011).

Kedward, H. R. *In Search of the Maquis: Rural Resistance in Southern France 1942–1944* (Oxford: Clarendon Press, 1993).

Kedward, R. *La Vie en bleu: France and the French since* 1900 (London: Allen Lane, 2005).

Keren, C. 'Autobiographies of Spanish Refugee Children at the Quaker Home in La Rouvière (France, 1940): Humanitarian Communication and Children's Writings', *Les Cahiers de Framespa*, 5 (2010), http://framespa.revues.org/268 (accessed 1 June 2010).

Kidd, W. 'From the Moselle to the Pyrenees: Commemoration, Cultural Memory and the "Debatable Lands"', *Journal of European Studies*, 35:1 (2005), 114–30.

King, P. *The Channel Islands War, 1940–1945* (London: Robert Hale Ltd, 1991).

Laborie, P. *L'Opinion française sous Vichy: Les Français et la crise d'identité nationale 1936–1944* (Paris: Éditions du Seuil, 2nd edn, 2001).

Lafourcade, M. (ed.), *La Frontière Franco-Espagnole: Lieu de conflits interétatiques et de collaboration interrégionale* (Bordeaux: Presses Universitaires de Bordeaux, 1998).

La France et l'Allemagne, 1932–1936 (Paris: Editions du CNRS, 1980).

Laharie, C. *Le Camp de Gurs, 1939–45: Un aspect méconnu de l'histoire du Béarn* (Biarritz: Société Atlantique d'Impression à Biarritz, 1993).

La Libération dans le Midi de la France (Toulouse: Service des Publications de l'Université de Toulouse-Le Mirail, 1986).

Laroche, G. *On les nommait des étrangers: les immigrés dans la résistance* (Paris: Les Éditeurs Français Réunis, 1965).

Léger, A. *Les Indésirables: l'histoire oubliée des Espagnols en pays charentais* (Paris: Le Croît Vif, 2000).

Leitz, C. and D. J. Dunthorn (eds), *Spain in an International Context, 1936–1959* (New York and Oxford: Berghahn, 1999).

Les Anarchistes espagnols dans la tourmente (1939–1945) (Marseilles: Bulletin du Centre international de recherche sur l'anarchisme, 1989).

Les Dossiers noirs d'une certaine résistance: trajectoire d'un fascisme rouge (Perpignan: Édition du CES, 1984).

Levitt, P. and B. N. Jaworsky, 'Transnational Migration Studies: Past Developments and Future Trends', *Annual Review of Sociology*, 33:129 (2007), 129–56.

Lewis, M. D. *The Boundaries of the Republic: Migrant Rights and the Limits of Universalism in France, 1918–1940* (Stanford, CA: Stanford University Press, 2007).

Lorenzo, C. M. *Les anarchistes espagnols et le pouvoir, 1868–1969* (Paris: Seuil, 1969).

Lormier, D. *La Base Sous-Marine de Bordeaux, 1940–1944* (Montreuil-Bellay: Éditions CMD, 1999).

Machado, A. *Campos de Castilla* (Madrid: Renacimiento, 1912).

MacMaster, N. *Spanish Fighters: An Oral History of Civil War and Exile* (Basingstoke: Macmillan, 1990).

Maga, T. P. 'Closing the Door: The French Government and Refugee Policy, 1933–1939', *French Historical Studies*, 12:3 (1982), 424–42.

Maitron, J. and C. Pennetier, *Dictionnaire Biographique du Mouvement Ouvrier Français*, 1914–1939, Vol. XIX (Paris: Éditions Ouvrières, 1983).

Mancebo, M. F., M. Baldó and C. Alonso (eds), *L'Exili Cultural de 1939. Seixanta anys després*, Vol. 2 (Valencia: Universitat de València, 2001).

Mandel, M. *In the Aftermath of Genocide* (Durham, NC and London: Duke University Press, 2003).

Mangini, S. *Memories of Resistance: Women's Voices from the Spanish Civil War* (New Haven, CT and London: Yale University Press, 1995).

Martín Ramos, J. L. *Rojos contra Franco: Historia del PSUC, 1939–1947* (Barcelona: Edhasa, 2002).

Mateos López, A. *Exilio y Clandestinidad. La Reconstrucción de UGT, 1939–1977* (Madrid: Universidad Nacional de Educación a Distancia, 2002).

Mauran, H. *Espagnols rouges: un maquis de républicains espagnols dans les Cévennes* (Nîmes: Lacour Éditeur, 1995).

Maux-Robert, M.-A. *La lutte contre le chômage à Vichy* (Panazol: Lavauzelle, 2002).

Maux-Robert, M.-A. 'Le commissariat à la lutte contre le chômage en zone sud', *Guerres mondiales et conflits contemporains*, 2:206 (2002), 121–46.

Messenger, D. A. *L'Espagne Républicaine: French Policy and Spanish Republicanism in Liberated France* (Brighton: Sussex Academic Press, 2008).

Milza, P. and D. Peschanski (eds), *Exils et Migration: Italiens et Espagnols en France 1938–1946* (Paris: L'Harmattan, 1994).

Mira Abad, A. and M. Moreno Seco, 'Españolas exiliadas y emigrantes: encuentros y desencuentros en Francia', *Les Cahiers de Framespa*, 5 (2010), http://framespa. revues.org/268 (accessed 2 June 2010).

Molina, J. M. *El movimiento clandestino en España 1939–1949* (Mexico City: Editores Mexicanos Unidos, 1976).

Naficy, H. *The Making of Exile Cultures: Iranian Television in Los Angeles* (Minneapolis: University of Minnesota Press, 1993).

Noiriel, G. *Immigration, antisémitisme et racisme en France (XIX–XX siècle): Discours publics, humiliations privées* (Paris: Fayard, 2007).

Noiriel, G. *Réfugiés et sans-papiers: La République face au droit d'asile XIX–XX siècle* (Paris: Hachette, 1999).

Noiriel, G. *Le creuset français. Histoire de l'immigration, XIX–XX siècles* (Paris: Seuil, 1988).

Nora, P. (ed.), *Les Lieux de Mémoire*. Vols 1–3 (Paris: Éditions Gallimard, 1997).

Ortiz, J. *Guerrilleros en Béarn. Guerrilleros, étranges terroristes étrangers* (Biarritz: Atlantica, 2007).

Ott, S. *War, Judgement, and Memory in the Basque Borderlands, 1914–1945* (Reno: University of Nevada Press, 2008).

Ott, S. (ed.), *War, Exile, Justice and Everyday Life 1936–1946* (Reno, NV: Center for Basque Studies, University of Nevada, 2011).

Pàmies, T. *Quan érem refugiats. Memories d'un exili* (Barcelona: Dopesa, 1975).

Pàmies, T. *Los que se fueron* (Barcelona: Martínez Roca, 1976).

Papy, M. (ed.), *Les Espagnols et la Guerre Civile* (Biarritz: Atlantica, 1999).

Parkin, D. 'Mementoes as Transitional Objects in Human Displacement', *Journal of Material Culture*, 4:3 (1999), 303–20.

Paxton, R. O. *Vichy France: Old Guard and New Order, 1940–1944* (New York: Columbia University Press Morningside Edition, 1982).

Paz, A. *CNT 1939–1951: el anarquismo contra el Estado franquista* (Madrid: Fundación de Estudios Libertarios Anselmo Lorenzo, 2001).

Peiró, J. *Trayectoria de la CNT* (Madrid: Ediciones Júcar, 1979).

Peschanski, D. *La France des camps. L'internement 1938–1946* (Paris: Éditions Gallimard, 2002).

Pigenet, P. 'La protection des étrangers à l'épreuve de la «guerre froide»: L'opération «boléro-paprika»', *Revue d'histoire moderne et contemporaine*, 46:2 (1999), 296–310.

Pike, D. W. *Jours de gloire, jours de honte, Le PCE en France* (Paris: Sedes, 1984).

Pike, D. W. *Vae Victis! Los republicanos españoles refugiados en Francia 1939–1944* (Paris: Ruedo Ibérico, 1969).

Pike, D. W. *In the Service of Stalin: The Spanish Communists in Exile, 1939–1945* (Oxford: Clarendon Press, 1993).

Plummer, K. *Documents of Life 2: An Invitation to a Critical Humanism* (London: Sage, 2001).

Pons Prades, E. *Los que Sí hicimos la guerra* (Barcelona: Ediciones Martínez Roca, 1973).

Pons Prades, E. *Republicanos españoles en la 2a Guerra Mundial* (Barcelona: Planeta, 1975).

Pons Prades, E. *Españoles en los «maquis» franceses (verano de 1944)* (Barcelona: Sagitario, 1976).

Pons Prades, E. *Los derrotados y el exilio* (Barcelona: Bruguera, 1977).

Pons Prades, E. *Las guerras de los niños republicanos (1936–1995)* (Madrid: Compañía Literaria, 1997).

Preston, P. *The Coming of the Spanish Civil War. Reform, Reaction and Revolution in the Second Republic* (London: Routledge, 2nd edn, 1994).

Preston, P. *Franco* (London: Fontana, 1995).

Preston, P. *A Concise History of the Spanish Civil War* (London: Fontana, 1996).

Pruja, J.-C. *Premiers camps de l'exil espagnol: Prats-de-Mollo, 1939* (Saint-Cyr-sur-Loire: Éditions Alan Sutton, 2003).

Rafaneau-Boj, M.-C. *Odyssée pour la liberté. Les camps de prisonniers espagnols (1939–1945)* (Paris: Denoël, 1993).

Républicains espagnols en Midi-Pyrénées: Exil histoire et mémoire (Toulouse: Presses Universitaires du Mirail, 2004).

Reviriego, B. *Les Juifs en Dordogne 1939–1944* (Périgueux: Éditions Fanlac, Archives Départementales de la Dordogne, 2003).

Rosal, A. del, *Historia de la UGT de España en la emigración (Tomo I)* (Barcelona: Editorial Grijalbo, 1979).

Rousso, H. *Le Syndrome de Vichy de 1944 à nos jours* (Paris: Éditions du Seuil, 1990).

Rubio, J. *La emigración de la guerra civil de 1936–1939. Historia del éxodo que se produce con el fin de la II República española.*Vols 1–3 (Editorial San Martín: Madrid, 1977).

Rubio, J. *La emigración española a Francia* (Barcelona: Ariel, 1974).

Rutherford, J. (ed.) *Identity: Community, Culture, Difference* (London: Lawrence & Wishart, 1990).

Sagnes, J. and S. Caucanas (eds), *Les Français et la Guerre d'Espagne* (Perpignan: Presses Universitaires de Perpignan, 2nd edn, 2004).

Samuel, R. *Theatres of Memory: Past and Present in Contemporary Culture.* Vol. 1 (London: Verso, 1994).

Samuel, R. and P. Thompson (eds), *The Myths We Live By* (London: Routledge, 1990).

Santos-Sainz, M. and F. Guillemeteaud, *Les Espagnols à Bordeaux et en Aquitaine* (Bordeaux: Éditions Sud Ouest, 2006).

Schor, R. *L'Opinion française et les étrangers, 1919–1939* (Paris: Publications de la Sorbonne, 1985).

Scott, J. C. *Weapons of the Weak: Everyday Forms of Peasant Resistance* (New Haven, CT: Yale University Press, 1985).

Seidler, F. W. 'L'Organisation Todt', *Revue d'histoire de la Deuxième Guerre Mondiale et des conflits contemporains*, 134 (1984), 33–58.

Seidman, M. 'Agrarian Collectives during the Spanish Revolution and Civil War', *European History Quarterly*, 30:2 (2000), 209–35.

Soo, S. 'Ambiguities at Work: Spanish Republican Exiles and the Organisation Todt in Occupied Bordeaux', *Modern and Contemporary France*, 15:4 (2007), 457–77.

Soo, S. 'Putting Memory to Work: A Comparative Study of Three Associations Dedicated to the Memory of the Spanish Republican Exile in France', *Diasporas. Histoires et sociétés*, 6 (2005), 109–20.

Soriano, A. *Éxodos: historia oral del exilio republicano en Francia 1939–1945* (Barcelona: Editorial Crítica, 1989).

Stein, L. *Beyond Death and Exile: The Spanish Republicans in France, 1939–1955* (Cambridge, MA: Harvard University Press, 1979).

Sweets, J. F. *Choices in Vichy France: The French under Nazi Occupation* (Oxford: Oxford University Press, 1986).

Tcach, C. and C. Reyes, *Clandestinidad y exilio. Reorganización del sindicato socialista, 1939–1953* (Madrid: Fundación Pablo Iglesias, 1986).

Téllez Solá, A. *La Red de Evasión del Grupo Ponzán: Anarquistas en la guerra secreta contra el franquismo y el nazismo (1936–1944)* (Barcelona: Virus, 1996).

Terrisse, R. *Bordeaux, 1940–1944* (Paris: Librairie Académique Perrin, 1993).

Teulières, L. *Immigrés d'Italie et paysans de France 1920–1944* (Toulouse: Presses Universitaires du Mirail, 2002).

Thalmann, R. 'L'Émigration du III Reich dans la France de 1933 à 1939', *Le Monde Juif*, 35:96 (1979), 127–39.

Thomas, H. *The Spanish Civil War* (London: Penguin, 3rd edn, 1986).

Thompson, P. *The Voice of the Past: Oral History* (Oxford: Oxford University Press, 3rd edn, 2000).

Thomson, A. 'Moving Stories: Oral History and Migration Studies', *Oral History*, 27:1 (1999), 24–37.

Thomson, A., M. Frisch and P. Hamilton, 'The Memory and History Debates: Some International Perspectives', *Oral History*, 22:2 (1994), 33–43.

Tuban, G. *Les séquestrés de Collioure: Un camp disciplinaire au Château royal en 1939* (Perpignan: Mare Nostrum, 2003).

Turner, V. *Dramas, Fields and Metaphors: Symbolic Action in Human Society* (Ithaca, NY and London: Cornell University Press, 1974).

Tusell, J. *La oposición democrática al franquismo (1939–1962)* (Barcelona: Editorial Planeta, 1977).

Ugarte, M. *Shifting Ground: Spanish Civil War Exile Literature* (Durham, NC and London: Duke University Press, 1989).

Valis, N. 'Nostalgia and Exile', *Journal of Spanish Cultural Studies*, 1:2 (2000), 117–33.

Valle, J. M. del, *Las Instituciones de la República española en exilio* (Paris: Ruedo Ibérico, 1976).

Vargas, B. (ed.), *La Seconde République Espagnole en Exil en France (1939–1977)* (Albi: Presses universitaires de Champollion, 2008).

Vargas, B. and D. Debord, *Les Espagnols en France. Une vie au-delà des Pyrénées* (Toulouse: Éd. de l'Attribut, 2010).

Vaughan, E. *Community Under Stress: An Internment Camp Culture* (Princeton, NJ: Princeton University Press, 1949).

Vernant, J. *The Refugee in the Post-War World* (London: George Allen & Unwin, 1953).

Viet, V. 'Vichy dans l'histoire des politiques françaises de la main-d'œuvre', *Travail et Emploi*, 98 (2004), 77–93.

Vilanova, A. *Los Olvidados: los exilados españoles en la segunda guerra mundial* (Paris: Ruedo Ibérico, 1969).

Villegas, J.-C. (ed.), *Plages d'exil. Les camps de réfugiés espagnols en France, 1939* (Nanterre-Dijon: BDIC-Hispanistica XX, 1989).

Villegas, J.-C. (ed.), *Écrits d'exil: Barraca et Desde el Rosellón. Albums d'art et de littérature Argelès-sur-Mer 1939* (Sète: Éditions NPL, 2007).

Viñas, A. *Los pactos secretos de Franco con Estados Unidos: bases, ayuda económica, recortes de soberanía* (Barcelona: Grijalbo, 1981).

Weil, P. 'Racisme et discrimination dans la politique française de l'immigration 1938–45/1974–95', *Vingtième Siècle: Revue d'histoire*, 47 (1995), 77–102.

Wood, N. 'Memory's Remains: *Les lieux de mémoire*', *History and Memory*, 6/1 (1994), 123–49.

Wood, N. *Vectors of Memory: Legacies of Trauma in Postwar Europe* (Oxford and New York: Berg, 1999).

Yagîl, L. *Chrétiens et Juifs sous Vichy, 1940–1944: Sauvetage et désobéissance civile* (Paris: Cerf, 2005).

THESES, DISSERTATIONS AND PAPERS

Bergouignan, J. 'Les Immigrés Espagnols à Bordeaux: Étude Statistique et Recherches sur l'Adaptation' (Mémoire, Institut d'études politiques de Bordeaux, 1967).

Blaizat, M-A. 'L'Opinion Publique et les Représentations des Républicains Espagnols dans la Région Toulousaine, 1936–1940' (Mémoire de maîtrise, Université de Toulouse-Le Mirail, 1987).

Bousquet, N. 'Les Espagnols dans le Lot de l'Entre-Deux-Guerres aux Années 50' (Mémoire de maîtrise, Université de Toulouse-Le Mirail, 1992).

Dreyfus-Armand, G. 'L'Émigration Politique Espagnole en France au Travers de sa Presse 1939–1975' (Thèse de Doctorat, Institut d'Études Politiques de Paris, 1994).

Laffitte, G. 'L'Encadrement par le Travail des Étrangers dans le Département du Gers 1939–1944: Au Cœur du Dipositif GTE' (Mémoire de maîtrise, Université de Toulouse-Le Mirail, 2003).

Salgas, E. 'L'Opinion Publique et les Représentations des Réfugiés Espagnols dans les Pyrénées-Orientales Janvier–Septembre 1939' (Mémoire de Maîtrise, Université de Toulouse-Le Mirail, 1989).

Soo, S. 'Exile, Identity and Memory: Spanish Republicans in the Southwest of France' (D.Phil. thesis, University of Sussex, 2005).

Zorzin, S. 'Le Camp de Septfonds (Tarn-et-Garonne): Soixante Ans d'Histoire et de Mémoires' (Mémoire de recherche, Institut d'Études Politiques de Bordeaux, 2000).

Index

Lightning Source UK Ltd.
Milton Keynes UK
UKHW020647201120
373694UK00011B/2709